CW01332865

With kind regards

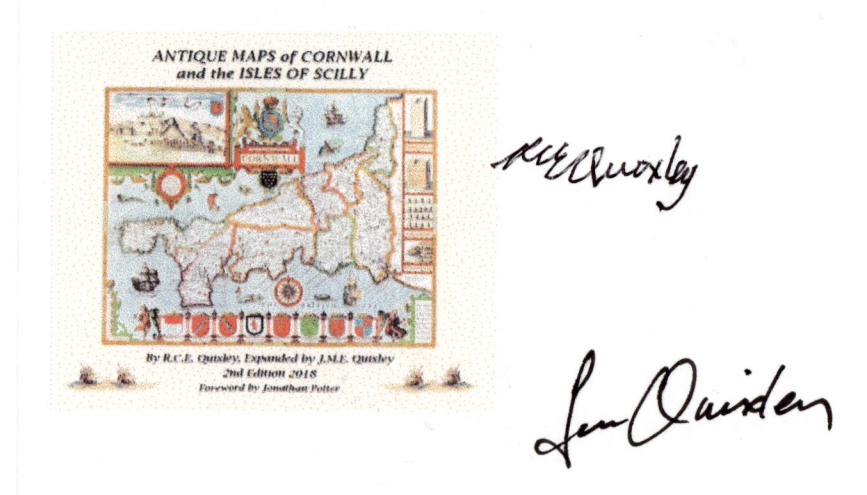

ANTIQUE MAPS of CORNWALL
and the ISLES OF SCILLY

By R.C.E. Quixley, Expanded by J.M.E. Quixley
2nd Edition 2018
Foreword by Jonathan Potter

RCEQuixley

Jan Quixley

ANTIQUE MAPS
of
CORNWALL
and the
ISLES OF SCILLY
by
R.C.E. QUIXLEY

2nd Edition
J.M.E. QUIXLEY

Published in the United Kingdom by:

R. C. E. Quixley
Sona Merg
Heamoor
Penzance, Cornwall TR18 3HA

Content Copyright © 2018 by R. C. E. Quixley

Illustrations © 2018 by J. M. E. Quixley

All rights reserved. No portion of this book may be reproduced, stored in a retrieval system, transmitted at any time or by any means mechanical, electronic, photocopying, recording or otherwise, without the prior, written permission of the publisher.

The right of R. C. E. Quixley to be identified as the author of this work has been asserted in accordance with the Copyright, Designs and Patents Act 1988

A CIP record of this book is available from the British Library

First printed August 2018

Layout and design by Jon Quixley

Printed by Short Run Press Ltd, Exeter

ISBN 978-1-5272-1503-0

Antique Maps of Cornwall and the Isles of Scilly

Foreword by Jonathan Potter

Congratulations to Bob Quixley on following up his 1966 work on the mapping of Cornwall.

The first publication "Antique Maps of Cornwall and the Isles of Scilly" appeared at a time when my own interest in old maps was developing and becoming what has turned into a lifetime career - it became one of my favourite "collector's" books. Following the lead of R. V. Tooley whose "Maps and Map-Makers" was the best general reference to the history of European cartography, Quixley's publication on maps of a specific county provided a focus which, although limited geographically, could be cross-referenced for any other county for which a map-maker's information remained constant. For many years, lacking the relatively recent influence of the internet, such books remained the prime source of information for the serious collector and amateur enthusiast. "Quixley" became a by-word for THE reference to go to when researching maps of Cornwall.

After fifty years of further research, I am sure reading the new edition, in terms of information, presentation and the facility of having the whole picture at one's fingertips, will prove a much more satisfying experience than staring at a screen!

Jonathan Potter,
Bath.
January 2018.

Acknowledgement

I would like to acknowledge my great indebtedness to Miss E. M. Rodger for allowing me to refer to her 'Bibliography Printed Maps of Cornwall', without which my task would have been considerably more arduous; to Dr R.A. Skelton for his advice and encouragement; and to Mr R. V. Tooley, for giving me the initial idea of attempting this work.

Over the intervening years, this project has been attempted several times. I would like to thank Stuart Forsyth, who ably assisted in starting this, the second edition, several years ago. Since then and with the help of my sons, the second edition has taken shape. The advent of the internet has become a boon in terms of accessing information; we have been fortunate to be able to draw upon copies of the various maps and advice from these sources, as well as our private collections.

Several maps have needed special permission to use due to their extreme rarity, and I would like to thank Dr Todd Gray of Devon and Cornwall Records Society for his help in accessing the Gasgoyne map facsimile.

The John Norden manuscript map is unique; few copies of it have been made. Helen Gannon at University of Exeter Press was instrumental in allowing us to use their facsimile copy, and Trinity College Cambridge also consented their permission as owners of the original map.

A special note of thanks is due to Philip Burden of Clive A. Burden Ltd for the considerable number of maps he has generously provided as illustrations, and wealth of knowledge he freely gave in helping to order much of the details.

- Bodleian Library, Oxford and the assistance and advice of Debbie Hall.
- Bonhams London and the assistance of Simon Roberts, plates thus: BON.
- Clive A. Burden Ltd, Buckinghamshire, and the assistance and advice of Philip Burden, plates thus: BUR.
- Chris Bond, plate thus: CMB.
- Devon and Cornwall Records Society, plate thus: DCR.
- Jonathan Potter Ltd, Bath, for his forward and supply of plates thus: JPL.
- Personal Collections (RCEQ and JMEQ), plates thus: PER.
- University of Exeter Press, plate thus: UEP.
- Photography: The following plates were photographed by Simon Cook of Penzance: 9.3, 42, 64, 86 and 87.

The typing, editing and compilation of the second edition was done by my son, Jonathan, and was proofed by Dr Philip Barham.

To all of them I extend my thanks.

R. C. E. QUIXLEY

Penzance,
Cornwall.
August 2018.

Editorial

The maps are presented in chronological order, from Christopher Saxton to Joshua Archer. Later maps by the same author are left with that first mention. There is an inevitable debate amongst carto-bibliographers concerning the crediting of maps in terms of authorship – this stems from the fact that there are a number of individuals involved with the process of taking the initial field sketch, to engraver, to author, to printer and finally publisher.

By way of an example: an early map such as John Speed's 1610 Cornwall map appears in his own publication 'The Theatre of the Empire of Great Britain', which was published as an expanded atlas in 1611. Speed surveyed (partially) and drew the Cornwall map. It was Jodocus Hondius who engraved the map and Sudbury & Humble who first published it.

So far as is reasonably possible, the indexing here references the originator of the map (surveyor if known), and/or the engraver.

This interplay of numerous personalities involved with the various stages of construction gets even more complicated in the 1700s and 1800s, with engravers lifting original work of others, slightly modifying it and selling it on to a ravenous market, scrambling to keep up with an insatiable public demand. Maps over this period tended to be incorporated into volumes written/compiled/produced by another person. The volume (be it atlas, directory &c.) is usually better known by its producer or author and not by the engraver of the map. In these instances, the indexing is done by Author/Publisher then Engraver. A full cross-referenced table is included in the appendices.

There are inevitable omissions to the collection presented here, but the intent is to present a selection of maps that show the evolution over the 270 years covered, and that are still ones a collector could expect to find at auction or even at a car boot sale. There are one or two here that are beyond that; these are included as historical markers. There are maps missing, hopefully not too many.

- The date given alongside the map-maker's name heading each section is the date at which the map was engraved, and sometimes differs from the date of publication of the atlas in which the map appeared.
- Titles and dates of atlases are given at the end of each section, together with a list of the dates at which reprints of the map or atlas were issued.
- Dimensions of the maps are given in millimetres measured inside the border, the first figure the width, and the second figure the height.
- Below each title is the name of the Surveyor/Engraver, to ~1740 where Publisher/Engraver is used.

Following this are some notes dealing with common aspects of some of these maps: location, language and geography.

ANTIQUE MAPS OF CORNWALL AND THE ISLES OF SCILLY
BY R. C. E. QUIXLEY

FOREWORD
ACKNOWLEDGMENT
EDITORIAL
CONTENTS
ILLUSTRATIONS
INTRODUCTION

1. SAXTON, CHRISTOPHER 1576
2. WAGHENAER, LUCAS JANSZOON 1584
3. DE BRY, THEODOR 1588
4. BOWES, WILLIAM 1590, 1595
5. VAN DEN KEERE, PIETER 1605
6. NORDEN, JOHN 1728
7. CAMDEN, WILLIAM 1586 et seq.
8. MERCATOR, GERARD 1595
9. KIP, WILLIAM 1607
10. BLAEU, WILLEM 1608, 1623
11. SPEED, JOHN 1610
12. HOLE, WILLIAM 1612
13. BILL, JOHN 1626
14. VAN LANGEREN, JACOB 1635
15. WEB, WILLIAM (after SAXTON) 1645
16. BLAEU, JOHANNES WILLEMSZOON (JAN) 1645
17. JANSSON, JAN 1646
18. BLOME, RICHARD 1673, 1681
19. OGILBY, JOHN 1675
20. MORDEN, ROBERT 1676, 1695 and 1701
21. REDMAYNE, WILLIAM 1676
22. LEA, PHILIP (after SAXTON) 1689, 1694
23. COLLINS, CAPTAIN GREENVILE 1689
24. DE HOOGHE, Sr. ROMAIN 1693
25. GASGOYNE, JOEL 1700
26. SELLER, JOHN 1694, 1773
27. NICHOLLS, SUTTON 1712
28. SCHENK, PETER & VALK, GERARD 1714
29. LENTHALL, JOHN 1717
30. BOWEN, EMANUEL 1720, 1748, 1759, 1764, 1767 and 1785
31. MOLL, HERMAN 1724, 1718
32. VAN KEULEN, GERARD 1735
33. PINE, JOHN 1739, 1740
34. BADESLADE, THOMAS & TOMS, WILLIAM 1741
35. COWLEY, JOHN 1741-3
36. ROCQUE, JOHN 1743, 1753
37. SIMPSON, SAMUEL 1744
38. OSBORNE, THOMAS 1748
39. KITCHIN, THOMAS 1749, 1750, 1764, 1769 and 1778
40. MARTYN, THOMAS 1748, 1749 and 1784
41. KITCHIN, THOMAS & JEFFERYS, THOMAS 1749, 1775
42. BICKHAM, GEORGE (Snr & Jnr) 1750, 1796
43. BORLASE, WILLIAM 1754, 1758
44. MEIJER, PIETER & SCHENK, LEONARD 1757

ANTIQUE MAPS OF CORNWALL AND THE ISLES OF SCILLY
BY R. C. E. QUIXLEY

45.	GIBSON, JOHN 1759, 1762		70.	LANGLEY, EDWARD & BELCH, WILLIAM 1817
46.	DURY, ANDREW & ELLIS, JOSEPH 1764		71.	CRABB, THOMAS 1819
47.	DE LA ROCHETTE, LOUIS STANISLAS 1765		72.	LEIGH, SAMUEL & HALL, SIDNEY 1820
48.	TOVEY (Jnr), ABRAHAM & GINVER, NICHOLAS 1779		73.	DIX, THOMAS & DARTON, WILLIAM 1821
49.	"WALPOOLE, GEORGE" & HATCHETT, THOMAS 1784		74.	SMITH, CHARLES & GARDNER, WILLIAM 1822
50.	CARY, JOHN 1787, 1789, 1790 and 1809		75.	PERROT, ARISTIDE & MIGNERET, Mme 1824
51.	MURRAY, JOHN & LODGE, JOHN 1788		76.	GREENWOOD, C & J 1827, 1829
52.	HARRISON, JOHN & SUDLOW, EDWARD 1790		77.	TEESDALE, HENRY 1830
53.	AIKIN, JOHN & JOHNSON, JOSEPH 1790		78.	MURRAY, T. LAURIE & HOARE & REEVES 1830
54.	BAKER, BENJAMIN 1791		79.	CREIGHTON, ROBERT & STARLING, THOMAS 1831
55.	TUNNICLIFF, WILLIAM 1791		80.	COBBETT, WILLIAM 1832
56.	SPENCE, GRAEME 1792		81.	FISHER, HENRY & DAVIES, BENJAMIN REES 1832
57.	FAIRBURN, JOHN & ROWE, ROBERT 1798		82.	DUNCAN, JAMES & EBDEN, WILLIAM 1811
58.	SMITH, CHARLES 1801		83.	BELL, JAMES & SCOTT, ROBERT 1833-4
59.	WILKES, JOHN & NEELE, SAMUEL 1802		84.	PIGOT, JAMES & Co. 1830
60.	DUGDALE, JAMES & NEELE, SAMUEL 1814		85.	PINNOCK, WILLIAM & ARCHER, JOSHUA 1833
61.	LYSONS BROTHERS & NEELE, SAMUEL 1814		86.	MOULE, THOMAS 1834
62.	PINNOCK, WILLIAM & NEELE, SAMUEL 1819		87.	DUGDALE, JAMES & ARCHER, JOSHUA 1846
63.	BUTTERS, ROBERT 1803		88.	APPENDICES
64.	LUFFMAN, JOHN 1803		89.	REFERENCES
65.	COLE, GEORGE & ROPER, JOHN 1805		90.	INDEX
66.	CAPPER, BENJAMIN & COOPER, HENRY 1808			
67.	WALLIS, JAMES 1812, 1812 (x2) and 1820			
68.	BAKER, BENJAMIN & ORDNANCE SURVEY 1813			
69.	ROWE, ROBERT 1816			

Illustrations

Wherever possible the maps used here are in as close to their original state as possible. With modern technology, the photographs we have used give the option to digitally correct blemishes such as spots and foxing. In some cases, this has been done in order to return the maps to a condition "as published" - the intent is to present the maps in a condition to enable the viewer to appreciate the cartographer's work in its near-original state, without the subsequent tarnish of years. Some of the photos are of maps still bound in their atlas - there is some distortion with these photos that has been left.

Key: BON - Bonhams, CAB - Burden Collection, CMB - Chris Bond, CRO - Cornwall Records Office, DCR - Devon and Cornwall Records Society, JPL - Jonathan Potter, PER - Personal Collections (RCEQ & JMEQ), UEP - University of Exeter Press.

1.	BON	Saxton 1576	*An Atlas of England And Wales, Christopher Saxton, London.*
2.	BON	Waghenaer 1592	*Thresoor der Zeevaert. Amsterdam.*
2.1	BON	Waghenaer 1584	*Spieghel Der Zeevaerdt. Amsterdam.*
3.	BON	De Bry 1588	*The Mariners' Mirrour, Anthony Ashley, London.*
5.	PER	Van Den Keere 1617	*Viri Clarissimi Britannia, W.J. Blaeu, Amsterdam.*
5.1	BON	Van Den Keere 1627	*England, Wales, Scotland and Ireland Described and Abridged.*
6.	UEP	Norden ~1596	*'Manuscript Map'.*
6.1	PER	Norden 1728	*Speculi Britanniae Pars. Bateman, London.*
6.2	UEP	Norden 1728	*Kerrier Hundred section.*
8.	BON	Mercator 1595	*Atlas Sive Cosmographicae..., Rumold Mercator, Duisberg.*
8.1	BON	Mercator 1595	*Detail: Cornwall Atlas Sive Cosmographicae...*
9.	PER	Kip 1607	*Britannia, sive florentissimorum regnorum Angliae... Camden, London.*
9.1	PER	Kip 1607	*Detail Launceston Castle.*
9.2	PER	Norden 1728	*Detail Launceston Castle.*
9.3	PER	Kip 1610	*Britain, or a chorographical description of the most flourishing kingdomes. Camden, London*
9.4	BON	Kip 1637	*Detail, Britain, or a chorographical description...*
10.	BON	Blaeu (Snr) 1608	*Het Licht Der Zee-Vaert, Amsterdam.*
10.1	BON	Blaeu (Snr) 1623	*Zee-Spieghel... Amsterdam.*
11.	BON	Speed 1610	*Britannia, The Theatre of The Empire of Great Britain. Sudbury & Humble.*
11.1	PER	Speed 1610	*Britannia, The Theatre of The Empire of Great Britain, Frontispiece.*
11.2	PER	Speed 1623	*Britannia, The Theatre of The Empire of Great Britain. Sudbury & Humble.*
12.	BON	Hole 1612	*Poly-Olbion, Or A Chorographicall Description... Lownes, Browne, Helme and Busbie.*
12.1	PER	Mixed	*Sea Monsters.*
13.	CAB	Bill 1626	*The Abridgement of Camden's Britannia.*
14.	CAB	Van Langeren 1635	*A Direction for the English Travailler by Matthew Simmons.*
14.1	BON	Van Langeren 1657	*Detail, A Booke of The Names of All Parishes... Thomas Jenner.*
14.2	PER	Norden 1625	*Mileage Table from England; an intended guyde for English Travaillers.*
14.3	BON	Van Langeren 1657	*A Booke of The Names of All Parishes... Thomas Jenner.*

Antique Maps of Cornwall and the Isles of Scilly

15.	BON	Web 1645	The Maps of All the Shires in England And Wales.
16.	BON	Blaeu 1645	Theatrum Orbis Terrarum, Amsterdam G & J Blaeu.
17.	BON	Jansson 1646	Novus Atlas sive Theatrum Orbis Terrarum, Amsterdam.
18.	CAB	Blome 1673	Britannia: Or, a Geographical Description of the Kingdoms of England... London.
18.1	CAB	Blome 1685	Speed's Maps Epitomiz'd. London.
18.2	CAB	Blome 1715	England Exactly Described. Or a guide to Travellers... London.
19.	PER	Ogilby 1675	Britannia Volume the First, Or an illustration of the Kingdom... London. Frontispiece.
19.1	BON	Ogilby 1675	Britannia Volume the First... London. Plate 28: Plymouth To Land's End.
19.2	BON	Ogilby 1675	Britannia Volume the First... London. Detail: Plate 28.
19.3	CAB	Ogilby 1675	Britannia, Volume the First... Plate 69: Exeter to Truroe.
20.	BON	Morden 1676	The 52 Countries of England And Wales, Described in A Pack of Cards.
20.1	BON	Morden 1680	Pocketbook of all the Counties.
20.2	BON	Morden 1695	Britannia, William Camden, published by E. Gibson, London.
20.3	BON	Morden 1708	Fifty-six new and accurate maps...London.
22.	BON	Lea 1689	All the Shires of England And Wales... Being the best and Original Mapps. London.
22.1	BON	Lea 1689	All the Shires of England And Wales ...Being the best and Original Mapps. London. Detail.
22.2	BON	Lea 1694	The Shires of England and Wales... London.
23.	BON	Collins 1738	Great Britain's Coasting Pilot, London 1738.
23.1	BON	Collins 1693	Great Britain's Coasting Pilot, London 1693.
23.2	BON	Collins 1686	Great Britain's Coasting Pilot, London 1686.
24.	BON	De Hooge 1693	Atlas Maritime, Amsterdam.
25.	DCR	Gasgoyne 1700	A Map of The County of Cornwall, published by Darker & Farley, London.
26.	JPL	Seller 1694	Anglia Contracta, Or A Description of the Kingdom of England & Principality of Wales...
26.1	CAB	Seller 1787	Supplement To The Antiquities Of England And Wales, published by Francis Grose, London.
27.	BON	Nicholls 1712	A New mapp of the county of Cornwall, Overton's Made-Up Atlas VI. London.
28.	PER	Schenk & Valk 1714	Atlas Anglois, Ou Description Générale De L'Anglettere. Mortier, London.
29.	BON	Lenthall 1717	Pack of Playing Cards, London.
30.	BON	Bowen 1720	Britannia Depicta, Or Ogilby Improv'd. T. Bowles, London.
30.1	BON	Bowen 1777	The Royal English Atlas, Bowen & Kitchin, London.
30.2	CAB	Bowen 1748	The Universal Magazine of Knowledge and Pleasure Vol IV, J. Hinton, London.
30.3	CAB	Bowen / Bowles 1785	Bowles's New Medium English Atlas. Carington Bowles, London.
31.	BON	Moll 1724	A New Description of England And Wales, H. Moll & Others, London.
31.1	CAB	Moll, 1718	Roads of ye South Part of Great Britain. Published by Bowles and Bowles. Detail - Firebasket.
31.2	CAB	Moll, 1718	Roads of ye South Part of Great Britain. Published by Bowles and Bowles.
32.	BON	Van Keulen 1735	Nieuwe Afteekening Van De Sorlinges Eylanden..., Amsterdam.
33.	BON	Pine 1739	The Tapestry Hangings of The House of Lords, London.
33.1	BON	Pine 1740	A Plott of All the Coast of Cornwall And Devonshire ... in 1588. London.
34.	PER	Badeslade 1741	Chorographia Britaniae, or a set of maps... T. Badeslade And W. H. Toms, London.
34.1	PER	Badeslade 1742	Chorographia Britaniae, or a set of maps... T. Badeslade And W. H. Toms, London.

Antique Maps of Cornwall and the Isles of Scilly

#	Cat	Author Year	Title
35.	CAB	Cowley 1744	*The Geography of England, R. Dodsley, London.*
36.	BON	Rocque 1753	*The Small British Atlas, Rocque & Sayer London.*
37.	CAB	Simpson 1744	*The Agreeable Historian, or the Compleat English Traveller... London.*
38.	CAB	Osborne 1748	*Geographia Magna Britanniae, Publishers Birt et al., London.*
39.	BON	Kitchin 1749	*The London Magazine. London (1786 reprint).*
39.1	JPL	Kitchin 1764	*England Illustrated... R & J Dodsley, London.*
39.2	BON	Kitchin 1779	*The Large English Atlas by Emanuel Bowen And Thomas Kitchin, London.*
39.3	CAB	Kitchin / Bowles 1778	*Bowles's Pocket Atlas of the counties of South Britain or England and Wales, London.*
40.	BON	Martyn 1784	*New and Accurate Map of The County of Cornwall, (Rashleigh) Pub. W Faden, London.*
40.1	PER	Martyn 1784	*New and Accurate Map of The County of Cornwall, (Hoblyn) Pub. W Faden, London.*
41.	CAB	Kitchin and Jefferys 1749	*The Small English Atlas being a New and Accurate sett of maps... London.*
41.1	BON	Kitchin and Jefferys 1775	*The Small English Atlas, London.*
42.	PER	Bickham 1750	*The British Monarchy, London.*
45.	CAB	Gibson 1762	*The Universal Museum and Complete Magazine... Published J. Payne, London.*
46.	PER	Ellis 1764	*A Collection of Plans of The Principal Cities of Great Britain And Ireland. Pub. Dury, London.*
47.	CAB	De La Rochette 1766	*Ellis's English Atlas: Or a Compleat Chorography of England and Wales. Pub. J. Ellis, London.*
48.	BON	Tovey and Ginver 1794	*Complete Channel Pilot. Published by Laurie and Whittle, London.*
49.	CMB	Hatchett 1784	*The New British Traveller: Or A Complete Modern Universal..., State 1 Walpoole, London.*
49.1	CMB	Hatchett 1784	*The New British Traveller..., State 1, detail. Walpoole, London.*
49.2	CAB	Hatchett 1784	*The New British Traveller..., State 3 Walpoole, London.*
50.	CAB	Cary 1787	*Cary's New and Correct English Atlas, London.*
50.1	CAB	Cary 1809	*Cary's New and Correct English Atlas, London.*
50.2	CAB	Cary 1805	*Camden's Britannia (Gough), Pub Stockdale, London.*
50.3	CAB	Cary 1790	*Cary's Traveller's Companion, London.*
50.4	CAB	Cary 1806	*Cary's Traveller's Companion, London.*
50.5	CAB	Cary 1822	*Cary's Traveller's Companion, London (rotated text).*
50.6	CAB	Cary 1809	*Cary's New English Atlas, London.*
51.	CAB	Lodge 1788	*The Political Magazine, &c., By J. Murray, London.*
52.	CAB	Sudlow 1790	*Maps of the English Counties, by John Harrison, London.*
53.	CAB	Johnson 1790	*England Delineated. Or, A Geographical Description of Every County... by John Aikin, London.*
54.	CAB	Baker 1791	*The Universal Magazine of Knowledge and Pleasure, Volume LXXXIX. Pub. W. Bent, London.*
55.	CAB	Tunnicliff 1791	*A Topographical Survey of The Counties...Western Circuit, Salisbury, Exeter & London.*
56.	BON	Spence 1792	*A Survey of the Isles of Scilly. HM Topographic Office. London.*

Antique Maps of Cornwall and the Isles of Scilly

57.	CAB	Rowe 1798	*The Game of English Geography. John Fairburn, London.*
58.	CAB	Smith 1801	*Smith's New English Atlas. London.*
59.	CAB	Neele 1802	*Wilkes's Encyclopaedia Londoniensis. Or, Universal Dictionary... London.*
60.	JPL	Neele 1814	*The New British Traveller. Or, a Modern Panorama... Pub. J. Cundee. London.*
61.	CRO	Neele 1814	*Magna Britannia, Volume the Third. Lysons & Lysons, Pub. Cadell & Davies, London.*
62.	CAB	Neele 1820	*Pinnock's The History & Topography of Cornwall. Pub. G. & W.B. Whittaker, London.*
63.	CAB	Green 1803	*An Atlas of England. London.*
64.	PER	Luffman 1803	*New Pocket Atlas and Geography of England And Wales. Pub. Luffman et al. London.*
65.	CAB	Cole and Roper 1805	*The British Atlas. Pub. Vernor, Hood & Sharp, London.*
66.	CAB	Cooper 1808	*A Topographical Dictionary of the United Kingdom. B.P. Capper, Pub. R. Phillips, London.*
67.	CAB	Wallis 1812	*Wallis's New Pocket Edition of the English Counties, or Traveller's Companion. London.*
67.1	CAB	Wallis 1812	*Wallis's A New and Improved County Atlas. London.*
69.	CAB	Rowe 1816	*The English Atlas. London.*
70.	CAB	Langley 1817	*Langley's New County Atlas of England And Wales. Pub. Langley and Belch. London.*
71.	CAB	Crabb 1821	*Miller's New Miniature Atlas. London.*
72.	CAB	Hall 1820	*Leigh's New Pocket Atlas of England And Wales, Pub. Samuel Leigh, London.*
73.	CAB	Darton 1821	*A Complete Atlas of the English Counties, Dix & Darton, London.*
74.	CAB	Gardner 1822	*Smith's New English Atlas, London.*
75.	CAB	Migneret 1824	*L'Angleterre ou Description Historique et Topographique..., Pub. G-B. Depping, Paris.*
76.	BON	Greenwood C&J 1827	*Atlas of the Counties of England. C. & J. Greenwood, London.*
77.	CAB	Teesdale 1830	*A New British Atlas, Revised and Corrected. London.*
77.1	CAB	Teesdale/Haywood 1868	*The Travelling Atlas of England and Wales. Pub. Simpkin, Marshall & Co, London.*
78.	CAB	Hoare and Reeves 1830	*An Atlas of the English Counties, Pub. T.L. Murray, London.*
79.	CAB	Starling 1840	*Topographical Dictionary of England, 4th Edition. Pub. S. Lewis and Co, London.*
80.	CAB	Cobbett 1832	*Geographical Directory. London.*
81.	JPL	Davies 1832	*Devon and Cornwall Illustrated. Pub. H. Fisher, Son & Co., London.*
82.	CAB	Hoare and Reeves 1835	*A Complete County Atlas of England & Wales. Pub. James Duncan, London.*
83.	CAB	Scott 1833	*A New and Comprehensive Gazetteer of England and Wales. Pub. A. Fullerton & Co., London.*
84.	PER	Pigot and Co 1830	*Pigot & Co.'s British Atlas of The Counties of England. London & Manchester.*
85.	JPL	Archer 1833	*The Guide to Knowledge. Pub. William Edwards, London.*
85.1	CAB	Archer 1847	*Johnson's Atlas of England. Manchester.*
86.	PER	Moule 1848	*Barclay's Complete and Universal Dictionary. Pub. George Virtue, London*
87.	PER	Archer 1858	*Dugdale's England And Wales Delineated. Pub. Lucinda Tallis, London.*

Antique Maps of Cornwall and the Isles of Scilly

Directions

The geography of Cornwall is familiar to many, and less so to others: many areas called Hundreds are mentioned frequently in the book, and the map below shows where these nine Hundreds are, Scilly is the 10th. There a still a few counties where Hundreds are part of the landscape - the name has a few possible derivations: the area from which 100-armed men could be provided appears the most likely.

Several places are also mentioned as orthographic markers, and these are shown on the map below. They are discussed later; however, in summary:

Marazion, to the east of Penzance, in Penwith, is frequently marked on maps as 'Market Jew'. This is a corruption of the original Cornish, 'Marghas Yaw' meaning 'Thursday Market'.

Coldwind Cross, to the west of Truro, became 'Blow Ye Cold Wind' on several maps and, having been placed there, remained on maps for some time.

The island off the coast near Looe has a story all of its own and can be used as a marker to assess the trail of how it is referred to, on which map.

Richard Carew wrote a treatise on the history of Cornwall, in the early 1600s - he owned an estate at East Antony, opposite Plymouth, and constructed a saltwater pond to raise and keep fresh fish. This pond was marked by Norden and can also be used as a cartographic marker.

To the east of Davidstow, in north-east Cornwall, lies what is now Hallworthy. Norden marked this area of moors as 'Half Drunken Downs'. This became 'Hall Drunkard' and remained so until the early 1800s, (and even then, lingered on several post Ordnance Survey (OS) maps).

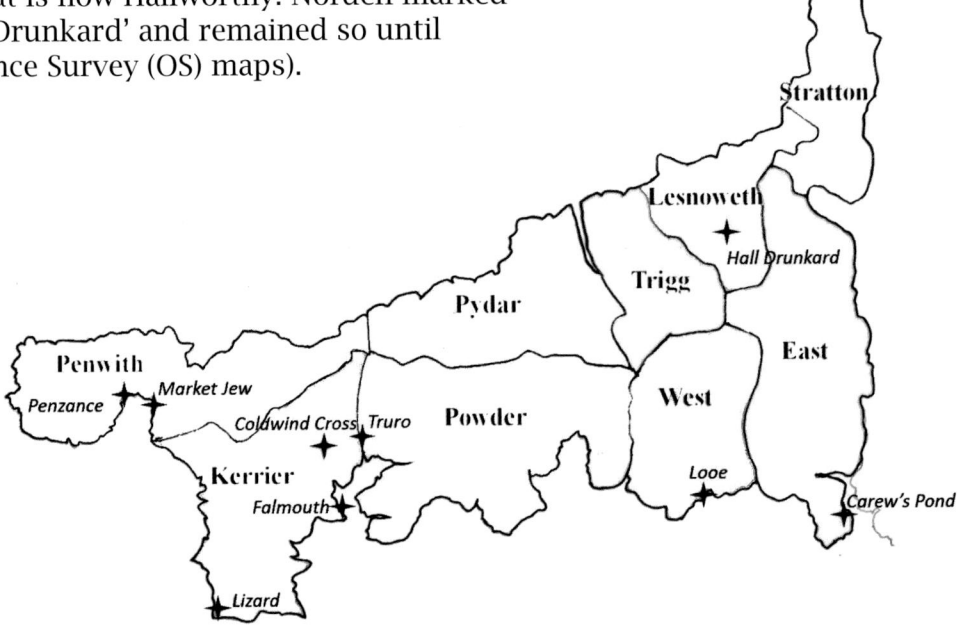

Antique Maps of Cornwall and the Isles of Scilly

Introduction

Map-making is among the earliest of the graphic arts acquired by man, and its origins are lost in antiquity. Primitive peoples have their own methods and conventions in map-making, but the important thing is that the art of constructing maps is common to all races, which suggests that the original skill developed independently and spontaneously among different peoples. It is not surprising, therefore, that maps hold a considerable fascination for many people, and in recent years a wealth of literature has grown up around the subject of old maps, and many devotees have become enthusiastic collectors.

County maps are probably the most popular of all the items sought after by the collector, and to assemble a complete set of the maps of any one county is an intriguing hobby. The maps of Cornwall hold an immediate and irresistible appeal for many who would not claim to be map collectors; the fact that Cornwall is almost surrounded by water gave the early map-makers an opportunity to incorporate ships and sea-monsters in the sea areas, thus adding to the decorative qualities already present in the shape of the coastline, so that the whole design becomes pictorially attractive.

This second edition has reworked and substantially enlarged the original 1966 version while keeping to the original date range. Each of the contributing maps is presented with a brief biography where possible, together with sufficient commentary to make possible the identification of the more important maps of the county from 1576 to 1846. Some important factors in differentiating later versions of the same maps are noted. After 1800 there appeared so many maps that space would not permit a full description of each, and therefore only a few outstanding examples have been included.

SECTION ONE:
1. SAXTON, CHRISTOPHER 1576
2. WAGHENAER, LUCAS JANSZOON 1584
3. DE BRY, THEODOR 1588
4. BOWES, WILLIAM 1590, 1595
5. VAN DEN KEERE, PIETER 1605
6. NORDEN, JOHN 1728
7. CAMDEN, WILLIAM 1586 et seq
8. MERCATOR, GERARD 1595

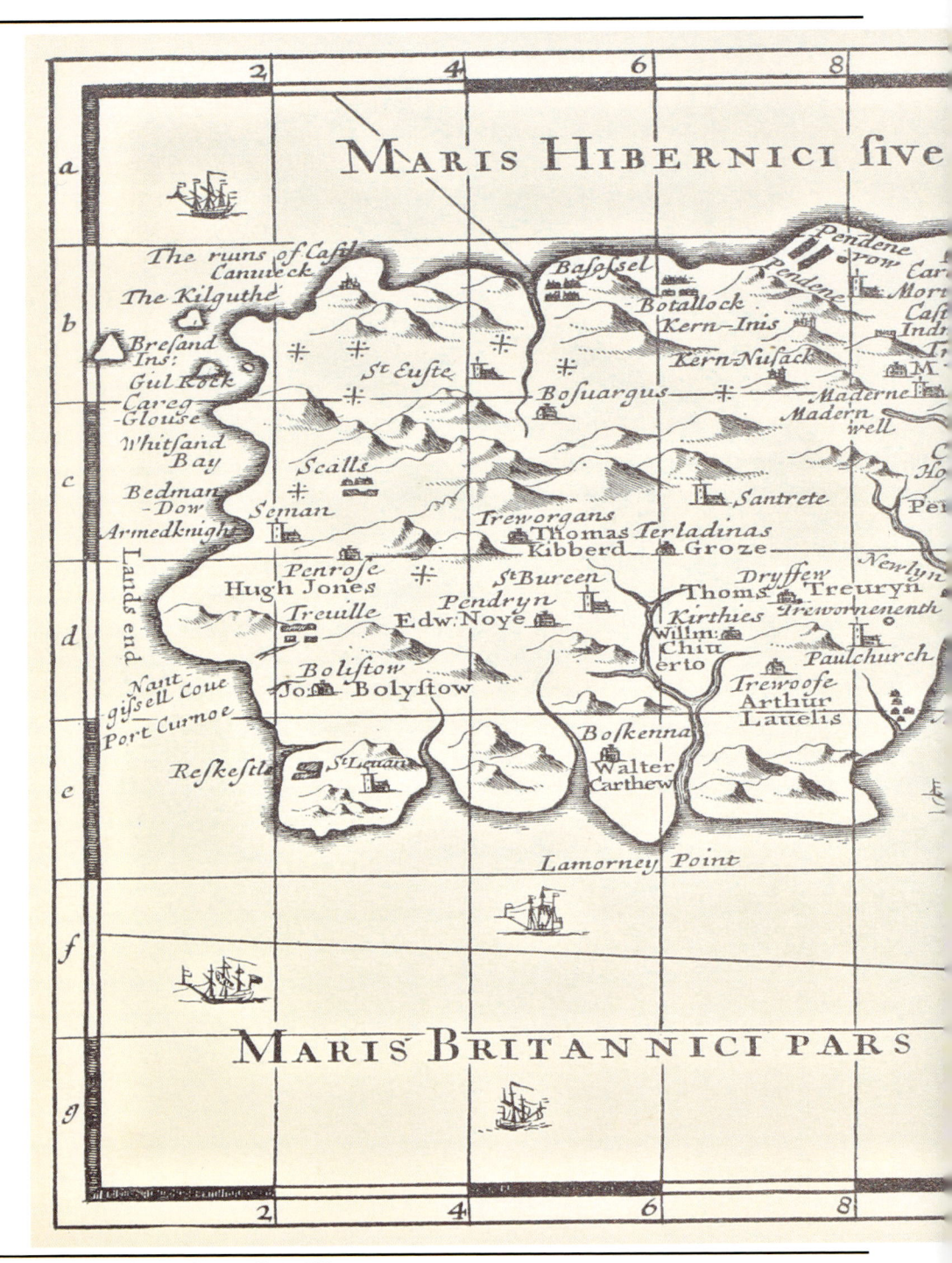

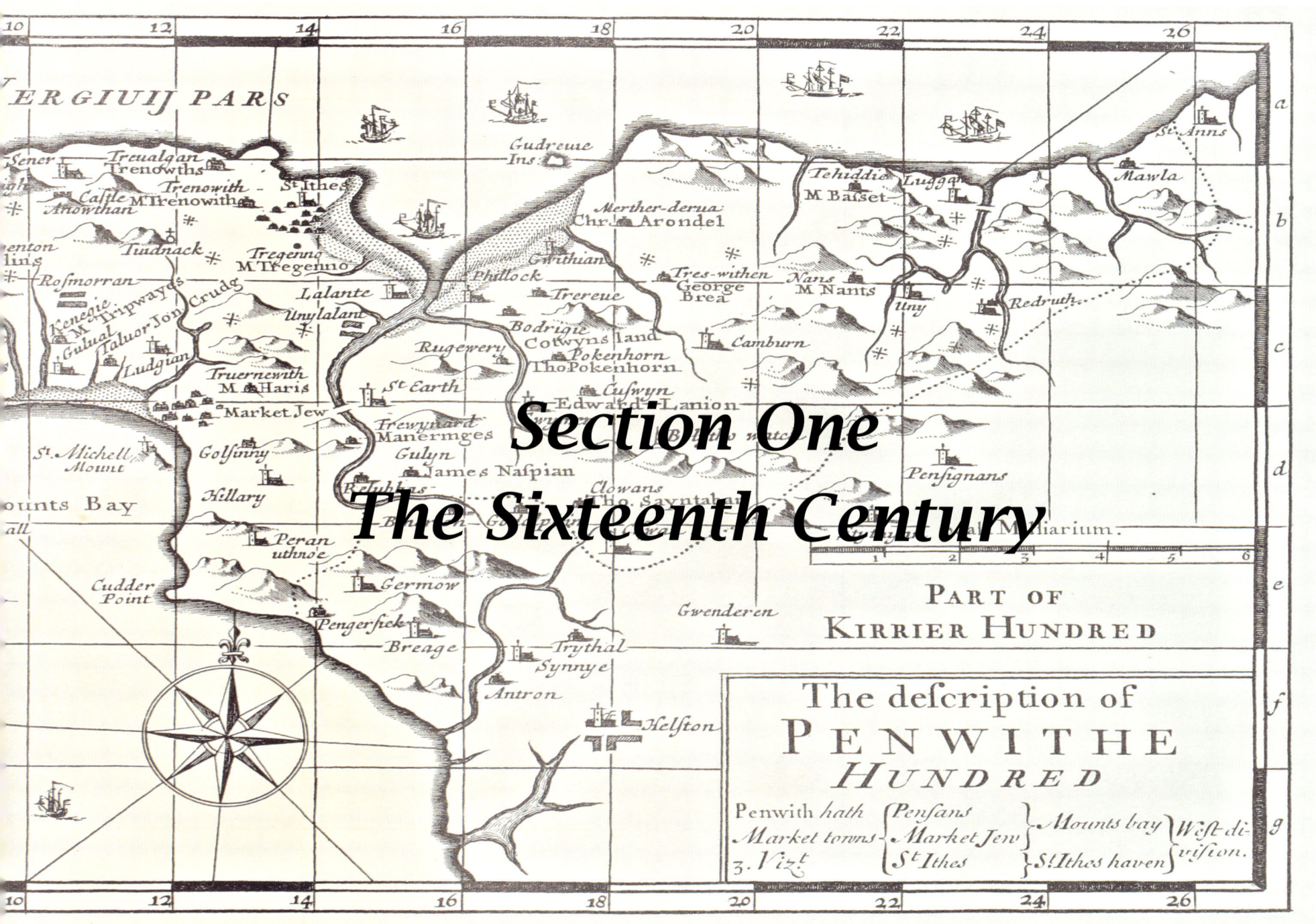

Section One
The Sixteenth Century

1. Saxton 1579 An Atlas of England And Wales, Christopher Saxton, London

1. SAXTON, CHRISTOPHER 1576

Eng. Terwoort, Pub. Saxton
(476 x 356)

Christopher Saxton was born at Dunningley (or Wakefield), about 1542, and after completing his education at Cambridge, he became attached to the household of Thomas Seckford, Queen Elizabeth's Master of the Court of Requests and Surveyor of the Court of Wards and Liveries. When he was about 30 years of age Saxton began his survey of all the English and Welsh counties. Working under the patronage of Seckford and the authority of the Queen, Seckford's open letter to local mayors and Justices ordered them to assist Saxton and guide him to any 'Towre, Castle or hill to view that countrey'.

The speed with which Saxton completed his maps, and the fact that surveying was possible only in summer, suggest that he must have had some access to existing manuscript maps of the period. Nevertheless, the feat of surveying the whole of England and Wales in detail was a prodigious one, and the maps produced are remarkable for their excellence. The map of Cornwall is delightful in a variety of ways; engraved on copper by Lenaert Terwoort of Antwerp, one of the Flemish refugees whom Seckford was fortunate enough to find working in London, is decorated in the ornate style of the Flemish school, with strapwork, fish, flowers, birds, galleons and sea monsters, the latter obviously very real in the mind of the artist who drew them! The Latin title is surmounted by the Royal Tudor arms of Elizabeth, supported by the lion and the Wessex dragon, thus symbolising the Queen's patronage, while below the map appear the arms of Thomas Seckford in acknowledgment of the gentleman's part in commissioning and financing the survey and publication of the maps. The narrow border is apparently an imitation of a carved and painted wooden frame, while the cartouches combine architectural devices and natural forms in a striking, if somewhat incongruous, manner.

However, the wealth of decorative details should not detract from the value of the map itself, which is indeed excellent. The general configuration is remarkably accurate when one considers the means at Saxton's disposal: evidently the map was intended to show the relative position of towns, and the omission of roads is rather surprising in view of the amount of travelling and the fact that at least one road-book had already been published. The cartographical innovations are worthy of attention here: firstly, the new conventional sign of a paling surrounding a piece of land, representing a park enclosed by the nobility ('Carabolok Parke'), and secondly, the use of different styles of lettering to show the relative importance of the various villages and towns, forests and Hundreds. Mapmakers used the former device for the next two centuries, while the latter is still employed today. The limits of the Hundreds (originally areas from which one hundred armed men were taken in times of war, but by that time administrative units) are marked by dotted lines, and their inclusion is unusual, appearing in only five of Saxton's county maps. Further distinction was made between villages and towns using one, two, or more towers alongside a place name, according to the size and importance of the settlement.

The map of Cornwall is dated 1576, and it is likely that single maps were sold separately from 1577 at which date Saxton was granted the right to print from the plates, although the complete atlas did not appear until 1579. Certain evidence, such as changes in some maps and variations in paper watermarks, suggests that the atlas was reissued several times before 1590, but the more important reprints, with alterations and additions, were issued in 1645 (William Web), c.1683-c.1693 (Philip Lea), 1720 (George Willdey), c.1749 (Thomas Jefferys) and c.1770 (C. Dicey & Co.). The Web and Lea editions show considerable changes that are described below (see #15 and #22). For over 200 years Saxton's map formed the basis from which many maps of Cornwall were copied, to a greater or lesser extent, each draughtsman copying his predecessors' work, so that mistakes persisted for a remarkable time! In this context, it may be noted that the island near 'Low' (Looe) is marked 'Sct Michael's Insul', since further reference to this point will be made in the section discussing John Norden (#6).

Several attempts to sort the various states of Saxton's Cornwall and later versions of the map have been made: Baynton-Williams supplies possibly the clearest version of what has been vexing cartologists for some time. This is a summary of that work:

State 1 — Pre-Atlas Proof, referred to as the Burleigh-Saxton – only one copy known (BM Royal 18 D. III, f.8.). The distinguishing features of this map are: The absence of the word 'Reginae' in the cartouche to the north of the county within the text 'Factum est hoc opus An Dm 1576 et D Elizabethe [Reginae] 18'. The scale in the lower left of the map has a scale of 1-10 miles. Below this the words 'Christophorus Saxton descripsit' are missing.

State 2 — Pre-Atlas Proof. Scale in the lower left now is 1-12 miles; the words 'Christophorus Saxton descripsit' have been added. Other details have been added. Atlas without title. The word 'Reginae' has been added to the cartouche 'Factum est hoc opus An Dm 1576 et D Elizabethe Reginae 18'. The county Hundreds have been added with their boundaries. Most copies in circulation are this state.

State 3 —

State 4 — A building symbol added to the top of St. Michael's Mount.

State 5 — William Web (1645).

State 6 — Postulated alterations post Web & pre-Lea; the engraver is unknown.

States 7/8 — Lea, (1689).

State 9 — Lea, (1694).

State 10 — Willdey (1732).

State 11 — Dicey/Jefferys (1770).

1579   An Atlas of England and Wales, by Christopher Saxton, London.

2. Wagenhaer 1592, Thresoor der Zeevaert. Amsterdam.

6   Antique Maps of Cornwall and the Isles of Scilly

2. WAGHENAER, LUCAS JANSZOON 1584

Eng. Deutecom, Pub. Waghenaer

(521 x 330)

Lucas Janszoon Waghenaer (1533-1606) was born in Enkhuizen, a port on the west side of the Zuider Zee - this is now the inland sea called the Ijsselmeer. Prior to producing his Spieghel der Zeevaerdt, Waghenaer was a sailor and very competent pilot. The book was first published in 1584 in Dutch and contained instructions for navigating the North Sea and Baltic. It was engraved by Baptist and Johannes van Deutecom - scions of a family of engravers from Deventer and printed by the Plantjin printing house in Leiden. Some versions of these charts of English coasts are signed by Jan Deutecom in the bottom right of the chart.

'The Rutter', as it was known, was reprinted four times in the first two years and sold for 4 guilders. A second volume was produced in 1585 and a Latin edition in 1586. A French edition followed in 1590. However, it was the English version published* in 1588 that propelled it as a popular and sought-after reference (see #3). The Privilege was acquired by Cornelis Claesz of Amsterdam in 1591 and sales fell away - it was too big and too expensive for the ordinary seaman.

This sea chart of the south-west coast of England is included because it contains the first printed map of the Isles of Scilly*, though in truth, the form shown is little more than a crude representation of the islands. The shape of the Cornish coast is surprisingly inaccurate, especially when one considers the superiority of Saxton's map which was published eight years earlier. Even the relative position of harbours was quite wrongly shown - Newlyn and Mousehole exchanged places. while Penzance did not figure on the map at all! Nonetheless the inclusion of soundings and safe anchorages (indicated by a small anchor) made the chart most valuable to mariners, while the addition of silhouettes of the coast as seen from two or three leagues out at sea was an important aid to navigation.

Quite apart from its utilitarian value, the chart is attractive in the decorative sense, charming in its incongruous combination of 'reality and fantasy'; the stylised sea is scattered with small ships with thundering cannon, sailing hither and thither among the most incredible sea monsters, while the land is embellished with sheep, horses and cattle set in a fairy-tale landscape of tiny fields, trees and houses.

* The family name appears variously as Waghenaer as well as Wagenhaer

* The English version - 'The Mariners' Mirrour' (see #3) should be considered as a separate publication.

1584   *Spieghel der Zeevaerdt by L.J. Wagenhaer, Reprinted four times between 1584 and 1586. Second Volume printed in 1585, Latin 1586, English 1588 (#3), French 1590, extended versions of the atlas were issued up to 1601.*

* *The Isles of Scilly: throughout the history of these islands and the maps presented, there are several variations of appellation. The 'Isles of Scilly' or 'Scilly' are locally preferred; other variants such as 'Scilly Islands' &c. are not favoured but do appear on various maps here.*

2.1 Waghenaer 1584 Spieghel Der Zeevaerdt. Amsterdam

8 Antique Maps of Cornwall and the Isles of Scilly

3. DE BRY, THEODOR   1588

Eng. de Bry, Trans. Ashley, Pub. ?Ashley
(508 x 330)

Theodor de Bry (1528-98) was a Protestant and was banished from his native Liège in southern Spanish Netherlands to Strasbourg in 1570. He moved to Antwerp in 1577, London in 1585 and Frankfurt in 1588 where he settled for the rest of his life. Sir Anthony Ashley, Bt (1551-1628), was a Wiltshire man who rose to the position of Clerk of the Privy Council (1587-1610). The Lord High Admiral Charles Howard I, Lord Howard of Effingham, persuaded the Privy Council that a translation of Waghenaer's sea atlas should be undertaken in English. Ashley did this accompanied by newly engraved plates by de Bry as well as other plates by Jodocus Hondius, Rutsinger and Augustine Ryther.

The Scilly to Plymouth chart is essentially a copy of the Waghenaer chart described above (#2) and is engraved by de Bry who signs the chart below the compass rose centre bottom. Many important changes were made, however, and this makes a comparison of the two charts most interesting. In the first place, the Dutch text is replaced by an English translation, and the admirable quality of de Bry's lettering immediately becomes evident. Secondly, the positions of place names are corrected at St. Just, St. Buryan and Newlyn, while this time it is the turn of Penzance to be included and Mousehole omitted. Further, there are subtle changes in the decoration used: the Tudor coat of arms is reduced in size and set within the Garter surmounted by a full crown with chapeau, the sphinx-like figure-head to the left of the cartouche now sports a beard, while small details, such as finials on the cartouche and figure-heads on the dividers above the scale, complete the design. The sea area in this chart is left plain, whereas the earlier version had a stylised wave decoration; in addition, the Lizard peninsula is shown running south-southeast rather than south-southwest. One small blemish mars these emendations, however; the Wolf Rock, marked on Waghenaer's chart as 'De Wolff', is unhappily called 'The Gulfe' on the revised version.

1588   *The Mariners' Mirrour*, by Anthony Ashley, London.

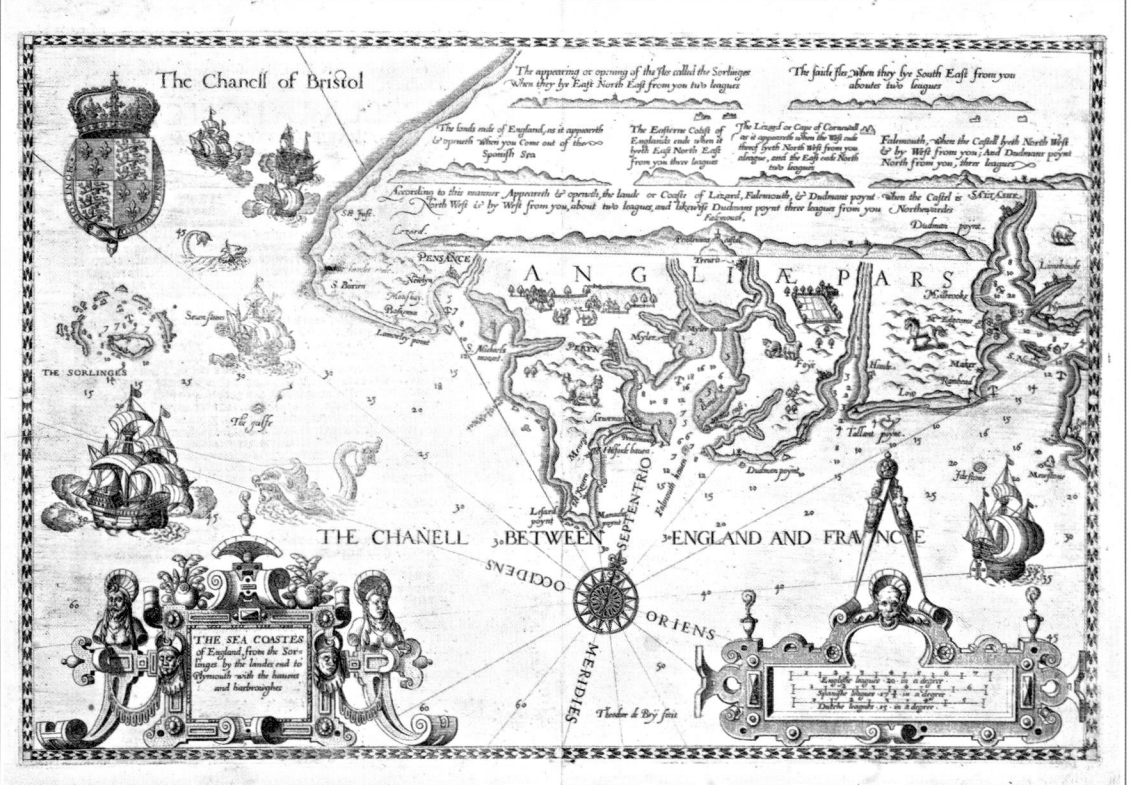

3. De Bry 1588 The Mariners' Mirrour, Anthony Ashley, London

Antique Maps of Cornwall and the Isles of Scilly

4. BOWES, WILLIAM 1590, 1595

Eng. Ryther, Pub. Bowes
(38 x 38) PLAYING CARDS

These tiny maps appeared on the first geographical playing cards ever issued, arranged in 'suits' corresponding to regions. No suit-marks were used, but the maps are numbered I to XIII; the map of Cornwall bears the number VIII at the top left and bottom right corners, showing it to be eighth in ascending order of size among the thirteen southwestern counties. The maps are on a uniform scale, with brief descriptive text above and below each county map, the card itself measuring 57mm x 95mm. Hills and rivers are shown, towns are marked by the initial letters and in addition to a compass rose, N., S., E. and W. are marked on the borders. These maps are copied from Saxton with the towns shown by initial letters only. It seems likely that the engraver used by Bowes was Augustine Ryther previously employed by Saxton.

1590   *Englan: Famous Plac: W.B. inuent*, London
1595   *Briefe descriptions shevving the contents of each particuler platt.* London.

---

5. VAN DEN KEERE, PIETER 1605

Eng. Van Den Keere, Pub. ?Claesz then Blaeu
(121 x 83)

Pieter van den Keere (1571- c.1646) was a Flemish engraver whose family moved from Ghent to London in 1584 as religious émigrés. He became an artist and bookseller and it was van den Keere's sister Collette who married Jodocus Hondius (1563-1612) in 1587; Hondius engraved most of John Speed's county maps and instructed van den Keere in the art of engraving. In 1593 Hondius and van den Keere moved to Amsterdam. The series of small maps was derived from those of Saxton and published in miniature atlas form (probably sold loose) in Amsterdam between 1605 and 1610. In 1617 the maps were reprinted by W. J. Blaeu in a small edition of Camden's 'Britannia', and from 1627 to 1676 they figured in a 'pocket edition' of John Speed's 'Theatre' for which reason they are often known as 'miniature Speeds'.

Van den Keere's map of 'Cornuwaillia' is a reduced copy of Saxton's; the number of place names is reduced as a function of the smaller map, with most of them marked as a circle with a small church tower perched atop. Some attempt at showing highlands has been made, along with the rivers. No roads or

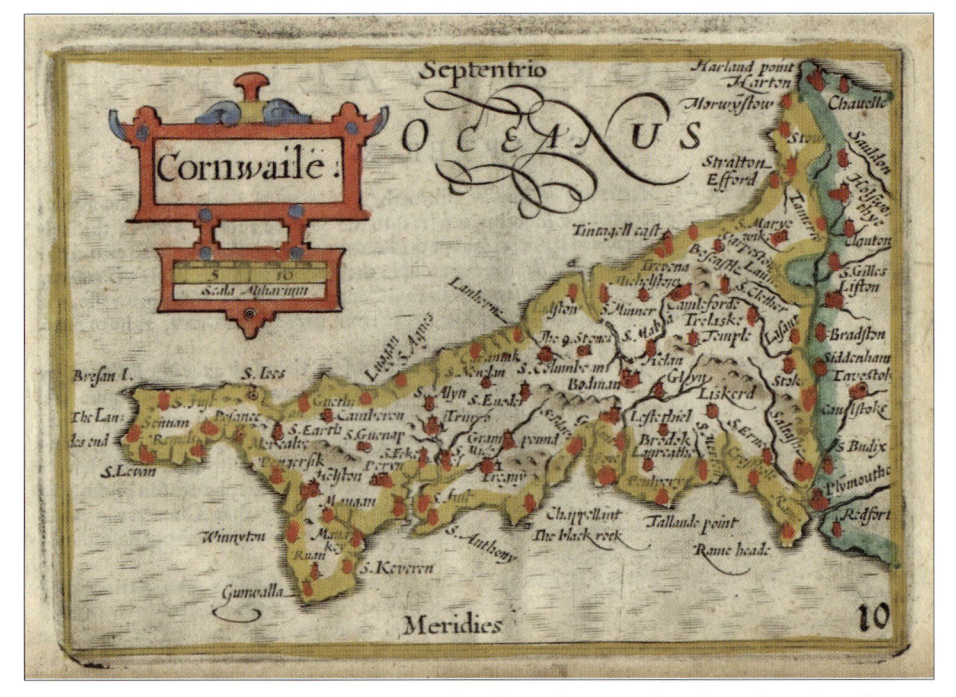

5.1 Van Den Keere 1627 England, Wales, Scotland and Ireland Described and Abridged. Humble, London

10 **Antique Maps of Cornwall and the Isles of Scilly**

Hundreds are marked. The sea area is dealt with by a series of horizontal lines (shot-silk) creating zigzags and giving the impression of calm waters. Speed (or more probably Hondius) continues using this device on his Cornwall map (#11). Rather at odds with the rest of the perfunctory style elsewhere, and engraved to the north of the county, is the very ornately flourished title 'Oceanus'. The rectangular cartouche labelling the county 'Cornuwaillia' with a basic scale of miles (Scala Milarium) lies below this, above St. Ives. The county outline has been canted slightly so the Devon-Cornwall border runs parallel with the right margin - an accommodation Saxton started and which leads to many maps incorrectly showing the county as lying east-west. The level of detail, especially in the shot-silk, gives an indication of the wear of the plate, with later copies showing a marked degradation.

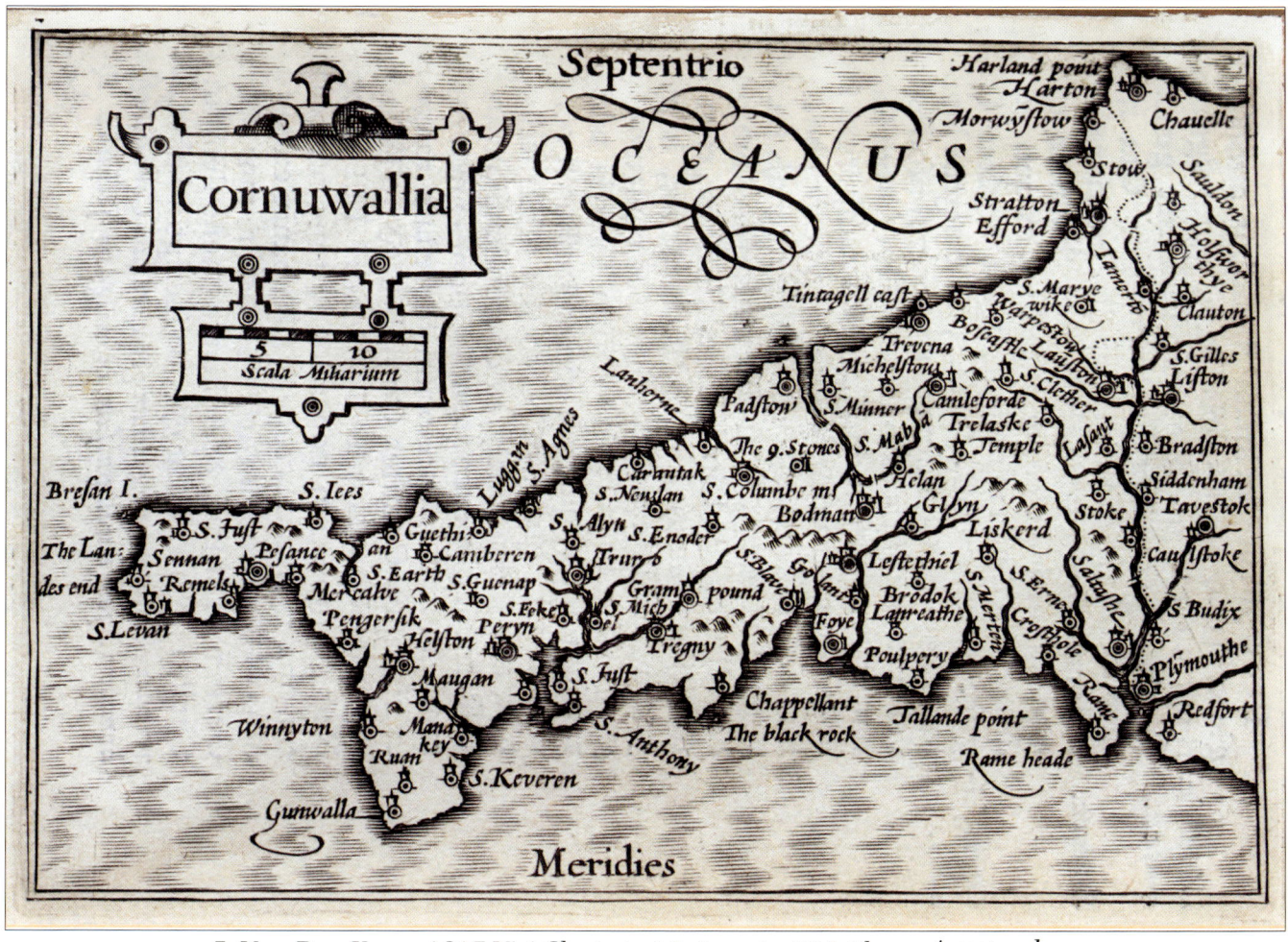

5. Van Den Keere 1617 Viri Clarissimi Britannia, W.J. Blaeu, Amsterdam

1605-10 Loose maps sold in Amsterdam. The English maps including Cornwall are based on Saxton; there is no text on the rear. Some are dated 1599, others are signed 'Petrus Kaerius' (Cornwall has neither marks). All plates were sold in 1609 by Cornelis Claesz possibly to Willem Blaeu. .

1617 'Cornuwaillia' Guilielmi Camdeni, Viri clarissimi Britannia, sive florentissimorum Regnorum Angliae, Scotiae, Hiberniae, & Insularum adjacentium … description. Amsterdam, Guilielmi Ianssonij Blaeu, Amsterdam. Latin text to the rear of the maps. Plate number (101) added to left border about 1 inch from the top. Reprints: 1617, 1627, 1632, 1646, 1662, 1666, 1668 & 1676.

1619 England, Wales and Ireland (1619/27) No text on rear of map.

1627 England, Wales, Scotland and Ireland Described and Abridged… from a Farr Larger Voulume Done by John Speed. London: G. Humble. Title renamed 'Cornwaile', plate number (10) added bottom right. Text on reverse in English from Speed. 1627 (1632); William Humble, (1646); Roger Rea, 1662, 1666, 1666, (1668); Thomas Bassett and Richard Chiswell, 1676.

Antique Maps of Cornwall and the Isles of Scilly

6. NORDEN, JOHN 1728

Eng. Pine, Pub. Bateman

(313 x 159)

This first section in italics is left here from the first edition of this book in 1966. The purpose here is to give the reader a refresher on the thinking at the time in terms of the connections between Norden's publication in 1728 and the as then undiscovered manuscript in 1970.

John Norden, a contemporary of Saxton, was born in 1548, possibly in Somerset. A lawyer turned estate-manager and surveyor, he became so enthusiastic about regional geography that he began a series of county handbooks under the general title 'Speculum Britanniae' but failed to complete the work because he lacked the backing of a wealthy patron. The few items which did appear in print during his own lifetime were published at Norden's own expense – descriptions and maps of Middlesex and Hertfordshire, maps only of Surrey, Sussex and 'Hamshire'.

Norden's 'Description of Cornwall' was not published in print until 1728, but the manuscript text and original drawings must have been used as source material by William Kip (#9) and John Speed (#7) when they drew their versions of the map of Cornwall.

The ten maps which were published with Norden's text in 1728 (nine of the individual Hundreds and one general map of the County) present something of an enigma; there is no record of maps actually drawn by Norden at the time of his survey work in Cornwall in 1584, and quite possibly the maps were 'fabricated' from material given in Norden's text and other maps (e.g. Kip and Speed) at the time of the 1728 publication. However, there are several considerations which detract from the force of the explanation. In the first place, the shape of the general map of Cornwall given in Norden's work is typically the shape used in maps of the late 16th and early 17th centuries, such as Saxton, Kip and Speed. Secondly, the map of East Hundred shows 'A Salt water pond' at Antony, the seat of Richard Carew; by 1728 this pond had fallen into such disrepair that it had virtually disappeared, having been neglected after the death of Richard Carew in 1620.

Thus, if the map had been compiled for the 18th century publisher, the draughtsman made a deliberate attempt to represent Cornwall as Norden (and Carew) had known it, and this is borne out by the names of the owners of the various houses and estates shown on the map, all of them being of the 1600 period as listed in Norden's manuscript. Neither of these two points would invalidate the possibility that the maps had been compiled by reference to Norden's MS. supplemented by Richard Carew's Survey of Cornwall, published in 1602. Now if we turn our attention to William Kip's map of 1607 (#9), we find that Kip had correctly inserted several place names not found on Saxton's map of 1576 (#1), and these additional place names are the ones given in Norden's text. It would not be possible to position these place names correctly from Norden's text alone, and there is no record of any original survey work having been done by William Kip. (Moreover, Kip's map shows items not mentioned in Camden's 'Britannia' or Carew's Survey, as for example, Trethevy Quoit and the house at Lanrest. Both places are recorded by Norden). This suggests that there must have been some form of manuscript map by Norden to which Kip had access, but unfortunately there is no conclusive evidence of its existence. In May 1606, Richard Carew wrote to William Camden in reference to a proposed revision of his Survey of Cornwall, thus: 'and if I wist where to find Mr. Norden I would also fain to have his map of our shire, for perfecting of which he took a journey into these parts'. Again, the evidence is inconclusive but at least Carew had the impression that such a map had been made.

Finally, however, we must return to the view that the 1728 maps were not merely engraved copies of original maps by Norden, if these did in fact exist. The one important clue that brings us to this conclusion is the naming of the island at Looe 'St. George's Island'. Nowhere in Norden's text is the island mentioned at all, and the only contemporary document to give it this name is Carew's Survey of 1602. This would explain why Kip retained the name 'St. Michael's Isle', as given on the Saxton map, and the version of the name continued to appear on all the 'copied' maps of the 17th century, through Speed, Blaeu and Jansson, down to Morden and, rather oddly, on the map by Herman Moll (#31), which in other respects is copied from Gasgoyne rather than the Saxton-Kip-Speed succession. Curiously enough, the name 'St. George's Island' does not occur again until the Greenwood map of 1827 (#75) and Pigot's map of 1831 (#84), by which time the Ordinance Survey maps had adopted the name. 'St. Michael's Isle' would appear to be historically correct, since from the 12th century there was a chapel of St. Michael de Lammana (Lemain) on Looe Island, Lammana being a cell of Benedictine Monks, subject to the Abbey of Glastonbury, on the mainland at Portloe Barton.

Updated 2018 Section:

Norden has been placed here before Camden, Kip and Speed. His 'lost' manuscript drove Cornish cartography at this time, despite his publication being delayed until 1728; our reasons for this will become evident herewith.

A postulation that there had to be an original manuscript <u>and</u> maps was made in the first edition (see italic section above); however, it took a further four years to solve the puzzle. The conundrum was finally unravelled by Professor William Ravenhill of Exeter University on 8 July 1970 and published in 1972. The entire story is complex and touches several aspects of national as well as local history. Ravenhill's write-up makes fascinating reading of Norden's struggle to survey and publish what is probably one of the main themes of the mapping of Cornwall. What follows is a summary of Ravenhill's conclusions.

In 1728 Christopher Bateman published a limited run (perhaps 200 copies) of a book ostensibly written by John Norden some 120 years previously – it contained nine maps of the Hundreds of Cornwall as well as a map of the whole county. The book is a 104-page attempt at cataloguing the county, but at the same time sparked a mystery that took 244 years to solve. What was missing was the suspicion that there had to be a forebear to the published book that was contemporaneous with the survey.

The manuscript in Norden's handwriting is in the Harleian Collection (Harl. MS 6252) in the British Library. In it are several illustrations Norden had done as part of the intended book. The original hand-drawn maps had been replaced by the engraved maps that appear in Bateman's publication in 1728 – the original manuscript maps were 'missing'. Ravenhill determined that the manuscript maps must be in Trinity College Cambridge's library, where they were eventually discovered: they had lain there since about 1738. The triangular mileage table that appears in the front of the 1728 publication was inserted by Bateman; it does not appear in the original manuscript.

The original surveying of Cornwall appears to have been done in several stages. Norden had noted that Camden's 'Britannia' in its earliest form (1586 et seq.) lacked maps to support the text. (Camden himself noted this and rectified it by the 1607 edition, where he added maps by Kip, Hole and Norden). Norden formulated a plan, sometime between 1586 and 1590, to combine a text and map treatise across the whole country and almost immediately ran up against the issue of finance. He was able to produce several manuscripts: 'Specvlvm Northamtoniae' (1591), 'Historicall and Chorographicall Discription of Middlesex' (1593) and a draft for the county of Essex (1594). It was this last one that threatened to curtail any further publications, and indeed could have cost him his life. The draft of a manuscript of Essex was done with the expectation that the Earl of Essex, Robert Devereux, along with Lord Burghley, William Cecil, who was Lord Lieutenant of Essex at the time, would agree to patronise the final production. At the same time, Norden was able to present to Elizabeth I a vellum volume of his endeavours over the counties of Middlesex, Essex, Surrey, Sussex, Ham[p]shire, and the islands of Wight, Guernsey and Jersey. Norden produced three county maps – Surrey, Sussex and Hampshire, with some direct and indirect help from Burghley. In 1597 Norden appealed to Lord Burghley for assistance in producing an account of Hertfordshire – it was unsuccessful, and the following year Burghley died, leaving Norden to complete the work at his own expense. An appeal to Elizabeth I where Norden pleaded, cajoled and might have overstated his predicament, came to naught and Norden was obliged to carry on alone.

It appears that Norden may have started work on Cornwall around 1580 and returned to it after his Hertfordshire

6. Norden ~1596. "Lost" Hand drawn Manuscript map of Cornwall. Compare to published version overleaf

William Ravenhill (ed.) John Norden's Manuscript Maps of Cornwall and Its Nine Hundreds, University of Exeter Press, 1972. Used with the kind permission of the Masters and Fellows of Trinity College, Cambridge.

work. At the same time, his association with Devereux, Earl of Essex, took on a more ominous aspect. Devereux talked Elizabeth into sending him to Ireland as Lord Lieutenant, in 1599, with the intent of ending the Nine Years' War. His conduct there infuriated Elizabeth and even more so when he returned to London without her permission later that year. Essex was tried in 1600 and again in 1601, this time for treason. He was executed on 25 February 1601. Into all this Norden had unwittingly wandered and evidently supported Essex with the possibly naïve publication termed 'Prayer for the Prosperous Proceedinge and Good Success of the Earl of Essex' published in 1599. Norden's support of Essex was there in print. When Norden appealed for funds to carry on his surveys his entreaties fell on deaf ears. With the death of Elizabeth I in 1603, things started to look more hopeful – James I came to the throne with a son, Henry Frederick (1594-1612). Henry automatically gained the title Duke of Cornwall with the accession of his father to the English throne. This state of affairs invigorated Norden to press his case for a patron of his Cornwall manuscript. After a number of exchanges, Norden, in January 1605, found himself granted the surveyorship of the lands of the Duchy of Cornwall for life. However, following the survey of the vast estate in Dorset belonging to Lord Burghley's son, Viscount Cranborne, it appears that Norden's dream of a 'Speculum Britanniae' and thereby Cornwall died for lack of funds.

Norden's original manuscript and hand-drawn maps were presented to James I sometime after June 1604 (the last death noted in the book is that of Sir Jonathan Trelawny that month) and remained in the Royal Library until their removal during the Dispersion of the Royal Library in 1642. This document came into the possession of the Cecil family, Earls of Exeter. At some time in the late 1600s a copy was made possibly for Robert Bruce, 1st Earl of Ailesbury – this was a scribe's copy and had larger handwriting than Norden's. This caused all the page references &c. to be out of alignment and furthermore was bound together with Norden's work on Middlesex and Hertfordshire. The Cecil family sold their version, along with other items, at auction in 1687, where it came into the possession of Richard Chiswell (see Speed's publishers (#11)). By 1720, it came into the hands of Benjamin Cawse, another London bookseller and apprentice of Chiswell's. He sold the text only to Christopher Bateman for £20 in 1723. In the meantime, the copy made for Robert Bruce, which possibly never included the maps, was also sold at auction around 1685 and went to Dr Thomas Gale, Regius Professor of Greek at Cambridge and avid bibliophile. Dr Gale gave this to his son, Roger Gale. It is this copy of the text that ended up in Trinity College's library in Cambridge in 1738. Benjamin Cawse had the original version and maps – he loaned the maps to Roger Gale, so at one point the maps from the original version and the scribe's copy were together. In preparation to publish the text Christopher Bateman had bought for £20, Bateman borrowed the maps from Roger Gale and had John Pine engrave nine maps of the Hundreds, as well as the main Cornwall map. The book was published in 1728. The original maps were returned to Roger Gale, who bound them with the scribe's copy. In 1738 Gale sent this copy, together with a lot of other manuscripts &c., to Trinity, where it sat until Ravenhill unearthed it in 1970. The original text that Bateman still had was bound up with the newly engraved maps by Pine and presented by Christopher Bateman to Edward Harley, 2nd Earl of Oxford,, to whom he, Bateman, had dedicated the book. This bound copy went into the library of the Earl of Oxford and later this became part of the Harleian Collection.

William Ravenhill (1919-95) was Reardon Smith Professor of Geography at Exeter University. In his analysis of John Norden's maps of Cornwall, he brought modern geographic analysis to the questions around whether Norden surveyed and drew the maps alone or used pre-existing maps as a basis for his own. From this, he considers Norden's main map of Cornwall to be based on that of Saxton with an overall reduction in scale of about 15%. (This is discussed further in the appendices). The techniques used by Elizabethan cartographers were undergoing something of a revolution, it is likely that Norden did not use traversing alone – measuring the distances between known points (town to town distances were tabulated and used extensively). If this were the only method, then the paths between the towns would have naturally been recorded as well – in the maps of Saxton, Speed and Kip no roads are drawn. A

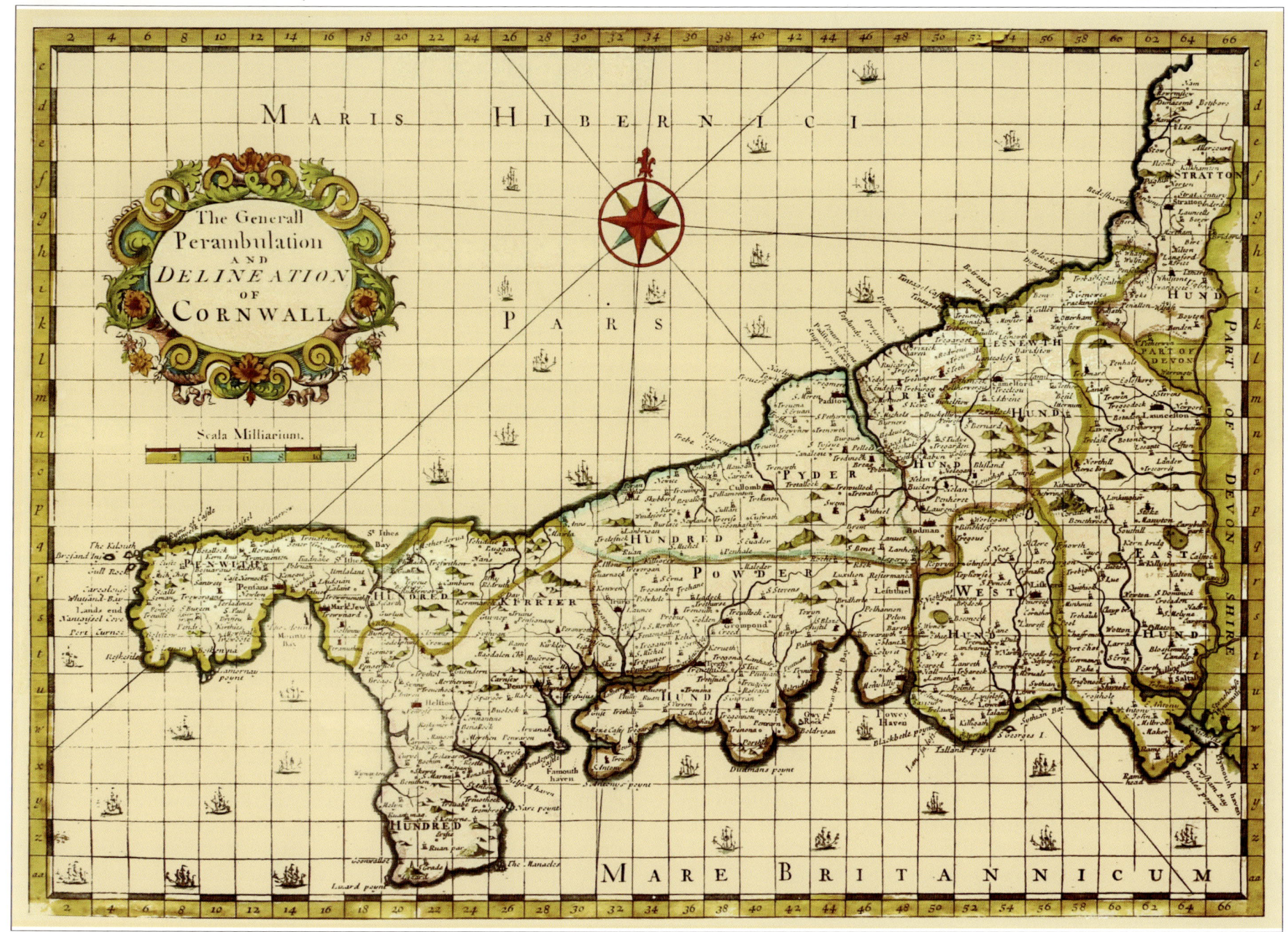

6.1 Norden 1728 Speculi Britanniae Pars. Bateman, London

quicker technique is triangulation. This was imported from Europe in the mid 1500s – Gerard Mercator had used it in his map of Flanders in 1540. This method focussed on tying suitable high spots together – church steeples, hilltops &c. were obvious candidates. Ravenhill contended that Norden would have taken a field copy of Saxton's map, and by using the already mapped church towers, spires, hills &c. would have added details, made corrections and so forth.

Further analysis of Norden's map in comparison with Saxton's strongly suggests that, while he may have referred to Saxton's map en route, Norden nonetheless produced some ground-breaking mapping of his own: he added a number of place names over those recorded by Saxton. In the Penwith Hundred alone, Norden recorded 101 place names, compared with Saxton's 58. Nonetheless, there are several major alterations in the outline of the county, which are discussed in the appendices. While Saxton's and Norden's outlines are comparable, there are several items that set Norden apart from Saxton and very much at the vanguard of subsequent maps.

The Island near Looe Story

Throughout these maps from Saxton to Moule, the island near Looe has proven to be an orthographic challenge. Since the 12th century there was a chapel of St. Michael de Lammana (Lemain) on Looe Island. Lammana, a cell of Benedictine Monks, subject to the Abbey of Glastonbury, was on the mainland at Portloe Barton (0.6 miles west of West Looe). In 1536, following the dissolutions of the monasteries, the small chapel on the island became the property of the Crown and in 1594 it was rededicated as St. George's Island. Within the text of the 1728 book by Norden (and one presumes the original manuscript), the island is only mentioned once, in the index of the general map as part of a preface ahead of the general map of the county itself. The East Hundred and general Cornwall maps (both in the hand-drawn pre-1604 versions and the 1728 published versions) show St. George's Island; however, the map of the West Hundred (to which the island belongs) does not show it, nor does the relevant chapter mention it. In the index to the general map, Norden offers two alternatives: 'S. Michael's Ins or S.

6.2 Norden ~1598. Extract of Kerrier map.
Note the enhanced relief on the south coast

George's', alongside the correct grid reference W54. The only contemporary document to give it this name is Carew's Survey of 1602: *'Almost directly ouer against the barred hauen of Loo, extendeth S. Georges Iland, about halfe a mile in compasse, and plentifully stored with Conies.'* At the stage of committing a single name onto the map, Norden, in line with Carew, opted for the newer 'St. George's Island'. 'St. Michael's Isle' is historically correct, right to the point that Saxton recorded the name during his survey sometime in the mid 1570s – obviously the change to

Antique Maps of Cornwall and the Isles of Scilly

'St. George's' in the 1590s didn't come to Kip's attention, or, since he had two common points of reference, (Norden and Saxton had both used 'St. Michael's Island' as one option), Kip went with the safer choice, and it became 'St. Michael's Island' for the next 230+ years.

Norden can be considered a pioneer of a few interesting cartographical innovations that can be seen in his Cornwall map:

- A marginal grid reference system which greatly facilitated map reading and is still in use today in a modified form, an innovation probably suggested to Norden by William Smith, who had acquired this art from his association with German cartographers while living in Nuremberg,
- A symbol denoting sand-dunes (as at Perranzabuloe and Padstow), another device that has survived in present-day maps.
- Finally, and only on the hand-drawn manuscript version: 3D shading of the south-facing cliff line, especially around the Lizard area, gives the map a perception of depth. Speed, Blaeu, Jansson, Lea and Nicholls took up this style.

1728 Speculi Britanniae Pars: A Topographical and Historical Survey of Cornwall, by John Norden. Printed by William Pearson, Sold by Christopher Bateman, London

7. CAMDEN, WILLIAM 1586 et seq

William Camden (1551-1623) is included here since he played a pivotal role in the advancement of cartography in the late 1500s and early 1600s. He gained a BA (Oxon) in 1573 before entering Westminster School as a teacher in 1575. He started on his magnum opus 'Britannia' in 1577. This was to be a description of the whole of Great Britain and Ireland, both in terms of history and geography. The first edition was published in Latin in May 1586 with a general map by Mercator, and ran to a further five editions: 1587, 1590, 1594, 1600 and 1607. It was the 1607 version that contained, for the first time, county maps based on the surveys of Saxton and Norden, featuring maps by Kip (34 maps, including Cornwall (#9)), Hole (21 maps) and Norden (6 maps). The first English version was translated by Philémon Holland and published in 1610; the final version of 'Britannia' was published in 1637. Edmund Gibson published later revisions with Morden's maps included in 1695, 1717, 1722, 1737, 1753 and 1772. In 1593 Camden was appointed headmaster of Westminster School, a post he held until his appointment by the College of Heralds as Clarenceux King of Arms in 1597. There is little doubt that this position would have brought him into contact with some highly placed members of Parliament, as well as the Courts of both Elizabeth I and James I – Camden himself is shown in Elizabeth's funeral cortège in full Herald's regalia.

This leads us into the puzzle of who knew what in the story of John Norden's manuscript and the maps that were presented to James I in about 1604 (see section on Norden (#6)). It seems reasonable that Kip, Speed and/or Hondius must have seen details of Norden's work in order to compile their own maps – Speed acknowledges Norden publicly; while there is little doubt Kip too had sight of Norden's work, he does not make any direct reference to it on the Cornwall map (#9). Camden does acknowledge both Saxton and Norden in his preface to the 1607 edition of his 'Britannia'. For Kip to have seen this, we have to assume that either he did so legitimately before Norden presented it to James I, (it is difficult to conceive how Kip would have had access to the Royal Library once Norden's work was placed in it), or was allowed access to it after it had been placed there by someone with access to the Royal Library – i.e. Camden. Or, there was a draft version long since lost. Kip had already engraved for Norden previously (Hertfordshire 1598), so it does not seem unreasonable for Norden to permit Kip sight of his Cornwall work. One of the issues we have with this is that Norden's intent, which matured at some stage in the late 1590s, was to produce a rival to Camden's 'Britannia', but including maps - this was to become his 'Speculum Britanniae'. Would Norden have given free, unimpeded access to anyone - even Kip - at this stage? It seems illogical to bruit the existence of a work that could eclipse Camden's 'Britannia' ahead of it being published (it never was). So, we are left with the possible conclusion that Norden presented his 'Description of Cornwall' to the Royal Court at some time around 1604 and realised soon thereafter that the dream of 'Speculum Britanniae' was just that and allowed Camden/Kip and Speed/Hondius sight of either a copy or draft of his Cornwall manuscript. Whichever route was used, it is evident that Norden was credited by Camden and Speed, and presumably therefore was aware that his surveys were being used.

In 1609 Camden moved to Chislehurst, in Kent; he died there in 1623 and is buried in Westminster Abbey, with a monument in the south transept featuring him clasping a copy of his famous 'Britannia'. The London Borough of Camden is connected to William Camden, though the route is not a direct one: Camden moved to Kent and into a house that became known as Camden('s) Place (it is now Chislehurst Golf Club). The house came into the hands of Charles Pratt in about 1760, who was the Attorney General and later Lord Chancellor. On his ennoblement in 1765 he took the title Baron Camden of Camden Place, and in 1786 became Earl Camden. One of his contributions in law was the opposition to perpetual copyright; (in the context of maps and rife plagiarism here, the irony is palpable!). Earl Camden had acquired land that was once the manor of Kentish Town through marriage. This land was used by him to develop a residential district in the 1790s; this became known as Camden Town.

William Camden's legacy to British cartography was the inclusion of maps to his guide that reflected the public's increasing interest in understanding their land and history - that the book continued to be popular for almost 200 years is a clear testament to this.

1586   Britannia, Latin without maps: Reprints 1587, 1590, 1594 & 1600.
1607   Latin with maps (#9).
1610   English with maps, 1637 (#9).
1695   Edmund Gibson Pub: 1695, 1717, 1722, 1737, 1753 and 1772 (#20).

7. William Camden 1623
From Camden's Britannia 1695

Antique Maps of Cornwall and the Isles of Scilly

8. MERCATOR, GERARD 1595

Eng. Mercator?, Pub. Mercator Jnr then Hondius
(368 x 466)

Gerard Mercator (1512-94) is renowned for creating a projection that bears his name even today. He is credited with the first use of the word 'Atlas' to mean a collection of maps. There is an immense amount of information elsewhere on his extensive output; however, his inclusion here is for three reasons:

The 1595 'Atlas' (using the word for the first time) was published posthumously by his son Rumold and ran to many editions, being later acquired and republished by Jodocus Hondius from 1604. The Atlas contains sixteen maps of Britain, one of which plate XV is the south-west quadrant of England and Wales, encompassing South Wales and the south-west of England, including Cornvbia (Cornwall).

Three things are of note here: the outline of Cornwall could be easily compared with Saxton's outline: with the space available, Mercator omitted Newlyn near Penzance but included its eastern counterpart St. Newland; Marazion (Market Jew) has become Mercatu; Henry VIII's castles at Pendennis and St. Mawes are shown. Mercator placed sticks on the circles indicating towns/villages, pointing to the place names to avoid confusion.

The second point to be made is the use of latitude and longitude. Mercator shows both and is one of the earliest cartographers to do so. Penzance is clearly marked as 50° 24' North and 13° 58' East (of The Azores). Today's co-ordinates are actually (from Greenwich) 50° 06' North, 5° 31' West. The error with longitude is to be expected - it wouldn't be resolved for more than a century hence. His location of Penzance would appear to be fairly good; however, upon checking his latitude in whole degrees, he has used about forty-eight miles to a degree; this is about 70% of its correct value. Prime meridians and Greenwich especially are discussed under the section dealing with Smith (#58).

Finally, the Latin inscription bottom left, and shown in the detailed illustration: 'Lethowsow qua recedente esta nudata tantum apparet, vulgo "The Gulf"', loosely translated as 'Lethowsow exposed at low tide, commonly known as The Gulf'. Lethowsow is Cornish and means 'Milky Ones'. It refers to the Seven Stones reef mid-way between Land's End and the Scillies, but also to the much older Cornish folklore of Lyonesse. Mercator has noted it as a fair-sized island at quite a distance off the coast. It is curious that he has not shown the Sorlinges or Scillies, which had been shown on maps at least 100 years previously; indeed, he had himself shown the Sorlinges on his 1554 map - so why not here?

1595   *Atlas Sive Cosmographicae Meditationes de Fabrica Mundi et Fabricati Figura. Edited by Rumold Mercator, Duisberg.*

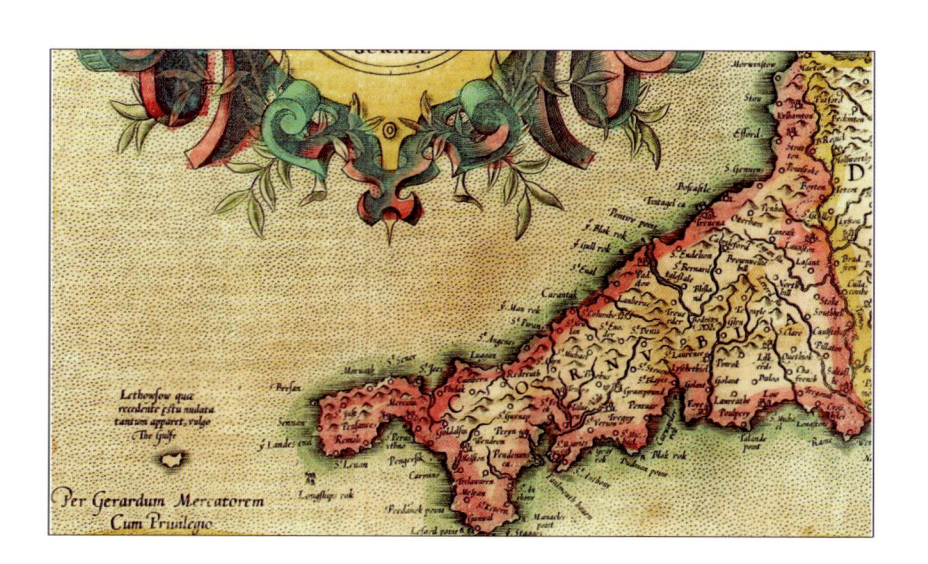

8.1 Mercator 1595: Detail of Cornwall

8. Mercator, 1595 Atlas Sive Cosmographicae... Duisberg

SECTION TWO:
9. KIP, WILLIAM 1607
10. BLAEU, WILLEM 1608, 1623
11. SPEED, JOHN 1610
12. HOLE, WILLIAM 1612
13. BILL, JOHN 1626
14. VAN LANGEREN, JACOB 1635
15. WEB, WILLIAM (after SAXTON) 1645
16. BLAEU, JOHANNES WILLEMSZOON (JAN) 1645
17. JANSSON, JAN (JOHANNES) 1646
18. BLOME, RICHARD 1673 and 1681
19. OGILBY, JOHN 1675
20. MORDEN, ROBERT 1676, 1695 and 1701
21. REDMAYNE, WILLIAM 1676
22. LEA, PHILIP (after SAXTON) 1689 and 1694
23. COLLINS, CAPTAIN GREENVILE 1689
24. De HOOGHE, Sr. ROMAIN 1693

Section Two
The Seventeenth Century

Antique Maps of Cornwall and the Isles of Scilly

9. Kip, 1607. 1st Edn. Britannia, sive florentissimorum regnorum Angliae, Scotiae, Hiberniae. Camden, London

9. KIP, WILLIAM 1607

Eng. Kip, Pub. Camden
(394 x 298)

William Kip (?-1649) was a Dutch émigré who probably arrived in Great Britain about 1585 from Utrecht. He is known to have lived in Candlewick Street (now Cannon Street) for about 30 years, until at least 1618, and was known as a goldsmith as well as an engraver. His daughter, Deborah, married Sir Balthasar Gerbier sometime around 1618. A painting of her and their children by Rubens in 1629 is in the Royal Collection at Windsor.

Kip and William Hole (#12) became known as English engravers who succeeded in establishing a reputation for themselves at a time when cartographical engraving was virtually the monopoly of The Netherlands. Between them and Norden they engraved the county and general maps which appeared in the 1607 edition of Camden's 'Britannia'.

The frontispieces of atlases probably originated with Ortelius's 'Theatrum Orbis Terrarum' in 1570. It was quickly adopted by others, though Kip does not seem to have produced an atlas of his own. Notwithstanding this, there is an interesting connection between Kip and frontispieces. Elizabeth I died in 1603 and the crown passed to James VI of Scotland. He was crowned James I of England in July 1603, with a planned ceremonial procession thereafter. Due to an outbreak of plague in London, this was postponed until the following March. Along the route, seven huge (approximately twenty metres high) triumphant arches were erected (and re-erected eight months later). These were designed by Stephen Harrison who produced a publication 'The Arch's of Triumph' (sic) in 1604, with seven plates of the various arches engraved by William Kip. Taking the 'Arch of the Italians', sited on Gracechurch Street, as an example, the strong similarity between this style and the frontispiece of Speed's 'Theatre' (#11) is remarkable. Whether these arches prompted Speed's frontispiece is intriguing.

Kip engraved the map of Cornwall, using as a source Saxton's map and manuscript notes, together with the notes and map by Norden, who had employed Kip to engrave his map of Hertfordshire in 1598.

The most remarkable feature of Kip's map is the

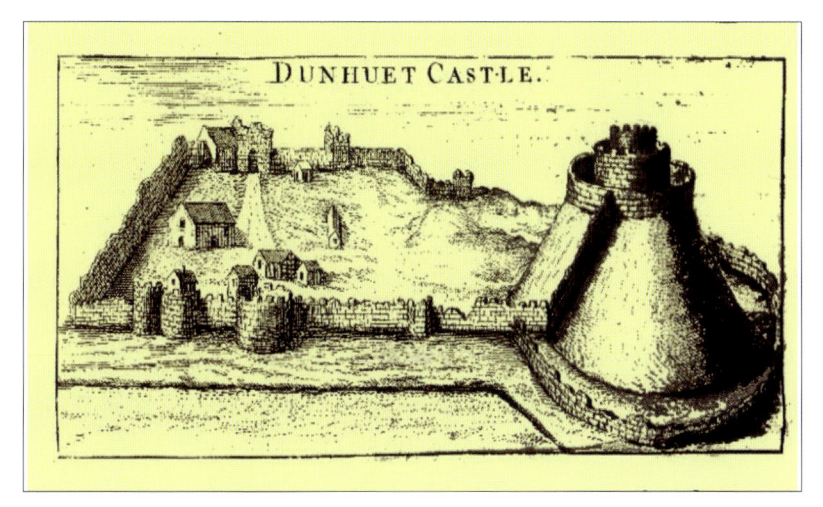

9.1 & 9.2 Detail of Kip's engraving of Dunheved Castle, left. Compare to Pine's 1728 engraving reproduced from Norden's original manuscript, right. Note the added buildings, church etc.

9.3 Kip. 1610   *Britain, or a chorographical description of the most flourishing kingdomes...*

beautiful engraved view of Dunheved (Launceston) and its motte and bailey castle. It is full of intricate detail and yet splendidly balanced. Deducing the source of the illustration is not straightforward – Skelton suggested that the engraving might have been derived from a field sketch by Norden. In Norden's much later publication, in 1728, an engraving of the castle is present, though it is not as detailed as Kip's. ('Description of Cornwall', by John Norden, page 93). The manuscript version (Harl. MS 6252 in the British Library) is a hand-drawn sketch comparable with this later engraving; however, Kip's and the later Speed engraving are substantial elaborations on the original – they may have had sight of the original sketch, but neither is a 'copy'.

The first state of the map (1607) may be recognised by the Latin text printed on the back (pages 133/4), while the map was reprinted unaltered in 1610 without text on the back (State I). Before the text setting of 1610 was exhausted, two alterations were made to the map itself; firstly, a compass rose was inserted in the sea area south of Looe (State II), and, later, plate numbers were added: number 2 above the scale (the correct number), and number one, also to the left of it (State III).

Thus, the maps may be found in States I, II or III with 1610 text; the final issue of State III was in the 1637 edition of Camden's 'Britannia', by which time the plate was badly worn, and retouched in places. This is a charming map of the period; the small ship and discreet sea monster are most sensitively drawn, and much of the lettering is beautifully engraved.

1607 *Britannia, sive florentissimorum regnorum Angliae, Scotiae, Hiberniae... chorographica descripto... chartis chorographicis illustrata. Guilelmo Camdeno authore. London, George Bishop and John Norton.*

1610 *Britain, or a chorographical description of the most flourishing kingdomes, England, Scotland and Ireland... Beautiful with mappes of the severall shires of England: written first in Latine by William Camden... Translated newly into English by Philémon Holland...London, George Bishop and John Norton.*

1637 *Britain, or a chorographicall description of the most flourishing Kingdomes, England, Scotland, and Ireland, and the Islands adjoyning, out of the depth of antiqvitie: beavtified with mappes of the severall Shires of England: Written first in Latine by William Camden, Clarenceux King of Arms (1597). Translated newly into English by Philémon Holland Doctour in Physick: Finally, revised, amended, and enlarged with sundry Additions by the said Author. London, Printed by Felix Kingston, Robert Young and John Legate for Andrew Crooke.*

William Kip's Cornwall from Camden's Britannia underwent three evolutions:
1607: No additions, Latin on rear (Previous page) Subsequent states may be found WITH text and alterations to map
1610: Text removed: State I, 1610: Add Compass: State II (Opposite), 1637: Add plate number 2 above scale bar and number 1 to the left of "Scala Milarium": State III (Below).

9.4 Kip 1637 Detail. *Britain, or a chorographicall description of the most flourishing Kingdomes....*

Antique Maps of Cornwall and the Isles of Scilly

10. BLAEU, WILLEM 1608, 1623

Eng. Blaeu, Pub. Blaeu
(248 x 555), (360 x 260)

Willem Janzoon Blaeu (1571-1638) was born in the North Holland area in either Uitgeest or Alkmaar. He was the son of a successful herring salesman but studied under the Danish astronomer Tycho Brahe around 1595 and qualified as a globe and instrument maker.

'The Light of Navigation' of 1608 ('*Het Licht der Zee-vaert*') was the company's second publication. Several interesting things immediately come to the fore here. Firstly, Willem Jan Zoon does not use the name Blaeu anywhere; he did not add Blaeu to his name until after 1623. Secondly, '*Het Licht der Zee-vaert*' promised more than it delivered. The sub-titles on the frontispiece offered descriptions of the coasts and ports of western, northern and eastern seas, along with the Mediterranean and, rather more ambitiously, Guinea, Brazil and the Indies (both East and West). The publication appeared in two parts (Vol. 1, 'West Seas' and Vol. II, 'North and East Seas') and was republished in Dutch five times, to 1634. The Mediterranean section finally appeared in 1618; Guinea et seq. were never published. A French version, '*Flambeau de la Navigation*', was published in 1620 and 1625, still under the name Guillaume Ianzoon. 'The Light of Navigation' appeared in English in 1612, published by William Johnson; it was republished in 1620 and again in 1622. The history of publication is further complicated with the expiry of Blaeu's privilege, around 1620, and thereby Jan Jansson was able to publish Blaeu's work at a lower price than the original.

This chart covers southern Cornwall, including the Scilly Islands, Devon and Dorset, and extends from Cape Cornwall, north of Land's End, around the south coast to Portland. In Blaeu's book, the plate (18) is discussed in the text (Vol. I, Ch. XVI), with the various points of navigational interest detailed, depth soundings around the coast, hazards such as Wolf Rock between Land's End and the Scillies &c. There are alterations to the 1608 original that were done before 1623, since they appear in the Dutch version of that year. The scale of miles located between the compass roses at the base of the map has been erased and the title 'De Canael tusschen Engelandt en Franchrijck' has been lowered to sit between the compasses. Within the text are views of the lay of the land from various points offshore, with explanations that were designed to aid a navigator in locating himself. The map has graticles for latitude on both sides of the page, with 50° North drawn clipping the tip of the Lizard Point. There are rhumb lines crossing the map, with two compass roses on either side of a scale table for German, Spanish, French and English miles and leagues. The lines of longitude are drawn but they are unlabelled, making any determinations beyond this problematic.

The detail contained around the coast is rudimentary, though no more so than other sea charts of the time. Anchor points and depth soundings are given in sheltered areas. There are, as to be expected, some errors of placement – St. Just and St. Buryan, for instance, are exchanged. The castles at Pendennis and St. Mawes are shown (built by Henry VIII in 1539); Blaeu has also marked with large script a place called 'Vaelmuijen' on the west side of the Fal – this is Dutch for Falmouth almost 60 years before its Charter. Waghenaer and de Bry also mark this location, yet it does not appear on any county maps until Blome's 1673 map (#18).

1608   *Het Licht der Zee-vaert, Amsterdam. (Dutch), Republished in 1617, 1620, 1627, 1629 and 1634.*
1619/20 *Flambeau de la Navigation, Amsterdam (French), Pub Jean Jeansson. Republished 1625.*
1612   *The Light of Navigation, Amsterdam (English), Pub William Johnson. Republished 1620 and 1622.*

In 1623, having by now expanded his name, Blaeu published his *'Zee-Spieghel'* and ran it in parallel with its sister publication for about 25 years. This was presented in two parts, the first being a brief education on the art of seafaring (*'Konst de Zeevaert'*); in fact, this is a volume that dealt with navigation, tides, compass use, moon phases &c.

The second part, the *'Zee-Spieghel'*, covered sea areas from The Netherlands, north into the Baltic and south as far as the mouth of the Mediterranean; a later volume covered the Mediterranean. Of interest here is the retreatment of the southwest England area covered by the 1608 chart from 'The Light of Navigation'. Plate 63 of the *'Zee-Spieghel'* shows the whole of southern England and Wales, with northern France, as one general chart. As previously, there is little detail inland and only the ports are shown. Drawn on the left side is the only indication of latitude, with the main compass south of Portland aligned with about 50° 05' North; the line cuts the Lizard in half and passes just to the south of the Penwith peninsula. This is important since, on the subsequent three maps that cover the same area at a larger scale, there are no marks of latitude, but the rhumb lines are the same, meaning we can locate the chart at least to latitude. The three charts covering this section of the south England coast appear in east–west order: No. 69: Portland to Start, No. 70: Start to Lizard and No. 71: Lizard to Cape Cornwall. This last plate is shown overleaf.

The chart is titled *'De Engeliche Cust van Lizart af tot de C. Cornwal en Englanden van de Sorlinges'*. The Sorlinges, or Scillies, as they are today, are still shown as an atoll-like cluster of islands, with slightly better detail than previously. The Seven Stones reef mid-way between Scilly and Land's End, as well as the Wolf Rock, are shown. Additionally, but unlabelled, is the Runnel Stone. The mainland perpetuates some of the placement errors that the 1608 chart marked and adds some others. Although Land's End is not marked per se, England's End is shown where Tol Pedn Penwith is today. This ambivalence was not uncommon, however; to the north of this, Blaeu has placed Port Curdo, which we can take to be Porthcurno. Compounding this is the misplaced St. Justin (St. Just), which should be nearer Cape Cornwall. Perhaps of greater significance is the alteration of the shape of the Lizard. The 1608 chart had shown this as a tapered headland pointing south-south-east. On the *'See-Spieghel'* chart, this is shown with a far flatter base (see Kip et seq.) and is now oriented a little further around to the south. In Mount's Bay the tidal flats surrounding St. Michael's Mount are shown, as too is the unlabelled St. Clement's Isle opposite Mousehole. The charts of Lizard to Start (Point) and then to Portland are, if anything, less detailed than the older *'Licht der Zee-vaert'* chart. Several place names have been omitted and the coastline is only lightly altered.

The English version of the *'Zee-Spieghel'* was translated by Richard Hynmers and published in Amsterdam in 1625. The charts themselves were unaltered from the original Dutch, and, without the atlas, are indistinguishable.

1623 *Zeespiegel: Inhoudende Een korte Onderwysinghe inde Konst Der Zeevaert. Willem Jansz Blaeuw, Amsterdam. Republished 1624, 1627, 1631, 1638 (w/4th Vol), 1640, 1643 (w/4th Vol), 1650, 1652, 1655 and 1658.*

1625 *Sea Mirror (English), Translated by Richard Hynmers, Amsterdam. Republished 1625, retitled Sea Beacon 1643 and 1653.*

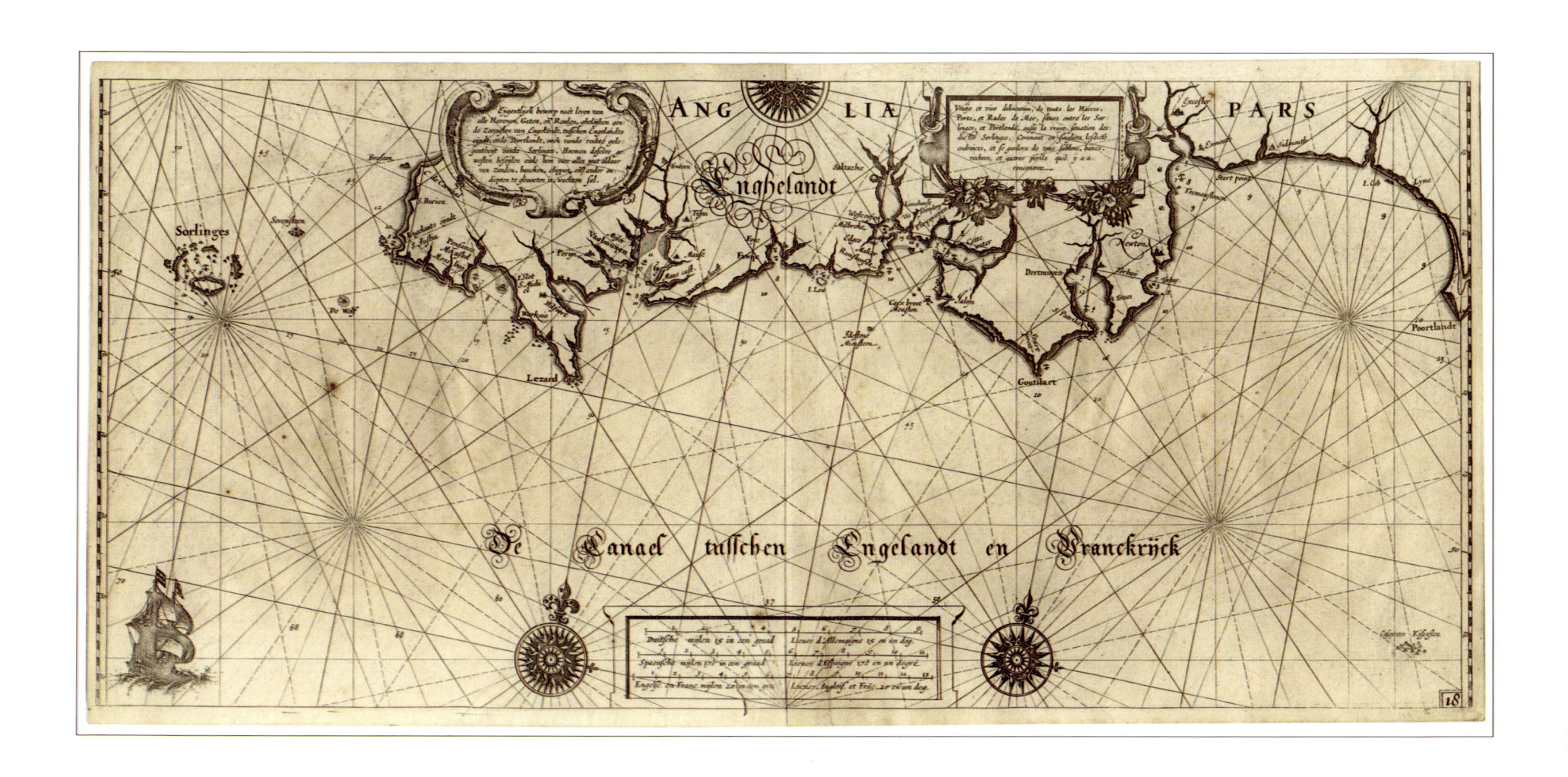

10. Blaeu (Wm), 1608 Het Licht der Zee-vaart , Amsterdam

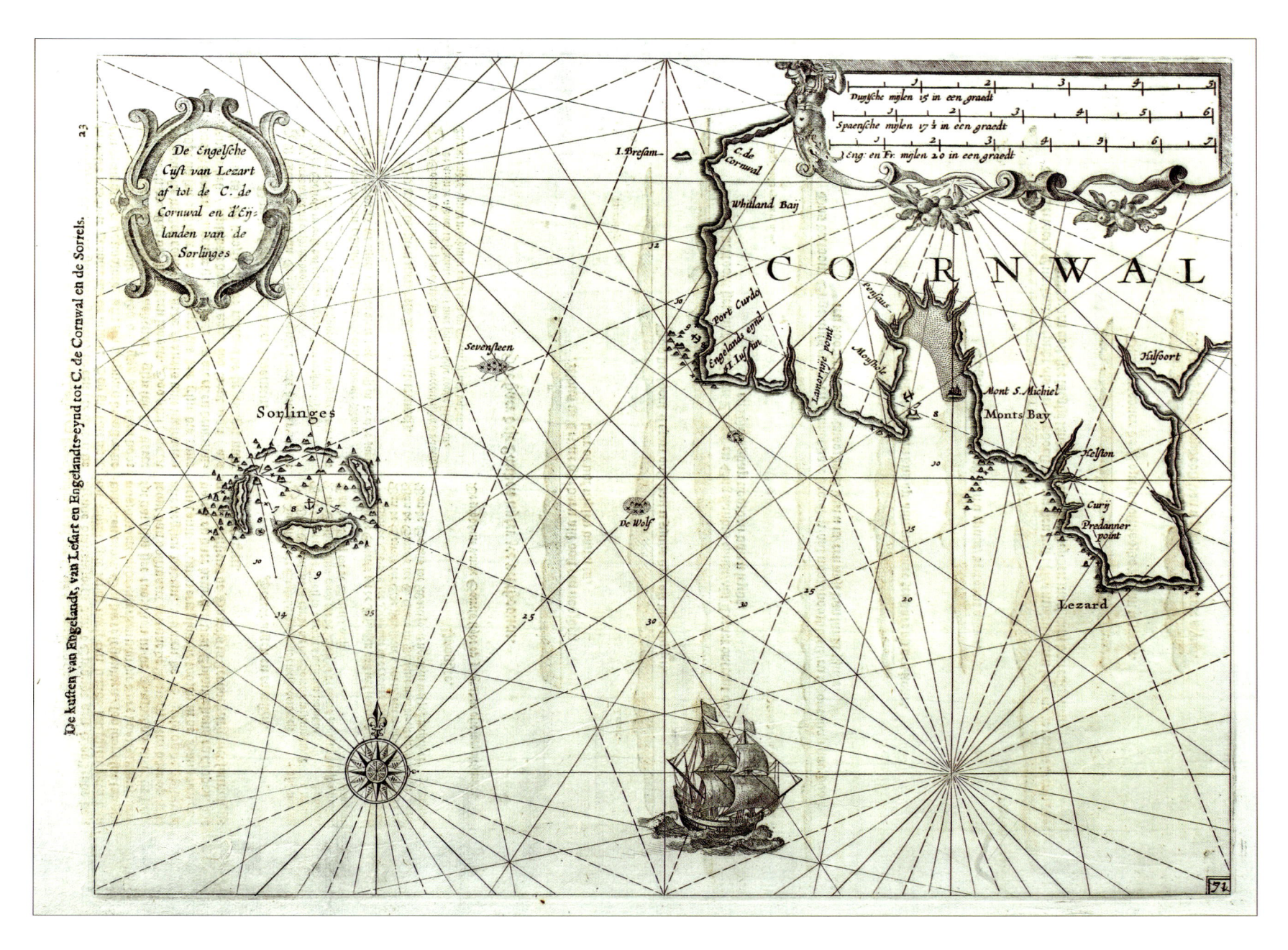

10.1 Blaeu (Wm), 1623 Zee-Spiegel, Amsterdam

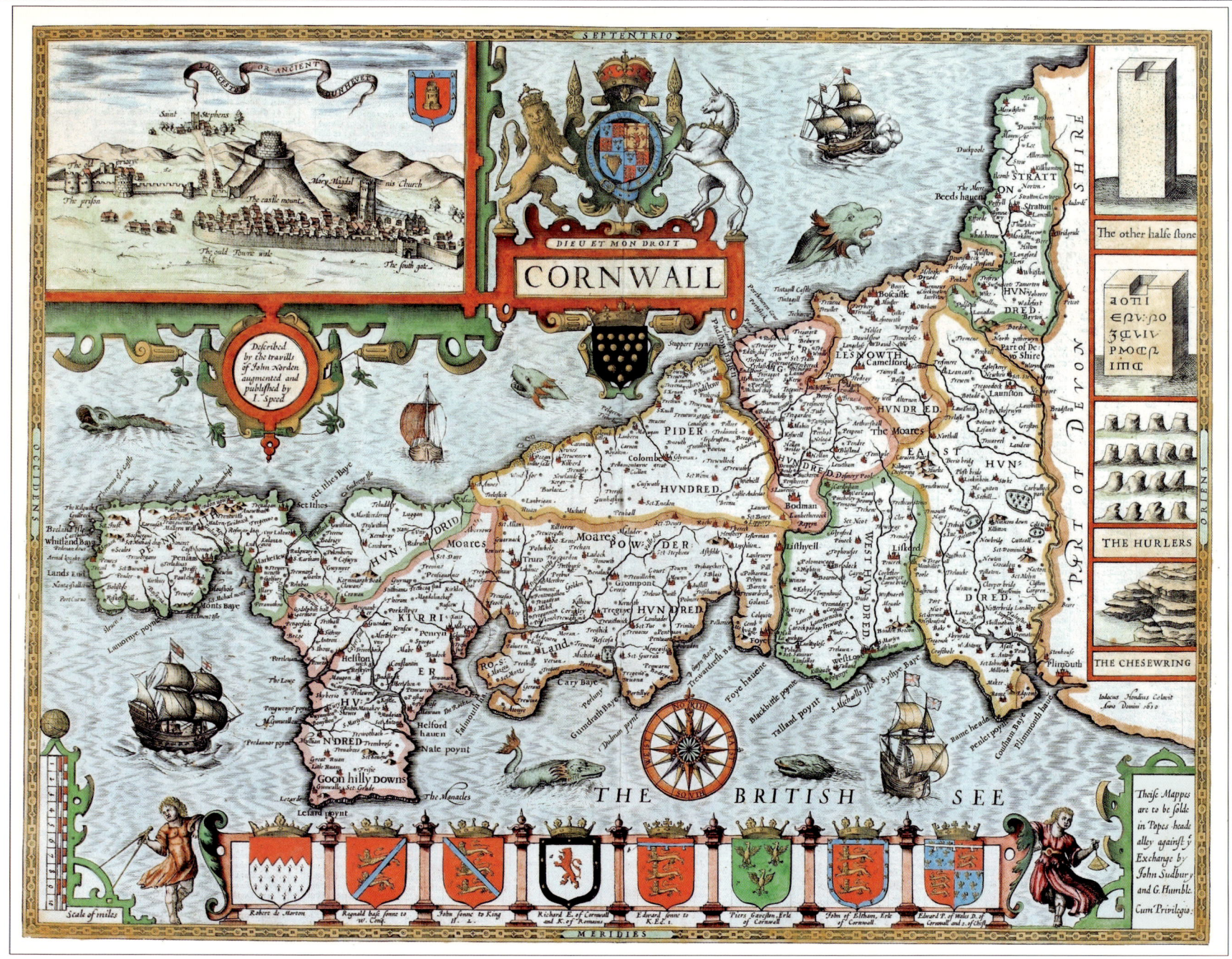

11. Speed 1610 (1st Ed.) Britannia, The Theatre of The Empire of Great Britain

11. SPEED, JOHN 1610

Eng. Hondius, Pubs. 1. Sudbury & Humble, 2. G. Humble, 3. W. Humble, 4. Rea, 5. Bassett & Chiswell, 6. Brown, 7. J. Overton, 8. H. Overton, 9. Dicey & Co.
(495 x 368)

John Speed's map of Cornwall is undoubtedly the best known and most popular of the county, and indeed the name Speed comes most readily to mind for whatever county map one might mention in England and Wales. Speed (1552-1629) was born in Farndon, in Cheshire, and although for many years he followed his father's trade as a tailor, he was by inclination an antiquary, and by about 1600 he had begun to collect geographical and historical material with the intention of publishing it. Most of the information and cartographic detail was copied from the maps and surveys of Saxton and Norden; on the map of Cornwall, the acknowledgment reads 'Described by the travills of John Norden', while in his writing, Speed makes the amusing comment 'I have put my sickle into other mens corne'. Although an early version of one county map, Cheshire, was engraved by William Rogers, who died in 1604, all the maps which finally appeared in Speed's atlas were engraved by Jodocus Hondius in Amsterdam between 1605 and 1610, the last atlas being published in 1611 or 1612, after loose maps with plain backs had already been issued.

Speed's preparation of the necessary material was most painstakingly done, and he sent to Hondius a wealth of illustrations to be included on each county map - town plans, drawings of buildings and antiquities, heraldic devices and portraits - all of which were ingeniously woven together by the engraver, as an integral part of the design.

11.1 Speed 1610 Frontispiece
Britannia, The Theatre of The Empire of Great Britain

Antique Maps of Cornwall and the Isles of Scilly

11.2 Speed 1623 Britannia, The Theatre of The Empire of Great Britain, London

Antique Maps of Cornwall and the Isles of Scilly

The view of Launceston in the top left of the Cornwall map is at odds with most of the other plans contained in his county maps forming his 'The Theatre of the Empire of Great Britain'. During the address to the reader, Speed clearly states authorship of the majority (50/73) of the town plans – these are easily recognised and they are clearly performed by the same hand in either plan or bird's eye view. Launceston is neither of these; there are some other views that are lightly comparable with the Launceston view – Buxton, on the Derbyshire map, being one (compare the hills). The view is the third iteration from Norden's original sketch and is discussed further in the appendices. Within this vignette are the arms of Launceston: 'Gules, a triple circular tower in a pyramidal form Or, the first battlements mounted with cannon of the last, all within a bordure Az. charged with eight towers domed on the second'. The origin of this coat of arms is interesting in itself – Launceston, or Dunheved, as it was known in ancient times, was fortified with a castle built by Robert de Mortain, the half-brother of William the Conqueror, in about 1070. This first element is reflected in the centre of the arms (a gold triple circular tower on a red ground). William had also given eight manors to de Mortain at the same time – thus the eight smaller towers in the border. This is notable as it gets used incorrectly thereafter as the Arms of Cornwall on several later maps; (all the subsequent Speed derivatives, Bowen (#30), De La Rochette (#47) and Hatchett (#49)).

Along the south coast, Speed and Hondius constructed a form of 3D shading designed to illustrate the cliffs as would be seen from an imaginary bird's eye view off the south coast. This trick of depth of field is notable, but not original to Speed's map. Neither Saxton nor Kip, his contemporaries, used this device. Norden's map in its engraved state of 1728 (#6) does not contain any evidence that Norden had used this device. However, reference to the hand-drawn manuscript maps that were found by Ravenhill clearly show that Norden had tried this as an illustrative device. From this we can postulate that both Speed and Kip had had sight of at least the manuscript maps, if not the whole document, of Norden's 'Description of Cornwall' at some time, presumably prior to it being presented to James I in 1604 when it was placed in the Royal Library, or possibly with Camden's access after this date (#6). It also appears that Kip and Speed were selective in which details they chose to include in their own maps. It is noteworthy that Speed had no private patron to support him, but his atlas was a great commercial success in the attraction it held for the map-buying public, a fact that must have gladdened the hearts of its publishers, John Sudbury and George Humble.

The popularity of Speed's county maps may be gauged from the fact that at least sixteen editions of the atlas were published between 1611/12, when the first edition appeared, and 1770. In addition, there were many reprints of the maps for sale as single sheets. Identification of certain editions of Speed's Cornwall is a comparatively easy matter, but in some cases the map itself remains unchanged through several editions, and reference must be made to the type setting of the text on the back of the map. The following is a list of the variations that mark the bibliographical history of the map of Cornwall; these should make it possible to identify most of the editions.

1611-12 *Britannia The Theatre of the Empire of Great Britain. Published by John Sudbury and George Humble, whose imprint appears in the label at the lower right corner. Note the <u>absence</u> of the words 'The Irishe or Virgivian Sea' in the sea area below the inset view of Launceston, (these words being absent until the 1623 edition). The engraver's name and date (Jodocus Hondius. 1610), below the view of the Cheesewring, are present on all editions except one and are thus of no value in dating the map, the only exception being the proof state where these items are lacking, and the map has a plain back, and maps in this condition are extremely rare. Text on the back of the first edition proper, Fol.21 (F2 v), Fol.22 (E iv); note the spelling of 'The aire' and 'The Soyle' in left margin, and the decoration of the capital 'C' of Cornwall at the beginning of the text.*

1614-16 *The map remains exactly as in the 1611-12 edition but the English text is reset, Fol.21 (P iv), Fol.22 (P 2v).*

1616 *Map unchanged, but Latin text on back Fol.21 (P iv), Fol.22 (P 2v).*

1623 The first alterations appear on the face of the map, viz.: 'The Irishe or Virgivian Sea' below the view of Launceston and north of the western half of Cornwall, with Latin names (copied from William Kip's map of 1607) at Land's End, the Lizard, Lostwithiel and the mouth of the River Tamar. English text as for 1614-1616. The atlas was issued by George Humble alone, but the imprint of Sudbury and Humble remains unchanged.

1627 Map as 1623, but with English text reset.

1631-2 Map as 1623, but English text reset.

1646 The first of a series of editions published by William Humble, but the face of the map remains unaltered, while the text is reset again.

1650-4 Five reissues of the map during this period, all in exactly the same state as the 1646 edition, so that it is impossible to date them individually from the Cornwall map alone.

1662 The comparatively rare edition of 'Roger Rea the elder and younger, at the Golden Crosse in Cornhill, against the Exchange, 1662', as the changed imprint shows clearly enough. This is only the second significant alteration to the face of the map, which has remained unchanged from 1623 to this date. The text is reset yet again.

1676 A third change in the face of the map, the new imprint which was placed in the margin immediately below the view of Launceston reading 'Are to be sold by Thomas Bassett, in Fleet Street, and Richard Chiswell, in St. Paul's churchyard'. The imprint of previous publishers in the lower right label is now replaced by the coat of arms of 'Henry eldest son of King James'. (This refers to Prince Henry, eldest son of King James I, who died at the age of 18 when his father was still on the throne). By this time, the copperplate had become so worn that the print was very pale in some places and showing signs of retouching in others. The text is reset.

1696 The previous imprint is erased and replaced by 'Corrected and sold by Christopher Brown, at the Globe, near the west end of St. Paul's church, London'. The back is plain.

1700-7 The map was reissued by John Overton (1640-1713) with no further changes.

1707-1743 John Overton's son, Henry Overton (1676-1751), reissued the map unchanged at first, but about 1720 added the roads and his own imprint below Brown's, reading 'And now sold by Henry Overton, at the White Horse, without Newgate, London'. There were probably several sheet issues, all with a plain back, and finally an atlas in 1743.

1770 The last atlas of Speed's maps, bearing the new imprint 'And now sold by C. Dicey and Co., in Aldermary Churchyard, London'. Plain back, plate retouched and evidence of erasure of previous imprint.

THE EARLS AND DUKE OF CORNWALL

Along the base of Speed's map and on some maps thereafter are the eight arms of the earls and Duke of Cornwall. There follows a description of each of these coats of arms, with their correct colouring. Most maps were published uncoloured, with some rudimentary guide of the colours often shown as a letter (tricking) and/or line shading (hachure) signifying the required colour. It should be noted that the codification of heraldry in terms of engraving/printing was still in its infancy in the early 1600s and several systems were vying for supremacy at this time. Hachuring is a process of showing the colour as lines (see side box). The use of hachure was unpopular since it tended to over-complicate the engraving; engravers preferred the lettering system (tricking), especially in confined spaces. Speed's uncoloured map has avoided hachuring and uses tricking instead.

Piers Gaveston's arms have gold eagles on a green ground; this is correctly marked as 'v' on the field of the shield as 'vert', or green. There are many occasions where an uninformed colourist has unwittingly taken the 'v' to mean violet and coloured this shield thus.

There are other shields on this map that are dealt with differently. The arms of James I are left untouched, with no hachuring or tricking; we assume Hondius considered them well enough known to not need further explanation – trying to add anything to the whole device would have severely detracted from it. The arms of Cornwall get a different treatment. The actual shield is: Sable, 15 bezants or roundels (or). Hondius dealt with this by cross-hachuring the ground to indicate sable (black) but left the roundels clear and added some shading to indicate their sphericity. They are gold and should be stippled. Bearing in mind that the coding of colour to hachure was at this time still evolving, the unevenness of coding might be forgiven. Having introduced the shields to the map of Cornwall, subsequent versions after Speed produced shields with colour instructions with varying success. If these shields have been, or intend to be, coloured, the rules of heraldry should be followed.

Some relevant Heraldic Components

Or:	Gold, Hachured as regular dots or stippled, 'o' or 'or'.
Argent:	Silver, Hachured as clear 'a', 'ar' or 'arg'.
Gules:	Red, Hachured as vertical lines, 'g' or 'gu'.
Azure:	Blue, Hachured as horizontal lines. 'az' or 'b'.
Vert:	Green, Hachured as diagonal lines top left-bottom right, 'v'.
Sable:	Black, Hachured as cross-hatch, 's' or 'sa'.
Bend:	Diagonal line normally L to R. In illegitimacy this is reversed.
Lions:	Traditionally, a lion is defined as being Rampant (on rear legs). French heralds termed a Passant (walking lion) a 'Leopard'. The Coat of arms of Richard I are sometimes referred to as leopards not lions There are no stripped or spotted cats in heraldry.
Label:	Mark of Cadency of Eldest son. Horizontal bar across top of shield with three prongs. Subsequent sons bore different marks of cadency.
Bezants:	Roundlets or balls, gold. There are other less common roundlets of other metals or tinctures.

The Earls and Duke of Cornwall

Robert of Mortain (c.1038 – 1095) Half-Brother of William the Conqueror.
Ermine with A Chief Indented Gules.

Reginald De Dunstanville, Earl of Cornwall (? – 1175) Illegitimate son of King Henry I.
Gules, Two Lions Passant Guardant Or, Bend Sinister Azure.

John, Earl of Cornwall (? – After 1175) Son of Reginald above.
Gules, Three Lions Passant Guardant Or, Bend Azure.

Piers Gaveston (1284 – 1312) Earldom bestowed by King Edward II.
Vert with Three Eagles Displayed Or.

Richard, Earl of Cornwall (1209 – 1272) Son of King John I.
Argent, A Lion Rampant Gules Crowned Or A Bordure Sable Bezantée.

Edmund, Earl of Cornwall (1249 – 1300) Son of Richard above.
Gules, Three Lions Passant Guardant Or. A Label Azure with Three Fleur De Lys Or.

John of Eltham (1316 – 1336) Son of King Edward II.
Gules Three Lions Passant Guardant Or With A Bordure Azure semy of Fleur-De-Lys Or.

Edward, Prince of Wales, Duke of Cornwall (1330 – 1376) Son of King Edward III.
Quarterly 1st and 4th Azure semée Of Fleur-De-Lys Or (France Ancient); 2nd and 3rd Gules, Three Lions Passant Guardant Or (England) Overall a Label of Three Points Argent.

Antique Maps of Cornwall and the Isles of Scilly

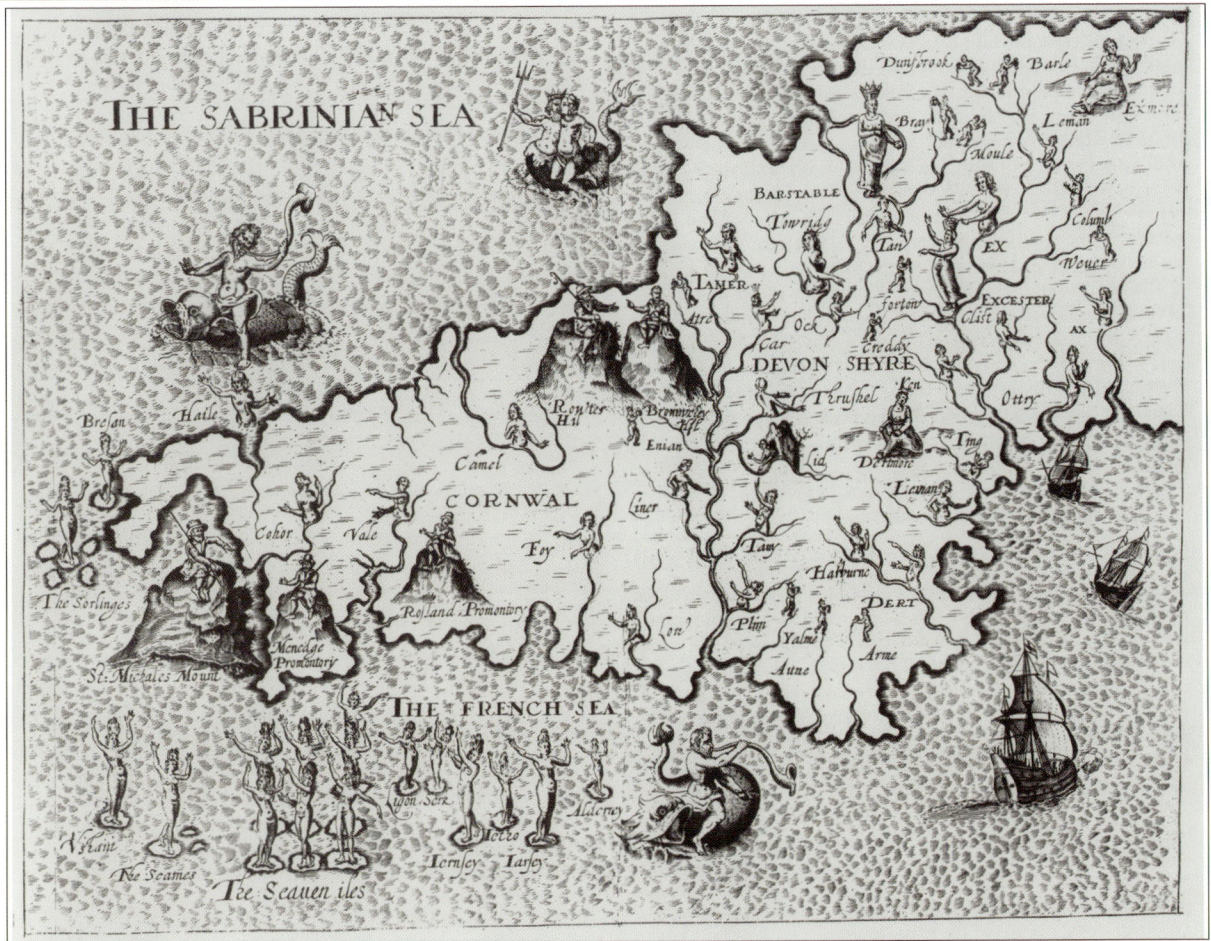

12. Hole 1612 Poly-Olbion... Michael Drayton, London

12.1 Sea Monsters by Saxton, Wagenhaer and Kip

38 *Antique Maps of Cornwall and the Isles of Scilly*

12. HOLE, WILLIAM 1612

Eng. Hole, Pubs. Lownes, Browne, Helme & Busbie
(311 x 241)

William Hole (? - 1624) had collaborated with William Kip in the engraving of the series of maps used in the 1607 edition of Camden's 'Britannia'. In 1612 he engraved eighteen maps to illustrate a curious work named 'Poly-Olbion'*, by Michael Drayton, a poet (1563-1631). The maps are quite extraordinary, each river being endowed with a water nymph, hills surmounted by seated shepherds and towns represented by female figures crowned with civic battlements, while in the sea King Neptune and his mermen ride upon their sea monsters, and small ships go their way in quite impossible perspective. The map includes not only Cornwall and Devon, but also the Isles of Scilly, Channel Islands, as well as the Sept Îles and Ushant in Brittany; the 'crowns' upon the heads of the sea-nymphs representing these islands are clearly symbolic of the rocky nature of the islands themselves. The fact that the map has little cartographical value becomes quite unimportant in view of the fascinating presentation of the beauties of the countryside in this allegorical manner, and indeed Drayton states quite clearly to his reader that the map is 'lively delineating...every Mountaine, Forrest, River and Valley; expressing in their sundry postures; their loves, delights and naturall situations'. A song appropriate to the area of the map accompanies each of the eighteen maps.

"Or, A Chorographicall Description of Tracts, Rivers, Mountianes, Forests and other parts of the Renowned Isle of Great Britaine", published with a second part in 1622.

1612   *Poly-Olbion London. M. Lownes, I. Browne, I. Helme, and I. Busbie. (1612).*

1613   *Poly-Olbion or A Chorographicall description of Tracts, Rivers, Mountaines, Forests, and other Parts of this Renowned Isle of Great Britaine. London. M. Lownes, I. Browne, I. Helme and I. Busbie. 1613.*

1622   *Poly-Olbion or A Chorographicall Description (in two parts). The Second Part, or A Continuance of Poly-Olbion... London. Iohn Marriot, Iohn Grismand, and Thomas Dewe. 1622 (Poly-olbion, by Michael Drayton. London 1612).*

SEA MONSTERS

Hole is, here at least, the last cartographer to incorporate sea monsters into his design. This was obviously done to enhance the overall feel of Drayton's rather fabulous composition. From Saxton to Kip we see various monsters wending their way into oblivion. For centuries, sea monsters had been a cartographic staple, though they do not appear on every map or chart with sea areas. Duzer (2013) suggested that their inclusion may be for several reasons, from the purely decorative to the financial – clients could opt for extra monsters!

The Renaissance briefly re-invigorated the trend for sea-borne beasts and, with the new techniques of visual depiction, they got a new lease of life. However, by the early 1600s, their popularity was waning and the use of monsters this late on is probably somewhere between decorative and infill. Hitherto, they had been used to indicate the edges of the 'known world', as a warning of dangers or even to ward off competing fishermen.

Saxton has included several monsters, including perhaps a twin-spouted, toothless Roider. If so, it was first described in the 13th century Old Norse text 'Konungs skuggsjá' or 'King's Mirror' and later used by Ortelius. Waghenaer's more generic styled monster is depicted attacking a ship, a fate that appeared to befall sailors frequently, and happily predates insurance claim forms. Of the limited number of monsters here, by far and away the best is Kip's. Almost as the last swansong of a dying form, he engraves a wonderful solitary dolphin perhaps playing in the Cornish surf.

13. BILL, JOHN 1626

Eng. Bill, Pub. Bill
(121 x 89)

John Bill, (1576-1630) was born probably in Shropshire. He worked in London from around 1590 until his death in 1630. In 1592 he was apprenticed to John Norden and by 1601 was a successful businessman and Master and Freeman of the Stationers' Company. He was commissioned by Sir Thomas Bodley (the collection became the genesis of the Bodleian Library, Oxford) to travel abroad collecting books. There are only two publications he is associated with: John Norden's version of the Ortelius Atlas in 1606 and 'The Abridgement of Camden's Britannia' in 1626.

The small map of Cornwall is, at first glance, somewhat similar to that of Pieter van den Keere; both are miniature versions of Saxton's map, but the style of engraving on Bill's map is quite different, and, although it has slightly fewer place names, its title cartouche and scale are more decorative than those used by van den Keere. The name of the county is divided on two lines as Corn/wall, but the most remarkable feature is the inclusion of latitude and longitude for the first time by an English map-maker. The method used to show latitude and longitude is interesting; on most of Bill's county maps appropriate divisions are made along the left and bottom borders of the map, but because of the alignment of Cornwall it was more convenient to draw two lines crossing the map at an angle to show North-South and East-West, with calibrations in degrees and minutes along them, the prime meridian being that of the Azores. (It used a meridian through San Miguel, the main island of the Azores, and, even as late as Arrowsmith's 1796 map, they are shown 70 miles too far east). The atlas appears to have been projected some years before publication, for the work is entered in the Stationer's Register in 1620.

1626 The abridgement of Camden's Britannia, with the maps of the severall shires of England and Wales. Iohn Bill 1626.

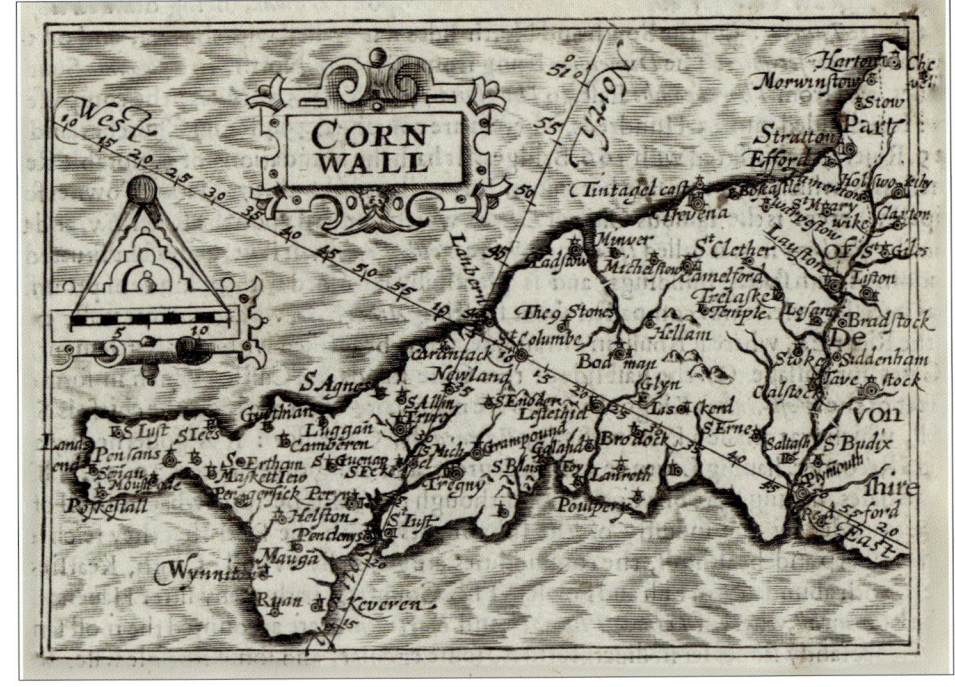

13. Bill 1626
The Abridgement of Camden's Britannia

14. VAN LANGEREN, JACOB 1635

Eng. Van Langeren, Pub. Simmons then Jenner
(102 x 102)

Matthew Simmons (1608-1654) was a member of the Stationers' Company, a printer, bookseller and publisher.

The first edition of 'A Direction for the English Traviller' was produced by Simmons in 1635 and engraved by Jacob Van Langeren. The Van Langeren (sometimes spelled Langren) family originates with Jacob Floris Van Langren, born in about 1525 in Gelderland, a province of The Netherlands to the east of Amsterdam. He moved eventually to Amsterdam, married and produced two sons; Arnold and Henricus. Jacob and Michael Van Langeren are the sons of Arnold. Jacob may possibly be the engraver in question.

Each map, of which there are 36, contains in the upper left a triangular table of distances between towns, with a copy of William Bowes' 1590 playing card in the bottom right. The distance table is a copy of that devised by John Norden and used in his 1625 book 'England: an intended guyde for English Travailers'. This triangular cross-table continued to be a feature of road maps until the advent of GPS devices after the turn of the second millennium.

Simmons's tabulation is similar to Norden's and is almost a direct copy – the order of towns along both sides is almost the same, with three places added: Mousehole, Milbrook and Grampound, and one removed ((St.) Austell). The towns shown by initials on the map are those listed in the distance table, though only with intimate knowledge of the county would one be able to match the letters to the towns. The map has been drawn with a simple compass set behind it. The Irish and Brittaie Seas are shown, along with the 'Maine' sea or Atlantic. In the bottom left below Plymouth is a basic scale of 0-10 with no further elaboration. At the base of

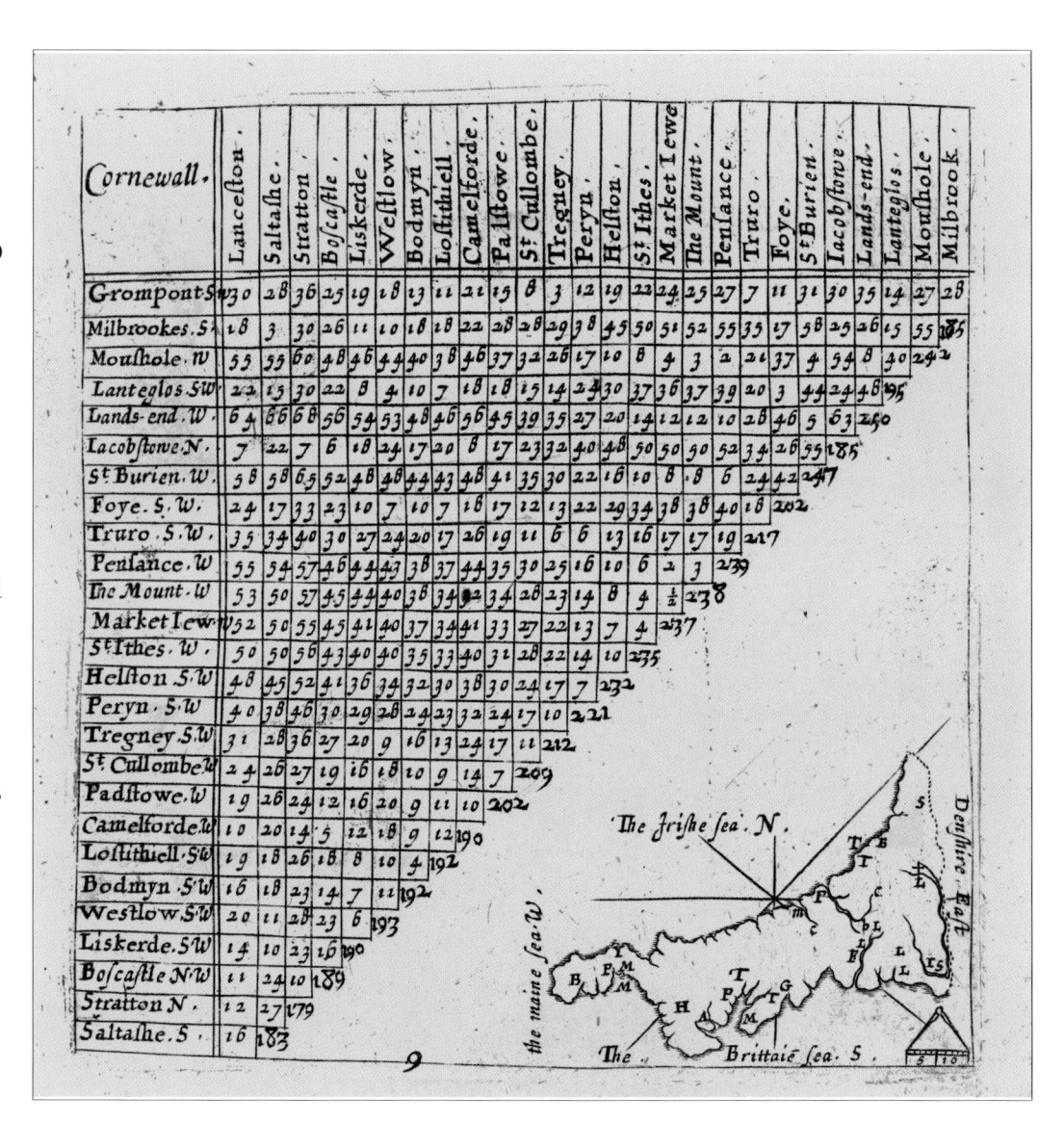

14. Van Langeren 1635
A Direction for the English Travailler by Matthew Simmons

the frame is the number 9 – presumably the plate number.

The third edition, published the same year (1636), contained an addition to the table: the distances to London were added to the end of each row. In 1643, the plates came into the possession of Thomas Jenner, he erased the original maps, redrew them at twice the original scale and gave the place names in full.

These larger maps may have been for use by the Parliamentary armies during the Civil War, and possibly this preparation was rather hasty: the name of St. Michael's Mount is engraved backwards across Mount's Bay (see below). On the north coast, St. Agnes and St. Sener (Zennor) appear in each other's places, while Padstow is shown at about the position of Hayle and St. Ives has moved to Newquay.

The 1649 edition by Jenner is rare – there may only be one copy known. The volume uses the re-drawn maps of 1643 – Cornwall is one of several maps missing.

The 1657 edition published by Jenner is like the 1649 edition, using the same maps and text. Set below the triangular table and map is a three-column list of towns in the county and their Hundreds, which, on the Cornwall map (page 23), commences at Camelford to Cortether (Cartuther south of Liskeard).

1635 *A Direction for the English Travviller, by Matthew Simmons. Reprints: 1636, 1636.*

1643 *Reprinted by Thomas Jenner, erased, re-engraved and enlarged. Added three maps (England, Wales and Yorkshire) 1657, 1662, 1668, 1677 & 1680.*

1649 *A Booke of the names of all the Hundreds contained in the Shires of the kingdom of England…Printed for Thomas Jenner and to be sold at the Royal Exchange.*

1657 *A Booke of the Names of all Parishes, Market, Towns, Villages, Hamlets and Smallest Places in England and Wales by M.S. (Mary Simmons, wife of Matthew) for Tho: Jenner at the south entrance of the Royall Exchange, London.*

1662 *Reprinted 1668 (twice).*

1677 *Reprinted by S.S (Samuel Simmons, son of Mary & Matthew) for John Garrett and sold at ye Royall Exchange in Cornhill… and later the same year with a slight alteration in the title.*

14.1 Detail of Mount's Bay reversed to show "S Michael's mount" engraved incorrectly.

14.2 John Norden's distance table first published in 1625 and reproduced by Bateman in the 1728 "Description of Cornwall". This was used by Simmons and later Jenner as a template.

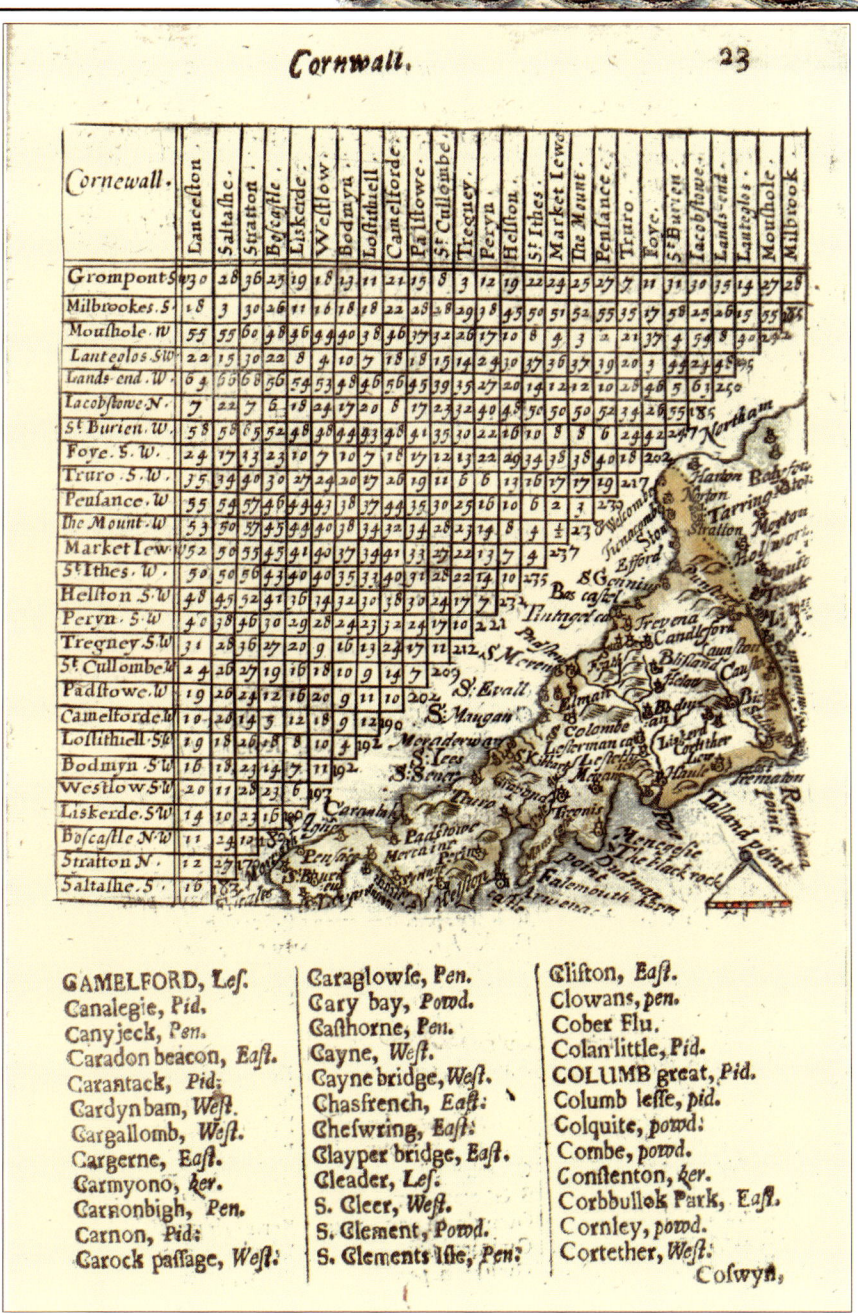

14.3 Van Langeren 1657
A Booke of The Names of All Parishes... Thomas Jenner

Antique Maps of Cornwall and the Isles of Scilly

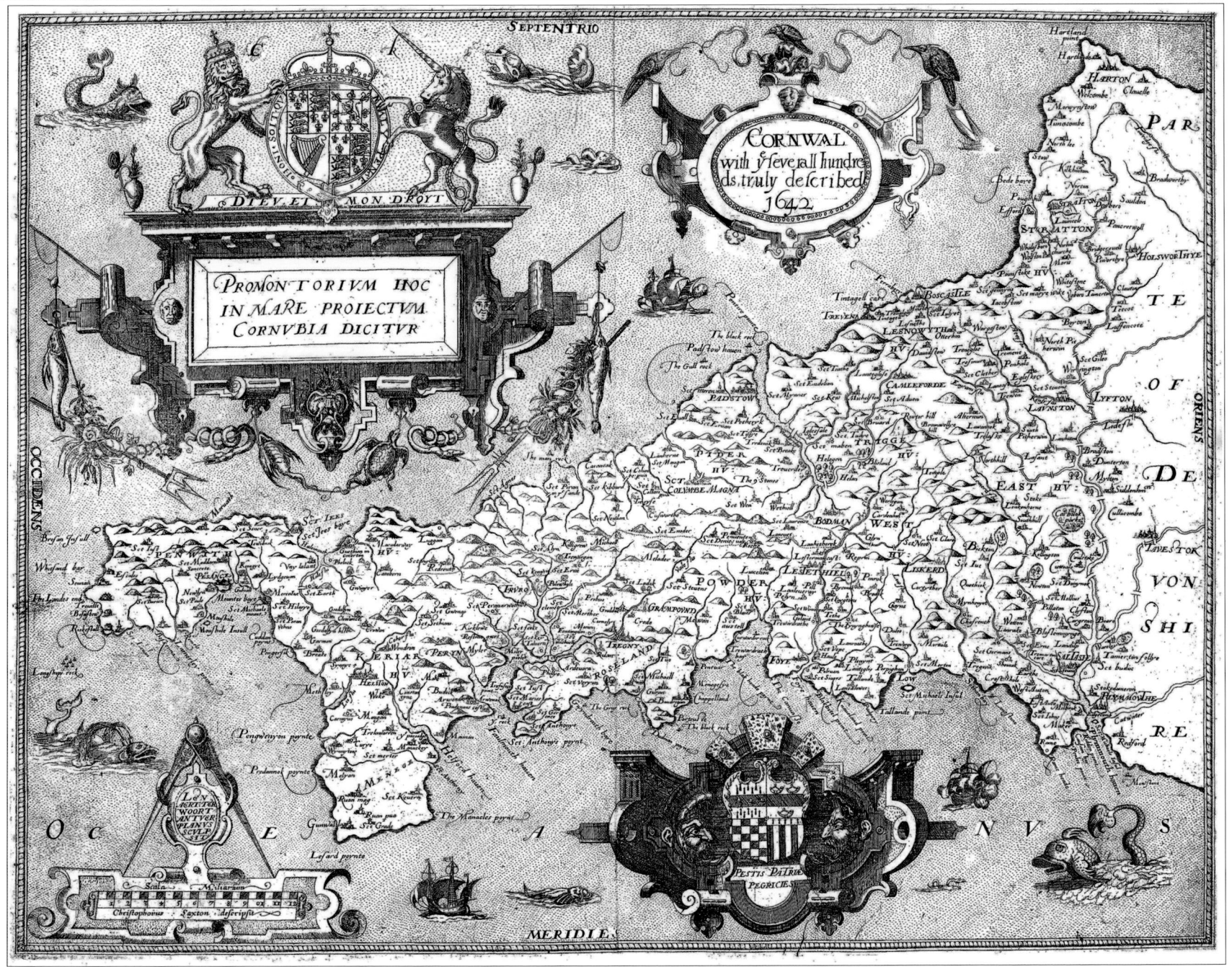

15. Web 1645 *The Maps of All the Shires in England And Wales*

44 **Antique Maps of Cornwall and the Isles of Scilly**

15. WEB, WILLIAM (after SAXTON) 1645

Eng. Terwoort/Unknown, Pub. Web

(470 x 356)

William Web (fl.1628-c.1647) was a publisher whose main line of work was in the production of portraiture. From his address in Cornhill at the Globe against the Exchange he produced numerous prints from the late 1620s. His output appears to have diminished during the 1630s, but then he published a map of Ireland in 1641. Given this background, it seems unlikely that Web himself undertook the actual re-engraving.

The Cornwall map is printed from the Saxton plate of 1576, but small though important changes have been made to alter the overall appearance of the map.

The Royal Tudor arms of Elizabeth I have been replaced by the Stuart arms of Charles I, with the initials C.R. (Carolus Rex) set above the arms where previously they were E.R. On the sinister side of the arms, the Wessex Dragon has been replaced by the chained Scottish Unicorn supporter in reference to Charles' Scottish origins – it is worth looking carefully at the unicorn: Web's engraver has added a cheeky smile!

The Latin title remains unchanged below the arms, but a new English title 'Cornwal with ye severall hundreds described', with the date 1642, has been inserted in the upper right cartouche in place of the dedication. The plate has been retouched - on the bottom edge of the plate, below the arms of Thomas Seckford, there is a small crack in the plate extending in an almost vertical line though the narrow scroll-worked border. (See inset below).

1645 *The Maps of all the Shires in England and Wales. Christopher Saxton. Printed for William Web at the Globe in Cornehill.*

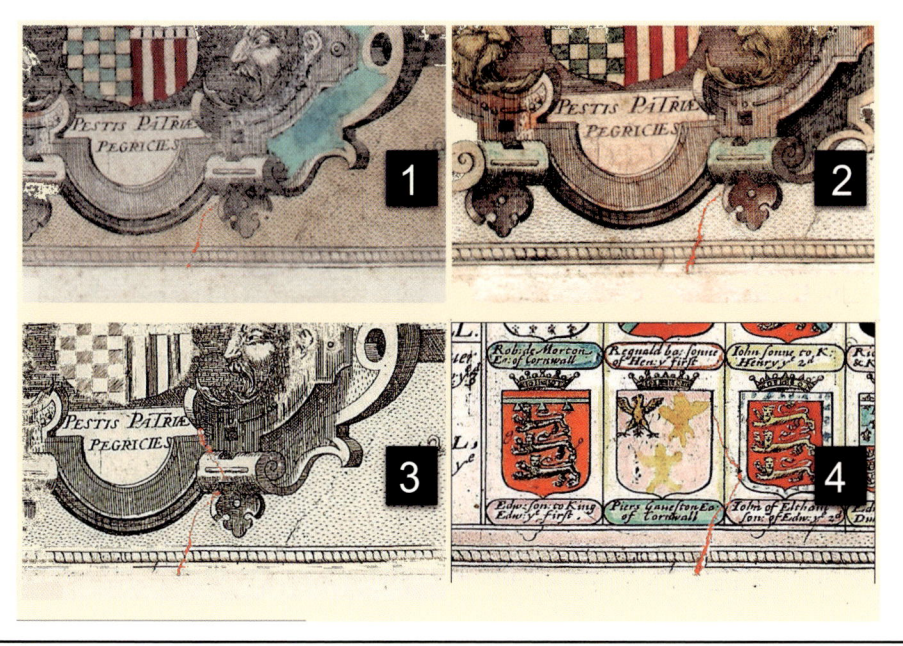

The Saxton Plate Crack

This crack appeared in the Saxton plate very early on in the life of the plate. It is shown here enhanced in red.

1: Early stage of the crack in a State III issue of the Saxton Cornwall map 1576.

2. Over the lifespan of the State III plate, crack develops

3. Web (full map left). Crack has extended into coat of arms of Seckford, but is comparatively narrow. 1645

4. Lea (full map #22). Seckford arms erased, Evidence of deepening/widening.

16. BLAEU, JOHANNES WILLEMSZOON (JAN) 1645

Eng. J. Blaeu, Pub. G.& J. Blaeu
(483 x 368)

Jan Blaeu (1596-1673) was the eldest son of Willem Janszoon Blaeu (1571-1638) and Maria van Uitgeest. In 1596 Blaeu senior started a business in Amsterdam as a maker of instruments and globes. It was natural that such a business should flourish; at that time in Amsterdam, there was a school of Dutch pilots, and most of the overseas enterprises leading to the establishment of the Dutch commercial empire originated here. Even so, the success of the Blaeu family business was chiefly due to the practical genius of both father and sons. Engraving and printing soon became important among the activities of their workshop, and the value of their services brought recognition in the appointment (1633) of the Blaeus as mapmakers to the Republic and hydro-geographers to the Dutch East India Company (Verenigde Oostindische Compagnie). By 1635 they had published their first world atlas in competition with the rival firm of Honricus Hondius (son of Jodocus Hondius, the engraver of Speed's maps) and his brother-in-law, Jan Jansson, who had brought out a similar atlas in 1633.

There followed a commercial battle in which both publishing houses brought out improved and enlarged atlases in successive attempts to outstrip each other. By 1640 the competition had centred on the preparation of county maps of England and Wales for a fourth volume of the atlas. Jansson had already eighteen 'British' plates available from a previous atlas; Blaeu copied six of his maps from these. The remaining 53 maps in Blaeu's atlas were copied from those of Speed, and the volume appeared in 1645, beating Jansson to the market by one year.

Blaeu's map of Cornwall is copied from the Speed map in its post-1623 state: the Latin titles of the headlands and mouth of the Tamar are included. The eight coats of arms of the various earls and Duke of Cornwall have been arranged in columns of three in the top-left corner, with three blank shields added to balance the design. To the right of the Royal Stuart Arms at the top centre is added the original arms of England (senso-stricto this is the arms of Plantagenet King Richard I: Three lions or leopards on a red ground – the distinction between lions and leopards from a heraldic perspective is subtle – French heralds consider a lion passant guardant to be termed a leopard, lions are depicted only as rampant) - a somewhat curious inclusion, since these arms had not been used by the Kings of England since 1340, when Edward III claimed the French throne and quartered the arms of France (gold fleur-de-lys on a blue ground) with those of England.

Fish and ingots of tin, the most important economic products of the county, flank the title-piece in the lower right corner. Even though the map is copied from Speed, its appearance is markedly different; the composition being much lighter and more open in effect. The engraving is superb, the calligraphy magnificent and the restrained use of decoration gives a clarity which greatly facilitates map reading without any loss of charm or beauty, although, in the absence of the sea monsters, the slightly archaic character has disappeared. The superlative quality of the paper and the typography is typical of the work produced by Blaeu and these qualities make this map one of the most sought-after 'collectors' maps.

1645   Theatrum Orbis Terrarum sive Atlas Novus, Guil. et Joannis Blaeu Amsterdam. Latin, Reprinted 1648.
1645   Le Theatre du Monde ou Nouvel Atlas. French, 1646, 1648.
1645   Novus Atlas, Das ist Welt-beschreibung. German, 1646, 1648.
1646   Toonneel des Aerdrycks, oft Nieuwe Atlas. Dutch.
1648   Vierde Stuck der Aerdrycks-beschreibung. Dutch, 1664.
1659   Nuevo Atlas del Reyno de Ingalaterra. Spanish, 1662.
1662   Geographiae Blavianae, Volumum Quintum, quo Anglia. Latin.
1662   Cinquieme Volume de la Geographie Blaviane, Contenant l'Angleterre. French, 1663, 1667.

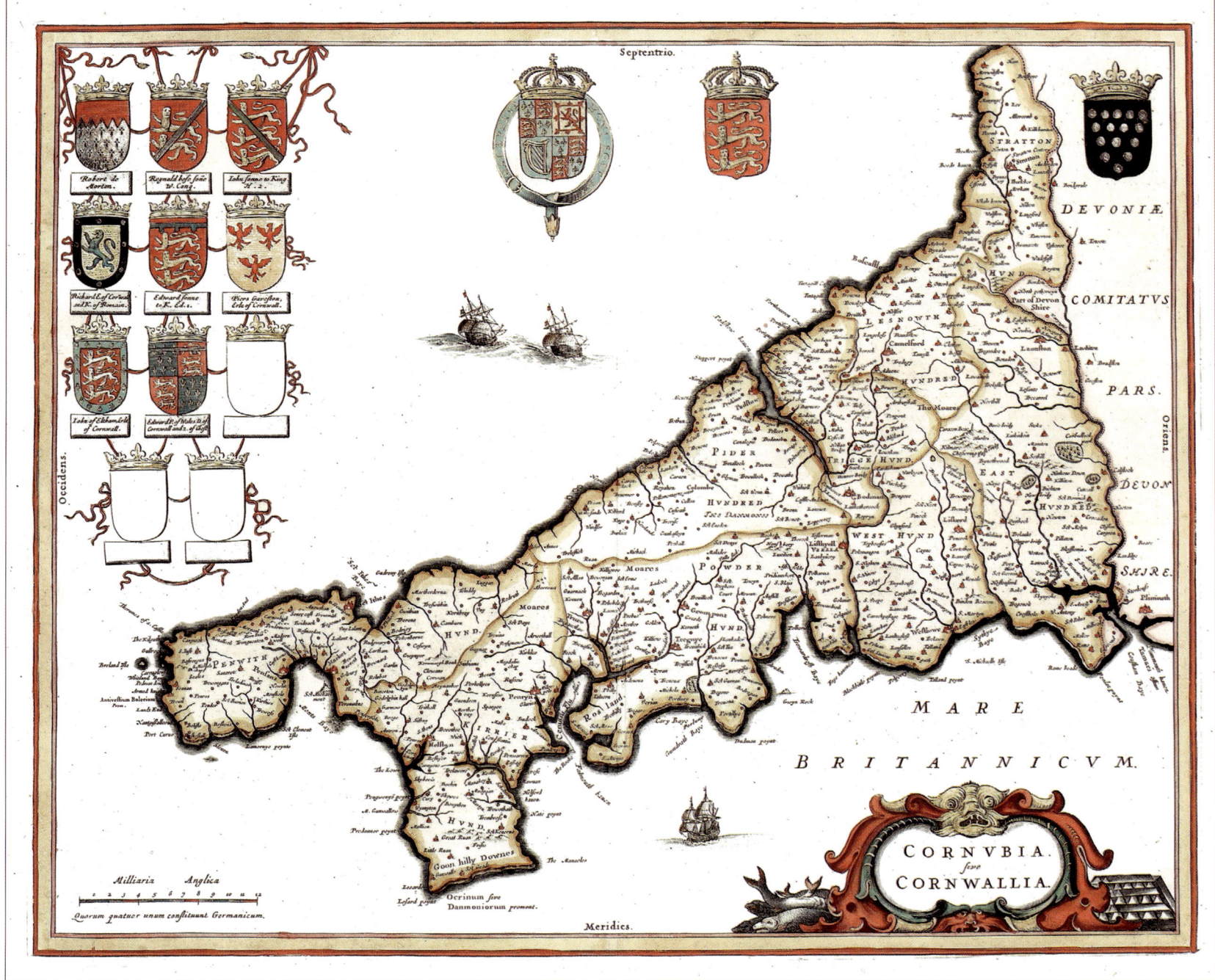

16. Blaeu 1645 Theatrum Orbis Terrarum, Amsterdam G & J Blaeu

Antique Maps of Cornwall and the Isles of Scilly

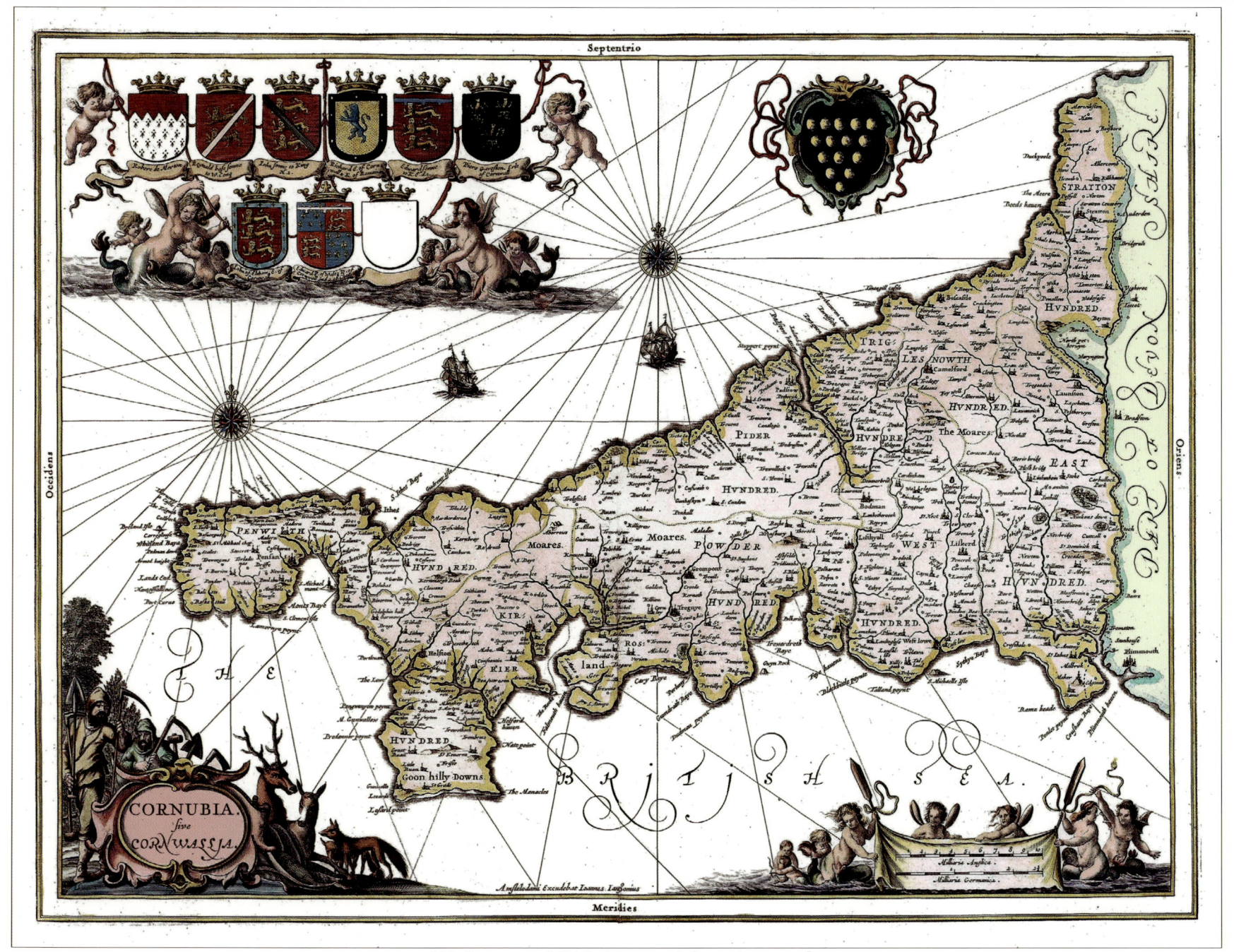

17. Jansson 1646 Novus Atlas, Amsterdam

Antique Maps of Cornwall and the Isles of Scilly

17. JANSSON, JAN (JOHANNES JANSSONIUS) 1646

Eng. Jansson, Pub. Jansson
(457 x 349)

Jan Jansson (1588-1664) was born in Arnhem, and as a young man went to live in Amsterdam, where he married Elizabeth de Hondt, the daughter of Jodocus Hondius, in August 1612. He thus became associated with that family's publishing business. It is interesting to note that Hondius had acquired the business as a flourishing concern built by three generations of the Mercator family, so that when Jansson finally took over in 1639, just 102 years after Gerard Mercator had started on his own, there was already a long tradition of map engraving behind him. One important difference between the works of Mercator and Jansson should be made - Mercator is distinguished for his original work as a map-maker and engraver, a systematic and scientific geographer, whereas Jansson was a reproductive engraver copying much of his work from the existing works of other cartographers. This, in fact, was symptomatic of the age - there was no law of copyright and the rapidly increasing public demand for new atlases encouraged many map-makers to copy from the works of others, usually without any serious attempt to either correct mistakes or to disguise the fact that they were copies. Remarkably enough, many publishers collaborated with each other by selling or lending plates and impressions. However, in the case of the Blaeu family and Jansson, this piracy seems to be rooted in a family feud almost certainly over the use of highly similar plates. It is interesting to note the very similar titles of the two atlases from Blaeu and Jansson: an obvious attempt to lure the unwary.

Not surprisingly, the outline of Jansson's Cornwall is almost identical with that of Blaeu's map, but there is an important difference in the way in which each has 'set' his map within the frame. This is most obvious in the direction of the Cornwall-Devon border, which in Blaeu lies somewhat to the west of North (though Blaeu gives no compass rose or north sign apart from 'Septentrio' at the top margin), whereas in Jansson, where two compass roses are included in decorating the sea area, the direction followed by the county boundary is almost parallel to the right-hand border of the map.

If anything, the Jansson map is somewhat the more decorative; the coats of arms copied from Speed are arranged in two rows in the upper left corner, the six shields above supported by two cherubs, while below are two shields, with a blank shield completing the design, supported by mermaids. The title in the lower left corner has a delightful cartouche with workmen bearing tools of their trade symbolising the activities of the county, while deer and foxes are representative of the plentiful wildlife of the area. In the lower right corner are mermaids supporting the scale of miles, while at upper right the arms of Cornwall appear embellished with ribbons. It is interesting to see that Jansson has chosen to fill in the open spaces of the sea area with compass roses and direction lines in the style of Italian portolan charts of the 14th century.

See also Nicholls 1712 (#27) and Schenk and Valk 1714 (#28).

1646 Novus Atlas sive Theatrum Orbis Terrarum, Joannis Jannsonii, Amsterdam. Latin, Reprinted 1659.

1646 Le Nouvel Atlas ou Theatrum du Monde. French, Reprinted 1647, 1652.

1647 Nieuwen Atlas, ofte Werelt-Beschrijvinghe, Vertonende Groot Britannien. Dutch, Reprinted 1652, 1653, 1659.

1649 Novus Atlas Oder elt-Beschreibung in welcher. German, Reprinted 1652, 1658.

18. BLOME, RICHARD 1673 & 1681

Eng. Lamb/Hollar/Palmer, Pub. Blome
(324 x 235 and 254 x 178)

Richard Blome (1621-1705) may have been born in Brecknockshire and may have attended Jesus College Oxford, matriculating in 1638 and created Bachelor of Civil Law in 1642. His entry into the DNB quotes Bishop Nicolson decrying Blome's 'Britannia' as a 'most entire theft out of Camden and Speed'. In fact, the story is a little more complex and not limited to Camden and Speed. Despite these criticisms, Blome's 'Britannia' and the later 'Speed's Maps Epitomiz'd' publications do contain a certain charm and decorative sense. Beyond this, the 1693 map's dedicatee, James Tillie, has a back story that may rival any others here.

'The Britannia' (1673) map measures 324mm x 235mm and was dedicated to John Granville, Earl of Bath, showing his coat of arms at top centre. In Blome's introduction, he describes himself as the 'Undertaker' rather than author as a justification for selectively using various sources in the compilation of the book. In the context of the maps, he, at one stroke, cuts Camden down and raises Speed as his preferred source (at least for the 'Britannia' maps).

The map of Cornwall appears within 'Britannia' as a double page insert between pages 58 and 59, with no text on the rear. It is quite evidently a 35% reduction of Speed's post 1623 map (#11) with all the elaboration removed. The cartouche top left titles it as 'A mapp of the county of Cornwal; with its hundreds, by Ric: Blome, by his Ma^{tys} comand' and is supported by a splendid pair of sea monsters that are almost Art Deco in style. To the right of this are the arms of John Grenville, Lord Lieutenant of Devon and Cornwall, set in a square frame resembling a theatre stage with open curtains. Of much more interest is the construction of the map itself, especially when compared with the later 1681 et seq. maps.

There is little doubt that the Cornwall map here is derived or copied from the Speed (#11) in its post 1623 state. This can be confirmed by the simple expedient of considering the Latin inclusions at Land's End, Falmouth, the Lizard, Lostwithiel and Plymouth Sound. Further evidence can be seen with the presence of the beacons seen on Speed's map, the tell-tale ramp of the north Cornish coastline at Trevose Head and the bulge at Tintagel. Blome's engraver/s (it is uncertain who engraved the Cornwall map, though it appears to be one of three – Francis Lamb, Wenceslas Hollar or Richard Palmer) have quite faithfully reduced and reproduced John Speed's post 1623 map.

The adornment is limited to four ships and a scale of 10 miles. Blome has copied the 3D effect cliff-line on the south coast first used by Norden. The label for Falmouth has moved over to the Roseland side of the Fal, with no obvious mark for the town. Evidently Blome knew of the existence of the town (founded 1661) but not its location. This is the only addition to Speed's place names. The map generally is a fair reproduction of one of the best examples of the engravers' art – hardly surprising that Blome spends two paragraphs apologising for its quality.

1673   *Britannia: Or, a Geographical Description of the Kingdoms of England, Scotland and Ireland…The like never before published. London. Printed by Tho. Roycroft for the Undertaker Richard Blome.*

1677   *Britannia: Or a Geographical Description… Printed for John Wright at the Crown on Ludgate Hill.*

Blome's 'Speed's Maps Epitomiz'd' maps were produced initially in 1681, but had been started as early as 1667, in other words at about the same time as the 'Britannia' maps, thus Blome was endeavouring to produce two atlases simultaneously. According to Skelton (p158), the maps were engraved by Hollar and Palmer (who sign some of the 38 county maps, but not Cornwall), but due to the poor performance of the 'Britannia' atlas, Blome sold and then recovered the smaller plates which became the 'Speed's Epitomiz'd' volume designed to continue the exploitation of the popular Speed maps without infringing the

18. Blome 1673 Britannia: Or, a Geographical Description of the Kingdoms

copyright held by Bassett & Chiswell. At this point, we need to point out that the maps used by Blome in his 'Speed's Epitomiz'd' are not copies of his 'Britannia' maps or Speed's either – or at least the Cornwall map is not, it is a 50% reduction of Saxton's famous map of 1576 (#1), which would side-step any copyright issues completely. Given the fact that the 'Britannia' maps are Speed copies, and poor ones at that, Blome may well have found himself at loggerheads with Bassett & Chiswell over copyright challenges, (their ten-years' privilege expired in 1686), and this may explain the poor sales.

The first edition of Blome's 'Speed's Maps Epitomiz'd' was better received and ran to a second edition in 1685. The 1681 map of Cornwall measures 254 x 178mm, and this first edition was dedicated to Hender Roberts, MP for Bodmin (1661-87); this version is very rare.

The 1685 edition returned to the patronage of John (Grenville), Earl of Bath, but is a poor version compared to the 1673 map. The surface of the map shows extensive evidence of re-working – one must assume that this is due to the plate being altered while out of Blome's possession and before the first edition dedicated to Roberts. The title cartouche has been moved from top left inwards to centre left. In outline it is the same design, with the art deco sea monsters on either side. The map title reads 'A Generall Mapp of the County of Cornwal with its Hundreds'. There is no mention of Blome, though it is evident that some previous detail has been hastily removed (e.g. the Tintagel label has been almost obliterated and scratch marks can still be seen behind the Padstow Haven label &c.). Alongside this cartouche is a newly drawn shield for John Granville. This shield is missing supporters and has below it a freestyle inscription which is almost verbatim from the earlier 1673 detail and initialled 'RB'. In the top left corner is a table of the Cornwall Hundreds numbered 1 – 9, again with evidence of a previous engraving below it.

Of the map itself, it is simply a 50% reduction of the Saxton 1579 with the following characteristics: Mount's Bay is wider at its southern end, the

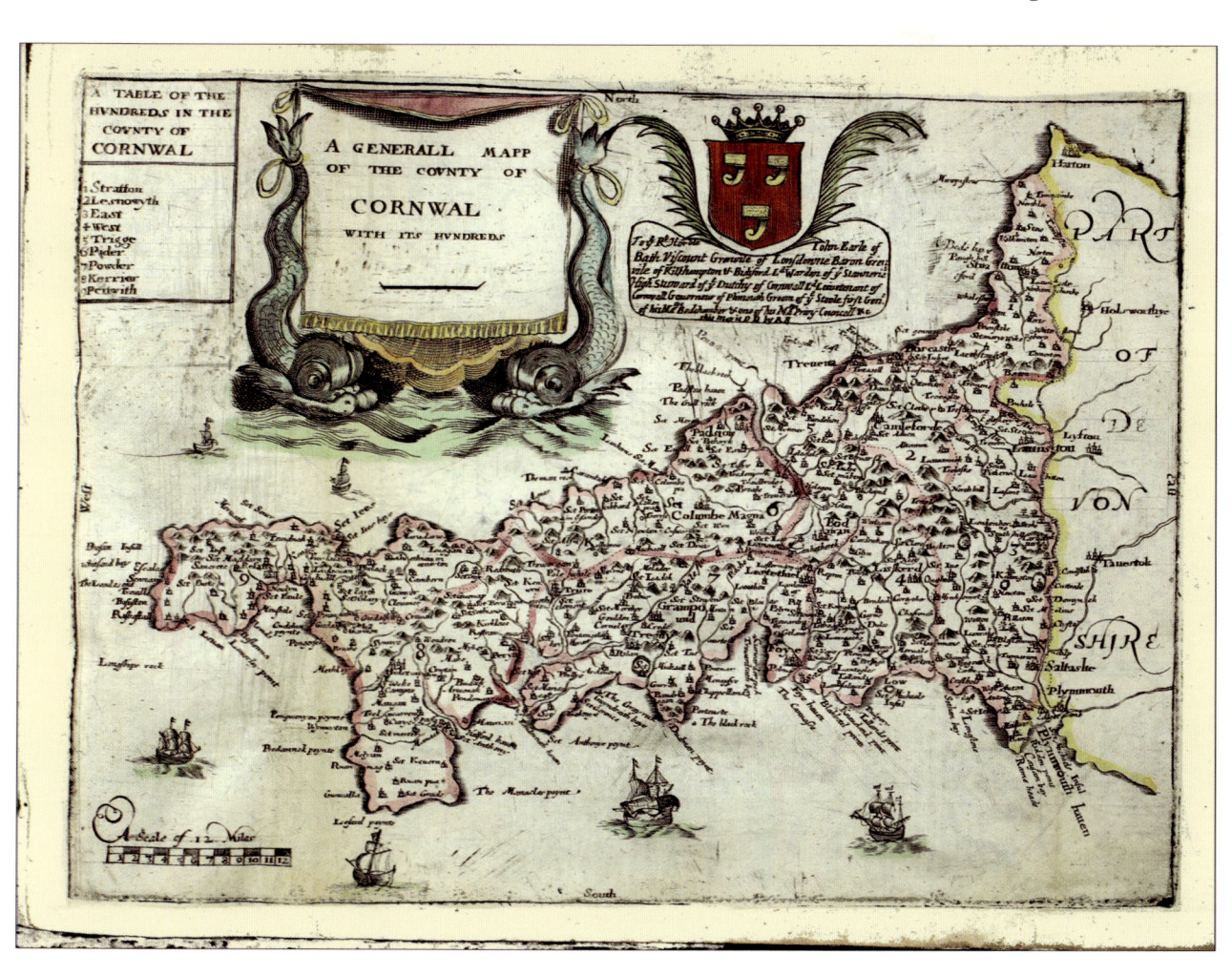

18.1 Blome, 1685 Speed's Maps Epitomiz'd ... London.

18.2 Blome, 1715 England Exactly Described ...

Antique Maps of Cornwall and the Isles of Scilly

Lizard base is inclined eastwards, Trevose Head near Padstow does not show the ramp seen on Speed's map (and thereby the 1673 'Britannia') and Tintagel is less prominent. There are no Latin labels, as detailed previously, nor are the beacons drawn. The scale of 0 - 12 miles is a Saxton scale; Speed uses 0 - 10 miles. For all this, the whole map feels unfinished and slightly rushed. The detail of the county has been completed but the engraver's construction lines are still present and the surrounding embellishments are untidy.

Blome produced 'The Cosmography and Geography…' in 1693 and the Cornwall map was altered again. It is still the same 50% reduced Saxton map, the table of Cornwall Hundreds in the top left is retained from the 1685 edition, the scale of 0 - 12 miles and the six galleons of various sizes are also kept. The title cartouche and arms of Granville have been replaced by a large stylised view of Pentillie Castle. Beneath this, in a very florid style, is a dedication to Sir James Tillie.

A prospectus to possible subscribers, offering them the map of their choice for the sum of £4, was produced, which must have piqued Tillie's ego in the light of the following story.

James Tillie (1645-1713), the son of a labourer at St. Keverne, had been taken as a groom into the service of Sir John Coryton, 1st Bt. (1621-1680) and eventually became his attorney, steward and the guardian of his children. 'In these situations, and by two advantageous marriages', according to William Hals* (1655-1737), 'and by other means, incommensurate with honesty and the laws, he became very affluent, secured the estate and by 'false representations' and 'a great sum of money,' obtained the honour of Knighthood from James II', (i.e. before 1688). Sir John was succeeded by his eldest son, also John (2nd Bt.), MP for Callington, and husband to Elizabeth Chiverton. The second baronet died under strange circumstances in 1690 and Tillie married his widow at All Hallows Church, London Wall, in November 1691. Thus, elevated and advantageously married, Tillie built Pentillie Castle near St. Mellion on the banks of the Tamar.

The curious tale has a more curious ending, for when he died Tillie left orders that his body (in his usual garb and in his elbow chair with table, bottles, glasses, pipes and tobacco before him), should be placed in a tower built on a nearby hill to await the Resurrection. His servants continued supplying the corpse with food and drink for a further two years. They abandoned further efforts and, at some stage, a seated statue of their dead master was made, to replace the body. In 2007 the new owners of Pentillie commenced restoration works of the house and gardens and discovered, in 2012, a vault below the tower. In the vault, Sir James Tillie's remains were found, along with those of a leather chair!

From 1715 to 1731 nineteen issues were made. These contain slight variations of the map, including the addition of a plate number (7) from late in 1715 and roads from 1717.

1681   *Speed's Maps Epitomiz'd or the Maps of the Counties of England, Alphabetically placed. London.*

1685   *Speed's Maps Epitomiz'd … London, Printed and Sold by Sam Lownes over against Exeter Exchange in the Strand.*

1693   *Cosmography and Geography, in Two Parts: … Illustrated with Maps. To which is added the County-Maps of England, drawn from those of Speed. London. Printed by Samuel Roycroft, for Richard Blome, dwelling near Clare.*

1715   *England Exactly Described Or a Guide to Travellers In a Compleat Sett of Mapps of all the County's of England… Printed Coloured and Sold by Tho: Taylor at ye Golden Lyon in Fleetstreet, London. Reprinted 1717 as 'England Exactly Described… Printed Coloured and Sold by Tho: Taylor.*

1731   *England Exactly Described … Sold by Tho: Bakewell, next ye Horn Tavern in Fleet Street. Later section of the dedication to Tillie has been erased (The great encourager…&c).*

William Hals wrote a history of Cornwall in about 1685 but never finished it, the reason for this may well have been the scandal created by some of his articles and their accuracy. His assessment of Sir James Tillie appears to be accurate or even perhaps generous.

19. OGILBY, JOHN 1675

Eng. Ogilby, Pub. Ogilby
(445 x 343)

John Ogilby (1600-1676) is described by Ereira (2016) as having nine lives. While there seems little doubt that his greatest legacy is 'Britannia', which will be discussed below, it came at the end of an eventful life of several episodes, which Ereira covers in detail. In very broad terms, Ogilby's life can be divided into pre- and post-Restoration. The pre-Restoration story, from his family's arrival in London, through Merchant Taylor's School, his life-changing injury while dancing at a masque in 1619 and appointment as master of revels in 1637 in Dublin, speak of a man who was making the best of his hand. Before returning to England in 1648, Ogilby had translated Virgil's complete works and published them that year.

Ogilby started using a coat of arms in 1653, deduced by Ereira as being those of the Earl of Airlie. There are at least three examples of Ogilby using three different variants of an achievement, which is curious, not least of which is the fact that it appears to simplify with age. The last example can be seen atop of the preface to 'Britannia' (1675), hiding in plain view. This is a lion statant guardant (all four paws on the ground, face looking towards the viewer); if it is wearing a crown, it is a small, three-pointed affair. On the ground above the lion is a star, or more correctly a mullet, signifying the 3rd son.

The next example can be found on a portrait of Ogilby by Pierre Lombart (1612-1680) in the National Galleries of Scotland's collection. From the title, we know it post-dates Ogilby's publication of Virgil in 1648, and obviously predates the death of the artist. The coat of arms shown here has the lion, but it is 'passant guardant' i.e. standing on three legs with the front right paw raised. The lion is wearing a crown with three fleurs-de-lys, c.f. the Great Seal of Henry III. Above the lion, the mullet is still present, however, above this are three further additions. A grated helmet used by the peerage below the rank of duke, and above this is a five-pointed crown denoting an earl, and above that the crest of the Airlie family – a lady from the waist up, facing forwards, in blue, holding a portcullis.

The last example is also in the possession of the National Galleries of Scotland and is engraved by George Fairthorne, and considered to date about 1660. This is a simplified version of the Lombart work; the shield still has the lion bearing the three-pointed fleurs-de-lys crown and is passant guardant. Above the lion is the mullet, but there are no helmets, additional crowns or suggestions of any association with the Airlie crest.

To understand the similarities and differences, the 7th Lord Ogilvy was created Earl of Airlie on 2 April 1629 by Charles I. The grant of arms is: 'Argent, a lion passant guardant gules crowned with an Imperial crown and collared with an open one proper. Over this is a crest of: A lady from the waist upwards, affrontée azure holding a portcullis gules'. There are elements of this that are highly similar but not similar enough to those used by Ogilby, at least in the portrait by Lombart. If we take the assertion by Ereira that Ogilby is the lost 3rd son of the 6th Lord Ogilvie, and thereby brother to the 7th Lord, who becomes Earl of Airlie, the mullet becomes important and where the problems start. The family history of the lords of Ogilvie and those of the Earl of Airlie are well documented; the third son of the 6th Lord was John Ogilvie of Newbigging, who died 22 November 1625. There are two scenarios: that Ereira's research is correct and Ogilby has the authority to bear arms, or Ogilby decided to up his profile by adding a bit of class.

Following the Restoration and the publishing of various Greek classics, John Ogilby's chief contribution to the art of map-making was his road atlas of strip maps in which were shown the Post Roads of the day. The postal services had been regularised after the Restoration, when the Duke of York (later James II) was given a monopoly of organising the conveying of letters, and Ogilby, appointed as Cosmographer Royal and Geographic Printer in 1674, made possible a considerable improvement in these services by his invention of the strip map.

Several points are worthy of note; the very ingenuity of the map is remarkable in itself and anticipated the modern route map by some 250 years: each road was carefully surveyed and measured by means of a 'Wheel Dimensurator', which recorded one revolution per 10 miles on a dial as it was pushed along. It seems likely that the circumference of the wheel was a ½ Pole or 8¼ feet: this becomes a wheel of 1ft 4 ins in radius. Ogilby was the first mapmaker to use, throughout a complete atlas, the statute mile of 1760 yards, (which had been prescribed for London and Westminster as early as 1593, though considerably longer 'county miles' persisted until the 1824 Act of Uniformity of Measures, and unofficially until even later). Within the preface we are given a detailed explanation for the English Mile. The definition is illuminating and stems from the lowly barleycorn. There are, says Ogilby, three corns to an inch, 12 inches to a foot and 3 feet to a yard. There are 5½ yards to a pole, 40 poles to a furlong. An English mile is 8 furlongs, or 320 poles, or 1760 yards, or 5280 feet. All the maps were drawn on a scale of one inch to the mile, with most of the plates covering about 70 miles per sheet; the cartouche of each map shows the distances in terms of miles and furlongs. The use of a consistent mile to an inch scale was another important development in the history of map-making. Within a few years, roads were being included in most maps, not only on the productions, but also the revised editions of earlier ones, such as Henry Overton's edition of the Speed atlas (#11) and Philip Lea's reissue of Saxton (#22).

Ogilby's 'Britannia' was planned as three volumes, though he was only able to complete the first one before his death in 1676. The road maps are laid out in landscape format of 12in x 18in in a scroll form that reads from left to right, bottom to top. In summary, there are 85 itineraries, covering 100 plates. Some of these routes cover only one plate while others extend to two or more plates. The London - Land's End route is one such sequence, covering four plates (Plates 25-28 incl.). In total, there are three plates related to roads passing through the county of Cornwall:

Plate 28. The fourth section of a continuous route from London to Land's End (starting at Plate 25: London - Andover, Plate 26: Andover - Crookhorn (Crewkerne) and Plate 27: Crookhorn - Plymouth) which features the last section from Plymouth to Sennen. This sequence has a bifurcation whereby the route splits at Andover, with Plate 32 from Andover to Bridgewater. Plate 33 continues from Bridgewater to Hatherley (Hatherleigh, Devon).

19. Ogilby 1675 Frontispiece Britannia, Volume 1

56 **Antique Maps of Cornwall and the Isles of Scilly**

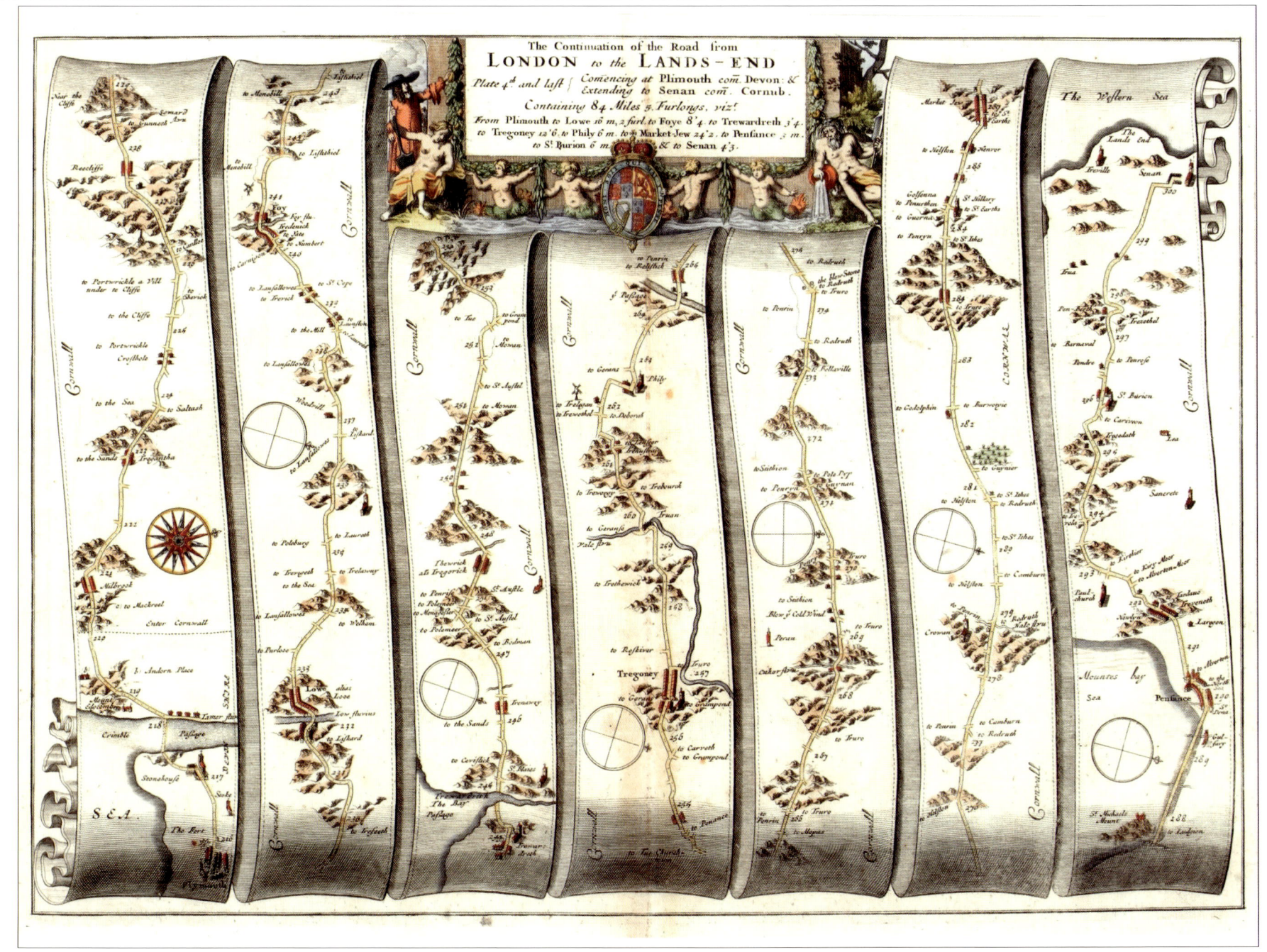

19.1 Ogilby 1675 Britannia, Volume 1: Plate 28; Plymouth To Land's End

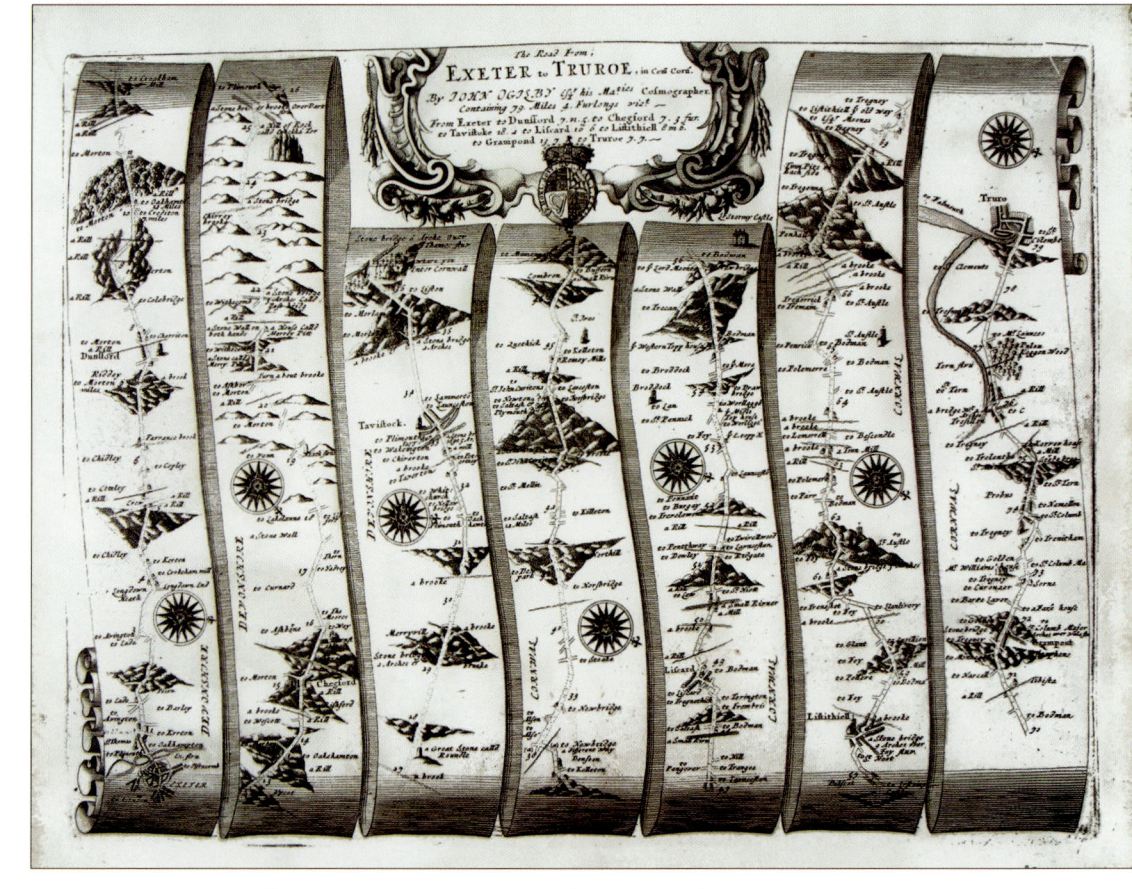

19.3 Ogilby 1675 Britannia, Volume 1: Plate 69; Exeter to Truroe

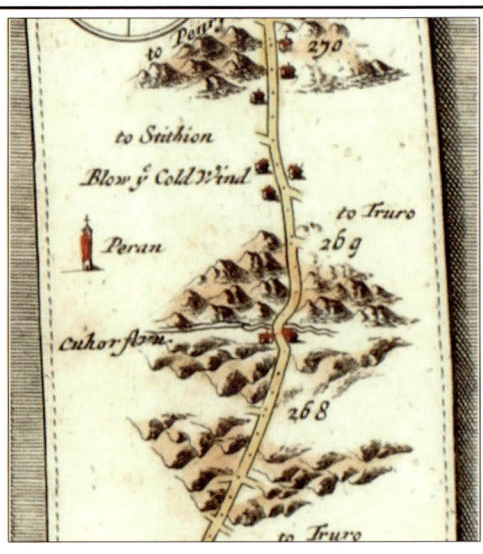

19.2 Detail: Coldwind Cross

Plate 34. From Hatherley in Devon to Truro.

In cross-reference, these plates correspond with the later Bowen strip maps, (#30) thus Ogilby's 28th becomes Bowen's 66th and 67th. Ogilby's 34th becomes Bowen's 82nd and 83rd; finally, Ogilby's 69th becomes Bowen's 181st and 182nd.

The preceding illustration shows the fourth plate of the route from London to Land's End (Plate 28), the section of road commencing at Plymouth and extending to Sennen. It is titled 'The Continuation of the road from London to Land's End' and details the route from Plymouth to Stonehouse, over the Tamar and into Cornwall. The route passes Looe, Foy (Fowey) and Tywardreath near St. Austell, and then to Tregony before crossing the Fal at Carrick Roads. The route continues through the centre of mid Cornwall to St. Hillary and then to Market Jew (Marazion), to Penzance, St. Buryan and finally Sennen.

This route is discussed further in the section detailing Bowen's comparable strip map of 1720 (#30). The inclusion of items of interest or use, uphill and downhill, ferry and bridge, town and village, are all that one might ask of such a simple map, and the comment 'Blow ye cold wind' is obviously the origin of the present-day Coldwind Cross which is south of Bissoe.

The success of these road maps was such that other cartographers and publishers almost immediately plagiarised Ogilby's work. Bassett & Chiswell lost little time in incorporating copies of these strip maps into their issue of the 1676 edition of Speed's 'Theatre of the Empire of Great Britain'. John Ogilby wrote, on what must have been his deathbed, complaining they had 'Rob'd my book'.

1675 *Britannia, Volume the First: Or, an illustration of the Kingdom of England and Dominion of Wales by John Ogilby, Printed by the author at his house in White Fryers, London. Reprints: Three editions issued in 1675, Reprinted in 1698.*

20. MORDEN, ROBERT 1676, 1695 & 1701

Eng. Morden, Pub. Morden
PLAYING CARDS (64 x 64)

Within a year of the appearance of Ogilby's road maps in 1675, Robert Morden (c.1650-1703) produced a pack of geographical playing cards of the 52 counties of England and Wales. The map is divided into three sections, with the top section used to title the card: Cornwall is the 10 of Diamonds. The red diamond is stencilled over the number 10 to the left; the Roman X is to the right of the title. The map itself is a rough outline of the county, with a limited number of towns and other features shown. Above the county, in the sea, is a very simple compass rose with north canted slightly to the right – this was done to align the county boundary with Devon to the right margin. These were the first county maps to show roads, though of course the limitations of size meant that only a single-lined diagrammatic version of the roads could be depicted. Below the map are the details of the length and breadth of the county, along with the distance from Launceston to London, as well as Launceston's latitude. In the earliest versions of these cards, only Launceston is denoted, with a small church tower; all the other towns are marked with a simple circle. The second edition, also published in 1676, named the adjacent counties, as well as marking the boundaries. From 1680 the retouched plates had many of the towns upgraded to a small symbol of a church tower, and the cards were bound into a small atlas. The map of Cornwall, in this state, has had the red diamond stencil omitted, suggesting that its use as a playing card may have been superseded.

1676 The 52 Countries (sic) of England and Wales, described in a Pack of Cards. Sold by Robert Morden at the Atlas in Cornhill, Will. Berry at the Globe in the Strand, Robert Green in Budge Row and George Minikin at the King's Head in St Martin's. Reprints: 1676.

1676-80 Untitled atlas by Robert Morden, London.

1680 Pocketbook of all the counties by Robert Morden, London.

1764-87 Brief description of England and Wales, Homan Turpin. London.

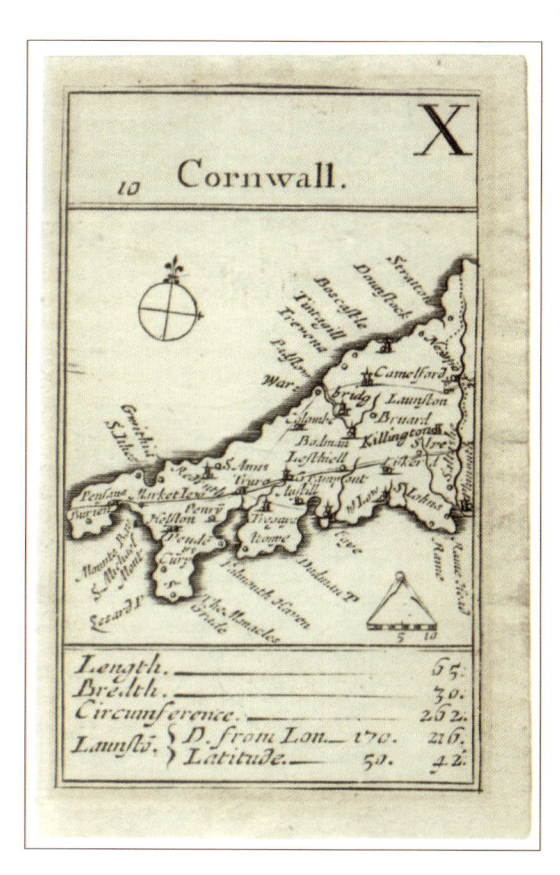

20. Morden 1676 The 52 Countries...

20.1 Morden 1680 Pocketbook of all the Counties

Antique Maps of Cornwall and the Isles of Scilly

1695 CAMDEN'S BRITANNIA
Eng Morden, Pub Camden
(406 x 343)

The most important of Morden's maps of Cornwall was used in Edmund Gibson's translation of Camden's (#7) 'Britannia', in 1695. It ran to six editions of this work, up to 1772. In most respects, it is a copy of the work of earlier cartographers such as Saxton and Speed, although Morden sent his manuscripts to 'Knowing Gentlemen' in each county for appropriate emendations, and claimed them to be 'much the fairest and most correct of any that have yet appear'd'. In effect, the map of Cornwall is somewhat coarse in appearance, although it has some claim to be called decorative by virtue of its ornamental cartouche.

In some respects, however, the map is worthy of special comment: it is the first large map to show roads, (copied from Ogilby and shown as single lines meandering through the landscape and occasionally embarking on detours – Coldwind Cross is avoided entirely). Morden shows many bridges crossing rivers, yet few, if any, show roads attached to the bridges. The county Hundreds are marked as dotted lines. Much of the cartographic content is derived from preceding publications, along with many of the inherited errors – e.g. Carn Marth beacon (See Lea #22) and Richard Carew's salt pond at Anthony (Norden #6). The isle near Looe continues to be termed St. Michael's - it won't be corrected until the 1800s.

Opposite St. Ives, near Gwithian, on Saxton's 1576 map is the dwelling of Maradarway. On Norden's map of about 1598 this is shown as Mertha-Derua and the 'Howse of Mr. Xtofer Arrondel'. The background to this is the Arundel family, an ancient armorial family of Cornwall with their main seat at Trerice (near Newquay and now owned by the National Trust). Christopher Arundel (1565-1604) had inherited the manor at Mertha-Derua from his father, Robert (Illg. 1535-1580), who in turn had been given it by his father, John Arundel (1495-1561), master of Trerice. Robert's legitimate half-brother, John (1530-1580), went on to inherit the seat at Trerice (and was father-in-law to Richard Carew). One of Robert's sons, Francis, bought Trengwainton, near Madron, in 1668, and moved this arm of the Arundel family seat from Mertha-Derua to Trengwainton, possibly around the time Gasgoyne was surveying the county. Mertha-Derua was sold in 1755, to Sir Francis Basset, Lord de Dunstanville, who was, by several generations, related to Reginald de Dunstanville, Earl of Cornwall. Morden's 1695 map shows 'Madern' placed both near Penzance and (in lieu of Mertha-Derua) opposite St. Ives; quite why is impossible to determine. Gasgoyne (surveying around the same time) has placed 'Matherderna' on the location of Madron and named the old location of Mertha-Derua as 'Menadarva'. It is 'Matherderna' instead of 'Madern' (Madron in Penwith) that is problematic and may be connected with the seat move of the Mertha-Derua Arundels to Trengwainton. Note that 'Trimguenton', near Madron, was noted by Norden and Morden, but not shown by Gasgoyne.

Thomas Martyn's 1748 map (#40) had corrected this, but Kitchin's 1755 Large English Atlas (#39), Bowen's 1762 Royal English Atlas (#30), Hatchett 1784 (#49) and Lodge 1788 (#51) retain this error. Cary's 1787 map corrects 'Matherderna' to 'Madern' and Trengwainton is removed from subsequent maps.

Morden's is the first map of the county to show longitude based on the meridian of London - St. Paul's and the offset to local time. Prior to this, the prime meridian had been taken through islands in the Azores; many cartographers had used various islands, with apparent indifference and resulting confusion.

The 1722 edition features alterations in the naming of Austel (to 'St. Austel'), Colan (to 'Collan') and Lugham (to 'Ludguan', now called Illogan). The later 1753 edition replaces the single line roads with double lines.

1695 Britannia. William Camden published by E. Gibson, London. Reprints: 1715, 1722, 1737, 1753 & 1772.

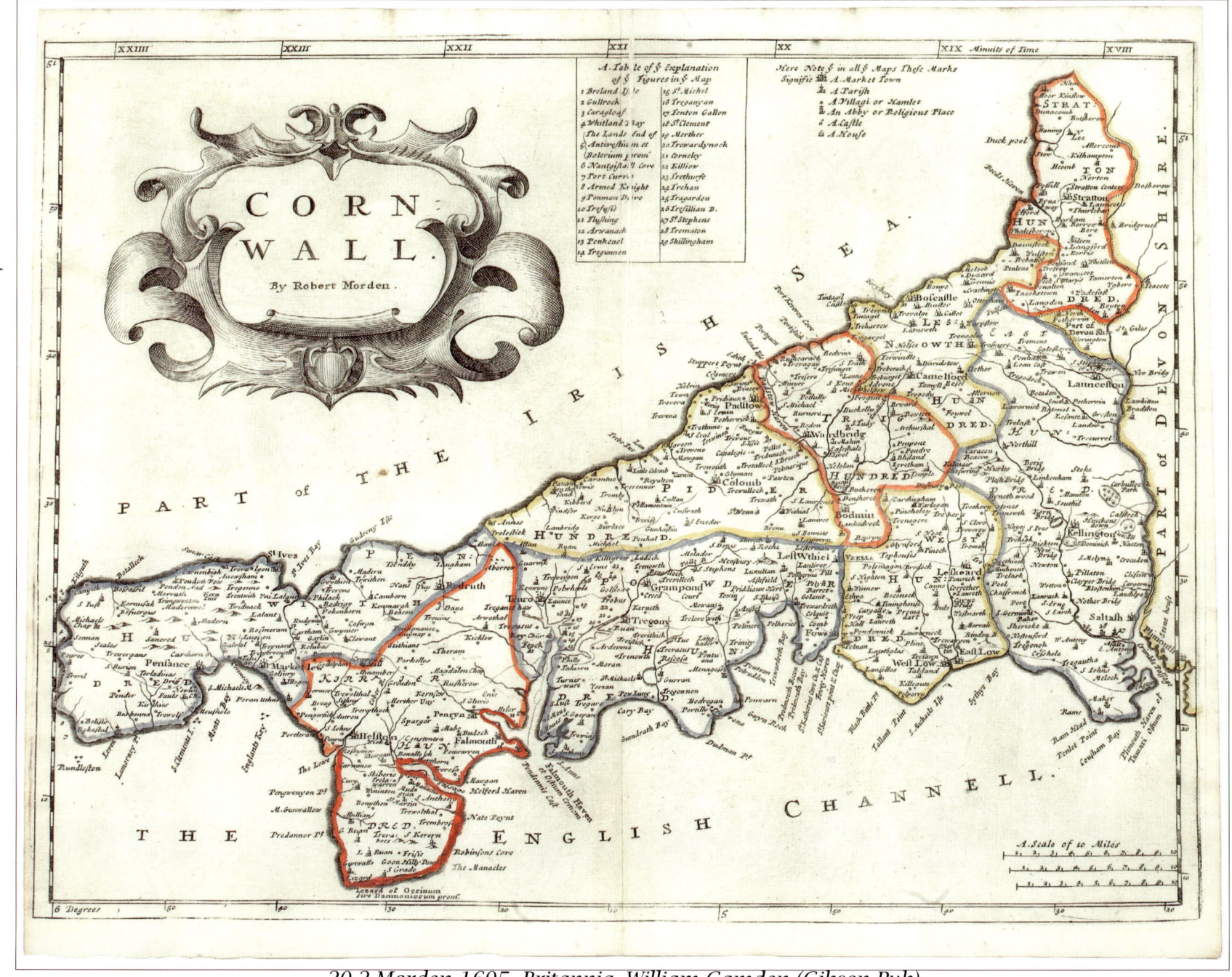

20.2 Morden 1695 Britannia, William Camden (Gibson Pub)

1701 THE NEW DESCRIPTION AND STATE OF ENGLAND
Eng. Morden, Pubs. 1. Morden, Cockerill & Smith. Later editions by a number of publishers
(220 x 170)

Morden's third map of Cornwall (1701) was rather plain and showed much the same information as the 1695 map. There are, however, some key changes: Morden's 1695 map was a rather low-level copy, lacking in coastal detail, among other deficiencies. Skelton (p193) suggested that Morden's 'Britannia' maps may have been originally smaller plates which were rejected by Gibson, and that these were revived here as the 'New Description...' and could date as early as 1693. There is no evidence to contradict this entirely, but it creates a problem vis-à-vis Gasgoyne's position in the chronology of the evolution of Cornwall's mapped outline, particularly the Lizard. Firstly, it is reasonably certain Morden never surveyed Cornwall; secondly, Ravenhill's (1991) analysis demonstrates Gasgoyne did so from c.1694 to the publication of his map in 1699. The outline of Morden's 1701 map is too similar to Gasgoyne's to be anything other than a copy. We have to conclude that Morden engraved the Cornwall map after Gasgoyne's publication, and not earlier.

Comparing the two Morden maps side by side reveals some big changes in the labelling of place names or their locations. Some of these can be justified by the reduction in the size of the later map, yet there are some omissions/changes/additions that are surprising. If the 1695 map can be considered a reproduction of the 1623 Speed (with some alterations), this 1701 map appears to be an amalgam of several sources. By illustration, there are several coastal labels that appear on the 1701 map and are not on (1) the 1695 'Britannia' or (2) any of Speed's or Saxton's maps. On the north coast are Illuggan and St. Agnes Well, on the south coast are Gull Rock, near Mullion, Porthallo (Porthallow) and St. Mich Charhays (St. Michael's Caerhays). All these appear on Gasgoyne's map.

In 1708 the map was issued in an atlas, corrected and enlarged by Herman Moll, (Morden died in 1702/3) - this is the 'Fifty-six new and accurate maps...', and enhanced the previous maps with the addition of roads, a compass rose and asterisks denoting the parliamentary boroughs. The atlas unashamedly made full use of Ogilby's road maps.

The 'Magna Britannia et Hibernia', in 92 instalments, started in 1714; it would take the buying public until 1731 for England alone to be completed, and the remainder of Great Britain and Ireland was never completed. Within this, Cornwall appeared in January 1715/16.

The 'Magna Britannia' (1720) also contains another rendition of the mileage table originally drawn by Norden, reproduced by Van Langeren (#14) and with its later variants by Jenner. The map has been replaced with details of the county (MPs, size, inhabitants &c.), and below this are some rather cramped and poorly drawn 'shields' of some of the county's towns.

The maps that followed Morden, particularly Moll's 1724 (#31), are of interest –Moll's 1724 is a copy of Morden. From this derive many other subsequent maps. For more, please refer to the discussion in the appendices.

1701 *The New Description and State of England, Pub Robert Morden, Thos. Cockerill & Ralph Smith. London. Second Edition: Pub S. & J. Sprint, J. Nicholson and S. Burroughs, A. & R. Smith.*

1704 *London. Second Edition in Quarto: Pub R. Morden, S. & J. Sprint, J. Nicholson, S. Burroughs, A. Bell & R Smith, London. Second Edition (reissued).*

1704 *Pub R. Smith, London.*

1708 *Fifty-six new and accurate maps...begun by Mr Morden...by Mr Moll. Pub John Nicholson, John Sprint, Andrew Bell and Ralph Smith, London.*

1720 *Magna Britannia et Hibernia Antiqua et Nova, Vol 1, Pub M. Nutt and J. Morphew, London.*

1739 *Magna Britannia Antiqua & Nova, Pub Caesar Ward and Richard Chandler. London.*

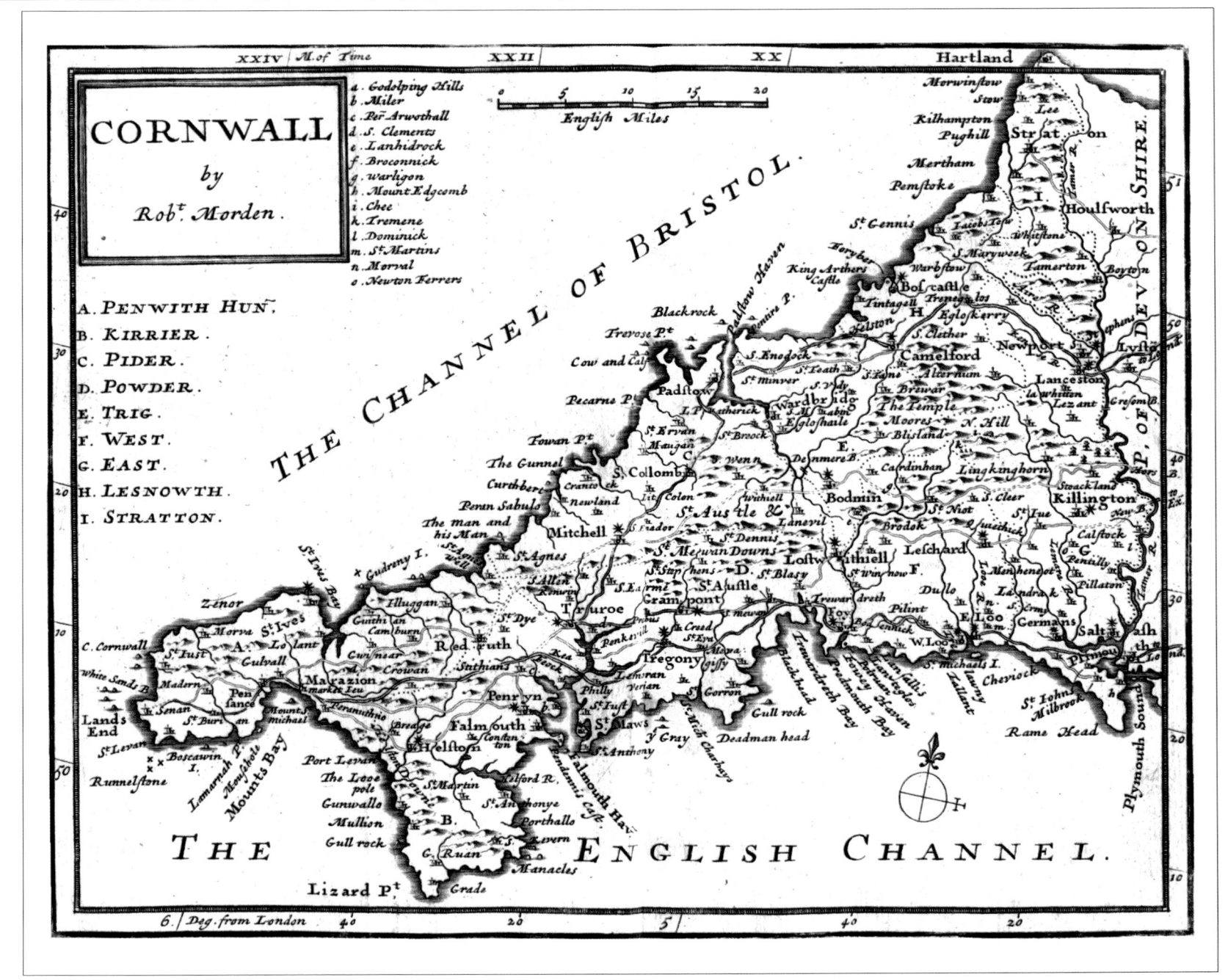

20.3 Morden 1708 Fifty-six new and accurate maps...

21. REDMAYNE, WILLIAM 1676

Eng. Redmayne, Pubs. 1. Redmayne, Mortlock, Turner, Cox & Billingsley, 2. Redmayne, 3. Lenthall
(89 x 53) PLAYING CARDS

William Redmayne produced a set of miniature cards at the same time as those by Morden and Bowes, though of lower quality. They are of little cartographic importance, small and cramped, with indifferent text, and they are crudely engraved. They are very scarce today.

The Cornwall card is enclosed with a lined double border on the top and sides. Top centre is the simple title in capitals, 'CORNWALL', with script text above and below the small map of the county in the middle. The map itself contains no labels, and only rivers and hills are depicted. Above the Penwith / St. Ives area is a pair of sailing ships as the only decoration. Printed over the county, and obscuring some of it, is the symbol for Clubs and the Roman numeral VIII.

The text above the map reads, including the title: 'CORNWALL is enclosed on the south with the British Ocean, by Northward with the Irish See, on the West with Penwith and the French Ocean'. Below the map, this continues: 'On the east parted from Devonshire with the River Tamar. Its of a fruitful soyl and abounds wth mettal mines, it hath store of fruit and is full of Towns. In it are (..) parishes and divers rivers'.

The cards were re-printed by John Lenthall in 1717 (#29).

1676 *Recreative pastime by Cardplay, London. W. Redmayne, H Mortlock, R Turner, H Cox & B Billingsley*
1677 *The suit is engraved with cross-hatching. Geographical, Chronological and Historiographical Cards of England & Wales London, W. Redmayne*
1717 *Narrow foliated border engraved. Historical Cards. London, J. Lenthall*

22. LEA, PHILIP (after SAXTON) 1689 & 1694

Eng. Terwoort/Lea, Pub. Lea
(470 x 356)

Philip Lea (? - 1700) issued two further reprints of the Saxton map. Lea, with Seller and Overton, was one of the most important London map-publishers at the end of the 17th century. The issue of 1689 shows considerable changes from earlier editions, for much of the decorative material from the Speed map is incorporated - the view of Launceston and the antiquities replace the Latin title. The cartouche in the centre top of the map, with the dedication to Elizabeth's 18th year (1576), has been erased and replaced by a roughly engraved title 'CORNWAL with several Hundreds truly described by CS [Christopher Saxton] - Corrected by P. Lea'. Note the spelling of Cornwall.

In the area previously occupied by the achievement of Thomas Seckford, a rather plain table of the arms of the earls and Duke of Cornwall has been introduced as shown earliest by John Speed (#11). For an unknown reason, the arms of Piers Gaveston, First Earl of Cornwall, is incomplete – only one of the three gold eagles is shown, though the other two are poorly outlined and unfinished. This plate is evidently still a work in progress - the ghosts of the Seckford arms are visible around the edges of the new table and the relics of the motto can be still seen in the unfinished Gaveston shield ('Pestis Patriae Pegricies'). The area of Saxton's elaborate title cartouche below the Royal Arms has been erased, to be replaced with a copy of Speed's Dunheved view. This has left a section of clear space above Penwith. Lea has not attempted to reproduce Saxton's sea and in consequence it is left devoid of the stippling.

On a hill to the south of Camborne, Lea has added a post on the top of the hill, with an arm and basket suspended from it – this is a fire beacon and the only one shown for the whole county. Today this is Crowan Beacon – a 720ft (220m) granite tor. In Norden's Penwith map (see appendix), it is called 'Bolitho Watch' and is marked by an inverted Y; it appears un-named on Kip's map of 1607 (#9), also as an inverted Y. On Speed's map of

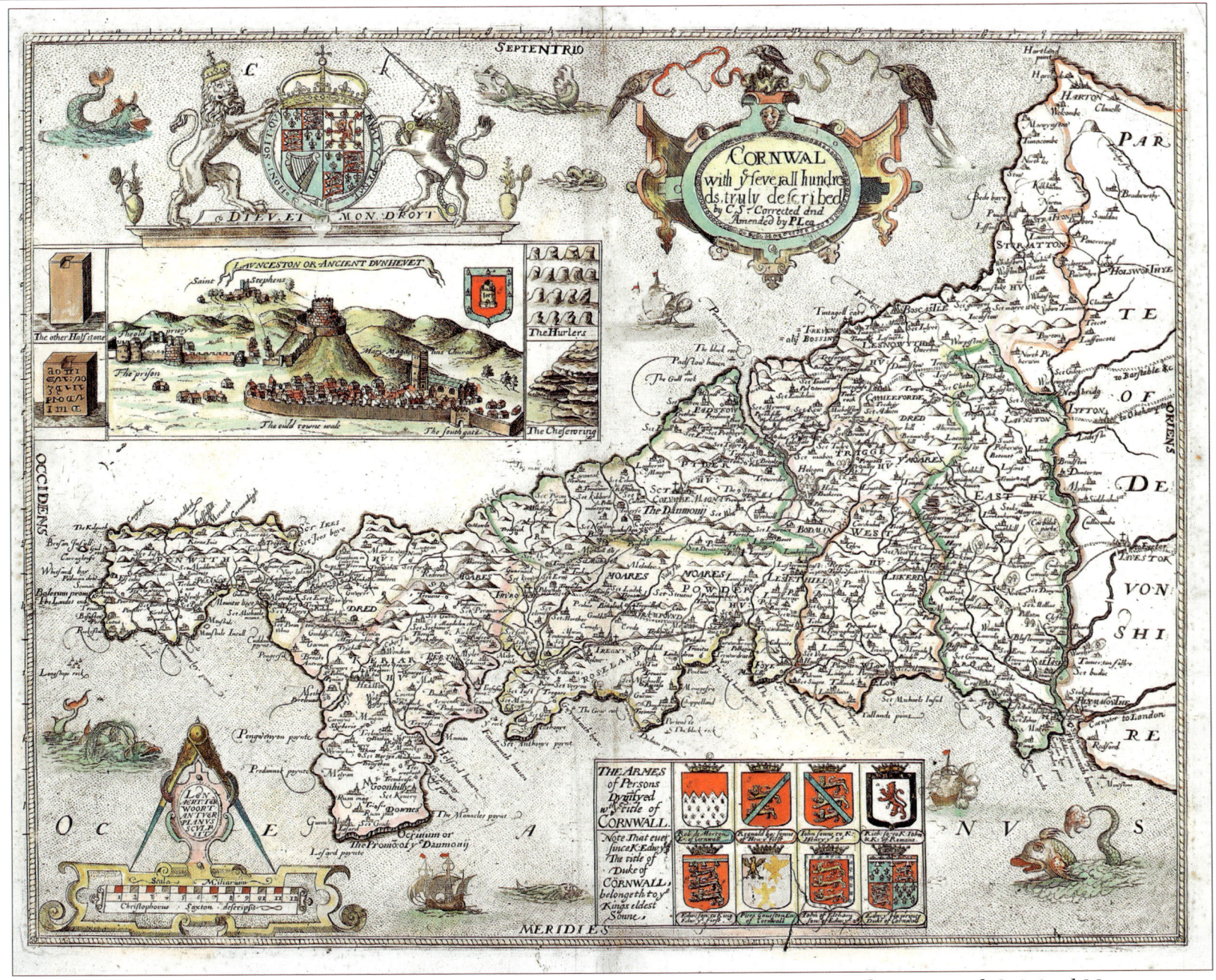

22. Lea 1689 *All the Shires of England and Wales by Christopher Saxton. Being the Best and Original Mapps. With many Additions and Corrections by Philip Lea*

1610 it is a simple mast almost hidden by the label of the Hundred but is mis-labelled 'Kernmargh Beac'. This is in error: Norden correctly places Kern Margh Beacon (Carn Marth) further east, to the south-west of St. Day, on his Kerrier Hundred map. In the process of compiling the detail of Cornwall, Speed has taken detail from Norden, (both Kernmargh Beacon and Bolitho Watch are present on the Hundred maps of Kerrier and Penwith, respectively), and compared this to Kip's. There is only an inverted Y at the location of Bolitho Watch (aka Crowan Beacon). Kip has not named either beacon. By Speed's own admission, he has copied detail from both Saxton and Norden. Neither of these beacons is mentioned on Saxton's map, so we are left with the conclusion that Speed obtained the detail from Norden and, in the process, exchanged Kernmargh with Bolitho Watch. Once this mistake was committed, all the subsequent maps (e.g. Jansson (#17), Blaeu (#16), Nicholls (#27), Morden (#20)) contain it. Web's version of Saxton's map (#15) did not make this addition.

22.1 Detail of Crowan Beacon Fire basket

Overleaf is a simple table showing the beacons named or drawn in Norden's original manuscript map, (both the main or the Hundreds' maps have been used); none of these beacons is marked as such by Saxton: he does indicate them as hills, but with no evident differentiation from other hills. We must consider that Norden has mapped these himself – since triangulation may have been his preferred method of mapping, marking these high points is logical. There are several possible reasons for the marking of these posts on the Norden map – we now know Norden's survey predates that of Kip and Speed. In preparation for the Spanish Armada (1588), beacons were set up throughout the Cornish peninsula and up-country to alert forces under Drake's command in Plymouth that the Armada had been sighted. Another beacon, mentioned by Norden, is at Hensbury, near Luxulyan. He notes that a man can see from this beacon as far as Devon and Land's End, as well as both the English Channel and Bristol Channel, weather permitting, from this one place. Evidently, 100 years later they were still in use.

There is some debate concerning whether much of the update from Web to Lea is in fact Lea's work, or whether there is an unidentified intermediate step, since there are a number of major alterations from the last seen version (Web #15), referred to by Baynton-Williams as State 5, and this State 7). There are a considerable number of additions to the Web plate, not least of which is the cramming of many, many new place names onto the Saxton/Web plate – this leads to the suspicion that there was a State 6 plate. Each of the county Hundreds has additions, as well as revisions to the previous (Web) plate.

The coat of arms of Elizabeth I on Saxton's 1579 map, above the title, has been replaced. In the process of less than 5 years (1685-1688), the throne of England changed three times: Charles II (1660-1685), James II (1685-1688) and William III (1688-1702). The coats of arms of all three kings are relatively similar; (Charles' and James' are identical, and William III added the Lion of Nassau inescutcheon as a differentiation and note of his Dutch ancestry). Lea's 1689 version left the arms as Web had changed them, from Tudor to Stuart, previously. Above the arms are the initials 'CR'; this denotes Carolus (Charles) Rex and refers to Charles I from Web's alteration.

Charles II acceded to the throne after the Reformation in 1660 and died in 1685. James II succeeded Charles II and reigned from 1685 until he was deposed in 1688. William III was then installed alongside his wife, Mary, on 13 February 1689. Thus, on the first (1689) edition, the arms and initials above them are technically incorrect by at least two kings. On some of the second edition (1694) county maps (e.g. Essex), Lea shows the new monarch by altering the letters above the (unaltered and incorrect Stuart) Royal Arms from 'CR' to 'WR' (William Rex). On the Cornwall map, however, the initials remain 'CR'.

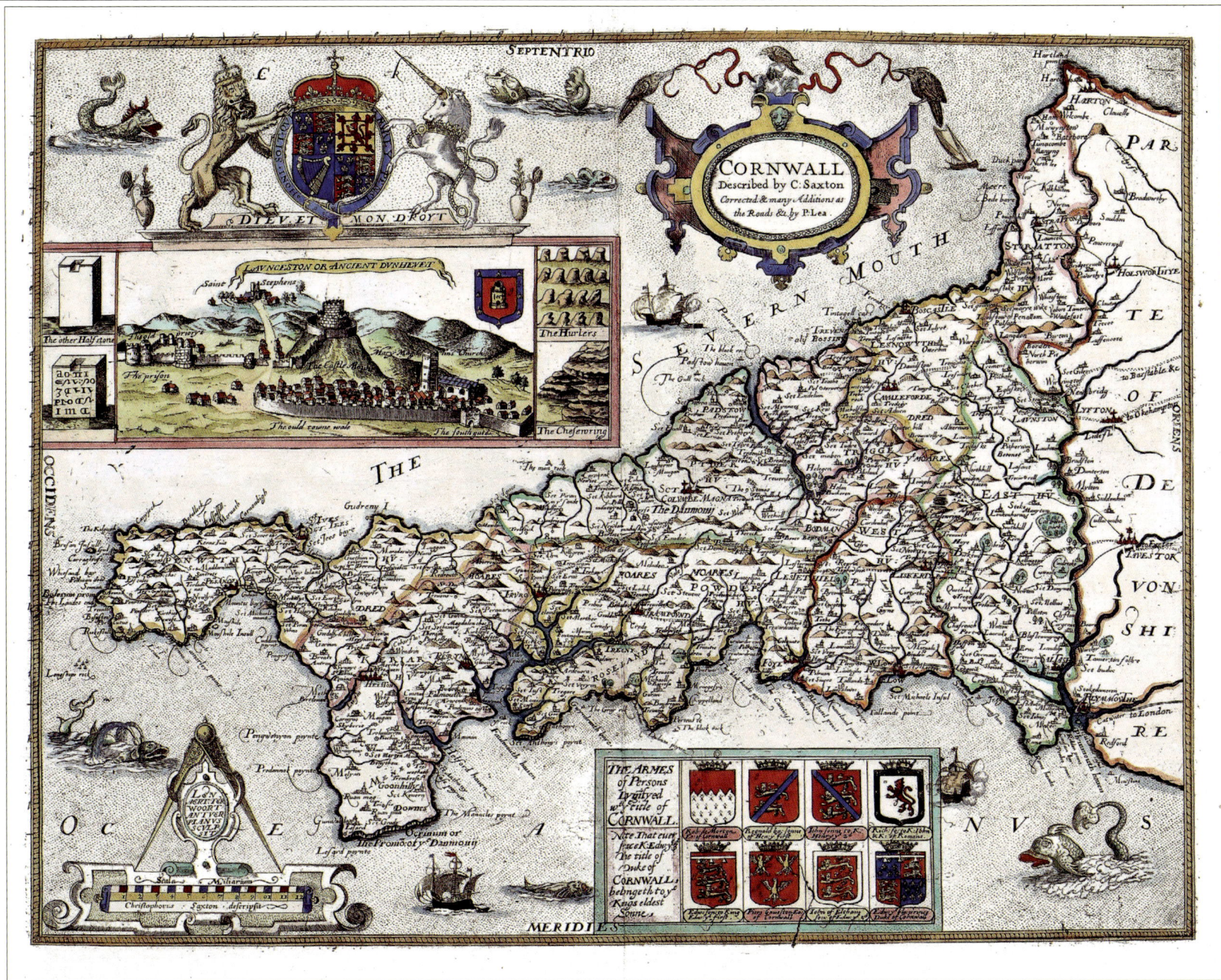

22.2 Lea 1694 *The Shires of England and Wales... Being the Best and Original Mapps with many Additions and Corrections Viz: ye Hundds, Roads. By Philip Lea. London*

More changes are found in the 1694 edition including three categories of roads, additional towns such as Falmouth, while crowns and crosses mark the borough towns and market towns respectively. Lea has taken the roads shown in strip map form by John Ogilby and inserted them into the Cornwall map, the route from Plymouth via Looe and Truro to Land's End is easily seen. Further, wrapped along the north Cornish coast is the label 'The Severn Mouth'. This is a novel addition and it is unique to Lea's 1694 edition.

The coat of arms of Piers Gaveston has by the 1694 version gained the correct number of eagles (3), however Lea has mistakenly transcribed the wrong coding for the colouring of the arms. On the field of the shield is the letter 'g' signifying gules or red, this should be 'v' for green, while the eagles are correctly marked 'o' or or, gold. Even with this second and tidier version, the remnants of the Seckford arms are evident - note the circle within a circle above the Mortain arms in the table's border - this is left from the Seckford embellishments. Around the outside of the border of the map Lea has added a basis for a grid labelled from the top left to bottom right - this commences with a blank and continues A to S across the top and A to N down the side. The purpose of this may be to aid in amending the plate details.

The crack that is seen on all Saxton maps has by this stage extended up to the upper third of the Gaveston shield. In the cartouche in the centre top of the map, the title has been altered from the 1st Lea version to a far neater: 'CORNWALL Described by C Saxton. Corrected and many Additions as the roads &c found by P. Lea'.

The edition by George Willdey in 1732 is unchanged except for his imprint in the lower right-hand corner. The last two editions by Jefferys (1749) and Dicey (1770) contain no further additions; Willdey's imprint has been roughly removed leaving the sea as an unstippled area.

1689 *All the Shires of England and Wales by Christopher Saxton. Being the Best and Original Mapps. With many Additions and Corrections by Philip Lea. Sold by Philip Lea at the Atlas and Hercules in Cheapside near Friday Street and at his shop in Westminster Hall near the court of common pleas where you have all sorts of Globes, Mapps &c. London.*

1694 *The Shires of England and Wales... Being the Best and Original Mapps with many Additions and Corrections Viz: ye Hundds, Roads. By Philip Lea. London.*

1732 *Republished and sold by George Willdey at the Great Toy Spectacle, Chinaware and Print Shop, The corner of Ludgate St near St. Paul's, London.*

1749 *The Shires of England and Wales...Saxton / Jefferys, London.*

1770 *The Shires of England and Wales...Saxton / Dicey, London.*

BEACON	CO-ORDINATES	NORDEN ~1598	KIP 1607	SPEED 1610	WEB 1642	LEA 1689
Menabilly, Nr Fowey	50° 20' 46" N 4° 40' 03" W	Shown	Shown	Not Marked	Not Marked	Not Marked
Binden Beacon, Nr Looe	50° 22' 39" N 4° 26' 31" W	Named	Named	Named	Shown	Shown
Hensbury, Nr Luxulyan	50° 25' 19" N 4° 43' 46" W	Named	Named	Named	Shown	Shown
Caradon Hill, Nr Liskeard	50° 30' 41" N 4° 26' 12" W	Named	Named	Named	Named	Named
Michelstow Beacon, Nr Camelford	50° 35' 04" N 4° 42' 31" W	Named	Shown	Not Marked	Not Marked	Not Marked
Crowan, Nr Godolphin	50° 10' 5" N 5° 16' 20" W	Named Bolitho Watch	Shown	Incorrectly Named (Carn Marth)	Marked	Incorrectly Named (Carn Marth)
Carn Marth, Nr St Day	50° 13' 24" N 5° 12' 17" W	Named	Not marked	Not Marked	Not Marked	Not Marked
Lizard	50° 00' 02" N 5° 14' 02" W	Shown	Shown	Not Marked	Not Marked	Not Marked

Table of the locations and names of Beacons drawn on the Norden manuscript map and subsequent maps

Sketch map of Saxton's outline and locations of the beacons.

1. Crowan
2. Carn Marth
3. Lizard
4. Hensbury
5. Menabilly
6. Michelstow
7. Caradon
8. Binden

23. COLLINS, CAPT. GREENVILE 1689

Eng. Yeats, Pub. Collins
(565 x 356)
SEA CHART OF THE ISLES OF SCILLY (Chart 20)

Captain Greenvile* Collins (1643-1694) served in the Navy and, as a younger brother of Trinity House he was appointed by Charles II to survey the coasts of Britain. The work began in 1681, until this time British seamen had to rely on Dutch charts which contained surprising inaccuracies. By the time that Collins' atlas was published, Charles had been succeeded by his younger brother, James II, who in turn was displaced by William of Orange, whose landing at Brixham in 1688 is commemorated in the Collins chart of Torbay.

'Great Britain's Coasting Pilot' forms a landmark in the charting of the British coasts, the charts being greatly superior to any previously issued. The chart of the Isles of Scilly is the first** printed map to be devoted exclusively to the islands, and because of this and its handsome presentation is much sought-after by collectors. The Scillies map was printed loose and predates the bound 'Pilot' by four years. The charming cartouche surrounding the title-piece shows rocks and cliffs crowded with goats, sea birds, rabbits, fish and shells, designed by Yeats to epitomise the life of the islands. The map is dedicated to Henry Fitzroy, Duke of Grafton, Vice Admiral of England, and his coat of arms, the Royal Stuart Arms debruised by a baton sinister, indicate that he was the second illegitimate son of Charles II. The great expanse of sea is decorated with rhumb lines, a compass rose and two small galleons, while the scale of miles is ornamented with a merman and mermaid supporting the Royal Crest within the Garter.

Down each side of the chart are two columns, labelled 'D' and 'M'; these refer to degrees and minutes of latitude, yet the columns are for the most part blank. Verner (1969) considered there to be three states of the chart in the context of latitude, with the first state (1689) containing latitude figures that, by the second state, (Pilot proper 1693) had been erased except for the number 1 to the left of the cartouche in column M. A final state, of 1781, further obliterates any remaining detail from the cartouche area.

Abraham Tovey (1687-1759) was a Master Gunner in command of a battery of guns in Star Castle, on The Hugh, St. Mary's, Isles of Scilly. His detailed knowledge of the islands, the channels and sailing marks used for making safe passage amongst them &c. made him a recognised authority on the navigation of the area. Tovey may have been born in Wiltshire. Following a military career, he was discharged, and arrived in Scilly in 1714 as the Board of Ordnance's resident man. Tovey's task of maintaining the Garrison's infrastructure was one of light maintenance. Politically, Britain was descending into a complicated European conflict, the War of Austrian Succession, and it was evident that the defences on Scilly were inadequate. Tovey's workload and submitted documents reveal that a major overhaul of the Garrison was undertaken from 1741 to about 1747. Such was Tovey's contribution to these improvements that his initials (AT) are inscribed below those of George III and Sir Francis Godolphin on the Star Castle in Hugh Town.

The 1723 edition makes a small amendment to the map, by marking 'Sir Clously lost' on the Gillstone. Collins has shifted the rocky outcrop of Pednanthys (and re-termed it 'Pednathis') about ⅜ of a mile eastward. Somewhere near the eastern side of the old Pednanthys location is the newly placed 'Gillstone'. This relates to the loss of *HMS Association* in 1707. Interestingly, the point where his body washed up (Porth Hellick on St. Mary's) was not included.

Collins' 'Pilot' added to the foot of the Scillies chart a text by Tovey on the tides and channels of the Isles of Scilly. These directions were printed and pasted onto the lower margin of Collins' chart in all its later editions. Note also that, with the addition of the Tovey text, the date within the cartouche has been erased.

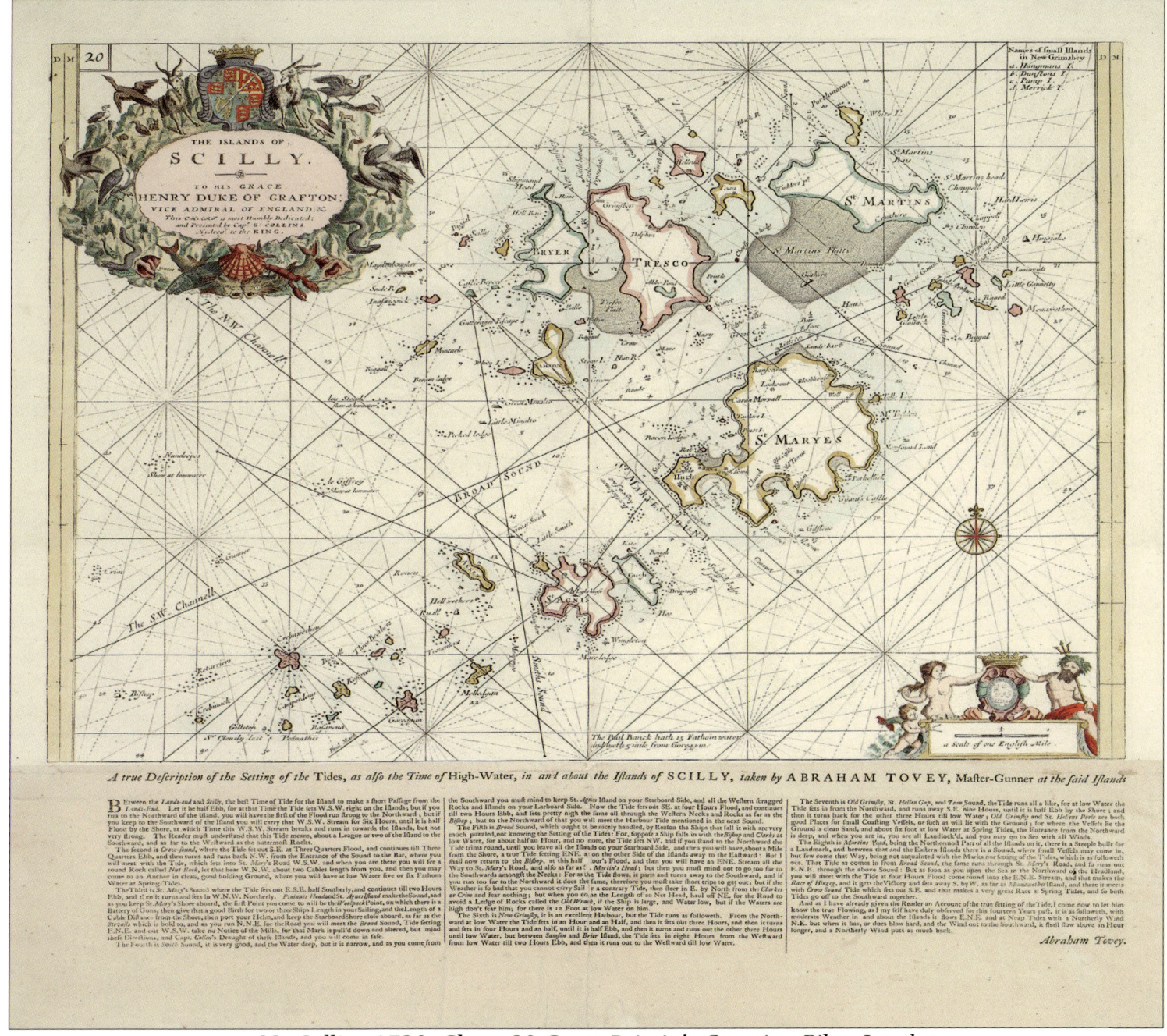

23. Collins 1738 Chart 20 Great Britain's Coasting Pilot, London

23.1 Collins 1693 Chart 20 Great Britain's Coasting Pilot

Detail of the 1693 edition showing the original position of Pednanthyes (rocks) offset from the alignment of Camperdeny and Crebawethen to its north

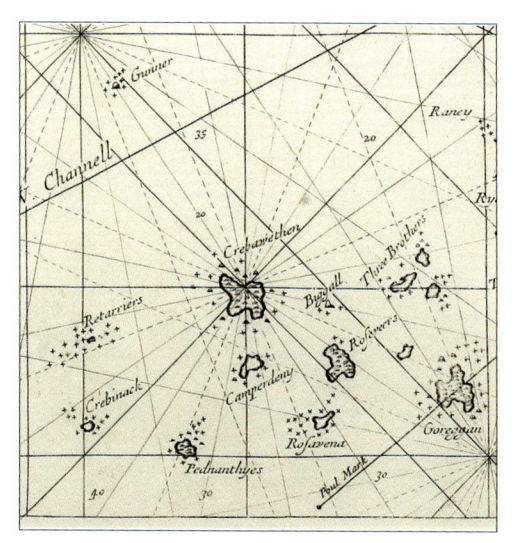

23.2 Collins 1686 Chart 19 Great Britain's Coasting Pilot, London

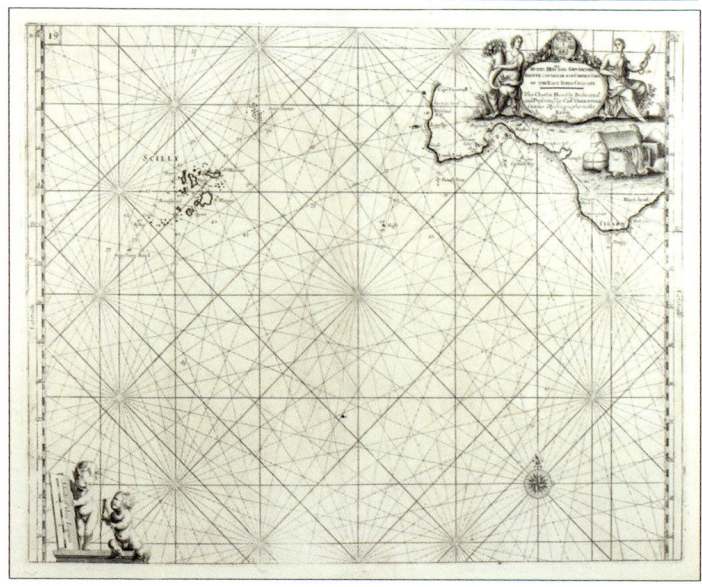

Chart 19 of the 'Coasting Pilot', 'Approaches to Land's End and Lizard including Scilly Isles', was prepared and published in 1686 and, while being a now less popular chart of the Scilies and western Cornwall than chart 20, it has been included to illustrate a few points that mark the map of interest. In fact, this chart is of greater maritime importance in terms of relative navigation between the Scillies and Cornwall. Entering or leaving the English Channel required knowing the location of the Isles of Scilly, and chart 19 was more important in this respect than chart 20. To achieve this, (St.) Agnes lighthouse (built 1680) was used as a point representing the whole archipelago and marked on both charts (without much fanfare on chart 19, it must be said). The limited sections of Penwith and Kerrier that are shown top right are slightly obscured by the cartouche dedicating the map to senior members of the (British) East India Company. The coat of arms above the dedication were used from 1600 to 1709. The selection and position of place names around the mainland coast, (few, if any, inland names are present), is interesting. 'Cape Cornwall' and 'Gurnard's Head' are exchanged, 'Longships', opposite what should be Land's End, is correctly placed, but 'Land's End' has moved to Tol Pedn Penwith. Collins has included Penzance as well as Mousehole and marked St. Clement's Isle without naming it. Overall, his mainland can only be described as rudimentary. The Isles of Scilly are drawn much as the later plate 20, with the obvious limits of scale meaning only the names of the individual islands are shown; the one exception being the lighthouse on (St.) Agnes. As with chart 20, down either side, Collins has set two columns, for degrees and minutes of latitude – however, in this chart, the figures have been left intact so we get an idea of Collins' construction of latitude regarding the islands. The reason why chart 19 contains marks of latitude and chart 20 does not is discussed by Everard (2004).

In 1779 Tovey's son co-operated with Nicholas Ginver to produce another very fine chart of the islands (#48).

*Various spellings are seen: Collins himself used 'Greenvill'.
**Commercially available: The Cornwall Records Office has a 1655 map (CCRO GO 574), probably privately commissioned by the Godolphin family, who were Lord Proprietors / Lessees of the Scillies until 1835. The map was never published.

1693 *Great Britain's Coasting Pilot. Captain Greenvile Collins, Sold by Page and Mount at the Postern on Great Tower Hill, London. Reprints: 1723, 1738, 1749, 1753, 1756, 1761, 1763, 1781, 1785 & 1792.*

Antique Maps of Cornwall and the Isles of Scilly

24. De HOOGHE, Sr. ROMAIN 1693

Eng. de Hooghe, Pub. Mortier
(953 x 584)
COASTAL CHART FROM SCILLY TO PORTLAND

Born in The Hague in about 1638, de Hooghe became a famous engraver much sought after to provide compositions for frontispieces printed in The Netherlands. His support of William of Orange was reflected in many publications.

Pierre Mortier (1661-1711) was born in Leiden, the son of a French political refugee. He was granted the privilege of distributing French maps and atlases in The Netherlands, which he did by having copies of the originals made - 'Le Neptune François' was one such publication, which also appeared in French and English in 1693. The same year, Mortier published a second part titled 'Cartes Marines a l'usage des armées du Roy de la Grande Bretagne' - it is this part that is also referred to as 'Atlas Maritime' and is usually bound with 'Le Neptune'. Within the 'Atlas Maritime' are nine plates. Only plates seven (Thames to Portland) and eight (Sorlingues to Portland) are of the English coasts; the remainder cover the Dutch/Belgian/French coasts of the Channel, as well as the Bay of Biscay and the Mediterranean.

De Hooghe's plate eight, of south-west England, is a truly splendid example of the decorative art of the mapmaker being combined with useful and relevant information. The whole chart is covered with grid lines showing latitude and longitude, the longitude being measured eastwards from the Azores.

The shape of the coast of Cornwall is somewhat similar to the crude design used by Waghenaer, but de Hooghe seems to have had access to more information about the north coast of the county, though in some instances there are some serious errors of position, for Padstow is shown to the west of St. Agnes and Redruth! A few other points of interest appear with closer inspection. Wolf Rock (aka The Gulf, on Mercator's 1595 chart, #8) continues to be termed 'Lethousen' (Cornish: Lethowsow), while Land's End has been placed at Tol Pedn Penwith. In common with most sea charts, few inland places are noted, though Kernmargh Beak (Carn Marth) has been included close to its correct location. Only Powder, West and East Hundreds are marked; the other six are missing. In Plymouth Sound, there are some further errors. The border between Cornwall and Devon is clearly shown, but uses the Plym instead of the Tamar. Both Saltash and Plymouth are shown on the Cornish side of this (incorrect) border, and Saltash appears at the head of an estuary which one could take as the Lynher. Evidently there is some confusion, which is compounded with the upper reaches of the river/border striking across country in a straight line from Bradston to the north Cornish coast. The whole construction is very strange, in view of the preceding maps that are essentially correct. The sea area is scattered with a profusion of notes about tides and currents, views of landmarks and hazards to navigation, and the overall decoration of ships, compass roses and direction lines is reminiscent of the style of Jansson.

Two fine views, one of 'Land's End' and the other of 'Falmouth (Valmue) with Truro from Pendennis Castle', fill the top left corner, and a view of 'Portland' appears at lower right beneath a handsome cartouche bearing the arms of William Bentinck, Duke of Portland, to whom the chart is dedicated. The companion plate seven shows the remainder of the south coast from Portland to the Thames and completes an impressive cartographic panorama.

The large inset of the Isles of Scilly is surrounded by a figured framework, personifying the seas and winds, but although the representation of the individual islands shows a considerable advance upon the rudimentary form depicted by Waghenaer and most of the map-makers of the early 17th century, the map of the Isles does not approach the standard achieved by Captain Greenvile Collins (#23).

1693   *Atlas Maritime* by Romain de Hooghe, Published by Pieter Mortier, Amsterdam. Reprint: 1694.

24. De Hooge 1693 Atlas Maritime Amsterdam

SECTION THREE:

25. GASGOYNE, JOEL 1700
26. SELLER, JOHN 1694 and 1773
27. NICHOLLS, SUTTON 1712
28. SCHENK, PETER & VALK, GERARD 1714
29. LENTHALL, JOHN 1717
30. BOWEN, EMANUEL 1720, 1748, 1759, 1764, 1767 and 1785
31. MOLL, HERMAN 1724 and 1718
32. VAN KEULEN, GERARD 1735
33. PINE, JOHN 1739 and 1740
34. BADESLADE, THOMAS & TOMS, WILLIAM 1742
35. DODSLEY, ROBERT & COWLEY, JOHN 1744
36. THOMAS READ & ROCQUE, JOHN 1746
37. WALKER, ROBERT & SIMPSON, SAMUEL 1744
38. OSBORNE, THOMAS & HUTCHINSON, THOMAS 1748
39. KITCHIN, THOMAS 1749, 1750, 1764, 1769 and 1778
40. MARTYN, THOMAS 1748, 1749 and 1784
41. KITCHIN, THOMAS & JEFFERYS, THOMAS 1749 and 1775
42. BICKHAM, GEORGE (Snr & Jnr) 1750 and 1796
43. BORLASE, WILLIAM 1754 and 1758
44. MEIJER, PIETER & SCHENK, LEONARD 1757
45. GIBSON, JOHN 1759 and 1762
46. ELLIS, JOSEPH 1764
47. DE LA ROCHETTE, LOUIS STANISLAS D'ARCY 1765
48. TOVEY, ABRAHAM (Jnr) & GINVER, NICHOLAS 1779
49. HATCHETT, THOMAS 1784
50. CARY, JOHN 1787, 1789, 1790 and 1809
51. LODGE, JOHN 1788
52. SUDLOW, EDWARD 1790
53. JOHNSON, JOSEPH 1790
54. BAKER, BENJAMIN 1791
55. TUNNICLIFF, WILLIAM 1791
56. SPENCE, GRAEME 1792
56. FAIRBURN, JOHN & ROWE, ROBERT 1798

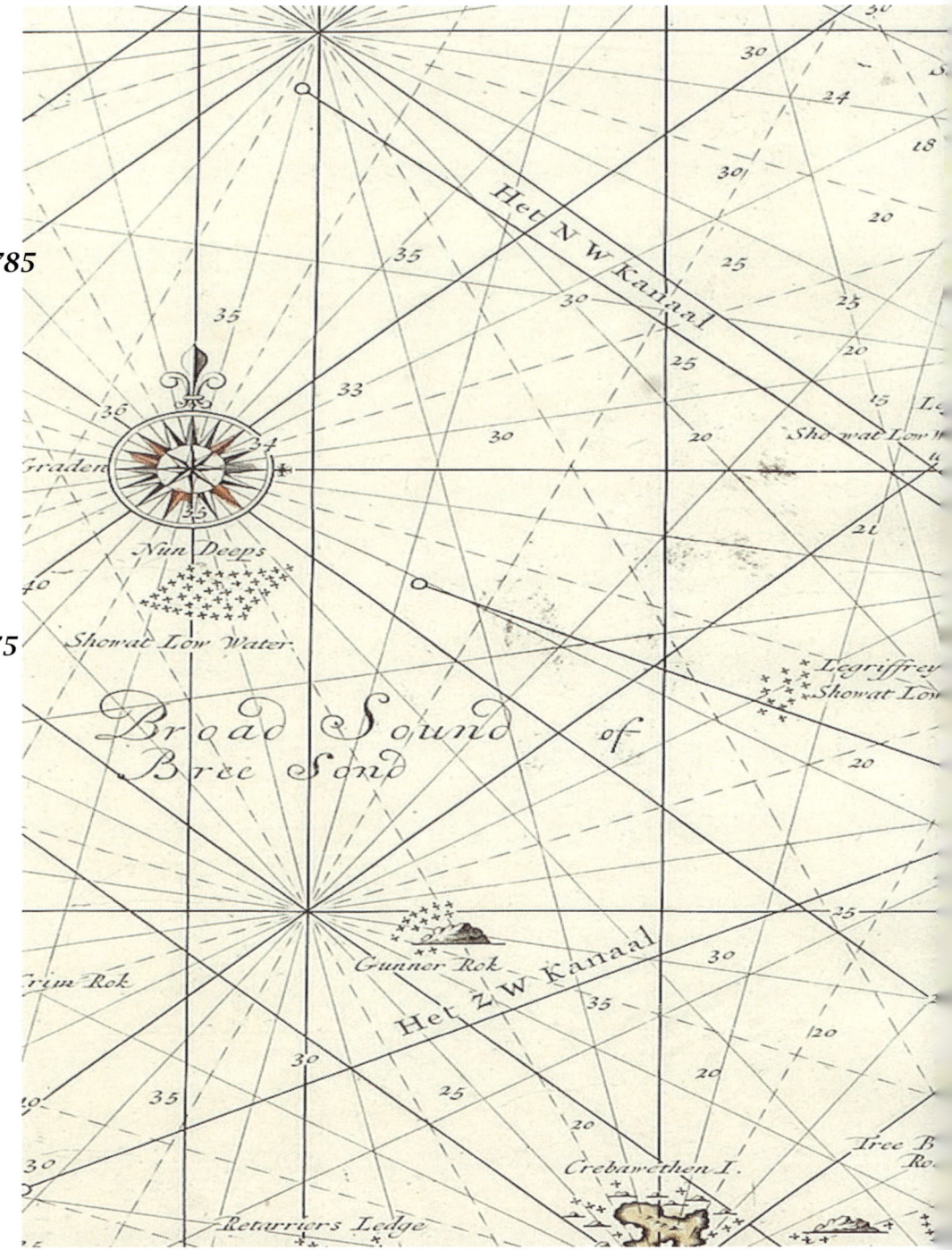

Antique Maps of Cornwall and the Isles of Scilly

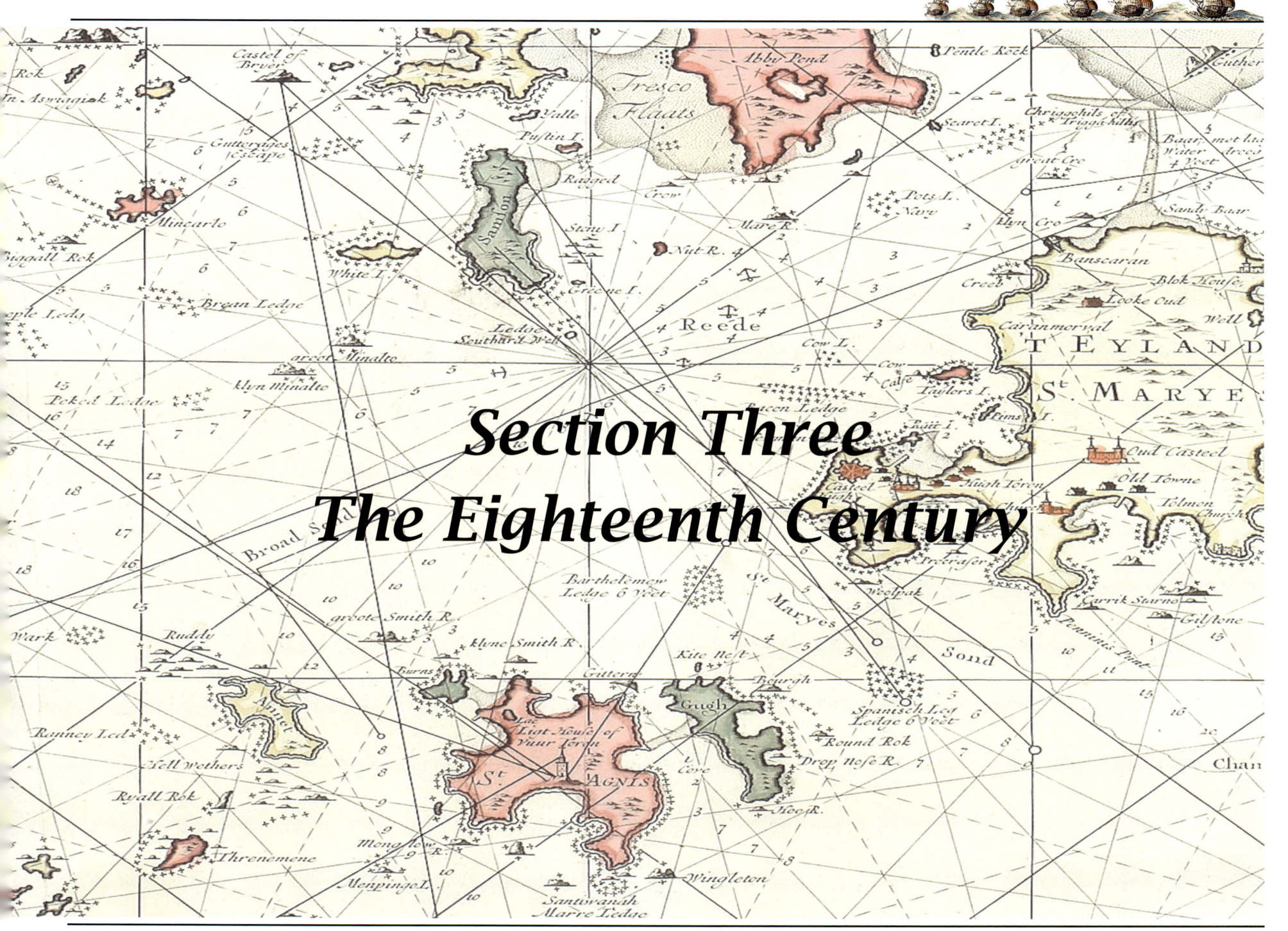

Section Three
The Eighteenth Century

25. GASGOYNE, JOEL 1700

Eng. Gasgoyne, Pub. Darker & Farley
(1829 x 1295)

Joel Gasgoyne was baptised in 1650 in Kingston Upon Hull, the name is sometimes spelled Gasgoine. He apprenticed himself to John Thornton, a platt-maker in the Minories in London, for a term of seven years, from 1668. A Platt-maker is, in fact, a chart engraver- the charts were drawn onto vellum and then pasted onto boards of oak for use at sea – this was the 'platt'. Thornton was, and presumably Gasgoyne also was, a member of The Thames School of Chart-makers.

This is the first large-scale map of Cornwall, or indeed of any county in England, the vogue for maps on the scale of one inch to one mile did not come in until the mid 18th century. Although Gasgoyne (1650-1705) had not given a scale to his map, it is about one inch to one mile, and naturally shows far more detail than any other previous map had been able to do.

The map itself is a truly remarkable piece of work, the result of an actual survey by Gasgoyne, and the accurate shape and improved information had a considerable influence on the maps of Cornwall that were to follow throughout the 18th century. It appears that Gasgoyne carried out his survey without any direct patronage, for in his 'Prospectus', dated 27 March 1699, he recommends his map to the Nobility and Gentry of Cornwall in the following way: 'May it please your Honours, I have with indefatigable Pains, with almost insuperable Difficulties, and all the Curiosity I could, completed the Map of your county of Cornwall; the publication of which, has proved beyond my Imagination, Chargeable and Expensive to me'. The prospectus goes on to state that the proof copy of the map was to be placed on show in the Grand Jury Chamber at Launceston, in order that any mistakes might be corrected before the final publication. The addition of the word 'Philomath' after Gasgoyne's signature is interesting: the close connection between surveying and the teaching of practical arithmetic is demonstrated in the case of not only Gasgoyne, but also Benjamin Donn (whose 1 inch map of Devon was the first to win the award offered by the Society of Arts, in 1765), and John Prior (Leicestershire, 1779). It is worth noting that the degree lines of latitude are drawn right across the map, and that pecked lines mark the ten-minute intervals, individual minutes being shown only by divisions along the borders; the calculation of the latitude has been done with a fair show of accuracy, unlike the attempts of earlier cartographers, which were as much as 30' in error. On the other hand, no attempt has been made to show longitude, possibly because of the confusion over what was the correct meridian, which was a problem confronting map-makers of that time. Parish boundaries are shown for the first time, using much the same symbol as is found on the Ordnance Survey maps today. The fenced and unfenced roads are also shown by devices familiar enough at the present day, but the hills are still shown by the conventional side views, which, though beautifully engraved, are of little value in the representation of their relief. The place-names at Newlyn and Newlyn East are both given as 'Newland', St. Day is written as 'St. Dye' and Madron given as 'Matherderna' (see #20). These mis-spellings persist through the maps of Kitchin, Bowen, De La Rochette and Walpoole, among others, and this, with other evidence, suggests that Gasgoyne's original work and mistakes were copied, either directly or indirectly, by many 18th century map-makers. Even so, Cornwall was at a distinct advantage, for most other counties had to wait a further seventy years before a 'genuine' survey provided the material which permitted cartographers to abandon the now outdated efforts of Saxton, Norden and Speed.

We cannot leave Gasgoyne's map without some comment on the decoration, which is really fine. In the top left corner, the title-piece is set in a grand cartouche in which two reclining figures represent the rivers Fal and Tamar, with the water gushing from the ewers on which they repose. Above the cartouche are the Royal Arms of William III, (the Stuart Arms with the Shield of Nassau in an escutcheon of pretence); within the title-piece itself, the list of those who sold the map includes not only important London booksellers, such as Richard Mount and

25. Gasgoyne 1699 A Map of the County of Cornwall. Pub Sam. Darker & Sam. Farley for Chas Yeo, London

Philip Lea, but also 'Cha. Yeo, Bookseller in Exon, Fr. Hill Grocer, in Plimouth and Cha. Blith in the White Hart, in Launceston'. The dedication to the 'Rt. Honourable Charles Bodville, (2nd) Earl of Radnor' &c., is set in an equally ornate cartouche at top right, with Bodville's arms above and a very busy mining landscape below. The central portion of the compass rose is filled with a delightful vignette of a surveyor at work, an unusual feature that was modified from Thomas Martyn's 1 inch map of 1748.

Clearly, Gasgoyne's map is a landmark in the history of Cornish cartography, and due credit must be given to the engraver, J. Harris, for the splendid presentation of the material. Perhaps the most significant comment about Gasgoyne's integrity as a cartographer is to be made by quoting his own words on the inset of the Isles of Scilly in his map: 'These islands were not surveyed by the Author of this map but by Capt. Greenvile Collins, whose skill and care is no ways questioned.'

Only three original copies of this map are known. The illustration above is from the 1972 facsimile by Ravenhill.

1699 *A Map of the County of Cornwall. Pub Sam. Darker & Sam. Farley for Chas Yeo, London*
Reprint: 1730. The imprint altered to "Sold by W. Mount and T. Page, on Tower Hill, London.

26. SELLER, JOHN 1694, 1773

Eng. Unnamed, Pub. Seller
(140 x 114)

John Seller (1632-1697) was a mathematical instrument maker to Charles II and James II. His chief work was the making of instruments for survey and navigation and the production of an atlas of sea charts. He should not be confused with John Seller Jr who published alongside William Berry at about the same time.

In line with others at the time, Seller oriented his map so the Devon border is parallel with the right margin - the map is a reduced copy of Speed's outline. At the same time, he eschews a compass rose, but marks his edges North, South &c. This has the effect of suggesting the peninsula is one of East-West orientation. The major towns are marked up with small church towers, while the lesser ones are marked with circles. Falmouth town is still unmarked, despite being officially in existence for over 30 years. The map contains no roads, and other geographical features beyond the county's rivers are lightly treated. The Penwith moors are shown, but none of the others; the Hurlers are marked south of Launceston, but not the Cheesewring. St. Michael's Mount and the island near Looe are both marked (neither are named), but are obscured by the coastline, which is shaded in horizontal

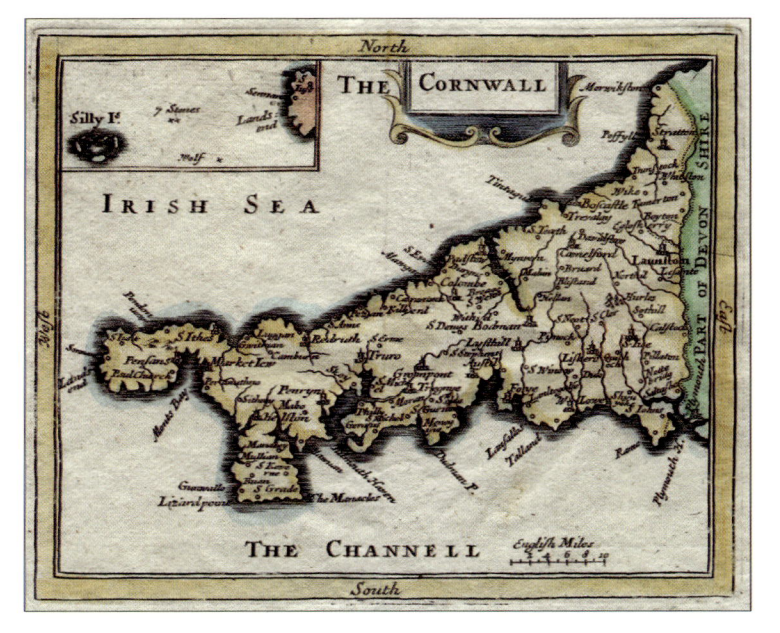

26. Seller 1694 Anglia Contracta. or A Description...

simplified the more decorative cartouche into a plain stamp. The word 'Silly' has been corrected, 'The Irish Sea' has been changed to 'St. George's Channel', the 'English Channel' is correctly spelt, and the scale title has been changed from 'English miles' to 'Scale of Miles'. Several changes of names on the map have been made: Removed: 'Poffyll' (Poughill near Bude), Added: Newport near Launceston, Wardbridge (Wadebridge), St. Michael, north of Truro and Falmouth.

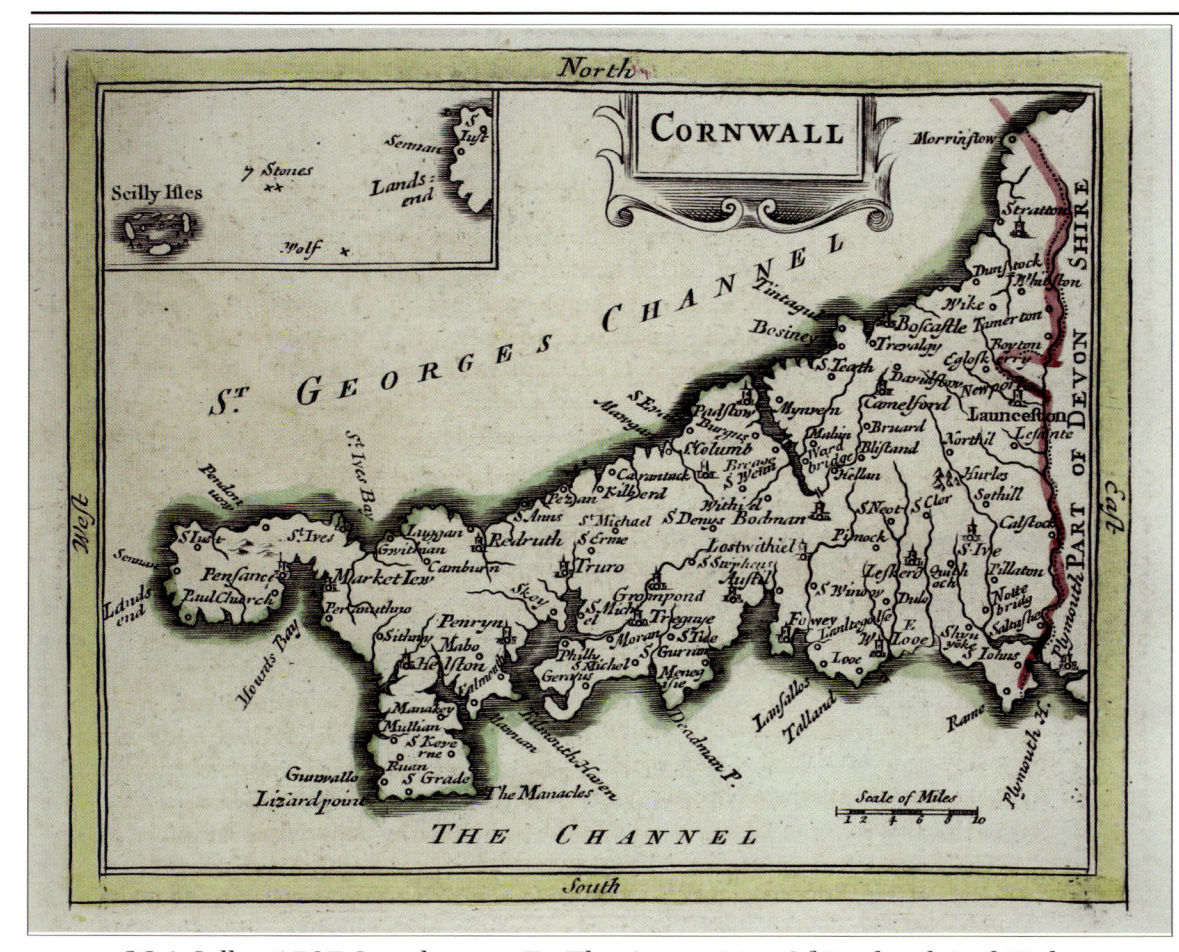

26.1 Seller 1787 Supplement To The Antiquities Of England And Wales

engraving that adds contrast to the overall map but is not especially appealing. In the top left corner is an insert, within a double border, of the 'Silly Is[lands]', with the Wolf rock and Seven Stones also marked. The position of the Scilly Isles is still shown due west of Land's End, and still as an apparent crude circle of islands. To the south of Looe is a simple scale of English miles. The word 'Channell' is mis-spelt.

After Seller's death, the plates for 'Anglia Contracta' were sold to Francis Grose (1731-1791), who added a rough hand printed block of text to the foot of each country map and

1694* *Anglia Contracta. or A Description of the Kingdom of England & Principality of Wales in Several new Mapps of all the Countyes therein Contained By John Seller Hydrographer to The King. John Seller, London.*

**Anglia Contracta contains no date or imprint.*

1696 *The History of England. ... With exact Maps of each County, John Seller. Printed by Job and John How for John Gwillim, against Crossby-Square in Bishopgate, London. Second Edition 1697.*

1701 *Camden's Britannia Abridge'd.... Printed by J.B. for Joseph Wild, at the Elephant at Charing Cross, London. Republished 1711 and printed for Isaac Cleave next to Serjeants-Inn in Chancery Lane, London.*

1703 *The History of England: ... With the Maps of all the Counties and Islands belonging to England...John Seller. Printed for J. Marshall, at the Bible in Grace-Church Street, London.*

1787 *Supplement To The Antiquities Of England And Wales. ... By Francis Grose, Esqr., F.A.S. London, Printed for S. Hooper, No.212, facing Bloomsbury-Square, High Holborn. Reprinted 1788, 1792, 1797 & 1809.*

Antique Maps of Cornwall and the Isles of Scilly

27. NICHOLLS, SUTTON 1712

Eng. Nicholls, Pub. Overton
(476 x 349)

Sutton Nicholls (1688-1729) engraved this interesting map that appeared in a composite atlas for Henry Overton (1676-1751). Henry's father, John, had been active in the map and print trade, following an apprenticeship with the Stationers' Company from about 1665. The Great Fire of London played a large role in the fortunes of several businesses connected to the print/engraving/publishing trades, with many businesses destroyed and others created out of the ashes of the fire. John Overton began collecting plates that had survived the fire from 1666, using them to create 'made-up' composite atlases. These are referred to as Overton Atlases followed by a Roman numeral. The Cornwall maps used were:

Atlas I, produced in 1670, used the Rea/Speed 1662
Atlas II, in 1675, used Jansson 1646
Atlas III, in 1685, used Bassett & Chiswell/Speed 1676
Atlas IV, in 1690, used Jansson 1646
Atlas V, in c.1700, used Browne/Speed 1696

Henry Overton took over his father's business in 1707 and continued issuing made-up or composite atlases. Atlas VI was issued in 1716 and it is to this atlas that Sutton Nicholls contributes his engraved version of Cornwall dated 1712 on the plate.

Nicholls' map is a re-working of the Jansson map of Cornwall from which it must have been derived, but many differing details serve to distinguish it from its predecessor. The border is marked with latitude and longitude, the engraving of the coats of arms of the earls and Duke of Cornwall, and figures in the top left corner, are bolder and simpler. The cartouche in the bottom left corner is simplified by the removal of the trees in the background, while the title is included within a simple oval line, and badly crowded with distracting information. The figures and scale in the bottom right corner of Jansson's map is replaced by a rectangular label that is even more crowded with miscellaneous information about the county of Cornwall. This refers to an apparently abridged version of the appropriate chapter in Camden's 'Britannia', or the reverse side of Speed's map. In the top right corner is a scale and key showing the symbols denoting post roads and cross roads on the map. A single compass rose with rhumb lines has been left to the north of Zennor from the Jansson map. Nicholls has corrected several items from the Jansson map that he has used as a base: The Latin titles Speed used for Land's End ('Bolerum Prom') and The Lizard ('Ocrinium...') have been added; Jansson's St. Clements Isle, off Mousehole, has unhappily become 'Mousehole Isle'. The Longships rocks have been added – by this time, several maps contained this navigational terror, unfortunately in the location of the Runnel Stone. Trinity House placed a lighthouse on the Longships in 1795. Nicholls added Falmouth to the area occupied by the port, though didn't mark it as a town, it seems more as if he's added it as a reference point to the mouth of the river, rather than as the port it was becoming. There are other light modifications to Jansson's map, as well as some notable items left on the plate that, were Nicholls walking the county, he would have noted. The salt pond at Anthony, built by Richard Carew and recorded by Norden on his actual survey in around the 1590s, has, by 1712, long since dried up and disappeared. The map is marked bottom left with 'Sutton Nicholls, Sculpt'.

The map was never reprinted and is consequently rather scarce.

1716 A New mapp of the county of Cornwall, Overton's Made-up Atlas (VI). Printed and sold by Henry Overton at ye White Horse without Newgate, London.

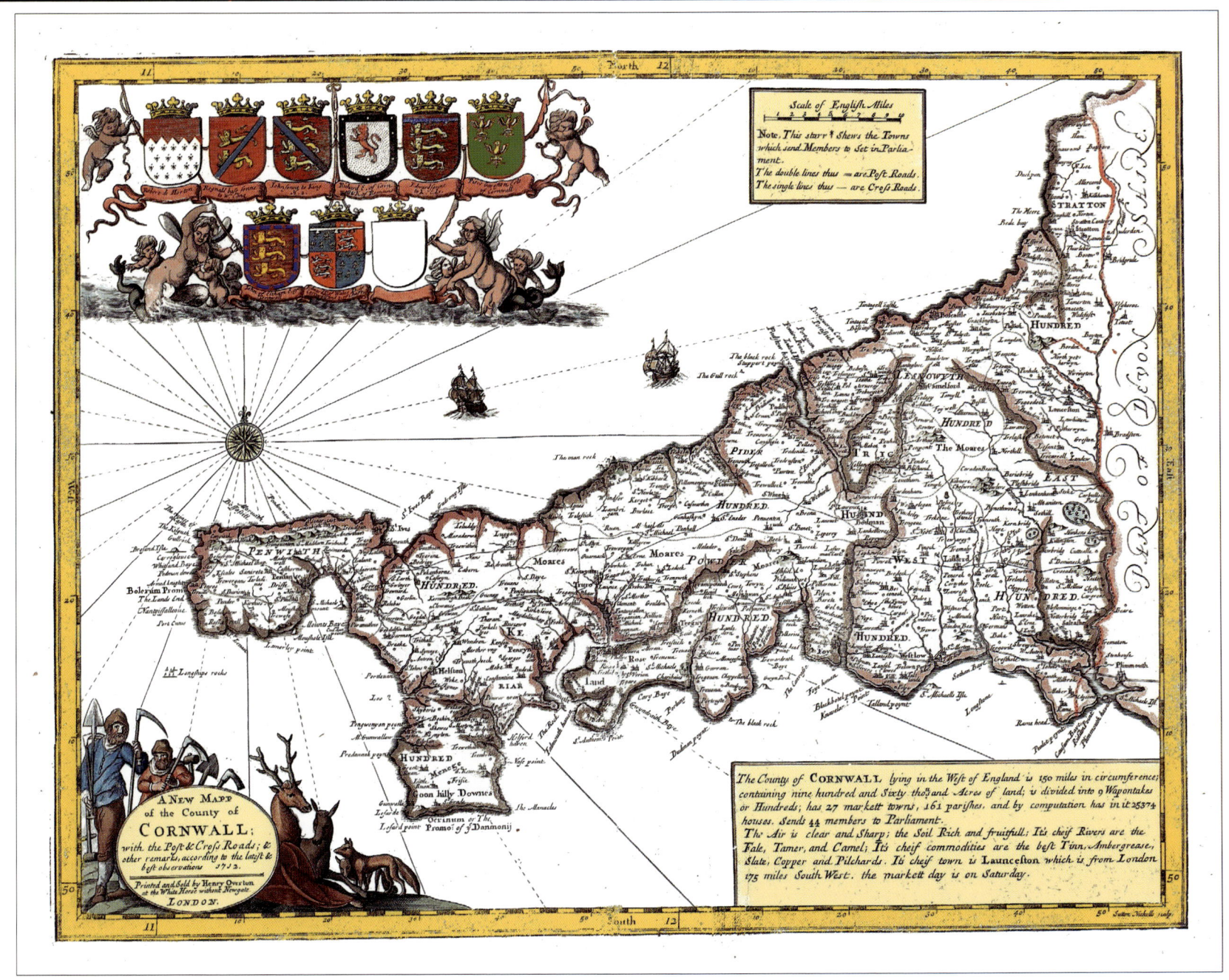

27. Nicholls 1712 A New mapp of the county of Cornwall, Overton's Made-up Atlas (VI)

28. SCHENK, PETER & VALK, GERARD 1714

Eng. Jansson/Schenk, Pub. Mortier
(380 x 508)

Peter Schenk (1655-1718) was from Elberfeld, near Essen, in Northern Germany. He married Agatha, sister of Gerard Valk (1652-1726). Schenk became a pupil of Valk's and learned the skill of 'Zwarte kunst', or mezzotint engraving. Jan Jansson (#17) had died in 1664 and his property had passed to his daughters. One of these, Elizabeth, married Jan van Waesberge. Their son, Janssonius van Waesberge, auctioned the plates to Schenk and Valk in 1694. These plates, with some updating, became the 'Atlas Anglois'.

'Britannia Illustrata' was first published (1707) by David Mortier (1673-c.1728). He was brother to Pierre Mortier (#24), who had published de Hooghe's 'Atlas Maritime' in 1693. This was a topographic work featuring 80 views of English houses and gardens, drawn by Leonard Knyff and engraved by Johannes Kip (1652-1722). Kip is a very common Dutch name and there is no obvious connection to the earlier William Kip (#9). 'Britannia Illustrata' was re-issued and expanded and re-titled, in 1708, as 'Nouveau theatre de la Grande Bretagne'. To this was added volume two in 1713, and finally volume three, the 'Atlas Anglois', in 1715. The maps were issued loose and later in atlas form, as part of this huge work, and published by David Mortier in 1715.

There are 41 maps, on 40 double page sheets- some 20 counties had the imprint of Schenk & Valk added, (Cornwall is one such county). A further edition was issued by Joseph Smith in 1724 - 38 maps had the imprint added. Without the atlases, the maps are indistinguishable.

The Cornwall map contains a number of changes from the Jansson (#17) original: the imprint of Peter Schenk and Gerard Valk, in place of Jansson's imprint at the lower border (Amstelodami Venditant apud, Petrum Schenk et Gerardum Valk. C Priv), has been added. The inner part of the border has been divided in a graticule pattern, to show latitude and longitude from the Azores. Lines of ten minutes of latitude and longitude have been added across the whole map.

Near the Black Rock off Pendennis Point, at the mouth of the Fal, are two changes to the Jansson map: the town symbol and name of Falmouth have been added, and on the east bank St. Mawes changes from a circle to a single towered town. These additions appear to have been copied from Sutton Nicholls (#27). No other changes to the map itself have been made. Within the bottom right border of the map is the number 2, being the second map in the atlas after the England map - the atlas works its way west to east and from the south to the north.

1715   *Atlas Anglois, ou description générale de l'Anglettere... David Mortier, London.*
1724   *Atlas Anglois..., re-issued Joseph Smith, Exeter-Exchange near the Fountain Tavern on the Strand. London.*

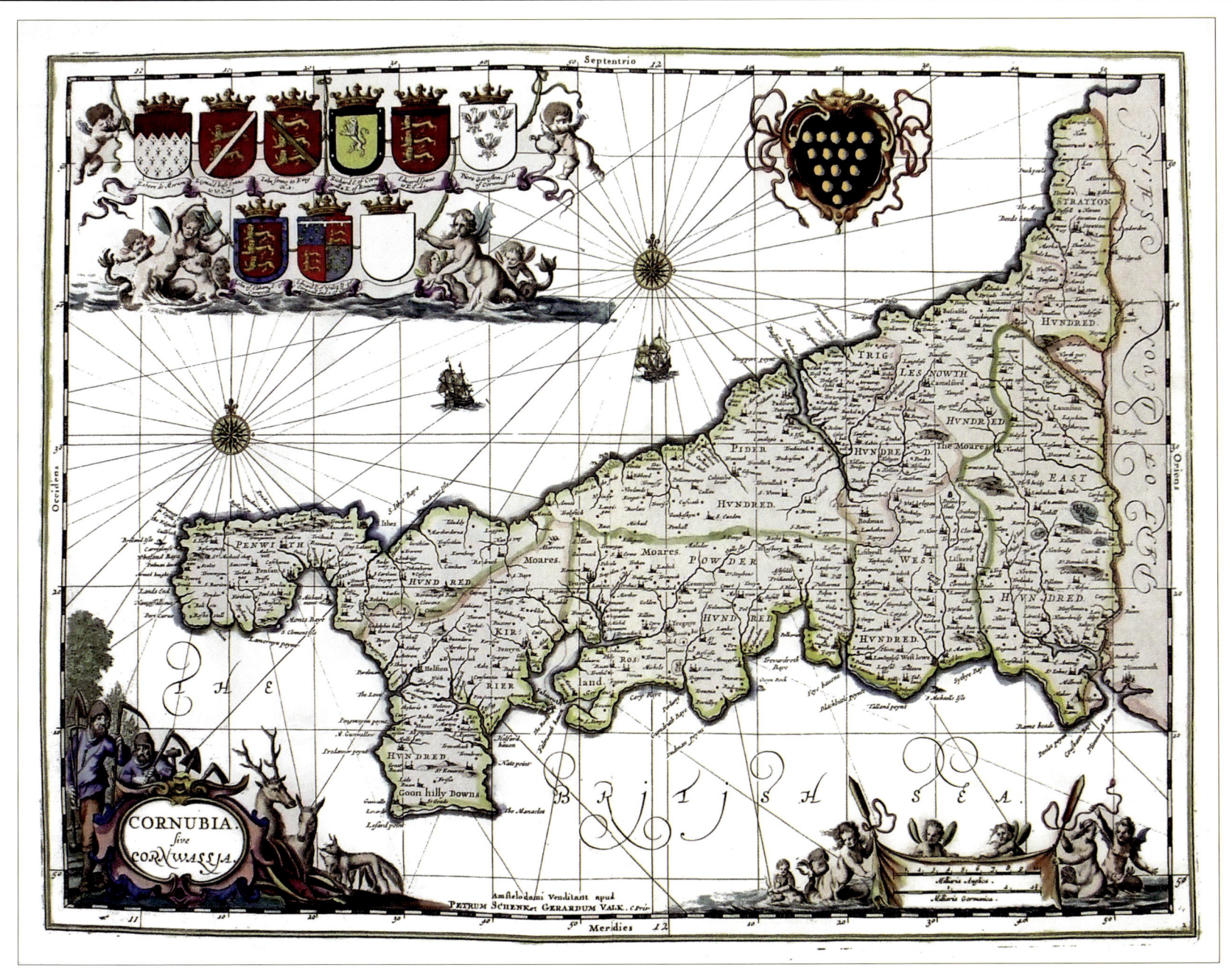

28. Schenk & Valk 1714 Atlas Anglois, Ou Description Générale De L'Anglettere... David Mortier, London.

Antique Maps of Cornwall and the Isles of Scilly

83

29. LENTHALL, JOHN 1717

Eng. Redmayne/Lenthall, Pub. Lenthall

(55 x 90)

PLAYING CARDS

John Lenthall was an apprentice and son-in-law to William Warter, a stationer based in Fetter Lane, off London's Fleet Street. They specialised in the production of playing cards, though Warter's trade card of the late 1680s indicates a wide range of printed material for sale. At some stage around 1716-17, William Redmayne's (#21) cards came into Lenthall's hands. These were reprinted and sold as County cards. A second set was produced in 1717 – these were copies of those produced by Robert Morden (possibly due to the Morden plates being melted down) in 1676 (#20), with some alterations.

The Cornwall card is the ten of Spades, (in the Morden issue it is the suit of Diamonds); the title is separated from the map by a double lined boundary, with the spade to the left. To the right is the Roman Numeral X. In the centre of the card is an outline map of Cornwall, with little other detail beyond place-names. The outline of the county is loosely comparable to Morden's, though it has to be said it is generally lacking in detail. To the south of the area around Looe is a set of dividers marking a scale in miles. To the north of the county is a simple compass rose. Below the map and bordered is a section showing the length, breadth and circumference of the county, along with the distance from London to Launceston, as well as its latitude (50 degrees 42 minutes North). A second edition of the maps was issued the same year, with a decorative twisted rope border around the edge of the card.

1717 Pack of playing cards, London, J. Lenthall

29. Lenthall 1717 Pack of playing cards, London

30. BOWEN, EMANUEL 1720, 1748, 1759, 1764, 1767 & 1785

1720 BRITANNIA DEPICTA
Eng. Bowen, Pub. T. Bowles (108 x 108)

Emanuel Bowen (c.1694-1767) is, in a sense, typical of the school of engravers, map-sellers and publishers which flourished in London during the 18th century. A vastly increased public demand for atlases of all sorts encouraged the growth of many publishing houses, and the capital which came to the map-trade thus paved the way for an enormous expansion, in which the export of English maps to the Continent played a considerable part. Bowen was important enough to bear the title of 'Geographer to His Majesty George II' and, in common with other large publishers, he had his business organised to deal with all branches of map-work, from original survey to the final printing and publication.

Bowen's first map of Cornwall was produced in collaboration with John Owen, who supplied the text below the map. Although it is so small, there is an extraordinary amount of information filling every spare piece of the plate. The portion of the page above the map has a splendid Baroque cartouche bearing the title 'The Road from Exeter to Truro in Cornwall'. The atlas in which the map appeared was based upon Ogilby's road maps.

In the top left corner of the map are the Royal Hanoverian Arms and a key to the Hundreds, and descriptive text dealing with historical and geographical details of the county appears under the arms and below the map. The map itself shows Hundreds, hills, rivers, towns, churches, roads and Parliamentary representation.

The map is marked top right with the page number (179), the reverse of this map (page 180) features a strip road map of the road from Exeter to Tavistock and the following page (181) shows the continuation of the road from Tavistock to Truro via Launceston. Re-constructing these routes using Bowen's road maps and modern OS maps, it is possible to follow the coaching routes of the early 1700s quite easily.

30. Bowen 1720 Britannia Depicta, Or Ogilby Improv'd. T. Bowles, London

Antique Maps of Cornwall and the Isles of Scilly

85

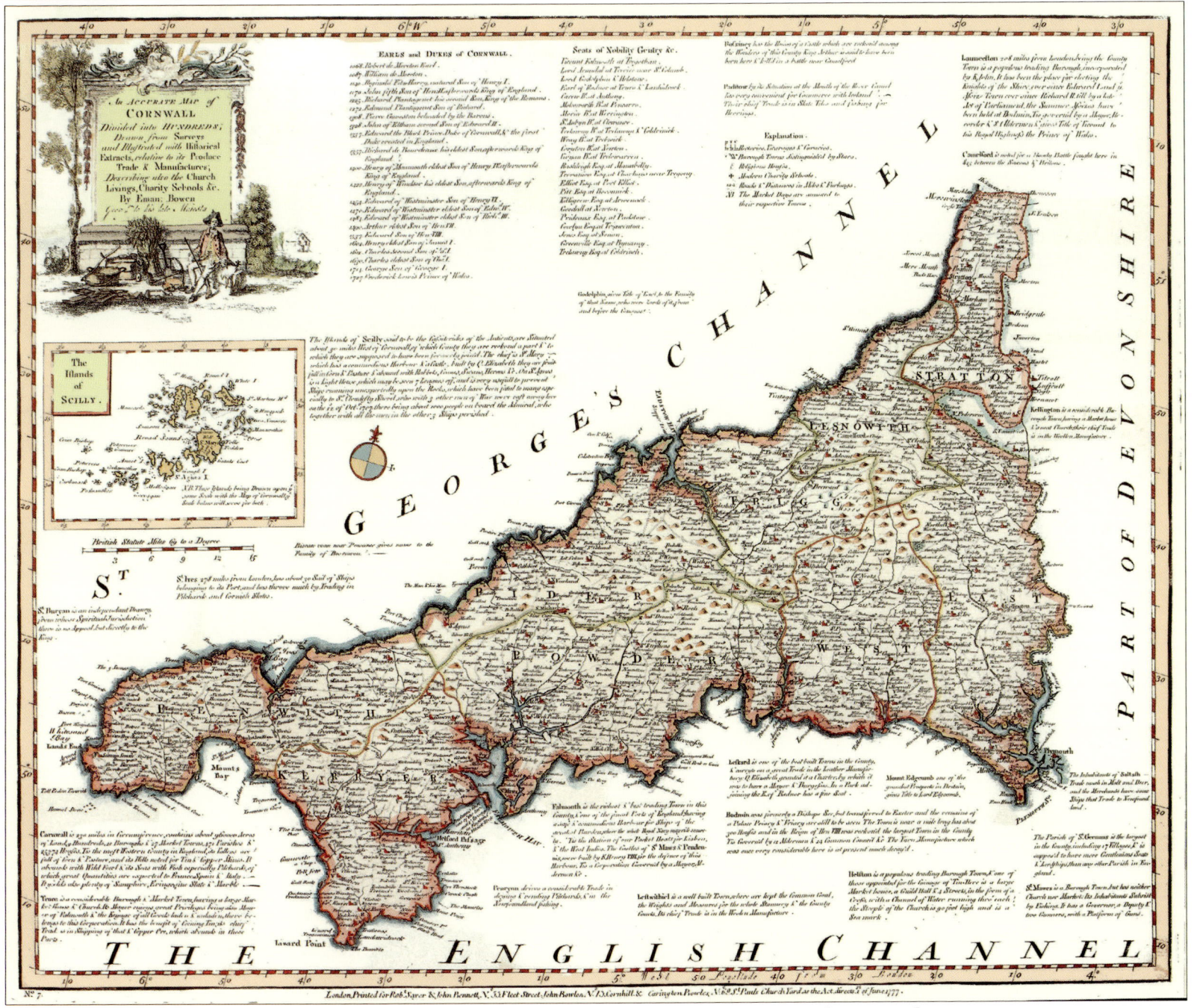

30.1 Bowen 1777 The Royal English Atlas, Bowen & Kitchin, London

Within the same atlas are the following strip maps involving Cornwall:

Page 59: London to Land's End (text only).

Page 66: Plymouth to Tregony. Bowen's road map starts in Plymouth, though it indicates a Priory; this must be the one in Plympton a few miles to the east of Plymouth. The road crosses the Tamar from Stonehouse to Cremyll while still (then) in Devon. The route is a general copy of that drawn by Ogilby (#19) passing Millbrook, Crafthole and follows the modern B3247 as it skirts its way across east Cornwall to Looe. From there Bowen's route passes near the house called Trelawne, then runs cross-country to Lanteglos, Bodinnick and Fowey. The route from Fowey to Tywardreath is shown briefly on Bowen's strip map, but is likely to have gone through Polmear, though this is not made clear. The third column of the strip map re-starts at Tywardreath and crosses the river at Par by ferry and past St. Blazey and Polgooth. The route passes through Tregony and Philleigh and crosses the Fal at Tolvern Cottage; this is upstream of the current crossing at Trelissick.

Page 67: Tregony to Land's End. This is a continuation of page 66 and runs from Halwyn on the west bank of the Fal to Playing Place, over the River Carnon to Coldwind Cross (50° 13' 24" North, 5° 7' 32" West), shown as 'Blow Ye Cold Wind'. From there the route runs across country, possibly through Lanner and Four Lanes before joining what is now the B3820. At the top of the middle strip, the road passes St. Hillary and Market Jew - there is still a turnpike there, now called 'Marazion'. From Market Jew, the road appears to cut across a segment of Mount's Bay to Penzance. From there it runs into Newlyn (correctly spelt), to St. Buryan. The route passes from here, via the head of Treen valley (the infamous hairpin bend is even shown!), and eventually to Sennen.

Page 82: Hatherly (Hatherleigh, Devon) to Camelford. From Hatherleigh, the route shown briefly follows the A3072, before cutting cross-country from a point near Pulworthy, heading south-west, passing to the north of Beaworthy and crossing what is now the A3079 at Halwill, from there to Lugworthy Cross and south-south-west to St. Giles on the Heath, and into the town north of Launceston called 'St. Stephens'.

Bowen's route runs through Egloskerry and Hallworthy. The notation 'Hall Drunkard' continues to be used as an alternative to Hallworthy. The route runs past the house named Tresoake, past Davidstow and onto the A39, (there is a turnpike gate on this road), and into Camelford.

Page 83: St. Teath to Truro. This page continues from page 82. The route has left Camelford on the A39, turning quickly into St. Teath, where there is an inn shown on later maps. It seems likely that the route takes a northern swing on the Treroosel road and into Pendogget, St. Endillion, St. Minver, Tredizzick and Porthilly, and from there a ferry across the Camel to Padstow. The route follows the present B3274 southwards from Padstow, and passes the farm at Trevibban, which is clearly marked and is still there today, to the junction with the A39. The route follows the old road passing through Gluvian, near Tregamere farm (which is referred to on the route map), before crossing the Menahyhl into St. Columb. From St. Columb the route runs south through Killaworgey to Fraddon, Summercourt and to Michell. From here the route runs through Trispen, near St. Erme, and into Truro.

Page 179: Map of Cornwall described above, and **Page 180**: Exeter to Tavistock (Devon).

Page 181: Tavistock to Truro. Bowen's road map shows the route out of Tavistock, on what is now the A390; it passes through two Newbridges, before arriving at St. Ive; (not St. Ives, which is further west). The route continues west through Liskeard and Liswithiel (Lostwithiel), St. Blazey, (St. Austell is a relatively small town at this time), and then to Dolgooth (Polgooth), Grampound, Probus, Tresillian and finally Truro.

1720   Britannia Depicta, or Ogilby Improv'd. T. Bowles, London. Reprints: 1720 (x3), 1722, 1723, 4th Ed 1724, 1730, 5th ed 1731 (x2), 1734, 1736, 1749, 1751, 1753, 1759, 1764, 1765

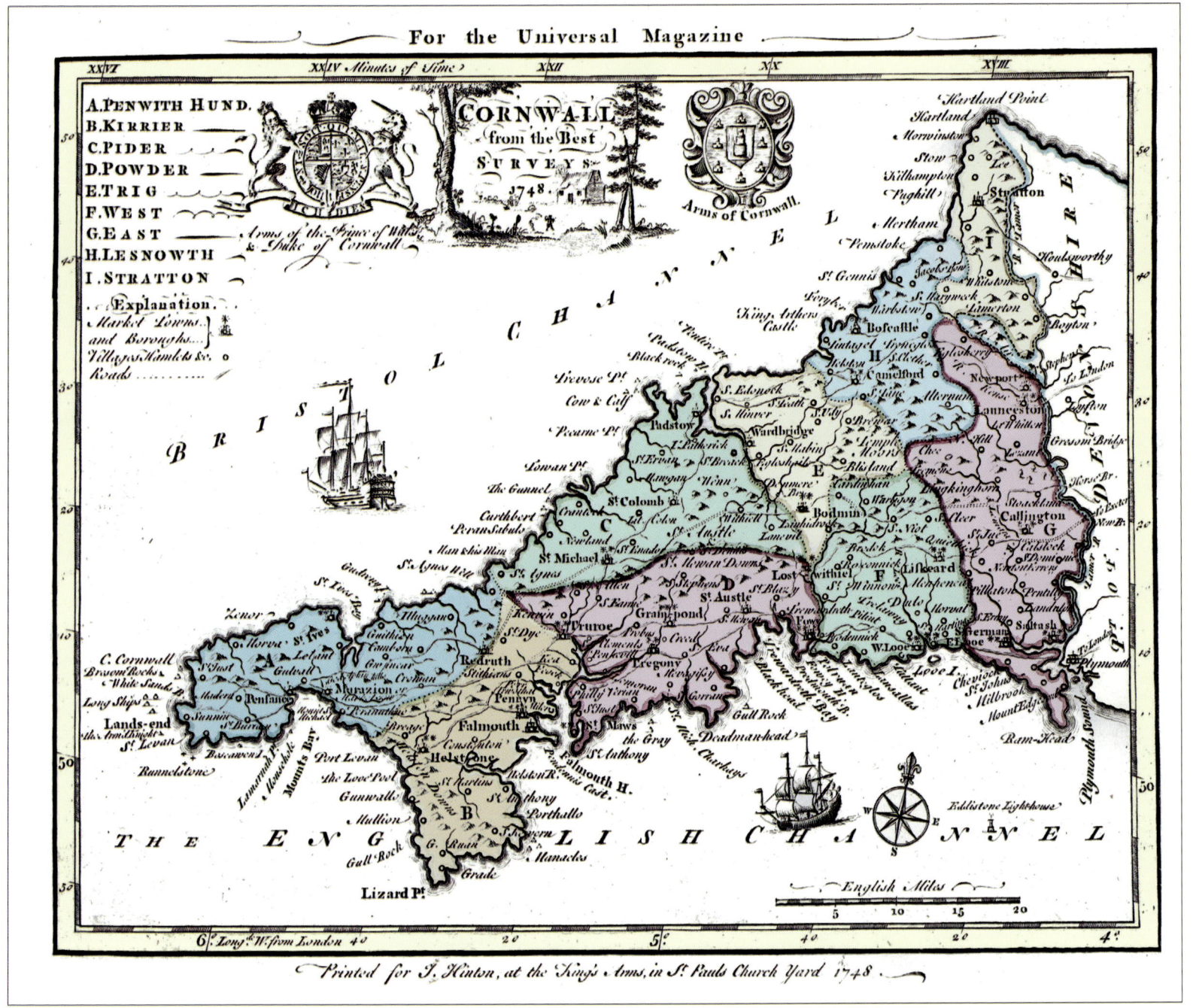

30.2 Bowen 1748 The Universal Magazine of Knowledge and Pleasure

1748 THE UNIVERSAL MAGAZINE
Eng. Bowen, Pub. Hinton (191 x 152)

John Hinton was a renowned book-seller and publisher, known especially for his publication of atlases and maps by Emanuel Bowen and Thomas Kitchin. He published 'The Universal Museum' and 'Complete Magazine of Knowledge and Pleasure' (1747-1803), 'The Universal Magazine' (1804-1814) and 'The New Universal Magazine' (1814-1815).

The Universal Magazine was published monthly, with two volumes per year. Between 1765 and 1773 a series of 39 road maps and counties appeared in the Magazine. The road maps were based on John Ogilby's 'Britannia' (1675). The county maps were well executed and engraved by Emanuel Bowen (?), Thomas Kitchin and Richard Seale. Hinton may have intended to produce maps of all the counties, resulting in an English Atlas, but only a few were printed.

Hinton's map is titled 'Cornwall from the best surveys 1748', in a nice cartouche in the top centre of the map, to the left are the arms of the Prince of Wales and Duke of Cornwall, to the right is the arms of Launceston, (not Cornwall, as titled). In the far right of the map is a list of the Hundreds of Cornwall from west to east (Penwith to Stratton). Below this is a key explaining the symbols used in the map, including market towns, boroughs and villages. The sea areas are decorated with two galleons, with a compass rose to the south of Looe and scale of English miles. The island near Looe is labelled Looe Is. The map is canted over slightly to align the Devon border with the right margin. Around the margin, the degrees of longitude from London are marked on the bottom with the time offset on the top. Latitude is marked off on either side of the map, however, they are mis-aligned by ten minutes. Below the map is the sub-title 'Printed for J Hinton at the King's Arms in St. Paul's Churchyard 1748'.

1748   The Universal Magazine of Knowledge and Pleasure ...Vol. IV. J. Hinton, London.

1759 THE GENERAL MAGAZINE
Eng. Bowen, Pub Martin (200 x 175)

In 1759 Bowen collaborated with Benjamin Martin (1704-1782) to supply maps to Martin's 'General Magazine of Arts and Sciences', a monthly magazine covering six volumes, produced in a somewhat chaotic manner with the buying public expected to reassemble the volumes themselves. The Cornwall map was produced in 1755, and, while it is somewhat less decorative than its predecessors, the map is remarkably clear for its size. In the top left corner is a list of the Hundreds, with the title piece in which appears, for the first time, mention of the fact that Bowen had become 'Geographer to His Majesty George II'.

1759   The General Magazine of Arts and Sciences, B. Martin London. Reprinted as The Natural History of England Vol 1 1759.

1764 THE ROYAL ATLAS
Eng. Bowen, Pub. Bowen & Kitchin (483 x 394)

The Royal Atlas map, the largest of the series by Bowen, was a slightly reduced version of the Cornwall map by Thomas Kitchin, engraved in 1750 and published as the 'Large English Atlas' in 1760 (#40). There are obvious differences in that the title-piece is simpler and no dedication cartouche is given. The seated figure of the gunman in a tricorne hat, the chest he is sitting on, the wheatsheaf and basket and scythe are all mirror copies from the Kitchin map of 1755 (#39). The two figures in the right of the Kitchin cartouche have been removed and the landscape is less grandiose, with cottages instead of mansions in the distance. The marginal information remains; however, the spelling of Newlyn is again given as 'Newland'. The map also includes an inset of the Isles of Scilly. At the foot of the map bottom left is the plate number, '7'.

The first edition of the map, in 1764, bears the imprint at the foot of the map and reads 'Printed for Messrs Bakewell and Parker, John Bowles and Son, Thomas Bowles, Thomas Kitchin, Henry Overton, John Ryall, Robert Sayer'. At the foot of the 1777 map illustrated is the inscription 'London, Printed for Robt Sayer & John Bennett, Nº. 53 Fleet Street, John Bowles No 13 Cornhill & _ Carington Bowles No 69 St. Paul's Churchyard as the Act directs 1st June 1777'. Note the extra space ahead of 'Carington', noted by Hodson (Vol. III, p21) as a possible correction to a spelling error ('Carrington').

1764   The Royal English Atlas, by Emanuel Bowen and Thomas Kitchin, London. Reprints: 1778, 1778, 1780 & 1784.

1767 ATLAS ANGLICANUS
Eng. Bowen, Pub. E. & T. Bowen
(311 x 216)

In 1767 'The Atlas Anglicanus' was published, in monthly parts, in competition to Ellis's 'English Atlas' of 1765. The last of Bowen's maps were comparatively plain. They were, in fact, published after his death by Thomas Kitchin, his partner in engraving and publishing for many years. The map differs from the previous 1762 edition; it is less cluttered in place-names. The insert of the Islands of Scilly has been re-engraved with the note of their relative position to Land's End moved outside the insert. The title cartouche in the top left is a new style, differing from the foregoing tabular style. The oval wreath style contains the title 'Cornwall divided into Hundreds... by Emanuel Bowen, Geographer to the late king'. Emanuel Bowen died a pauper in 1767. It seems likely that some of the engraving of this map was the work of Emanuel Bowen's son, Thomas Bowen (? - 1790), who carried on the business after his father's death. The project may have started to flounder, and Thomas Kitchin became involved – the last part is issued with his name as sole publisher. It appears that Kitchin may have acquired Bowen's plates, who then sold them with his own plates to Carington Bowles in 1775 (#39). From these ex-Bowen plates arose the 'Bowles New Medium Atlas' of 1785, see below.

1767   Atlas Anglicanus, by the late Emanuel Bowen and Thomas Bowen, London. Reprints: 1777, 1785.

1785 BOWLES'S NEW MEDIUM ATLAS
Eng. Bowen, Pub. C. Bowles
(324 x 230)

The Bowen and Kitchin plates were acquired by Carington Bowles in 1775. The 1785 'Bowles's New Medium Atlas' map is a reworking of the Kitchin 1750 and reduced Bowen 1764 map, though Bowles has altered much of the detail outside the map, as well as re-drawing the map itself. The map of Cornwall is titled 'BOWLES's NEW MEDIUM MAP OF CORNWALL...LONDON: Printed for the Proprietor Carington Bowles, No 69 in St. Paul's Church Yard'. The county is compressed horizontally and is not as balanced as the original. The engraving is heavier than Bowen's and the script lacks the finesse seen on the Bowen original. While there is little argument against the company's success – their portfolio was huge - the quality of cartography might not be considered as impressive. The detail contained within the map contains no departures from Bowen's, though Bowles has added distances from London onto the map - Bowen has them indicated on the key; however, they are absent from his map. The plate number (7) can be seen in the top right outside the border. The imprint at the base of the map simply reads 'Published as the Act directs 3 Jan 1785'.

1785   Bowles's New Medium English Atlas, Or Complete set of maps of the Counties of England and Wales... London: Printed for the proprietor Carington Bowles at his Map and Print Warehouse, No 69 St. Paul's Church Yard.

Carington Bowles died in 1793, and the business went to his son, Henry Carington Bowles, and Samuel Carver. They continued selling the original atlas unaltered. After this, the plates were updated. At some stage after 1793 the copyright date at the base of the map was altered, with the date of 3 Jan 1785 being erased. Later the title of each map was altered to read '... LONDON: Printed for the Proprietor Bowles and Carver, No 69 in St. Paul's Church Yard'. Thus, there are two states of the Cornwall map, both implying a date after the death of Carington Bowles. Firstly, the map appears as previously titled, with Carington as the sole proprietor <u>and</u> missing the copyright date of the original map. Secondly, again post 1793, the title is altered to Bowles and Carver. Sales of both versions were poor in the face of better value competition, and are now rare. The atlas was not re-issued.

Post 1793 Bowles's New Medium English Atlas...London: Printed for the Proprietor Bowles and Carver, No 69 in St. Paul's Church Yard'. Later the footnote at the base of the map was altered to read 'Published as the Act Directs', i.e. the previous date has been erased.

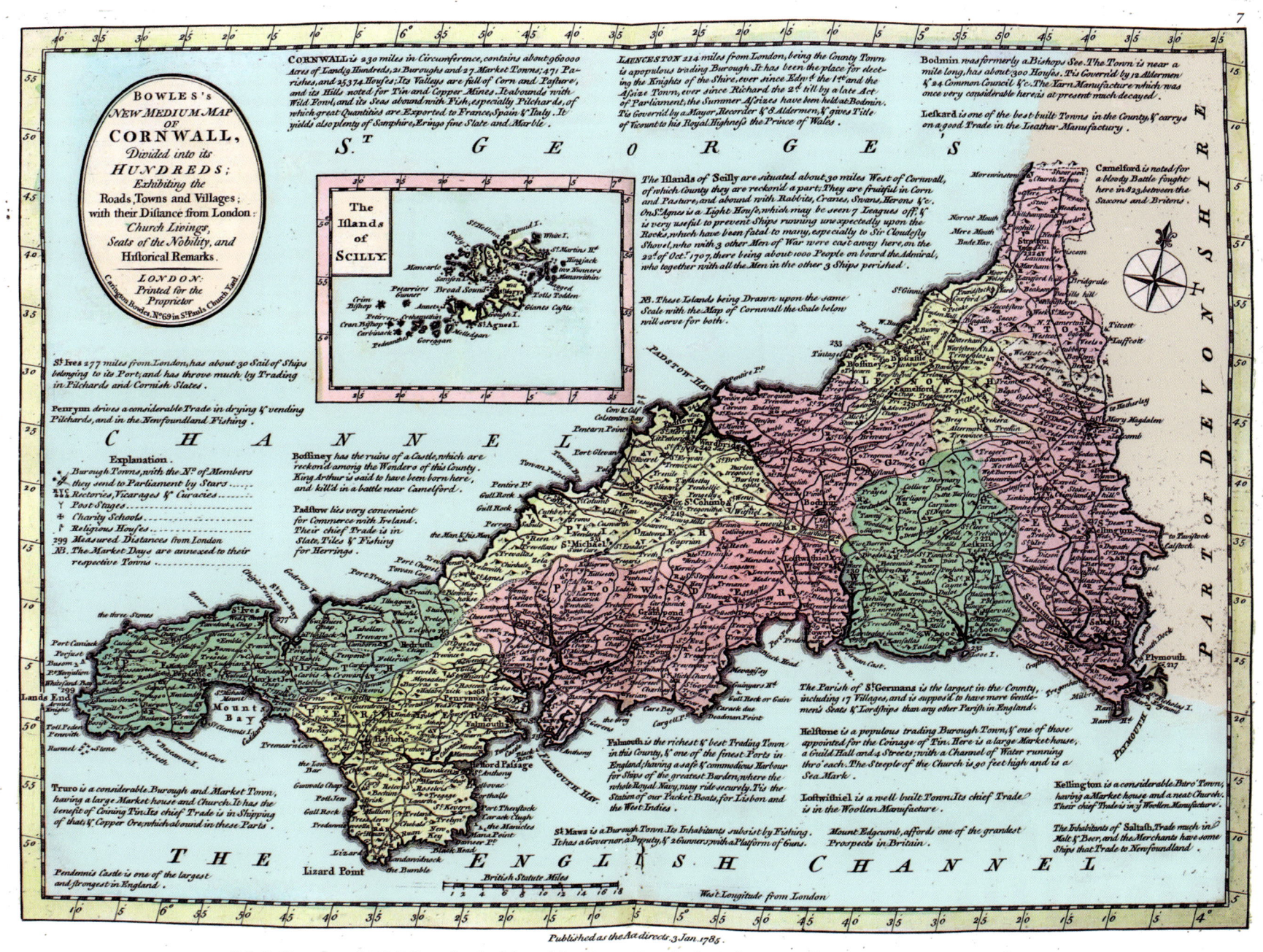

30.3 Bowles 1785 Bowles's New Medium English Atlas London. Carington Bowles.

31. MOLL, HERMAN 1724, 1718

Eng. Moll. Pub. Moll, T. Bowles, Rivington & J. Bowles
(241 x 171)

Herman Moll (c.1654-1732) was a Dutch engraver, (Moll's place of origin may have been Bremen, in north Germany), who settled in London about the year 1678. He engraved and published many atlases of all parts of the world, the maps varying from miniatures to very large productions. Moll worked as an engraver to Christopher Brown, Robert Morden and Philip Lea, from premises on the corner of Spring Gardens and Charing Cross, in London, before embarking on a career as a mapmaker in his own right around 1695.

'A New Description of England and Wales' was first issued in 1724 by Moll, along with the Bowles brothers and Rivington, as co-publishers, and then issued as an atlas without text under the name 'A set of fifty new and correct maps of England and Wales', the same year. The Cornwall plate contains, in the top left, the number '3' in brackets – this is missing from the first edition (1724).

His county maps are of medium size and are easily identified, in the earliest editions, by the inclusion of illustrations of antiquities found in the county. In Moll's map of Cornwall, the drawings of antiquities have been placed outside the border, to the left and right of the map, and the items illustrated appear to have been copied from Speed's map and the earlier editions of Camden's 'Britannia'. Certain features of the Moll map show that it was copied from the maps of Saxton and Speed, and, more recently, Morden; for example, the island at Looe is marked 'St. Michael'. On the other hand, the outline of the coast is much more accurate than the shape given by either Saxton or Speed; more roads are marked than those given in Ogilby's road-book of 1675, the usual source of information at that time.

The evidence suggests that Moll used some more reliable source of information in drawing his map, and the Gasgoyne map of 1700 (#25) provides the ideal answer to the problem. There is a similarity, not only in the general outline shape and the position of the more important roads, but also in certain idiosyncrasies in the spelling of place-names; for example, Bodmin Moor is given as 'Temple Moors' on both maps, and 'Hall Drunkard' is Hallworthy, near Camelford. Kitchin's map of 1764 is remarkably similar to Moll's map in shape and size, though the superiority of Kitchin's engraving enabled him to show more place names with greater legibility. Cape Cornwall to the north of Land's End has been abbreviated with the C left in the left margin, this becomes an interesting orthographic marker on later maps. Moll has set his Cornwall map with the Devon border parallel to the right margin and constructed indicators of latitude and longitude along the borders. There are two misleading labels. On the left margin, slightly below the Land's End label, is the figure '50' – this is (49°) 50 minutes north, the full 50th degree north occurring, unannounced, opposite the 'Breson' label. Similarly, on the right margin, there are errors: the label '30' next to the Cross at St. Blaise is correct (50° 30'North). Counting the divisions up the page, the full 51° North should occur next to the 'n' of 'Devon'; the label '51' opposite the 'e' of 'Shire' is misplaced by 10 minutes. In fact, both the 5° West and 51° North are wrongly located, by today's positioning.

1724   *A New Description of England and Wales, by H. Moll, T. Bowles, C. Rivington & J. Bowles, London. Re-issued same year with plate numbers – same publishers. Reprinted 1733 by H. Moll, T. Bowles, C. Rivington and J. Bowles.*

1724   *A Set of fifty new and correct maps. H. Moll, Tho. Bowles and J. Bowles, London. Re-issued same year with plate numbers – same publishers. Reprinted 1739 by H. Moll, T. Bowles, C. Rivington and J. Bowles.*

1747   *The Geography of England and Wales, T. Bowles and J. Bowles. Plate number of Cornwall changed to 9.*

1753   *H. Moll's British Atlas; Or, Pocket Maps of all the Counties. Tho Bowles and J. Bowles & Son. London.*

1755   *The Traveller's Companion; Or... John Bowles, London.*

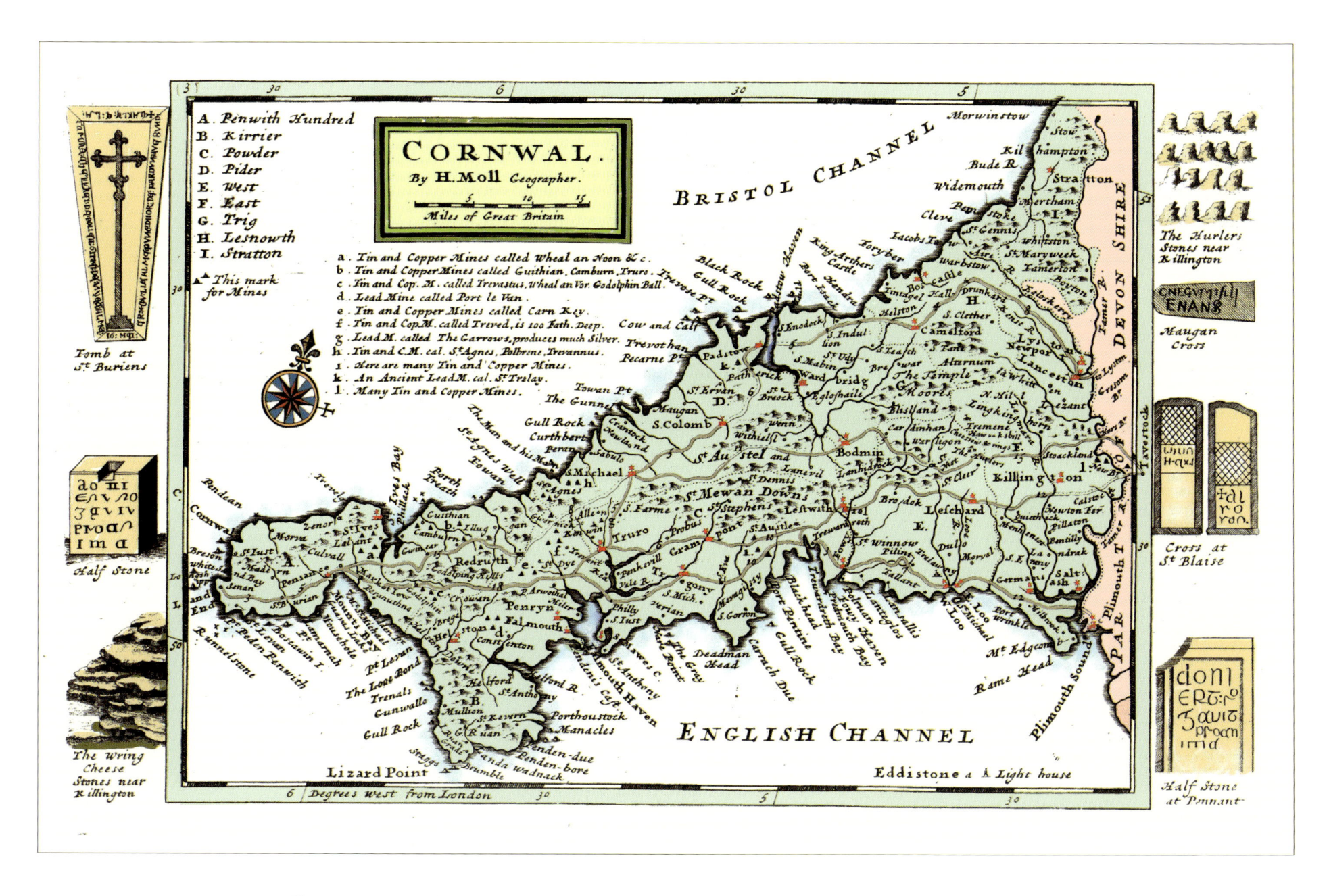

31. Moll 1724 *A Set of fifty new and correct maps.* H. Moll, Tho. Bowles and J. Bowles, London.

In about 1718 Moll started a road map series at a scale of approximately 6 miles to 1 inch. Only eleven sheets were completed, including a sheet from London to Land's End (opposite). The map is dedicated to Henry Hoare Esq, Goldsmith of London. Hoare was known as 'Henry the Good', who steered his family bank through the South Sea Bubble of 1720. Moll's project was never completed and all the strip maps are consequently rare*.

The route on the sheet including Cornwall passes from London, through Surrey, Hampshire, Wiltshire, Dorset and Devon, before entering Cornwall opposite Plymouth. From there, it traces the southern route through Looe, Fowey, Tywardreath and Tregony, crossing the Fal south of Truro (which is bypassed), Crowan, then Market Jew (Marazion), across a clear causeway to Penzance, and then to St. Buryan and Land's End. There is little change from Ogilby's map of 1675, at least with respect to the Cornwall section.

1718 *Roads of ye South Part of Great Britain, by Herman Moll, Published by T Bowles, St Paul's Churchyard, and J Bowles, Cornhill, London.*

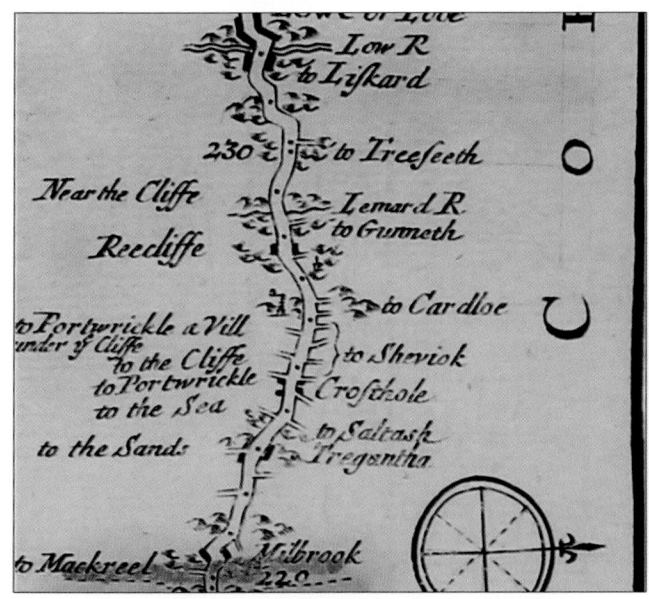

31.1 Moll 1718 Detail of Fire Basket

*In the same year as Moll's Road Map, two very similar other publications were issued. Thomas Gardner and John Senex had been each working on a reduced version of John Ogilby's 'Britannia', each with the same intent: to supply a truly portable or pocket-sized road book. Of the two, Gardner's is rarer now, mostly because of being published only once in 1719. The strip maps follow Ogilby's format almost faithfully, with a slight re-treatment of the towns depicted. The 100 road maps are set in the same way as Ogilby's, with each map dedicated to various local personages of note. The Gardner maps are quite easily distinguished by his name being prominently featured on the title of each map.

1719 *A Pocket Guide to the English Traveller; Being a Complete Survey... Printed for J. Tonson at Shakespear's Head, Strand and J. Watts at the Printing Office, Lincoln's-Inn Fields.*

John Senex's strip maps, produced the same year, went through many re-issues and was more successful than either Moll or Gardner until the appearance of Owen & Bowen's Britannia Depicta in 1720 (#30).

1719 *An Actual Survey of all the Principal roads of England and Wales; described by 100 maps...By John Senex, London. Re-issued 1757, 1759, 2nd Edition 1762, 3rd Edition 1775*
1757 *Re-titled The Roads through England delineated; Or...John Senex FRS, London. Re-issued 1762.*

Fire basket note: Between Portwrinkle and Looe is a beacon opposite the turn to Cardloe. This is shown as a post with a bar and a container on the top. and is certainly a fire basket. One is clearly shown on the Lea map (#41), as well as on the Ogilby road map (#34), though in the former there is a simple post with bars, whereas in the latter it is almost hidden from view. On the Lea map, this beacon is north of the route from Crafthole to Looe, but according to Ogilby and Moll this beacon is to the south of this route. It is tempting to consider these to be one and the same, yet Ogilby's, and thence Moll's, route shows the beacon to be under three miles from Crafthole - it cannot therefore be Bindon, which is at least five miles as the crow flies from Crafthole. No other beacon fire baskets are seen on either Ogilby's or Moll's road maps of Cornwall.

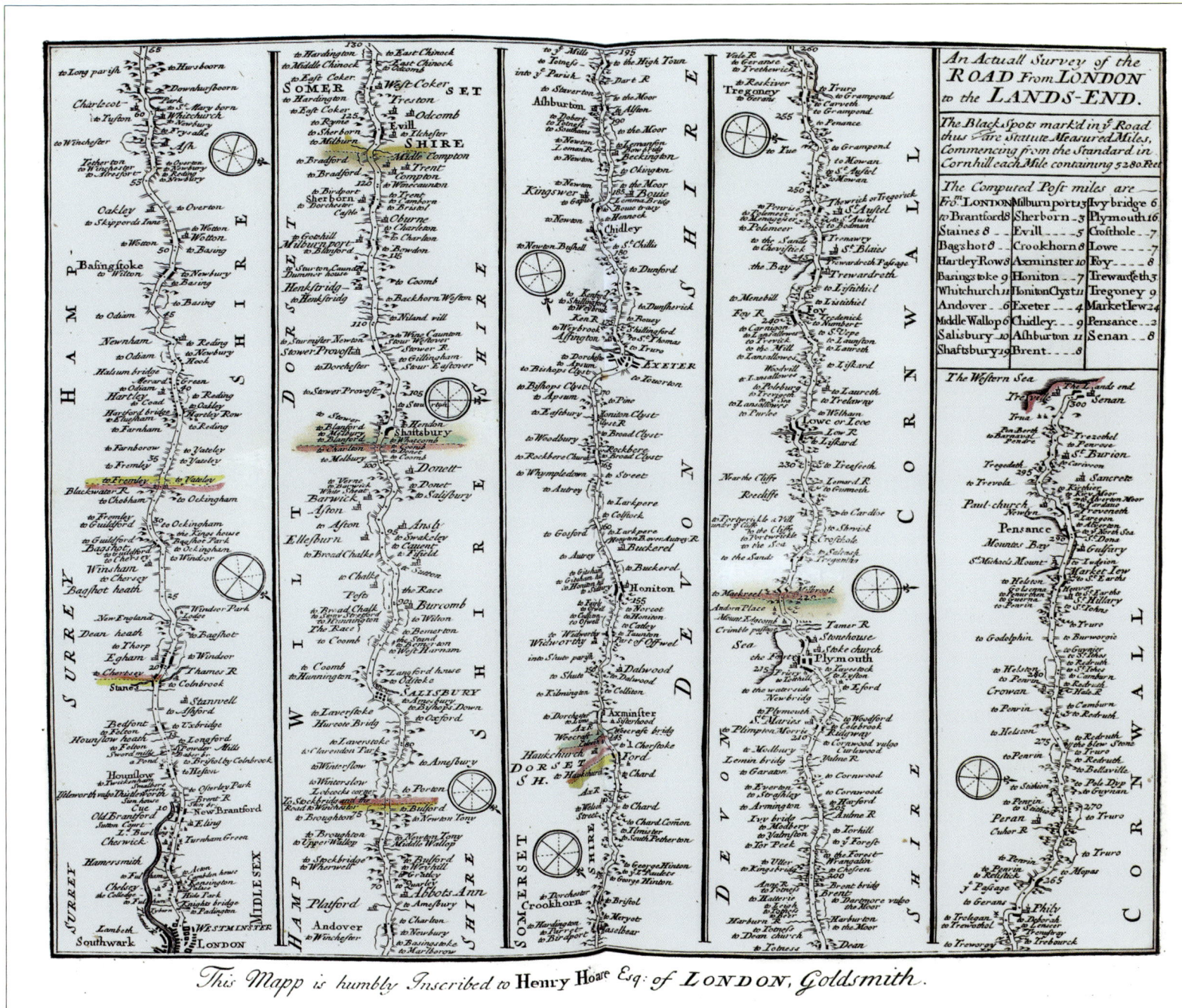

31.2 Moll 1718 Roads of ye South Part of Great Britain

32. VAN KEULEN, GERARD 1735

Eng. Van Keulen, Pub. Van Keulen
(522 x 595)
SEA CHART OF ISLES OF SCILLY

Johannes Van Keulen (1654-1715) established the Van Keulen firm around 1678 and produced his '*De Groote Nieuwe Vermeerderde Zee-Atlas ofte Water-Werelt*' in 1680, which would remain in production for the next 54 years, producing about 34 editions. His pilot guide '*De Nieuwe Groote Lichtende Zee-Fakkel*' (New large shining sea-torch) was published from 1681, and was expanded to five volumes, with the addition of river courses, Mercator's projections, depth soundings &c., and made the family famous. Johannes's son Gerard (1678-1726) and grandson Johannes (II) followed Johannes Senior into the nautical map business. Gerard took over his father's business in 1704 and went on to produce a total of over 120 issues of the '*Zee-Fakkel*', which continued in production until 1803. In 1714 Gerard was appointed cartographer of the East India Company (Verenigde Oostindische Compagnie or VOC). One of the major innovations made by Gerard was to move the '*Zee-Fakkel*' onto printed cards, at the recommendation of the VOC, thereby making them easier to handle at sea. At the same time, loose maps of the navigation routes outward from Amsterdam into the North Sea and Western Approaches were produced.

This 1735 map of the Isles of Scilly is one such example, and is particularly fine. With few other Scillies maps to refer to, this must have been based on the Collins map (#23), although there are several major differences, the first of which is the overall level of detail. Van Keulen's map is bursting with additional detail over Collins's. Although the cartouche and headings are in Dutch, much of the map itself is in English, and well done.

The outlines of the islands themselves have a greater rugosity, and appear more realistic in consequence, though the presence of hills might appear a little ambitious in view of the general altitude of the islands – nowhere is higher than 50m above sea level. The map is titled inside a cartouche in the bottom right, with a plan view of Hugh Town in the top left. Rhumb lines criss-cross the whole map, with sight lines into anchor points, depth soundings, sand banks, rocks and other hazards being marked clearly. Van Keulen has drawn vertical and horizontal lines over the map, though they are somewhat irregularly spaced, tending to compress towards the borders. Graticles of latitude are marked on either vertical side, but only align with the 50° North line of latitude; the rest are unaligned. The vertical lines of pseudo-longitude are unlabelled. Three compass roses are shown, pointing straight up the map.

The site of Sir Cloudesley Shovell's burial is marked at Porthhellick on St. Mary's, though the Gilstone rock, where *HMS Association* ran aground, is not. There are two Gilstone rocks, one south of St. Mary's and the other far farther west, and the site of the disaster. On Collins's 1723 edition of his Scillies chart, he has moved the small outcrop of Pednathes ⅜ of a mile east and inserted the Gilstone a little to the west of it. This has the effect of aligning the three outcrops of Crebawethen, Camperdeny and Pednathis. Van Keulen has not aligned these islands, his chart is therefore as per Collins 1689.

1735 Nieuwe Afteekening van de Sorlinges Eylanden, by de Engelsche genaamt Scilly Isles. Gerard Van Keulen, Amsterdam.

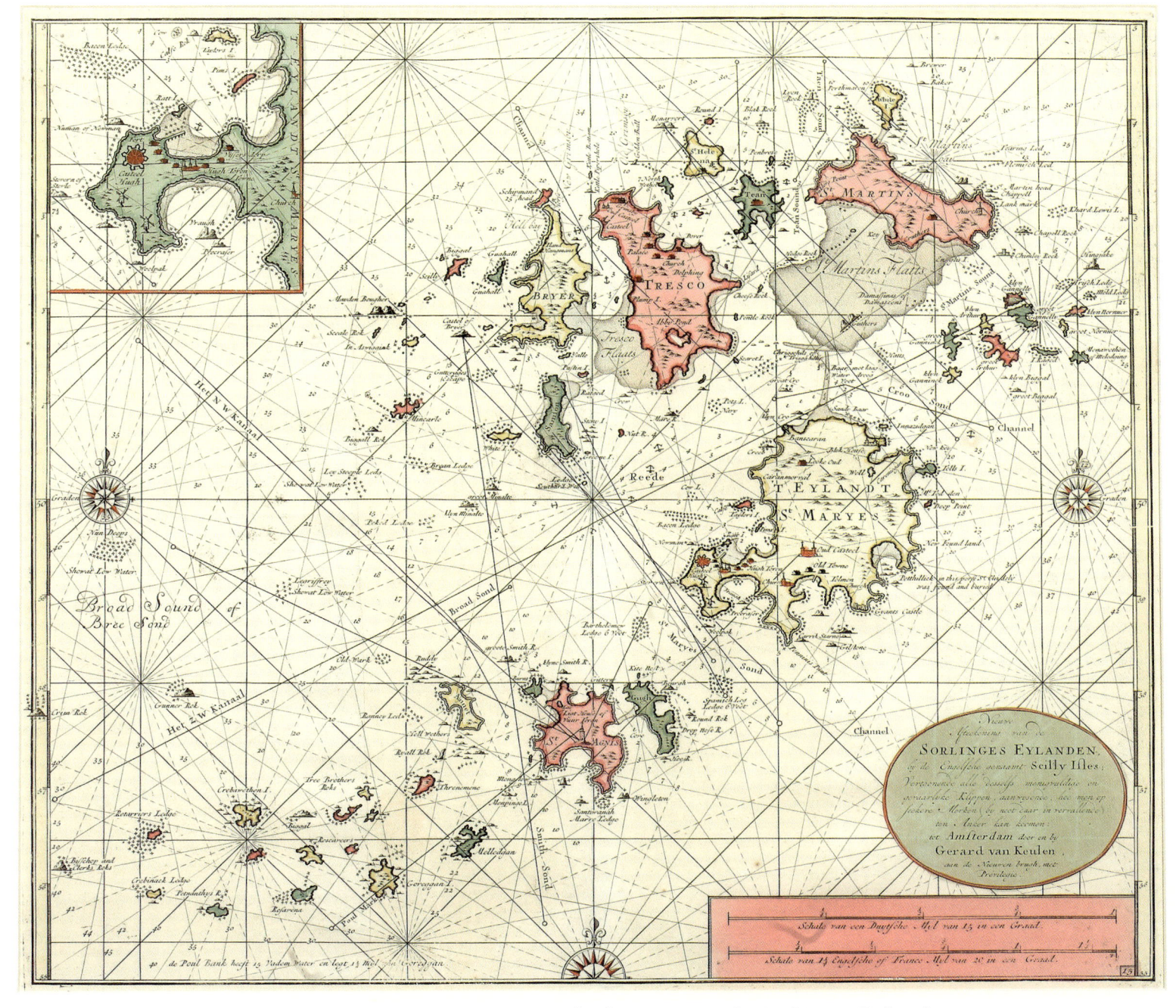

32. Van Keulen 1735 Nieuwe Afteekening van de Sorlinges Eylanden

33. PINE, JOHN 1739, 1740

1739 Eng. Pine, Pub. Pine (386 x 615)

1740 Eng. Pine, Pub. Pine (385 x 660)

John Pine (1690-1756) published many books illustrated with his own engravings. His copy of the 'Magna Carta' and several maps of London are amongst a number of his publications. One of his most noted accomplishments was the engraving of copies of the tapestries that were hung on the walls of the House of Lords. He was also engaged by Christopher Bateman to engrave the Norden manuscript maps that had been loaned to Bateman by Roger Gale in 1728 (#6).

Following the defeat of the Spanish Armada, in 1588, Lord Howard of Effingham commissioned Robert Adams to produce a series of eleven charts depicting the route of the ships as they made their way up the English Channel, encountered Drake's ships and the ensuing battle. These were titled 'Expeditionis Hispanorum in Angliam vera description, Anno Do MDLXXXVIII', published in 1590, and were engraved by Augustinus Ryther. These charts were sent to Hendrik Vroom, who produced ten tapestry designs based on the charts. These were woven by François Spierinck, in Haarlem, from 1592 to 1595, and depict the sea battle as it unfolded – these were huge works, measuring some 14ft x 28ft each. Having been sold to James I, they eventually were hung in the House of Lords.

Adams's 'Expeditionis...' features a frontispiece containing the arms of Effingham at the base and those of Elizabeth I at the top. It is the first map that is of interest here: that of the arrival of the Spanish fleet off the coast south of the Lizard. Adams/Ryther have drawn the coast line of south-west England, from somewhere near the Camel estuary on the north Cornwall coast, around to Start Point, in Devon. What is key here is the outline of Cornwall – it is that of Saxton (#1) drawn in 1579, with much detail stripped out of the map. The outline is unmistakeable.

In 1739 John Pine published a series of engravings based on drawings by Clement Lemprière, draughtsman to the Office of Ordnance, which were embellished by Hubert Gravelot, whose name can be seen in the bottom left corner. These combined the ten tapestries and eleven charts into six sheets of maps and ten copies of the ten tapestries. Pine's reasons for doing so were in tribute to the 'most glorious victory ever obtained at sea', and that 'time, accident or moths may deface these valuable shadows'. It turned out to be very prescient, for eight of the ten tapestries were lost to fire in 1834.

The six maps are loosely copied from Adams's maps, with the imprint at the base of each double page 'Publish'd by John Pine, June 24 1739, according to Act of Parliament'*. The first of these show Cornwall and a part of Devon on the left, and east Cornwall and west Devon to the right; both maps are surrounded by a very elaborate engraving with Elizabeth I at the top and horses, gods and angels &c. below. The left map shows the same view as Ryther's – Pine has, however, redrawn the Scilly Isles, from the circular cluster to something more modern and modified - the outline away from a Saxton copy to something more generic. One give-away is the inclusion of Falmouth as a town, (not 'Falmouth Haven', as shown on the Ryther map). Falmouth is unmarked, as such, on the Ryther map, and also missing from his source – Saxton. The town does not receive its charter until 1661 and does not appear on Cornwall maps until Blome's 1673 map (#18), but is marked on the sea charts of de Bry (#3), Waghenaer (#2) and Blaeu (#10). Note also the inclusion of 'The Gulphe' on Ryther's map, which reappears on Pine's. This suggests Ryther may have referred to de Bry. On the Waghenaer and Blaeu maps it is called 'de Wolfe'; Saxton terms these rocks, incorrectly, as 'Longships' – it is in fact the Wolf Rock. Much of what is contained on the page is a demonstration of Pine's mastery as an engraver, rather than his cartographic prowess – this is even more marked with the later 1740 map.

1739   *The tapestry hangings of the House of Lords: representing the several engagements between the English and Spanish fleets, in the ever memorable year MDLXXXVIII, John Pine, London, Reprinted 1745.*

33. Pine 1739 The Tapestry Hangings of The House of Lords, London

Pine produced a later edition of the Tapestry Hangings in 1753. In this edition, he included two new maps (though both are dated 1740) – the first is of the Thames as if viewed from an Essex viewpoint, looking to Kent. The second map is titled 'A plott of the coasts of Cornwall and Devonshire as they were to be fortified in 1588...' and is clearly dated 25 March 1740.

The title of the chart is set in an elaborate cartouche within the mainland area of Devon. Above the title is the Royal Coat of Arms of Elizabeth I, surrounded by the Order of the Garter. The title is 'A Plott of all the coast of Cornwall and Devonshire as they were to be fortified in 1588 against the landing of any enemy' and is 'taken from the original manuscript in the Cottonian Library'. This library was once the property of Sir Robert Cotton and forms the underpinnings of what is now the British Library. To either side of the Royal Arms, Pine has drawn a crouched crowned lion on the dexter side and an equally poised dragon on the sinister side – these are interesting adaptations of the more conventional style and seems to suggest the two animals are about to pounce. In the centre top, Neptune is seated holding Britannia's shield and a trident. Around him are cherubs, one of whom is firing a cannon.

Concerning the map itself, it is drawn to depict the fortifications that were set in defence of the country in 1588 – over 150 years previously. Pine's 1739 double spread was a redraw of the Ryther maps – this 1740 map is removed from both these by several large steps.

Pine's rendition of the same coastline in 1740 has been done to make the map appear older than this date; to add some *je ne sais quoi*. We have to assume that Pine deliberately deformed the line of the coast to give the 'feel' of a far older map – with a stretch of the imagination, one could compare it with the sea charts of de Bry (#3), Waghenaer (#2) or even Willem Blaeu's 1608 map of Cornwall, Devon and Dorset (#10). As one might expect, the detail of the inland areas is meagre, with only a few towns and other places named. Crammed around the coast, especially the south coast, are squads of men armed with pikes or muskets at port arms. The Tudor castles of Pendennis and St. Mawes are clearly shown, as too are the fortifications on St. Michael's Mount and the less well-known castle at St. Katherine's, opposite Fowey. Various places, including Penzance, Pendennis and Plymouth, are depicted with gun batteries readied and pointing out to sea. In the Bristol Channel, Pine has drawn an elaborate compass rose.

John Pine was created Bluemantle Pursuivant of Arms in Ordinary by the College of Arms in 1743. The college has been in existence since 1484 and in the same location, Derby Place, since 1555. It appears that Pine spent his remaining years living at the college. His will, written in August 1754, runs to only six lines, leaving everything to his wife (PROB11-822/101-151).

1753   *Second Edition: The Tapestries Hanging in the House of Lords, A plott of the coasts of Cornwall and Devonshire as they were to be fortified in 1588..., John Pine, London.*

*A Side-note to this, since it might explain why the Pine 1739 maps are similar but are not copies of the earlier Adams/Ryther maps: In 1734, the Engravers' Act (1735, 8 Geo.III,c13) was passed by Parliament – this was done with the petitioning of Pine and, amongst others, his friend William Hogarth. This was an extension of the 1710 Statute of Anne which protected authors of literature with copyright. The Act protected the engravers' work from plagiarists – something that had been rife to this point – recall Ogilby's dying words (#19). Hereafter we start to see at the foot of engraved maps words along the lines of '...According to Act...'.

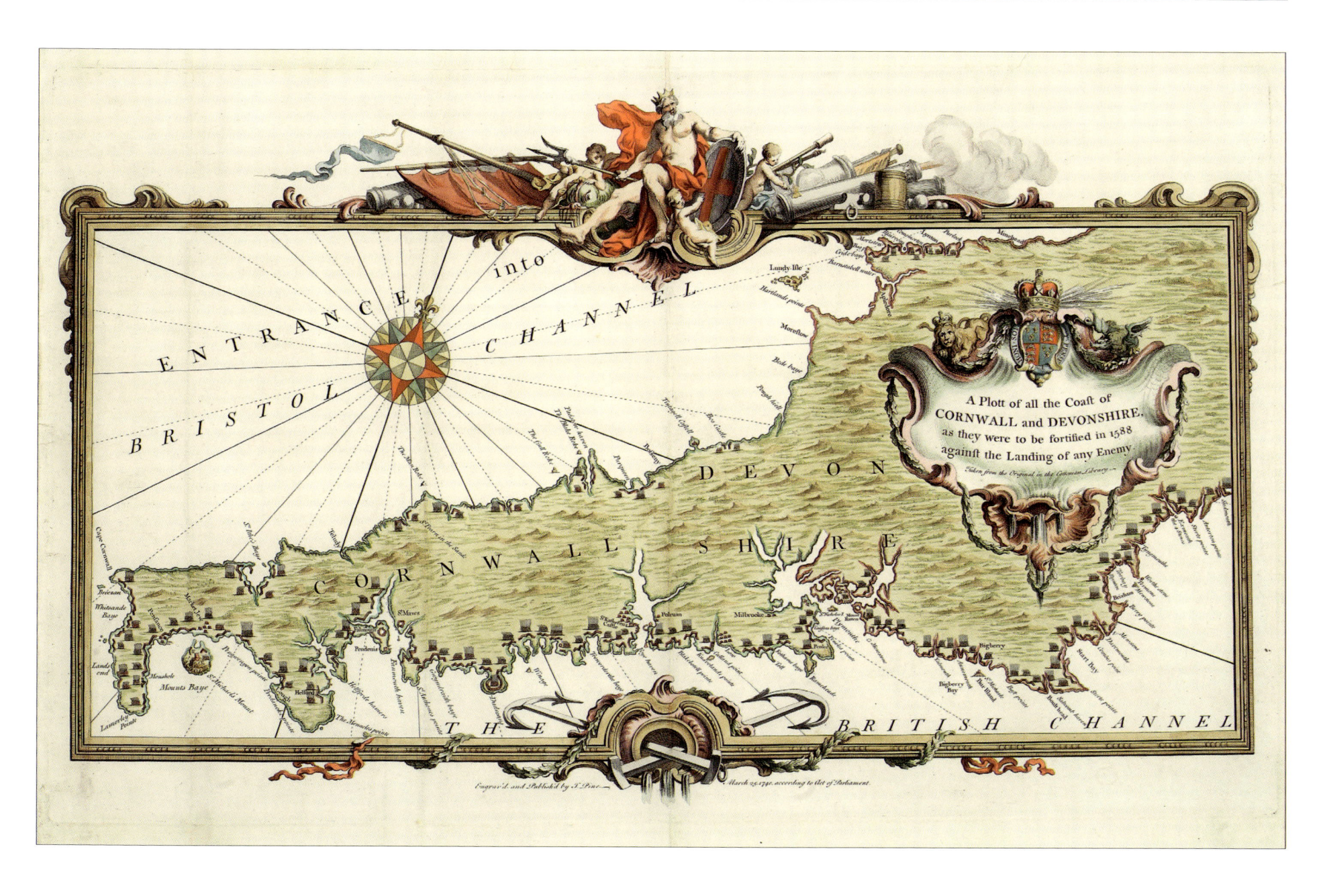

33.1 Pine 1753 *A plott of the coasts of Cornwall and Devonshire as they were to be fortified in 1588, London.*

34. BADESLADE, THOMAS & TOMS, WILLIAM 1741

Eng. Toms, Pub. Badeslade & Toms
(146 x 140)

The map is chiefly derived from earlier material, for, although Badeslade was a surveyor, he does not appear to have done any original work in the county. The engraving, which is clear and effective, was the work of Badeslade's co-publisher, William Henry Toms, and a good deal of information is given to the left of the map. The map itself is turned east end at the foot of the page. The section to the left summarises details of MPs returned to Parliament (44), as well as details of the major towns' market days and fairs. The border also lists the rivers of Cornwall. Badeslade's first state (1741) has drawn two principal roads through the county – one starts having crossed the Tamar west of Tavistock and proceeds to Liskeard, Lostwithiel, Grampound and Truro. From there, it passes Penryn and Market Jew (Marazion), and then meets the other route, before entering Penzance, where the two run to Land's End. His second road enters the county at Launceston (marked 173 miles from London); the road then travels north to Camelford and runs to Padstow, St. Columb and St. Michael's, and for the first time, Redruth is marked as a town, with a road passing through it*. Furthermore, the engraver has slightly enlarged the title of Redruth, above (e.g.) Tregony or Penryn. The closest map preceding Badeslade chronologically is Moll's (#31). Moll does mark these and other roads; however, this is the first map to single out Redruth above others. This road joins the other one between Market Jew (Marazion) and Penzance. The drawing of these two roads, at the exclusion of the others shown on the Moll map, is interesting – these two roads are the prototypes for the A30/A39 and A390/A394 routes that become the main arterial roads through the county. The foot of the map is dated Sept 29 1741; the plate number top right is 10.

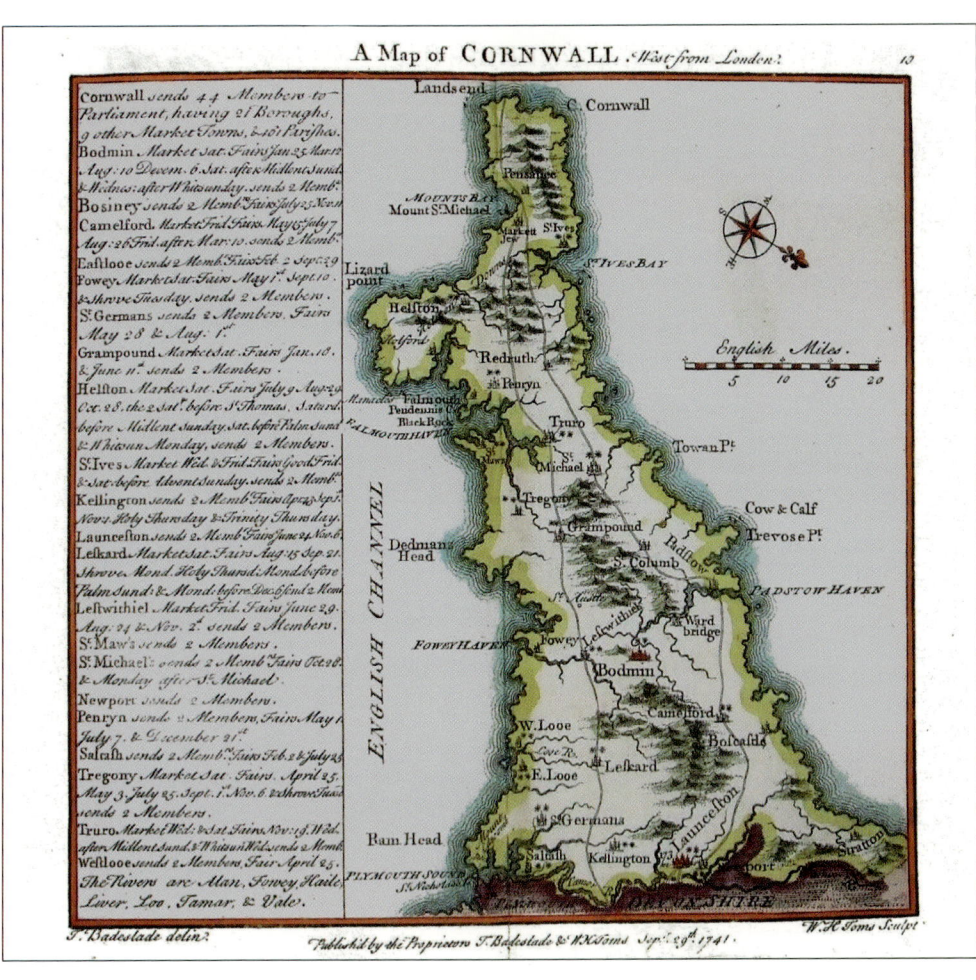

34. Badeslade 1741 Chorographia Britaniae, T. Badeslade And W. H. Toms, London

A Second state of this map was produced a year later (29 Sept 1742). The text in the insert to the left is unchanged, while the map's detail has been extensively enlarged. Major points around the coast have been added, as too have the inland towns. The routes through the county have also been elaborated with a further two main routes: the old southern coaching route delineated by Ogilby (#19, plate 28), and a mid-county route from Kellington to St. Michael (Mitchell) via Bodmin.

* Molls map (#31) shows Redruth at the end of a road from Penzance; the connection from Redruth to St. Michael's is still shown as a track.

1741   *Chorographia Britaniae. Or a Set of maps of all the counties.* T. Badeslade and W. H. Toms, London.

1742   *Chorographia Britaniae. Or a Set of maps of all the counties.* W. H. Toms, London. Numerous place names and two routes added.

1745   *Chorographia Britaniae… The Second Edition.* C. Hitch and W.H. Toms, London.

1746   Reprinted *Chorographia Britaniae…* J. Clark, C. Hitch & W.H. Toms, London.

1749   Reprinted *Chorographia Britaniae* C. Hitch W. Johnston & W.H. Toms, London.

34.1 Badeslade 1742 Chorographia Britaniae, T. Badeslade And W. H. Toms, London

Antique Maps of Cornwall and the Isles of Scilly

103

35. DODSLEY, ROBERT & COWLEY, JOHN 1741-3

Eng. Cowley, Pub. Dodsley & Cooper
(180 x 131)

John Lodge Cowley (1719-1768) was professor of mathematics at the Royal Military Academy, Woolwich, FRS and Geographer to King George II. Cowley also produced a number of works on geometry, including 'Geometry made easy' (1752), particularly notable for the fold-up figures of solid shapes such as tetrahedra and dodecahedra. He worked with Robert Dodsley to produce their atlas 'The Geography of England', which actually appeared in 1743, having been advertised in *The General Evening Post* on 24-26 November 1743.

Prior to the issue of 'The Geography of England' came a brief run of six county maps, including Cornwall, in 1741. These were published in the short-lived publication called 'The Publick Register' - Cornwall was issued in what was probably the last issue, in June 1741 (Hodson Vol. II, p5). 'The Publick Register' was killed off by Dodsley partially because of the expense of stamping, (Stamp Duty was liable on some sections of the magazine but not others, which made production difficult), but also due to an advertising boycott by Edward Cave, printer of the 'Gentleman's Magazine'.

Out of this, Dodsley produced 'The Geography of England', which contained an expanded compilation of descriptions of the counties of England, with maps. It quickly found itself in competition with similar publications, such as 'English Traveller' (#36) and 'Agreeable Historian' (#37).

The map shown is titled 'An improved map of CORNWALL containing the borough and market towns with those adjoining, also its principal roads and rivers By I Cowley, Geographer to his Majesty'. Cornwall was lightly revised from the 1741 map, with some corrections. Added: Temple Moors, S. Agnes, Helford. Changed: Mitchael from Michel, Marazion back to Market Jew. The title is contained in a simple cartouche in the upper left. In the centre top are marked English miles 0 through 10, and to the left of this a simple Kip-style compass rose is drawn. The boundary with Devon has been canted over slightly so it runs parallel with the right margin, thus perpetuating the misconception that Cornwall runs east-west. A rudimentary key is placed below the cartouche, indicating 'Borough' and 'Market' towns, as well as forts/garrisons. Points of interest around the coast are included; however, inland less detail is present, though the roads and distances between towns is shown, along with the highland areas drawn to resemble sand-dunes all heading east! Both Hall Drunkard and Temple Moors persist. Only one area of wooded or forested land is shown to the south of Launceston, probably Carabolok Park.

The plain border is marked by latitude and longitude from London, with the line of 5° West parallel with compass north. Setting today's line of 5° West against this reveals Cowley to be rotated 7° counter clockwise No county maps since Norden's preparative statement in 1596 have been drawn to magnetic north, (by the early 1700s this was 16° West of grid north), and while tempting here, it seems unlikely. This causes other problems with the construction of latitude, which should, at this scale, be perpendicular to longitude. It is not and has been mis-aligned by the same amount (7°). Additionally, 51° North has been mis-labelled '50' as the last number on the right border.

1741   *The Publick Register. London, Printed for R. Dodsley at Tully's head in Pall mall; and sold by T. Cooper at the Globe in Paternoster Row*

1744   *The Geography of England: Done in the manner of Gordon's Geographical Grammar, by R. Dodsley, London. 1765 Republished by Dodsley's brother James, re-titled as 'The geography and history of England', but with no county maps.*

1745   *A new sett of Pocket maps of all the Counties of England and Wales. Shewing the situation of all the Cities, Boroughs, Market Towns... London, R. Dodsley & M Cooper.*

1745   *A new sett of Pocket maps of all the Counties of England and Wales. In which particular regard has been had to the roads and rivers. London, R. Dodsley & M Cooper.*

1748   *A new sett of Pocket maps of all the Counties of England and Wales. London. R Dodsley and M Cooper.*

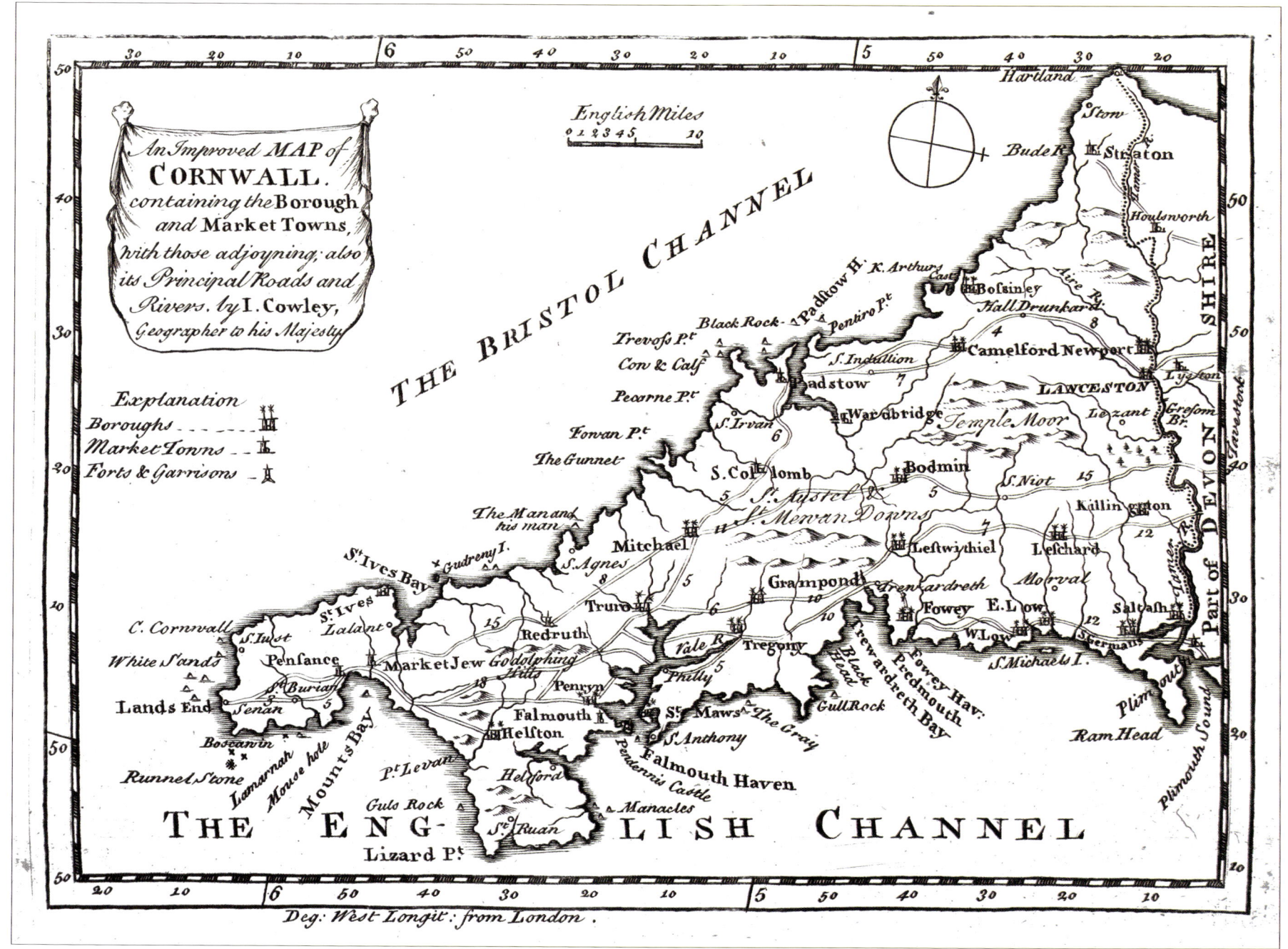

35. Cowley 1744 The Geography of England...

36. READ, THOMAS & ROCQUE, JOHN 1743

Eng. Rocque, Pub. Read
(197 x 152)

John (Jean) Rocque (c.1709-1762) was a Huguenot émigré, who, with his parents, like many others, moved to London from France. He initially worked with his brother as a landscaper and later produced plans of gardens. From this, he became an engraver who did most of his work in London.

'The English Traveller' was published, in weekly parts (with an occasional hiatus), from November 1743 to November 1745, (the title page is dated 1746). The descriptions and maps quickly became out of step with each other and, by the time the map of Cornwall was issued as part 6 in January 1743/4, the description was three issues behind, with part 9 issued at the end of the same month. The Cornwall map (not shown here) is an identical fore-runner to the later 1753 edition, the two differences being the mile scale above St. Ives and plate number. The scale is shown as 0-8 English Miles; this, by inspection, is an error. The distance, by the map's marks, from Penzance to Land's End is eight miles. Eight miles, from the scale bar, would extend from Land's End to Redruth. The re-issued map has boldly and simply replaced the scale bar with 0-20 Measur'd Miles. In the top right corner there is no evidence of a plate number.

Rocque bought Read's plates and issued his 'Small British Atlas' in 1753. The following describes that later map.

The outline shape and content of Rocque's Cornwall is a near copy of Moll's 1724 map. The placement of just about every place name is identical, with an error in the transcription of 'Cape Cornwall' - Moll has abbreviated this to 'C. Cornwall' and allowed the 'C.' to spill off the map and into the left border. Rocque has missed the 'C.' and thus the only cape in England now appears as 'Cornwall'. With that said, Rocque redeems himself with the correction of Moll's 'Godolping Hills' to 'Godolphin Hills', south of Redruth. For the first time on the maps of Cornwall, Penzance has been spelt using a 'z'; previous cartographers preferred either the common 's' or its long variant 'f'. The 'z' is taken up again by Kitchin in his 1764 map for Dodsley's 'England Illustrated', though its adoption across later maps is still uneven until Cary.

Rocque has, in line with the Moll map, marked mines, roads, towns, rivers &c. There are no lines of latitude or longitude, but the map contains a compass rose in the sea north of St. Ives, with a new mileage scale of 0-20 'Measur'd Miles'. Rocque has slightly compressed the map horizontally, but his compass is at least 10° further east than Moll's. From this, we can presume that he has referred to other, later, maps since his assumed (but un-shown) latitude-longitude 'grid' is aligned with today's true grid north. In the top right corner inside the border is the remains of a plate number (41) that has been scratched off the paper.

The 'Small British Atlas' was re-issued twice in 1753, with no changes to the maps; the last was issued bearing John Rocque's name and that of Robert Sayer at the Golden Buck opposite Fetter Lane on the title page. The 1762 edition was produced with a slight change to the Cornwall map – a plate number (6) was added outside the border top right, and Sayer's name has been removed from the title-sheet. The final edition, in 1764, contains no further changes to the Cornwall map.

1746 *The English Traveller, Giving a description of those parts of Great Britain called England and Wales... Printed for T. Read in Dogwell-Court, White-Fryers, Fleet Street. London.*

1753 *The Small British Atlas: Being a new Set of Maps of all the Counties in England and Wales...Publish'd according to Act of Parliament by John Rocque, Chorographer to His Royal Highness the Prince of Wales, near Old Round Court in the Strand,* (undated in title). Re-issued 1753 (dated 1753 in title), 1753 re-issued again with Robert Sayer's address in title.

1762 *The Small English Atlas,* Sayer's address removed, (plate number 6 added), Final Edition 1764 unchanged from 1762 except for date on title page.

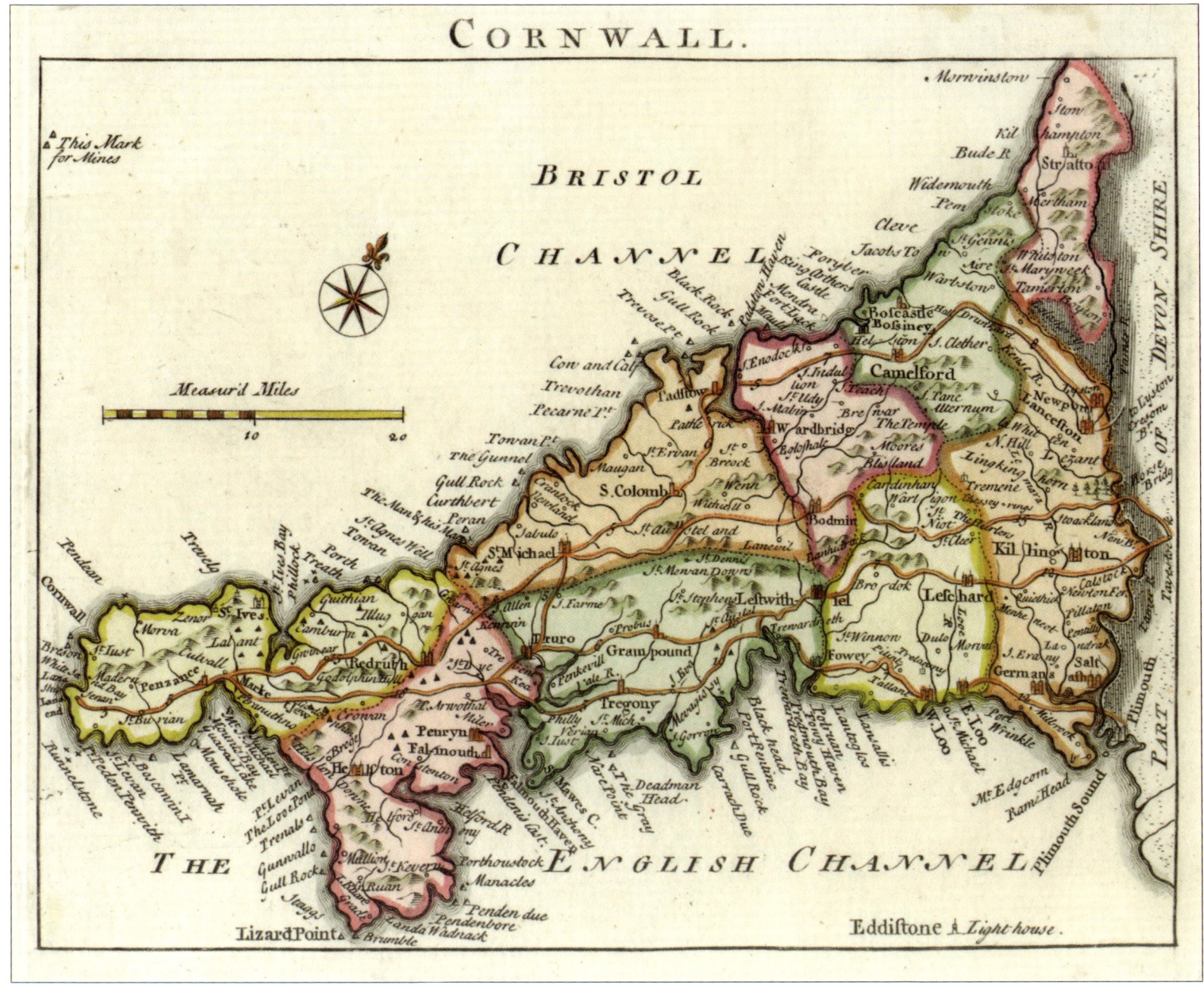

36. Rocque 1753 *The Small British Atlas*, Rocque & Sayer London

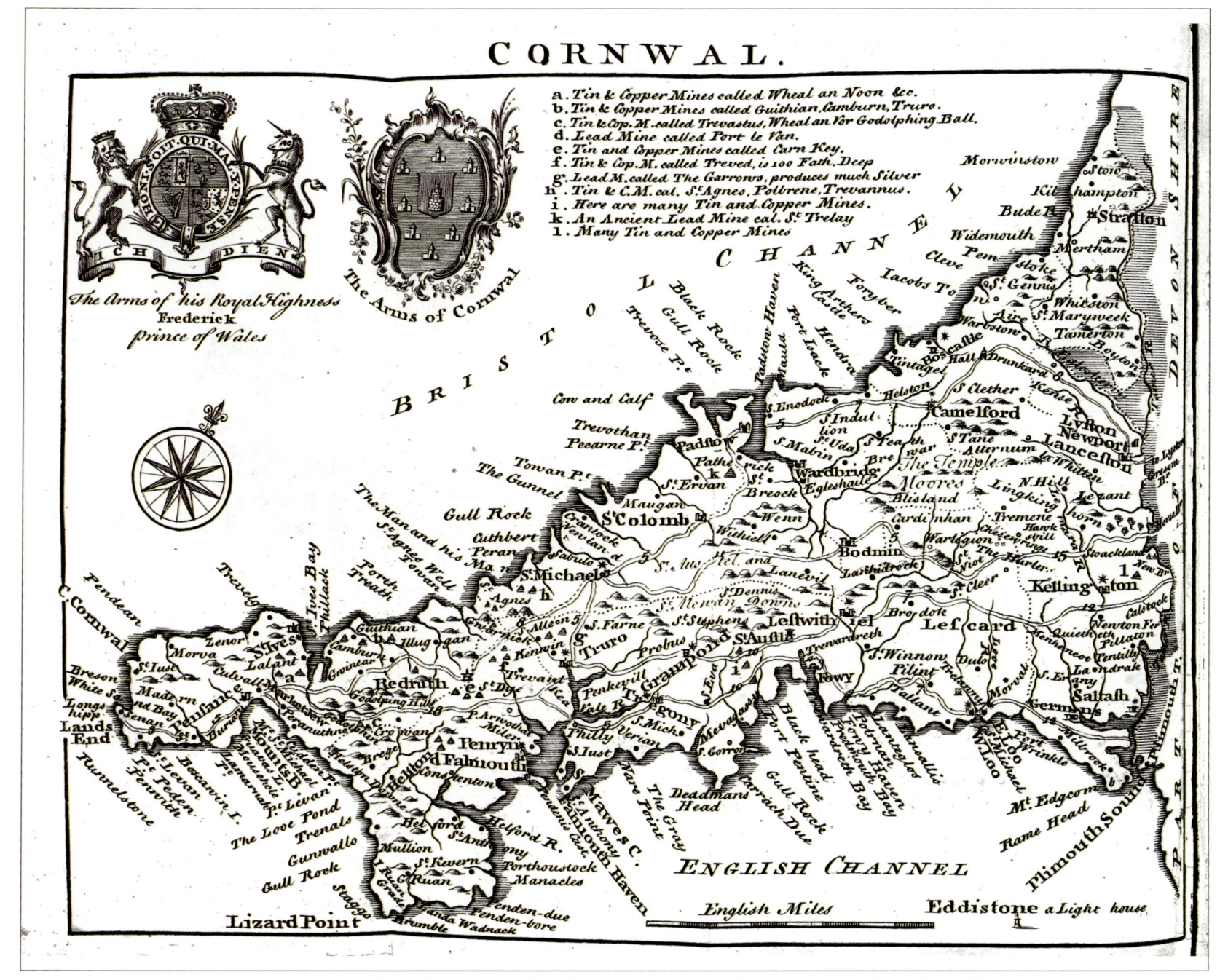

37. Simpson 1744 The Agreeable Historian, or the Compleat English Traveller

37. WALKER, ROBERT & SIMPSON, SAMUEL 1744

Eng. Simpson, Pub Walker
(196 x 150)

'The Agreeable Historian' was issued only nine days after 'The English Traveller' (#36), and there are some very similar passages of text between the two. It was issued in three volumes, and never again – in consequence it is very rare. The component parts that built into the three volumes were issued in 16-page pamphlets over 109 weeks, the final issue coming at the end of 1745. Hodson (Vol. II, p43) has noted the similarities between this and the earlier 'English Traveller' and offers three possible routes: that one was copied from the other, or a third source supplied both, or the two publishers, Read and Walker, used the same compiler. He concludes that the two publishers shared the same compiler.

There is some difficulty in determining the date of issue for Volume I. Hodson (as above) deduces from advertisements that it must have been issued from 5 December 1743 to about 30 July 1744. The counties were issued in alphabetical order, with Bedfordshire to Essex in Volume I, Gloucestershire to Middlesex in Volume II (August 1744 to April 1745) and finally Norfolk to Yorkshire (and Monmouthshire) in Volume III (May 1745 to December 1745).

The map of Cornwall is based on Moll's work, showing a good deal of useful information. The arms of Frederick, Prince of Wales and of Launceston (shown incorrectly as 'The Arms of Cornwal') appear in the top left corner. The mines that Moll had listed below his title cartouche are replicated verbatim; the 'C' of 'Cape Cornwall' has been correctly set, though it crosses the left border. St. Michael's Mount, while labelled, is not drawn. 'Godolping Hills' are still shown. These elements alone strongly suggest the map is derived with few amendments from Moll (#31).

Although Simpson has elected to not show the Hundreds by list, they are shown as dotted lines on the map. In line with many other maps of the time and later, the county has been rotated to fit the eastern border with Devon in line with the right margin. A compass rose north of Morvah has been rotated further eastwards than Moll's, by about 12 degrees. There are no lines or grid of latitude or longitude shown on the map, however the implied grid north from the rose is too far east by about the same value. A scale bar of eight divisions at the foot of the map is drawn as 'English Miles', though it is not numbered.

Samuel Simpson presents something of an enigma; in terms of cartographic production, 'The Agreeable Historian' appears to be his only venture, and there is little trace of Simpson elsewhere. One Samuel Sympson (fl 1726-1751) produced 'A New book of Cyphers' in 1726, and there are broad similarities between the Launceston arms (and similar illustrations elsewhere in 'The Agreeable Historian) and one of Sympson's trade cards, though it is quite evident the trade cards are done by a better hand. It is unlikely that Sympson is Simpson.

1746 *The Agreeable Historian, or the Compleat English Traveller: giving a geographical description of every county in that part of Great-Britain, call'd England. Together with the antiquities of the same. ... with a map of every country [sic] ... after the designs of Herman Moll, and others. ... Compiled from Camden, Leland, Dugdale, Ogilby, Morgan, and other authors, by Samuel Simpson, gent. Printed by R. Walker, Fleet Lane, London.*

38. OSBORNE, THOMAS & HUTCHINSON, THOMAS 1748

Eng. Hutchinson?, Pubs. Birt, Osborne, Browne, Hodges, Millar & Robinson
(159 x 133)

Thomas Osborne produced 'Geographica Magna Britanniae', possibly with his brother, John, though John is not mentioned on the frontispiece. The atlas contains 60 plates: Cornwall is No. 6, with the Isles of Scilly the last plate (No. 60). The frontispiece of the atlas shows Samuel Wale as engraver, though this may only refer to the frontispiece. Some of the other maps are signed Hutchinson and, for lack of better information, he has been used here.

Neither the Cornwall nor the Isles of Scilly map contains any indication of an engraver. The Cornwall map is simply titled 'A Correct Map of Cornwall', in a rectangular 'picture' frame that has been embellished with some clouds, waves &c. The map is set with the Devon border parallel with the margin, a compass rose is set in the sea to the north of Padstow and there is a scale of 0-20 miles below Fowey. The Isles of Scilly are shown as an inset hard against the left margin, mid-way down the map. The picture frame-like border is missing its left side. Only four labels are placed within the insert: St. Martin's, St. Mary's and St. Agnes. The last label is 'Saale', which might refer to Seal Rock, to the west of Bryher. The source of this is undoubtedly Gasgoyne (#25).

The outline of Cornwall appears to closely resemble that of Gasgoyne (#25) - some names have been ported over, though it is evident that Osborne has had to be selective and may have cross-referenced with others - Morden's 1701 (#20), Bowen's 1720 (#30) and Rocque's 1746 (#36) maps are all similar, though there are inconsistencies. Osborne has included Botallack, not generally shown on any mid-scale maps, but present on Speed's and Gasgoyne's. He has also included 'Newland', near St. Michael, in mid Cornwall. This is an error derived from Gasgoyne - it is Newlyn East. Rocque and Bowen carry the same error.

Finally, a comment on the construction of latitude and longitude with respect to the placement and orientation of Hutchinson's compass. As mentioned earlier, the county had been set onto the page with the east border parallel with the right margin. The compass rose had been rotated 14° east of straight up the page, which is tolerably close to the correct orientation of the county. The construction of latitude and longitude graticles around the map border are correctly numbered, however, there are several problems that arise after this. The mark of 50° North can be seen in the lower left corner; its counterpart on the right is incorrectly placed in the bottom right corner. It should be 8° further south and should intersect the bottom margin at 5° 40' West. This achieves the required 90° intersection with Hutchinson's compass. This then reveals the next issue - that of longitude construction. Hutchinson's 5° West line runs, incorrectly, straight up the page, at odds with the compass, and crosses the county from Looe in the south to Marham, near Stratton, in the north. This is quite some distance too far east (5° West crosses Cornwall from St. Anthony's Head in the south to Harlyn in the north).

1748 *Geographia Magna Britanniae, by S. Birt, T. Osborne, D. Browne, J Hodges, J Osborne, A Millar, & J Robinson. London.*

Second Edition same year (or ~1756 ?) by T Osborne, D. Browne, J Hodges, A Miller, J Robinson, W Johnstone, P Davey and B Law.

NOTE: From the late 1700s through into the 1800s relatively few cartographers' maps were used in a multitude of publications from 6d magazines to full sized multi-volume atlases. Amongst these Kitchin and Cary in particular were successful and in consequence one can find the same map in several publications with no evident differentiation. Identifying the map while still in its published document is one thing, without the document this can be difficult. There are considerably more publications than there are maps - our attempt here has been to cover the maps as comprehensively as possible - there are omissions due to space and access.

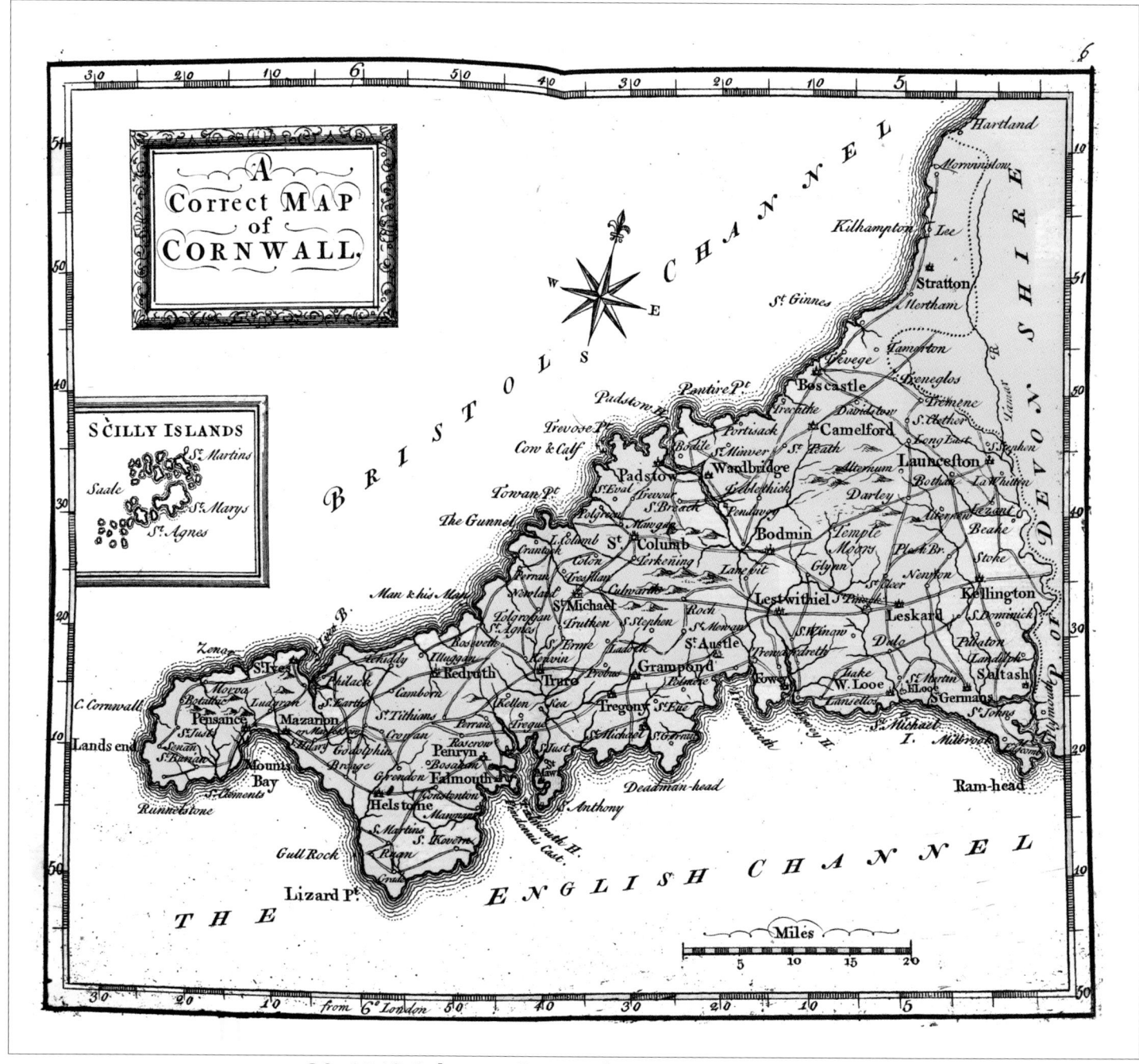

38. 1748 Osborne, Geographia Magna Britanniae.

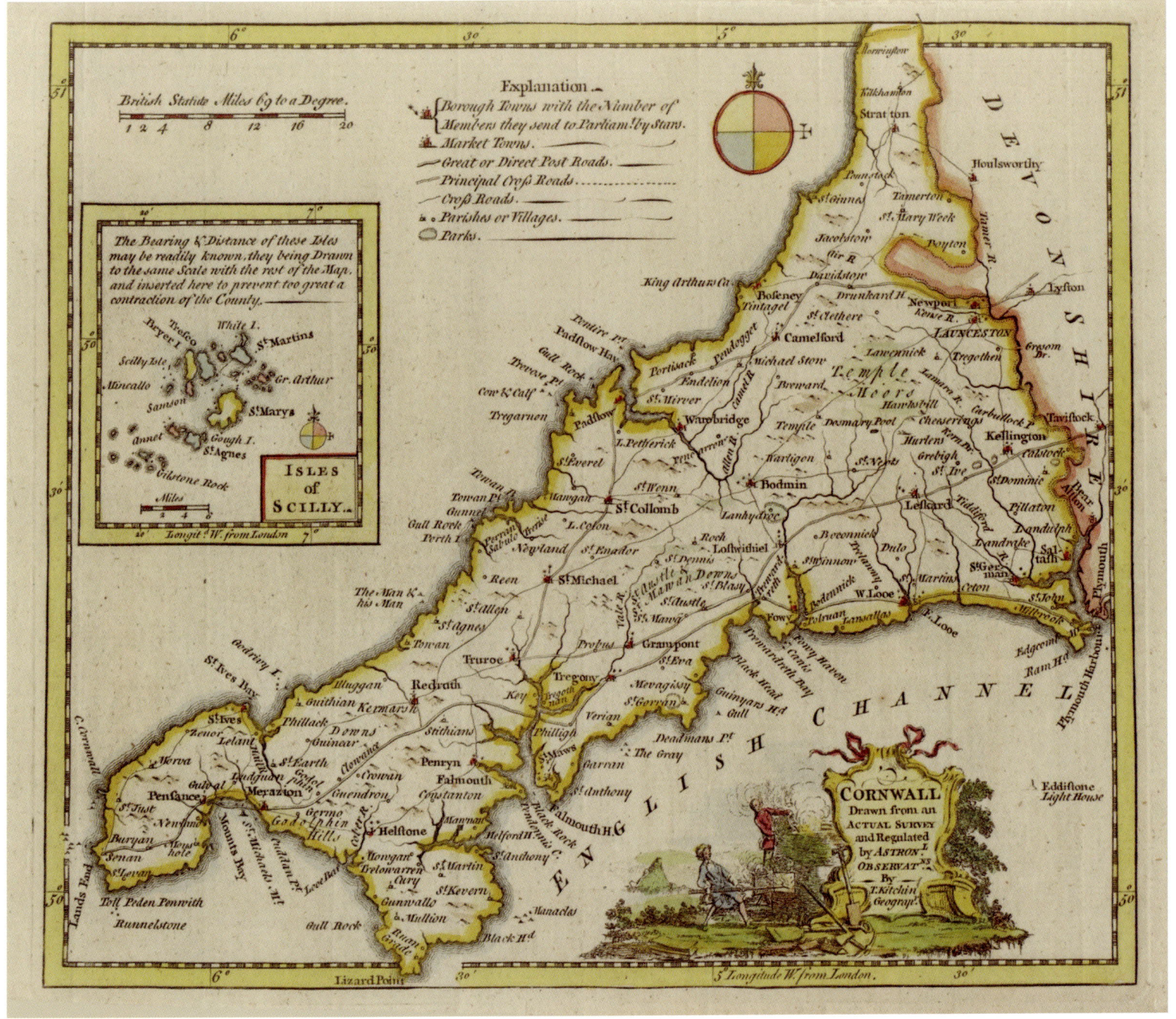

39. Kitchin (1786 Reprint) The London Magazine. London.

39. KITCHIN, THOMAS 1749, 1750, 1764, 1769 & 1778

1749 THE LONDON MAGAZINE
Eng. Kitchin, Pub Baldwin (222 x 191)

Thomas Kitchin (1718-1784) was a fine engraver and an important publisher whose premises were at the Sign of the Star at Holborn Hill. He was a prolific worker, engraving several atlases of county maps and others of different parts of the world. He was apprenticed to Emanuel Bowen, with whom he had a publishing association for much of his adult life. Kitchin married Bowen's daughter, Sarah.

'The London Magazine' started life in 1732, in monthly issues. From 1747 and at irregular intervals until 1763, county maps of England and Wales were produced. The Cornwall map was issued in Volume 18 in October 1749. (The Scilly Islands' map appeared in April 1753).

The 1749 Kitchin map of Cornwall was quite simple but well-engraved, the first edition identified by the publisher's imprint below the map, ('Printed for R. Baldwin Junr. at the Rose in Pater Noster Row'). The map has a title-piece in a small cartouche in the bottom right corner, showing mining tools and the figures of two tinners busy with a small furnace. There is an inset of the Isles of Scilly, and latitude and longitude from London are shown. Kitchin has placed his 5° West line of longitude about 20' too far east, but this is the first map here to NOT align the Devon/Cornwall border with the right margin – grid north is straight up the page.

1749   *The London Magazine, London. Reprints: 1786, 1795 & 1798. (Baldwin's imprint removed in all reprints).*

1750 THE LARGE ENGLISH ATLAS
Eng. Kitchin, Pubs. Bowen & Kitchin
(686 x 502)

The 1750 map is by far the most impressive and attractive map of Cornwall to appear in a complete atlas of the 18th century and appeared in the 'Large English Atlas' by Emanuel Bowen and Thomas Kitchin. The concept of designing a set of county maps to a standard format may have been John Hinton's, with each map to be printed onto large Imperial paper. In line with many other endeavours at the time, the maps were produced at monthly intervals, from May 1749, with the Cornwall map being produced in 1750. The final complete atlas was advertised as a single volume in May 1760.

The Atlas went through many re-issues over the following 30 years, with Hodson (Volume II, pp228) identifying 28 different examples. Regarding the map of Cornwall, there are seven states contained within these 28 examples. These are characterised by the imprint at the foot of the map as follows, (the inferred date is added in parentheses):

   a) *Printed for J Hinton, 1750 (1750)*
   b) *Printed for T Bowles, I Tinney, John Bowles & Son, and Robt Sayer (1756)*
   c) *Printed for T Bowles, John Bowles & Son and Robt Sayer (plate number 7 top right and bottom right added) (1762)*
   d) *Printed for Carington Bowles, John Bowles and Robt Sayer (1764)*
   e) *Printed for Carington Bowles and Robt Sayer (1767)*
   f) *Printed for Carington Bowles, Robert Wilkinson and Robt Sayer (1779)*
   g) *London. Printed for Bowles and Carver, R. Wilkinson and Laurie & Whittle (1787)*

The title-piece of the Cornwall map in the left corner is represented as an engraving upon a large memorial tablet, set in a landscape with trees, buildings and towers in the background. In the foreground are various agricultural and mining implements, a wheatsheaf, fishing nets and baskets, as well as three figures. The title reads 'A New Improved Map of Cornwall from the best surveys and Intelligence'; Kitchin makes no direct claim to having carried out the surveys himself, and the evidence on the map itself suggests that he copied directly from Joel Gasgoyne's large map (#25). In the top centre is a cartouche with a dedication to Richard Edgecumbe, 1st Baron Edgecumbe, whose

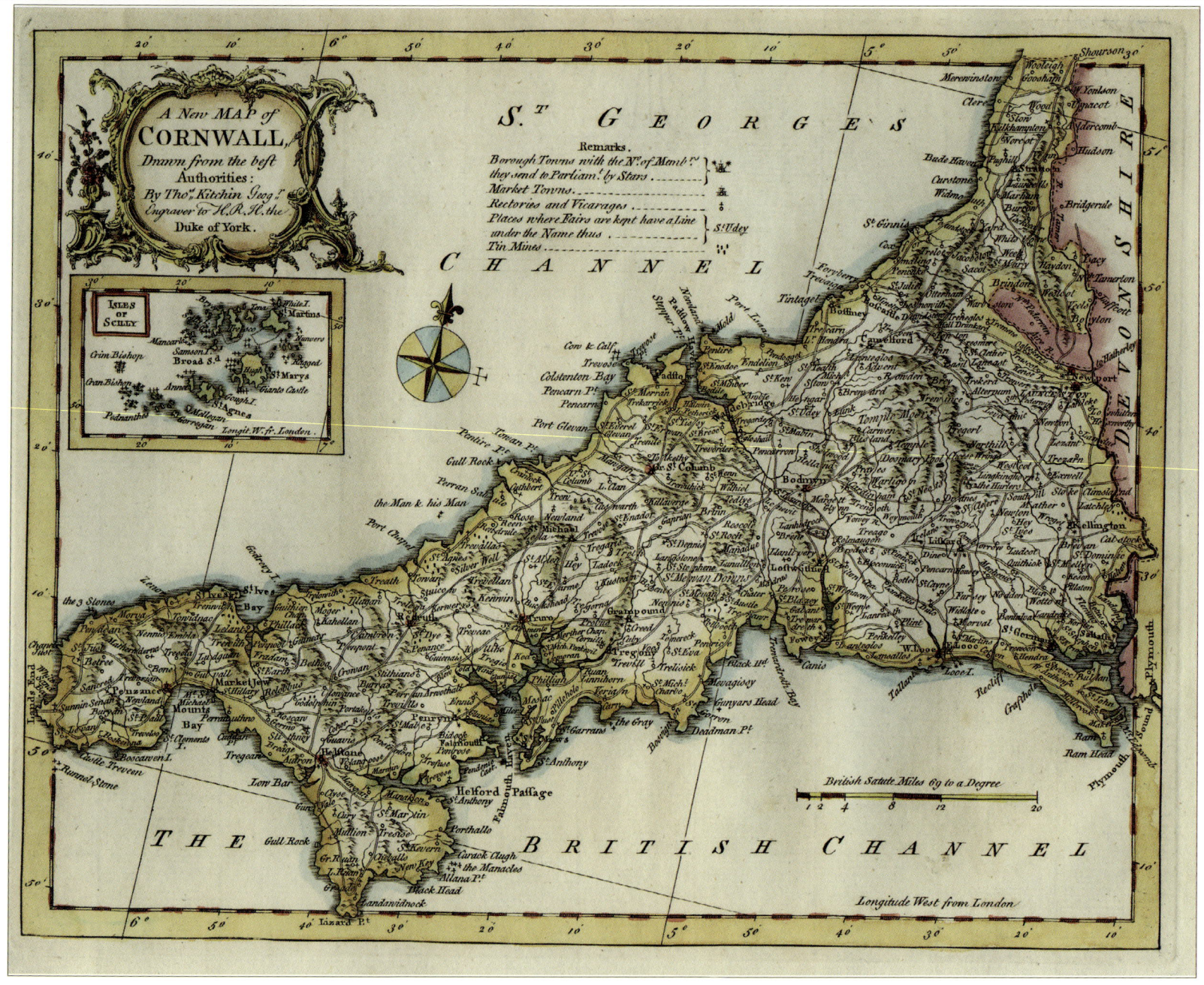

39.1 Kitchin 1764 England Illustrated... R. & J. Dodsley, London.

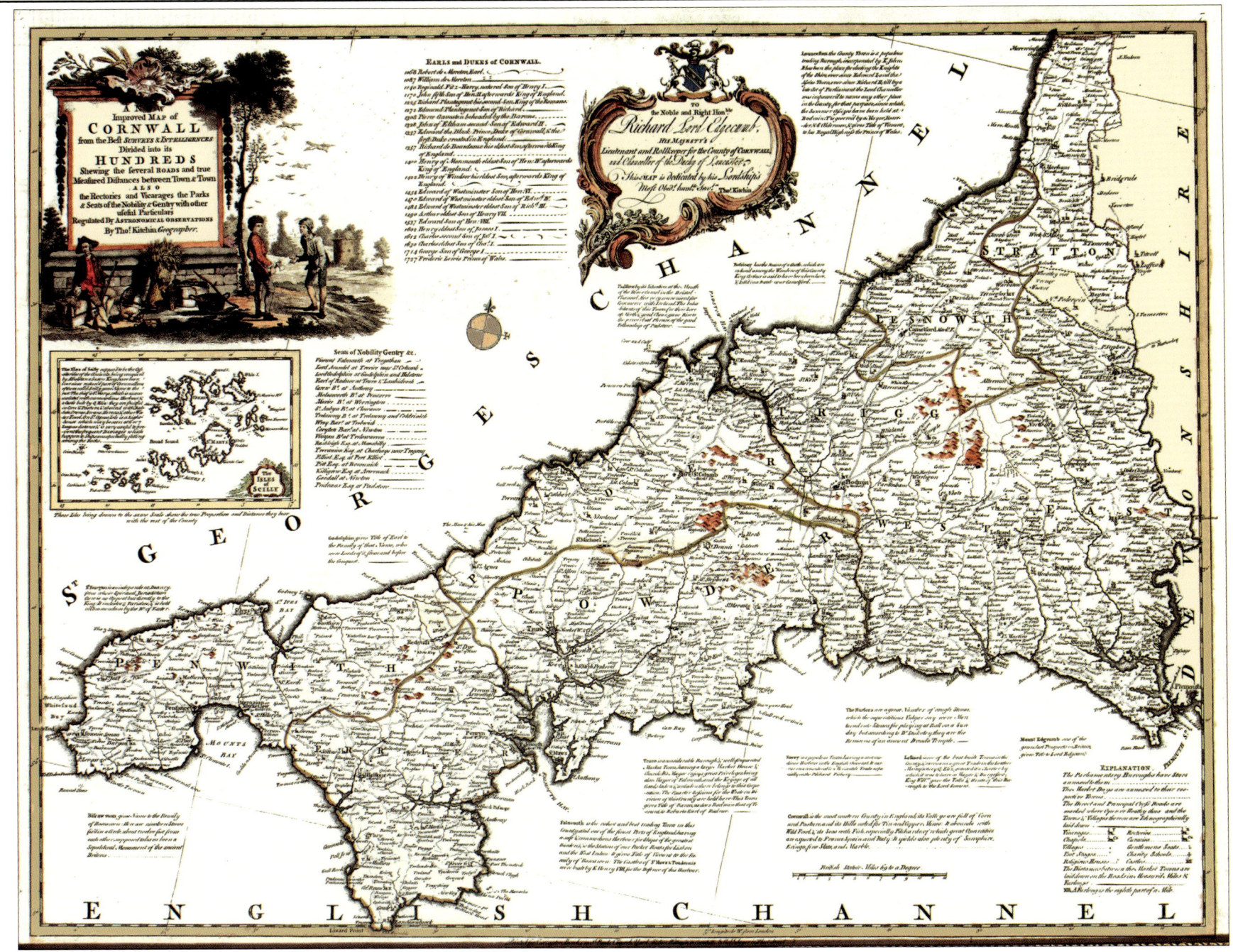

39.2 Kitchin 1779 The Large English Atlas by Emanuel Bowen And Thomas Kitchin, London.

coat of arms surmounts the cartouche itself. The most remarkable feature of the map is the inclusion of a vast quantity of information in the spaces around the county outline, without making the map at all difficult to read. (A reduced version of this map was engraved by Emanuel Bowen (#30) and was published in the 'Royal English Atlas' by Bowen and Kitchin in 1764). The Isles of Scilly are again included in an inset, and the degrees of **latitude and longitude west from London are carried right across the map.**

1749-60 The Large English Atlas: Or, A New set of maps of all the Counties in England and Wales... by Emanuel Bowen, Geographer to His Majesty, Thomas Kitchin and others. Printed and sold by T. Bowles in St. Paul's Church-Yard; John Bowles and Son at the Black Horse, in Cornhill; John Tinney, at the Golden Lion, and Robert Sayer, at the Buck, both on Fleet Street. London, 1760 Reprints 1762, 1763, 1764, 1767, 1779, 1787.

1764 ENGLAND ILLUSTRATED
Eng. Kitchin, Pubs. R & J Dodsley
(248 x 184)

In October 1763 Robert and James Dodsley announced the impending publication of 'England Illustrated ...'. The first of twelve parts was issued in December that year (but dated 1764). Cornwall appears as the 6th county map in Volume 1; there is no visible plate number on the map itself. The whole atlas notes that Kitchin was Geographer and Engraver to HRH the Duke of York, and in general terms its form is like that of its predecessors. The Cornwall map is drawn to a scale of 1 inch to 10 miles, with 69 British Statute miles to a degree of latitude. The county is set so the border with Devon is parallel with the right margin, though the county does spill into all four borders. The map still has a decorative cartouche, but it is less ornate and lacks the figures that had appeared in the two earlier maps, though the Isles of Scilly inset is still present, as are the lines of latitude and longitude. In line with other maps of the period, Kitchin's longitude line of 5° West is 20 minutes too far east. The co-ordinates of Penzance and Hugh Town can be read 50° 5' North, 6° 8' West and 49° 55' North, 7° 10' West, respectively. The distance between the two towns by Kitchin's scale is almost 48 miles – today this is 37 miles. The difference must be due to a shortfall in the number of miles allocated to one degree of longitude, (the offset of latitude between the two is only 10', on today's maps it is 12'), yet one degree of longitude read off the map at a latitude of 50° North corresponds to 42.8 miles, (today this is 44.5 miles). One obvious solution is that the Isles of Scilly are located incorrectly with respect to Cornwall: the error in **miles to one degree of longitude is insufficient to explain the 11 mile error.**

1764 England Illustrated, Or, A Compendium of the Natural History, Geography, Topography and Antiquities Ecclesiastical and Civil of England and Wales...In Two Volumes. Printed for R. & J. Dodsley in Pall Mall. London.

1765 England Illustrated Or, A complete set of maps of all the Counties of England and Wales... By Thomas Kitchin, Geographer to HRH the Duke of York, London. Printed for J Dodsley in Pall-Mall.

1769 POCKET ATLAS
Eng. Kitchin, Pub. Kitchin
(356 x 279)

The 1769 pocket atlas is an interesting publication for Kitchin introduces a novel idea to the discipline of county mapping: The maps of the counties of England and Wales would be drawn to the same scale. In order to achieve this, Kitchin needed to re-base old maps or find a solution to a self-imposed problem. All preceding maps had been drawn at various scales to fit a page and could not be used – the solution was to take a single map of England and Wales and re-scale each county drawn thereon as separate maps, this could have been done either using a pantograph or the squares method. The resulting maps derived from his 1752 map of England and Wales on four sheets are drawn at a scale of about 1 inch to 7¼ miles. Hodson suggests that this may well have been something of an experiment for Kitchin to which he did not place too much time or effort.

The Cornwall map, published therefore in 1769, is lacking in all the decorative work and marginal text that characterized his earlier maps, and there is no inset of the Isles of Scilly. However, the shape is good and the place-names clear and readable, the lettering varying with the importance of the town concerned. In all the maps, the name Newland is given both at Newlyn and Newlyn East, and in reference to the point the map by de la Rochette (#47) and Hatchett (#49) have the same version of the name at Newlyn. The source of this mistake in spelling is Gasgoyne's map of 1700 (#25). The only piece of information left in the sea is a brief set of remarks or legend detailing the symbols in use for Borough towns, market towns &c. At the top right outside the border is the plate number, 12. The maps in the atlas are arranged in full alphabetical order with a general map of England and Wales first, then Angelsea, Brecknockshire &c.

1769   Kitchin's Pocket Atlass of the Counties of South Britain or England and Wales, Drawn to ONE scale... Printed for the author T. Kitchin Engraver, Map and Printseller, No 59 Holborn Hill and J. Gapper, Map and Printseller, No 56 New Bond Street, London.

1778 BOWLES'S POCKET ATLAS
Eng. Kitchin / Unknown, Pub. Bowles

Carington Bowles' father, John ran a print shop in Cheapside before moving to Cornhill in 1733. He apprenticed Carington in 1741 and took him as a partner presumably at the end of this apprenticeship in about 1748. They operated as John Bowles & Son until Carington took over the business of his uncle Thomas Bowles II sometime around 1764 three years before Thomas died. The Bowles family had been in the printing trade for at least three generations and it was carried forwards by Carington's son (Henry) Carington Bowles who later went into partnership with Samuel Carver until 1822. The Bowles family had by that stage been involved with printing for about 130 years and can be found associated with many of the maps here.

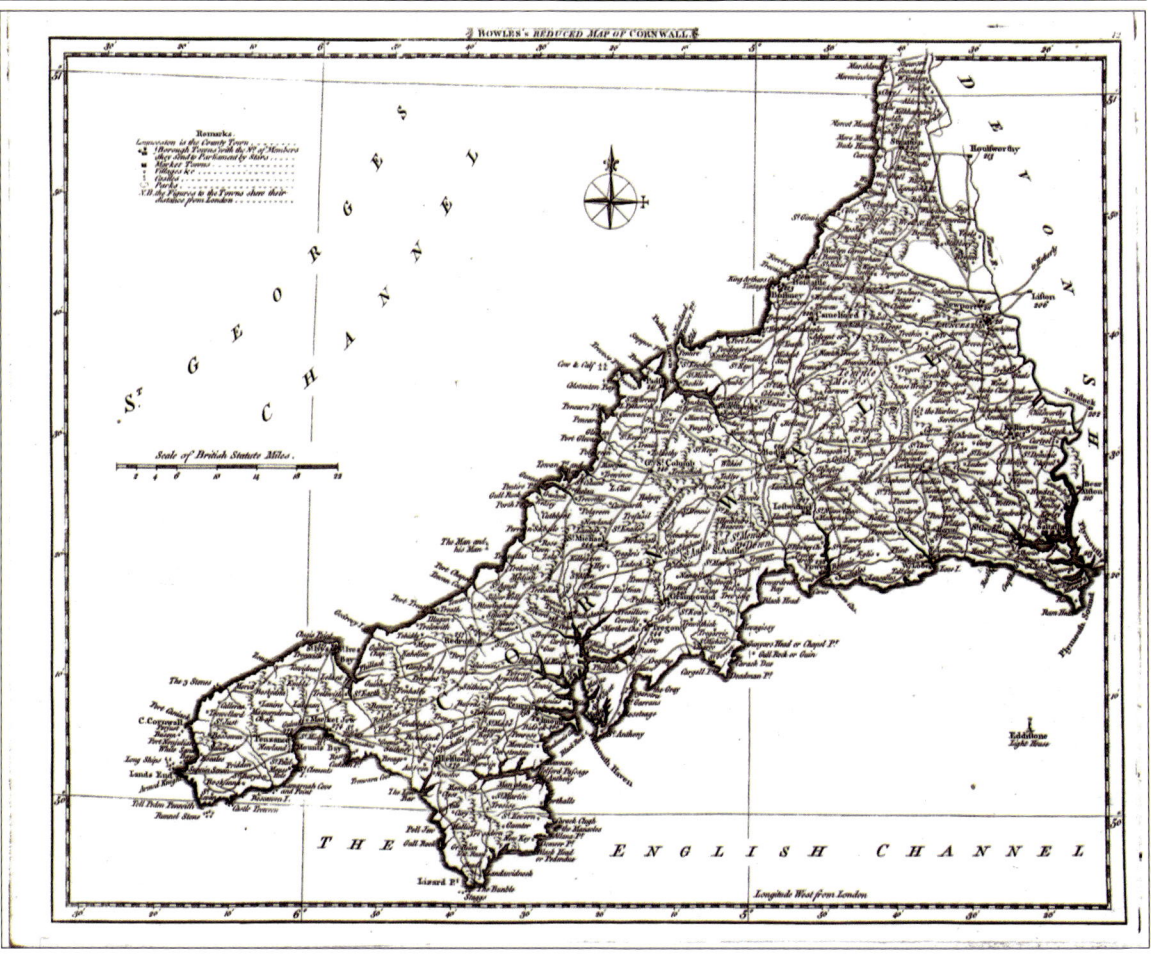

Kitchin's plates were acquired by Carington Bowles in 1775, he re-issued them under the title "Bowles's Pocket Atlas" in 1778. The Cornwall map is a re-work of the 1750 plate and the later 1769 Pocket Atlas. This and the Bowen 1777 map are almost identical. Bowles retitled the imprint above the top border reading 'Bowles Reduced Map of Cornwall'.

39.3 Bowles 1778
Bowles's Pocket Atlas of the Counties of South Britain or England and Wales.

1778   Bowles's Pocket Atlas of the Counties of South Britain or England and Wales...Being the only set of Counties ever published on this plan. Printed for & Sold by the Proprietor Carington Bowles, No 69 in St. Paul's Church Yard.

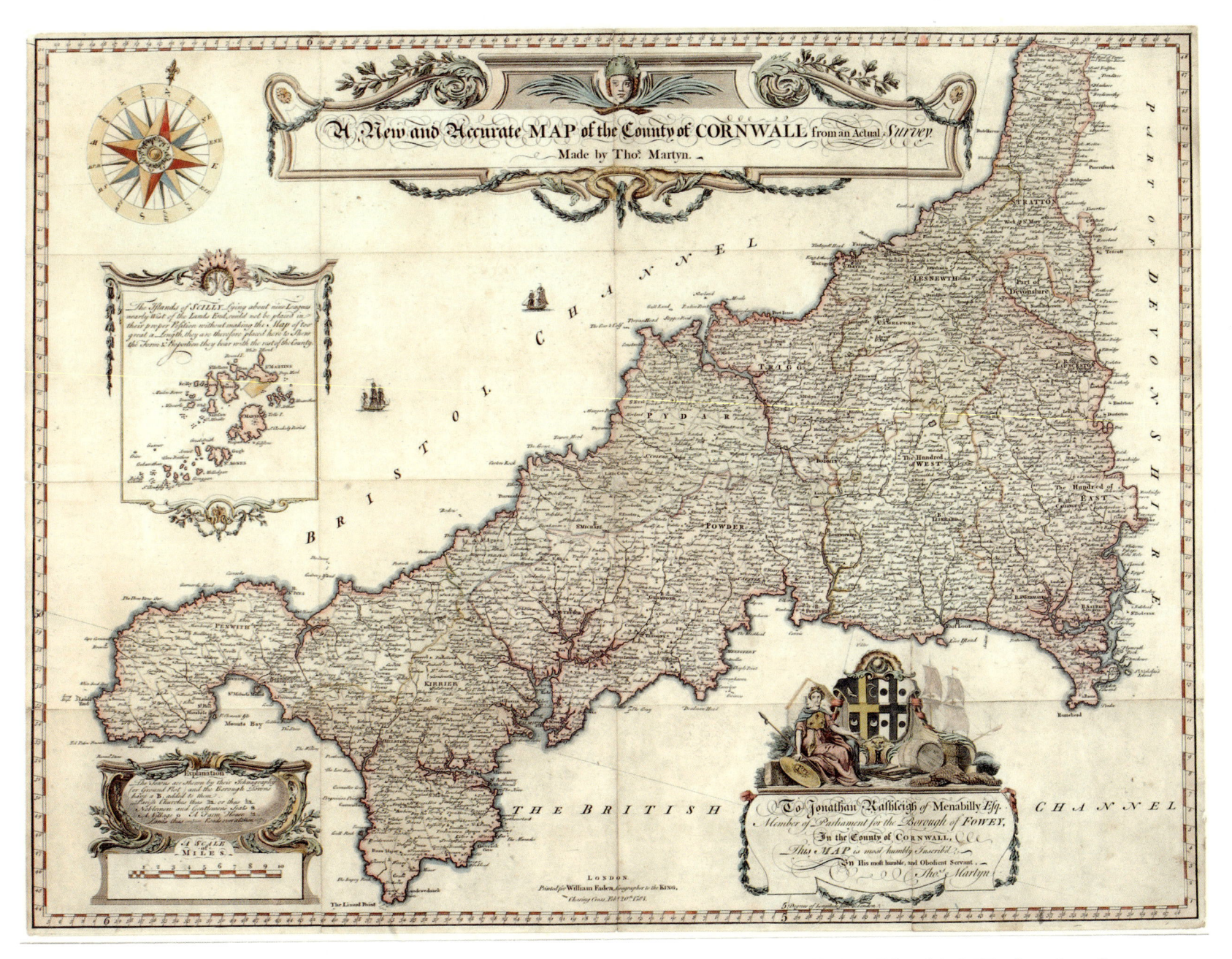

40. Martyn 1784 New and Accurate Map of The County of Cornwall, (Rashleigh). W Faden, London

40. MARTYN, THOMAS 1748, 1749 & 1784

1748 Eng. Unknown, Pub. Sayer (1778 x 1422)

1749 Eng. Unknown, Pub. Sayer also Faden (692 x 464)

1784 Eng. Unknown, Pub Fadden (991 x 699)

Thomas Martyn (1695-1751) was a Cornishman, born in Gwennap and baptised 22 March 1695. His parents, John and Leah, had eventually seven children and lived for some time at Little Trevince, near Gwennap. This is in the middle of the Redruth – St. Day mining area and many of the Martyn family were involved in that industry. Another growing influence at the time were the Methodist sermons of John Wesley, who, over about 50 years, visited Cornwall frequently. One of his favourite places was Gwennap Pit (near Busveal, 3km north-west of Gwennap). Thomas Martyn's older brother's grandson, Henry (1781-1812), would be strongly influenced by this and became a leading missionary in India and Persia, until his death. From about 1730 Martyn was engaged in surveying various Cornish estates, such as the Manor of St. Ewe (1732) and the Manor of Tolverne (1735). Rather like Gasgoyne before him, this led to surveying the whole county on foot, which, according to Daniel Lysons (#61), took him some 15 years to complete. There are no records of a wife or family and Thomas Martyn died on Christmas Day 1751, 'a stranger' in Ashburton, Devon, while working on a survey of Devon.

In 1748 Martyn completed a full survey of his native county and issued his 1 inch to 1 mile map of Cornwall. Hand-coloured copies of the map were available to subscribers at three guineas each, a considerable sum of money in those days, but the beauty and accuracy of the map made it well worth the price.

Since Gasgoyne had already produced a large-scale map of the county in 1700 (#25), it might be supposed that Martyn's work was little more than copying from the previous survey. However, a close comparison of the two maps shows that Martyn's map is the result of a much more thorough survey, in which practically every cove and headland was painstakingly examined, every road and lane minutely surveyed. Other significant features demonstrate Martyn's originality - St. Michael's Mount is shown in plan, with a small elevation view, whereas Gasgoyne indicated the Mount by a crude side view only. Martyn's method of showing hills is interesting: he is the only map-maker to show Brown Willy and Rough Tor as granite tors with rugged outlines and clitter slopes. Martyn gives the correct spelling of Newlyn (as against Gasgoyne's 'Newland') and gives both St. Day and St. Dye as alternative spellings of that place name. Martyn's map was printed on seven large sheets and two small ones, often mounted as one flat map, or mounted on canvas to be folded and stored in a case. It is dedicated to His Royal Highness Frederick Lewis, Prince of Wales, elder son of George II. Frederick was fated never to ascend to the throne, the succession passing to his son, who became George III. Above the dedication are the Royal Hanoverian Arms and below is a cartouche in which a female figure, holding a shield bearing the Cornish Arms, is placed between two god-like figures representing the Fal and Tamar. The coats of arms of numerous gentry, 146 of whom subscribed to the map, fill spaces in the four corners of the map, and provide not only decoration, but also a useful guide to the noble families of Cornwall at the time.

It is worthy of note that the large-scale maps by Gasgoyne (#25) and Martyn preceded the large-scale maps of other counties by many years, (Rocque's Shropshire, Middlesex, Berkshire and Surrey, are dated 1752 to 1768, while Donn's Devon was printed in 1765). In 1759 the newly-formed Society of Arts offered an annual award for an accurate survey of any English county on a scale of 1 inch to 1 mile, and it seems unfortunate that Gasgoyne and Martyn did not qualify for an award. Benjamin Donn's map of Devonshire was the first to win the prize, and its plainer style and more scientific approach were to set a new standard in cartography.

The inch to a mile map was printed on nine large sheets: such is the size of the original map, segments have been seen in auction as stand-alone maps. The map intact is a rare item indeed.

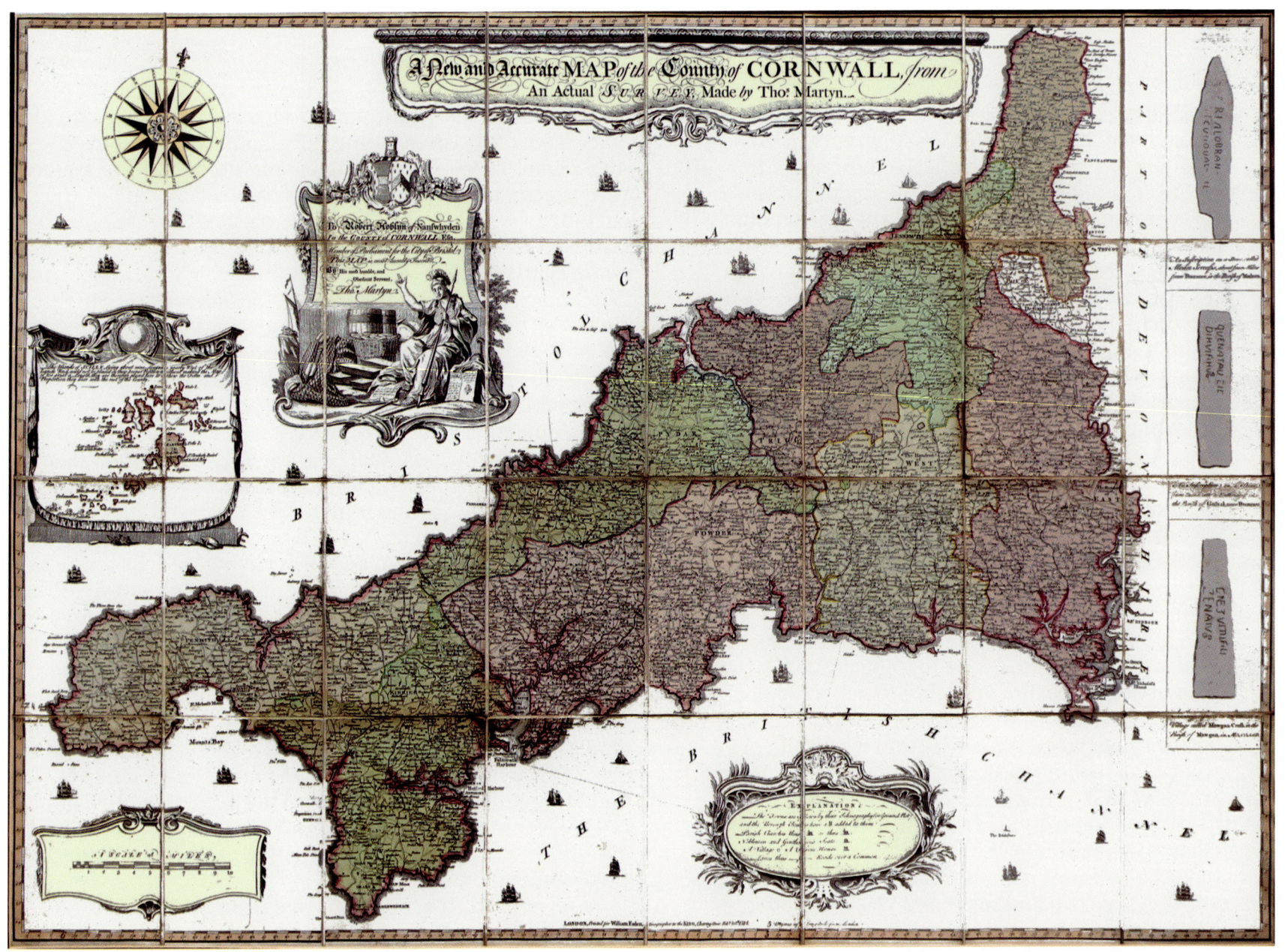

40.1 Martyn 1784 New and Accurate Map of The County of Cornwall, (Hoblyn). W Faden, London

1748 *New and accurate map of the County of Cornwall, from an actual survey. Sold by Robert Sayer, Fleet Street. Published according to Act of Parliament, Nov. 26, 1748. Scale: 1 mile to 1 inch. Re-issued by William Faden, who added his imprint bottom right 'LONDON, Printed for William Faden, Geographer to the KING, Charing Cross Feby 20th 1784'.*

The second map, measuring 690mm x 465mm, appeared in 1749; in effect, it is a scaled down version of the first map, with a dedication to Jonathan Rashleigh of Menabilly. The peripheral decorations have almost entirely been re-worked: the four blocks of coats of arms of the sponsoring families have been removed, and even the compass rose has been replaced, improved and repositioned. The inset border of the Isles of Scilly has been redrawn and improved. On balance, the 1749 version is a better balanced, de-cluttered and more pleasing map – more so for being of a more manageable size. A comparison of this map will give some idea of the differences between the work of Martyn and that of Gasgoyne, on which Kitchin's map is based. The map was re-issued by Faden following his purchase of the plates in 1783 – Faden inserted his own imprint at the base of the map: 'LONDON, Printed for William Faden, Geographer to the KING, Charing Cross Feby 20th 1784'.

1749 *A new and accurate map of the County of Cornwall from an actual survey made by Thos. Martyn, Lond., printed for and sold by Robert Sayer 1748-1749. Scale: ⅜ inch to 1 mile.*

1784 *Another edition printed for Wm. Faden, Scale: ⅜ inch to 1 mile. Reprinted: 1784.*

The third and last of Martyn's maps is on a scale of about ½ inch to 1 mile and is another plate based on the original survey. The coastal outline and geographies of the three maps are similar, but not identical. Notwithstanding this, the embellishments surrounding the three maps are sufficiently different to make identification straight-forward.

The 1784 version is dedicated to Robert Hoblyn (1710–1756), MP for Bristol and FRS. This is curious – Hoblyn had been dead almost 30 years before the date imprinted at the foot of the map. Since Martyn had died in 1751, one must assume that this third map had been completed by Martyn at some time in the late 1740s, but, for whatever reason, he did not publish it. We might consider that the three maps were engraved from the one survey at about the same time. None are signed by the engraver, who remains unknown. There are some slight differences in the cartographic content but they are only that.

Martyn's Hoblyn map is about 50% larger than the second map (dedicated to Rashleigh). While it is similar cartographically, it is not a copy, yet some elements of the former have been ported onto the latter – the delightful compass rose in particular. The right side of the map has been extended into Devon and used to illustrate three mênhirs or standing stones. The first stone, the Mên Scryfa, lies between Madron and Morvah, near Penzance. The second, the Bleu Bridge Inscribed Stone, is near a footbridge in Barlowena Bottom, Gulval. The final stone is in Mawgan Cross, in Kerrier. All three are probably from the 6th century, commemorating fallen Romano-Celtic chieftains or kings, about whom little is really known.

As with the other two maps, Faden has added his inscription at the base of the map: 'LONDON, Printed for William Faden, Geographer to the KING, Charing Cross Feby 20th 1784'.

1784 *A New and Accurate MAP of the County of CORNWALL from an Actual SURVEY by Thos Martyn. Dedicated to Robert Hoblyn, of Nantswhyden. Pub. William Faden, Charing Cross, London.*

41. KITCHIN, THOMAS & JEFFERYS, THOMAS 1749, 1775

1749 Eng. Kitchin, Pubs Kitchin & Jefferys (114 x 121)
1775 Eng. Kitchin, Pubs Sayer, Bennett, J. Bowles & C. Bowles (114 x 121)

'The Small English Atlas' was first published in 13 weekly parts, by a publishers' consortium, from November 1748. This nine-member consortium is mentioned in the advert which coincided with Issue 1. The title page was issued in the 13th part in early 1749, and by this stage only Payne is left. In the intervening time, Kitchin and Jefferys have gained some control of the publication, probably by simple virtue of capacity. Cornwall was issued, along with Surrey, Berkshire and Suffolk, in late November 1748 (Hodson, Vol. II p59).

Thomas Jefferys (c.1719-1771) is noted previously as one of the later re-publishers of Saxton's map (#1). He was apprenticed to Emanuel Bowen in 1735, and through him became associated with Thomas Kitchin. Jefferys became Geographer to the Prince of Wales in about 1746, yet this is not mentioned in the atlas until the 1751 edition. Much of Jeffery's output postdates this joint publication, and in particular, maps of the New World.

'Cornwall' is a small but informative map, in which the influence of Kitchin may be seen in the included marginal text. Penzance and Market Jew (Marazion) are written up in the top left corner, with details of market days. Information about other towns is given below the border. The map of Cornwall is slightly cramped and appears compressed horizontally. The island off the coast at Looe is shown as 'St. Michael's Is.'. Longitude is given from (St. Paul's Cathedral) London. The distance from London to Launceston is shown (212 miles), and the inter-town distances within the county are also shown. The first edition (1748) contains no plate numbers. At some point in time during the lifetime of this edition, and implemented unevenly, plate numbers were added. However, even within the 1751 edition, there are numberless maps. Cornwall and Isles of Scilly may have had plate numbers added comparatively late enough for them to be considered a 1751 addition, rather than a 1749 one.

The Isles of Scilly is shown in the atlas as a separate plate to Cornwall, and marks 'Porthhellick' where Sir Cloudesley Shovell's body was thrown up following the wreck of *HMS Association*, in 1707. In the text below the map it notes, incorrectly, that the Isles of Scilly are 60 miles from Land's End. From the two maps of Cornwall and Isles of Scilly we can read that the longitude west of St. Paul's to Hugh Town is 7° 5' and to Land's End it is 6°. In fact, both these are wrong, even corrected to present day Greenwich from St. Paul's, (a difference of 5'). Hugh Town (from Greenwich) is 6° 18'; Land's End is 5° 43' - a difference of 35', compared to the map's difference of 1° 5'!

1749 *The Small English Atlas being a New and Accurate sett of maps of all the counties in England and Wales, London. Publish'd according to the Act of Parliam^t by Messrs Kitchin and Jefferys 1749, London. Sold by M. Payne at the White Hart and M. Cooper at the Globe in Paternoster Row.*

1751 *New Edition: The Small English Atlas...Publish'd according to the Act of Parliamen^t by Messrs Kitchin and Jefferys 1751 and sold by Thomas Jefferys, Geographer to his Royal Highness the Prince of Wales at the corner of St. Martin's Lane, Charring Cross, by Mr George Faulkner in Essex Street, Dublin. A Paris chez le S^r le Rouge Ingenieur Geographe du Roy de France. Plate numbers added - Cornwall is 10, Isles of Scilly is 52.*

The 1775 Cornwall map is essentially the 1751 edition though there are some small changes both to the map and the text below it. The detail concerning Penzance and Market Jew has been removed from the sea area of the map and inserted in with the other text below the map. The area still contains remnants of the engraving that are just visible. A number of additional roads have been drawn onto this edition. Major (double line) roads have been added from Lostwithiel - Camelford - Stratton, St. Ives - St. Just, Launceston - Liskeard and Truro - Penryn. The Hundreds have been marked with dotted lines, though nothing on the page

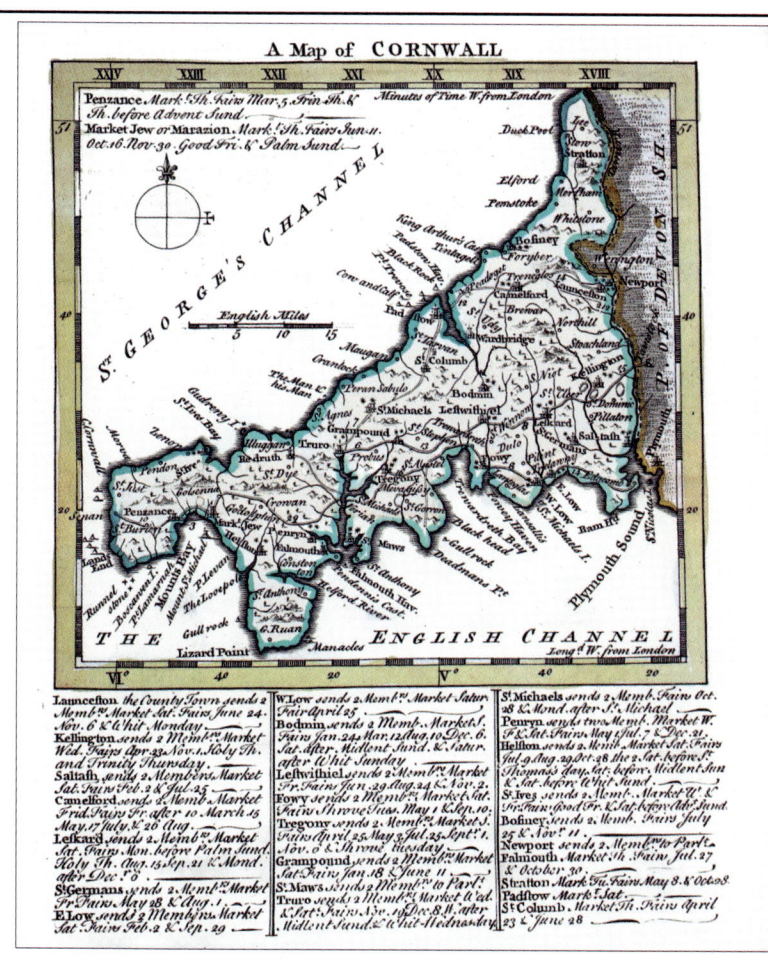

41. Kitchin & Jefferys 1749 *The Small English Atlas, London*

41.1 Kitchin & Jefferys 1775 *The Small English Atlas, London*

details this. The only other addition to the 1775 map is a small note indicating a section (a) belonging to Devon – this refers to the Cremyll area, a small piece of land opposite Plymouth.

The text below the 1775 map has been reset, previously the towns were ordered in a slightly haphazard way with Launceston at the top. The new version deals with the towns in alphabetical order and has added St. Austell, Redruth and Wadebridge. The table has been updated re: fairs, market days &c. No later alterations to the Cornwall map are known.

1775 *The Small English Atlas by T Jefferys, Geo to the King and Thos Kitchin Snr, London. Printed for Robert Sayer and John Bennett, No 53 in Fleet Street, John Bowles, No 13 in Cornhill and Carington Bowles, No 69 in St. Pauls Churchyard.*

1776 *An English Atlas: Or, A Concise View of England And Wales…On 52 plates. Published as the Act directs 1 Aug 1776 Printed for Robert Sayer & Jno Bennett. Map and Printsellers.*

1787 *Re-issued and published as the Act directs 1 Augt 1787 Printed for Robt Sayer No 53 in Fleet Street.*

1794 *Re-issued and published 12th May 1794 by Laurie & Whittle, 53 Fleet Street, London.*

1796 *Re-issued and published 12th May 1796 by Laurie & Whittle, 53 Fleet Street, London.*

Antique Maps of Cornwall and the Isles of Scilly

42. BICKHAM, GEORGE (Snr & Jnr) 1750, 1796

1750 Eng. Bickham Jnr, Pub Bickham Snr (140 x 229)
1796 Eng. Bickham Jnr, Pub. Laurie & Whittle (140 x 229)

George Bickham senior (1684-1758) was a famous engraver, who produced various books demonstrating his elegant calligraphy. On 1 October 1743 he advertised 'The British Monarchy: Or, a new chronographical description of all the dominions subject to the King of Great Britain', which would later carry 48 maps and 180 copperplate illustrations. The maps were engraved by his son, also George (c.1706-1771). These are very curious indeed: they take the form of bird's eye perspective views with the county shown in relief as if it were from some neighbouring eminence. 'The British Monarchy' was published in monthly parts, from 1743 to about 1749. The Bickhams then re-issued it in two-weekly parts from the end of 1749, bound into two volumes (1751 and 1755) - in this were included the county maps.

The section dealing with Cornwall commences on p41 (Volume 1), with the arms of Launceston heading the page. The county maps appear to have been produced later (1750), with the intent of inserting them into the county sections later - in the top right of the Cornwall map is the note: 'After page 41'. At the foot of the map under the distances table are the words 'Published according to Act of Parliament 1750'; opposite this is the script 'G. Bickham Ju Insc'.

The map of Cornwall shows, in the foreground, a horseman with a dog, a goat and other animals beneath a large tree on a hillside, while in the middle distance is a stream (presumably the upper course of the Tamar), beyond which the county stretches away into the distance, Land's End being on the horizon near the top of the page.

The first issue was entitled 'A Map of Cornwall West from London' and dedicated to the Earl of Radnor, with a list of distances between towns below the map; the 1796 edition was simply headed 'Cornwall', with all other matter erased and a plate number top right (6).

Bickham junior died in 1771, and his stock was sold - it may have passed to Robert Sayer, whose stock was bought in 1794 by Robert Laurie and James Whittle.

1750 *The British Monarchy, by George Bickham, James St, Bunhill Fields, London.*
1755 *Title and distances list removed.*
1796 *A Curious Antique Collection of Bird's Eye Views of the Several Counties in England and Wales by George Bickham Jnr. Title replaced and plate number added. Published by Robert Laurie and James Whittle.*

42. Bickham 1750 *The British Monarchy, London*

43. BORLASE, WILLIAM 1754, 1758

1754 Eng. Unknown, Pub Borlase, then Baker, Leigh, Payne and White (267 x 146),
1758 Eng. Unknown, Pub. Borlase (432 x 318)

William Borlase FRS (1696-1772) was born in Pendeen and educated at Exeter College, Oxford. He became Rector of Ludgvan, near Penzance, and later St. Just. Ludgvan was, at the time, a copper mining area and Borlase turned his interest to the natural history of his parish and thence to the county in general. He was admitted to the Royal Society as a Fellow in 1750 and published his 'Antiquities of Cornwall' in 1754.

It was Borlase who, in September 1755, wrote a letter to Henry Baker, a founding member of the Society of Arts, complaining of the lamentable state of British map-making, which led it to offer a reward for county surveys. The Society launched a map-making competition in 1759, with a prize of £100. The objective was to map the country at 1 inch to a mile, county by county, and 'join' the maps together. The final, and flawed, caveat was the stipulation that the map(s) should be completed within two years: Benjamin Donn started his survey of Devon shortly thereafter, but did not complete it until 1765, and took the prize. Thomas Martyn (#40) had produced a 1 inch to 1 mile map in 1748, but would not have been eligible, since his map had been completed ahead of the launch of the competition. The Society of Arts closed the competition in 1802 with the advent of the Ordnance Survey, which brought the rigour of a military establishment to the process. Borlase could be credited, one could argue, for suppling the germ of an idea that led to modern, standardised mapping.

Borlase's map is quite plain and shows the Isles of Scilly at about the correct distance from Land's End; the left margin is marked in minutes up to 50° North, and 5° West longitude from London is also shown. Below the title 'Map of the County of Cornwall and the Scilly Islands' is a brief key explaining the symbols used for ancient castles, Roman coins and Roman roads, as well as more recent castles, rivers and harbours. The Hundreds are labelled and the boundaries are very faintly drawn. There are a limited number of places indicated on the map – aside from Carn Brea, near Camborne, no other physical features are shown. In outline, the map is loosely similar to Martyn's 1748 map – Borlase sets his 5° West of London at the same place as Martyn.

The second map (1758) is larger, shows the Scilly Islands inset and has more detail and information generally. It is easily identified by the inclusion of a line marking the 'Latitude of Liskeard'.

Overall, the maps are of local interest, being one of two drawn by Cornishmen – of the two, Borlase's is perhaps the less accomplished.

1754   Observations on the Antiquities of Cornwall, by William Borlase, AM, FRS. Printed by W. Jackson in the High Street, Oxford.
1769   Second Edition used the larger map from the 1758 book. Printed by W. Bowyer and J. Nichols for S. Baker and G. Leigh, T. Payne and B. White, London.
1758   The Natural History of Cornwall, by William Borlase. Printed for the author by W. Jackson and sold by W. Sandby at the Ship in Fleet Street and the booksellers of Oxford.

44. MEIJER, PIETER & SCHENK, LEONARD   1757

Eng. Bowen/L. Schenk, Pub. Meijer
(200 x 175)

Benjamin Martin published a 'General Magazine of Arts and Sciences' in 1754, with maps predominately by Bowen (#30). Pieter Meijer was an Amsterdam publisher – whether he obtained a licence from Martin (unlikely) or simply copied Martin's work and had the maps reproduced by Schenk is debatable. The work produced was called '*Algemeene oefenschoole van konsten en wetenschappen*', or 'General Handbook of Arts and Science', and ran to six parts, with an index volume. Overall the entire project was immense – each part contained several volumes of hundreds of pages each. Part II contained the county maps of England – the rest of Great Britain was omitted, in line with the original Martin volume.

It is likely that Leonard Schenk (1696-1767) was the son of Peter Schenk senior and Gerard Valk's sister, Agnatha (see #28).

The Cornwall map is a mix of English and Dutch. Meijer credits Bowen with the original map in the title cartouche top centre. The Hundreds are listed in a mix of Dutch, where a translation is possible, (*Oost* for East gets translated, most of the others defeat translation and are left in English) and are shown as dotted lines on the map. There are some other Dutch/English challenges on the body of the map: 'Mounts Baai', 'Kaap Lizard' and 'Kamelfort' are but three. Major towns (Burghvlekken) and market towns (Markvlekken) are drawn, along with the three main routes through the county.

The whole county is set with the Devon border parallel to the right margin. Latitude and longitude are shown from London, with Schenk's 5° West line intersecting the Cornwall coast slightly west of Fowey, and a little further east than Bowen's maps. Note the advancing sand dune-like structures covering the map: John Cowley had tried this in 1744 but had limited himself – Schenk was not so restrained.

1757   *Algemeene oefenschoole van konsten en wetenschappen*, by Meijer, Amsterdam.

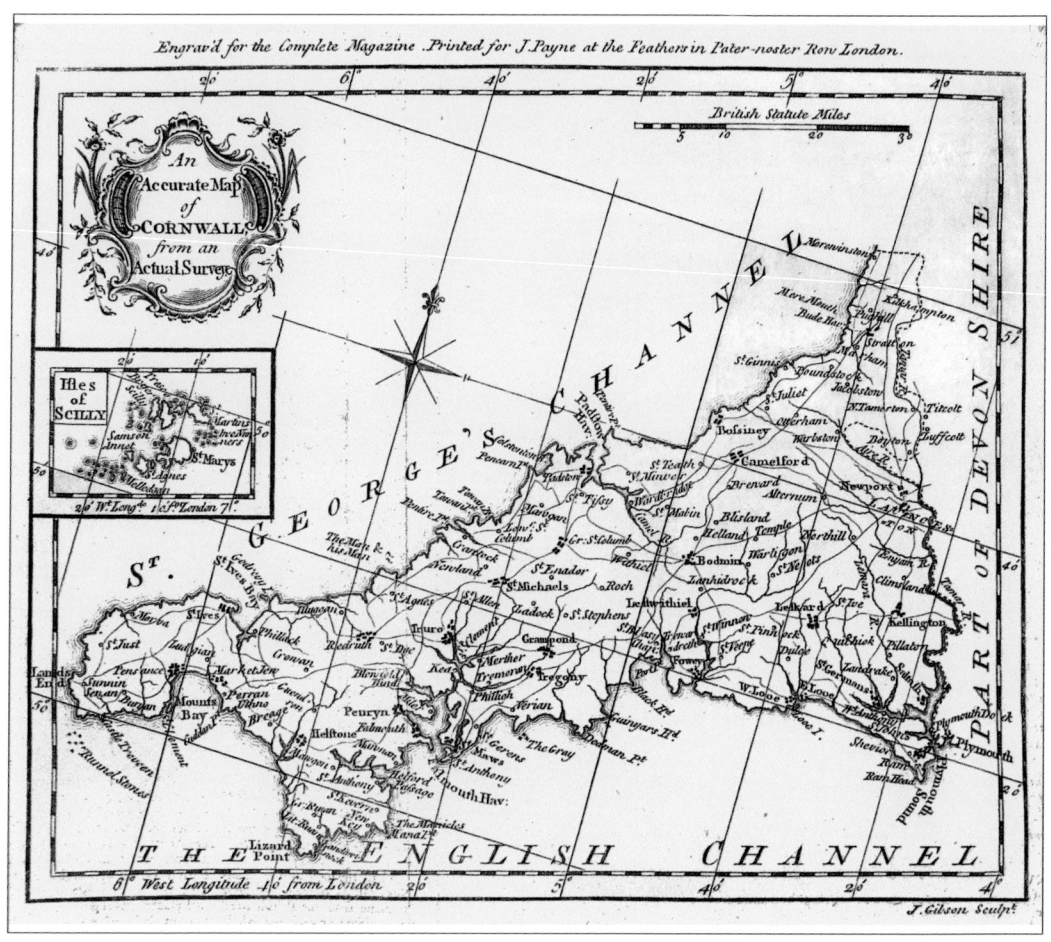

45. Gibson 1762 The Universal Museum and Complete Magazine. Payne. London

Antique Maps of Cornwall and the Isles of Scilly

45. GIBSON, JOHN 1759, 1762

1759 Eng. ?Gibson, Pub. Newberry, Carnan (1780)
(102 x 64)

Gibson (? – 1792) was a prolific engraver: there are hundreds of his maps, in numerous magazines and other publications. In the late 1700s there was a veritable explosion of publications informing the increasingly literate public of all kinds of information, from current affairs to politics, geography and science, and everything in-between. This hunger was fed by the publishers of London and elsewhere, with such magazines as 'Gentleman's Magazine', 'Universal Magazine', 'The Universal Museum' and 'Universal Traveller'. Gibson is perhaps best known individually for his two miniature atlases: Atlas Minimus was published by J. Newberry in 1758 but contained no county maps. Gibson's next atlas, in 1759, presented the 53 counties of England and Wales.

The 1759 Cornwall map has the plate number '7' but has no engraver's name. It is copied from earlier maps of the period, showing rivers, towns, roads, parliamentary representation and latitude and longitude from London.

The detail below the cartouche states: 'Cornwall is in the Diocese of Exeter and is 70 miles long and 40 broad near Devonshire. It contains 26760 houses, 163600 inhabitants, 161 Parishes, 27 Market towns and sends 44 members to Parliament. It is a hilly and rocky County and greatly exposed to winds and storms. It produces corn, cattle and fish but is most remarkable for its tin-mines and commodious harbours.'

Gibson's map of Cornwall (opposite) for the 'Universal and Complete Magazine' was published by John Payne, of Paternoster Row, London, in 1762. A cartouche in the top right proclaims the map to be new and accurate from an actual survey. In fact, this is an outline copy of the 1748 Bowen (#30), with much of the original detail incorrectly transcribed and the decoration missing. Below the cartouche is a simple insert of the Isles of Scilly, with what detail could be fitted into the cramped frame, along with lines of latitude and longitude from London. The main map of Cornwall is, as with several others, canted over so the Devon border runs parallel with the right margin. A scale of British Statue Miles is drawn in the top left of the map, with a simple compass in the centre of the map. After that, things take on a bit of a mix of old and new.

The roads through the county are haphazardly or imaginatively drawn as single lines, with little regard to foregoing maps. There is a non-existent road from St. Ives directly to Sennen, for instance, and the road to Redruth from Penzance has been deleted. Marazion stubbornly remains as 'Market Jew', Coldwind Cross has reverted to 'Blow Cold Wind' and Falmouth is still the lesser cousin of Penryn. Further east we find 'Wardbridge' (Wadebridge) and 'Lestwithiel' (Lostwithiel). The coast of Devon is missing, making Cornwall appear to have been cast adrift.

1759 New and Accurate Maps of the Counties of England and Wales. Pub. John Newberry, London. Thomas Carnan 1780.

1762 The Universal Museum and Complete Magazine of knowledge and pleasure. Pub. J. Payne at the Feathers in Paternoster Row, London.

46. DURY, ANDREW & ELLIS, JOSEPH 1764

Eng. Ellis, Pub. Dury
(121 x 95)

Andrew (André) Dury (fl1742-1778) was possibly a French Huguenot who lived and worked from Duke's Court, off St. Martin's Lane. Little else is known of Dury. His will (PROB11/1039/47-92) makes no mention of wife or children, though Jane Smith, who receives some of the inheritance, could be considered as his common law wife. Of note is his witness, one Aaron Arrowsmith.

The small atlas titled 'A Collection of plans of the principal Cities of Great Britain and Ireland. With maps of the Coast of Said Kingdoms...' was produced in 1764. This was divided in two sections; firstly, a series of plans and maps of coastal regions, and secondly, a series of town plans. The whole atlas was designed as a second volume to the 1761 publication 'A New General and Universal Atlas'; this was engraved by 'Mr (Thomas) Kitchin & Brothers (actually John Bayley, John Ellis, John Gibson and John Spilsbury), and printed for and sold by A. Dury at the Indian Queen in Dukes Court, St. Martin's Lane and by Robt Sayer at the Golden Buck in Fleet Street'.

'The Collection of plans...' is undated; the title page subtitle reads: 'Drawn from the most Accurate Surveys; In particular, those taken by Mr. J. Rocque, topographer to His Majesty'. The presumed date is revealed by the town plan of London listed in the contents: '...this present year 1764'.

The untitled map of Cornwall appears 6th in the first series, as it goes around the coast from Essex/Suffolk (1), Kent, Sussex & Dover (2), Hampshire (3), Isle of Wight (numbered 0 and the only one to have a title on the map), Dorset and Devonshire (4) and then Cornwall (plate 5). The series continues around the coast in a clock-wise manner. Cornwall is loosely based on Rocque's map (#36), and though only three of them (including plate 8, N. Wales) are signed 'Joseph Ellis', it reasonable that he may have done all of them.

A lot of the detail has been stripped out of the interior of the county, and it is little more than a coastal outline, with many coastal points marked - the rivers are marked, but not the hills. Most of the towns in the interior are absent; Launceston is shown in capitals. A note in the index of the maps states that: 'since one degree of latitude equates to 60 "Geographick miles" and contains 69½ British Statute miles and, since this is so well known, no scales are necessary'.

The plan border is marked up with latitude and longitude from London. Note that the longitude minutes are counted off in reverse: thus 5° West of London (which is 20' too far east) should increment by 15' divisions westwards to the 6° West mark - Ellis has counted them off 15-30-45, reading left to right. In line with many preceding maps, the Devon/Cornwall border is set parallel to the right margin. A simple compass rose in the top left is the only decoration.

1764   A Collection of plans of the principal Cities of Great Britain and Ireland. With maps of the Coast of Said Kingdoms..., by A. Dury, Dukes Court, St. Martin's Lane, London. Reprinted 1766 by Andrew Dury and Robert Sayer.

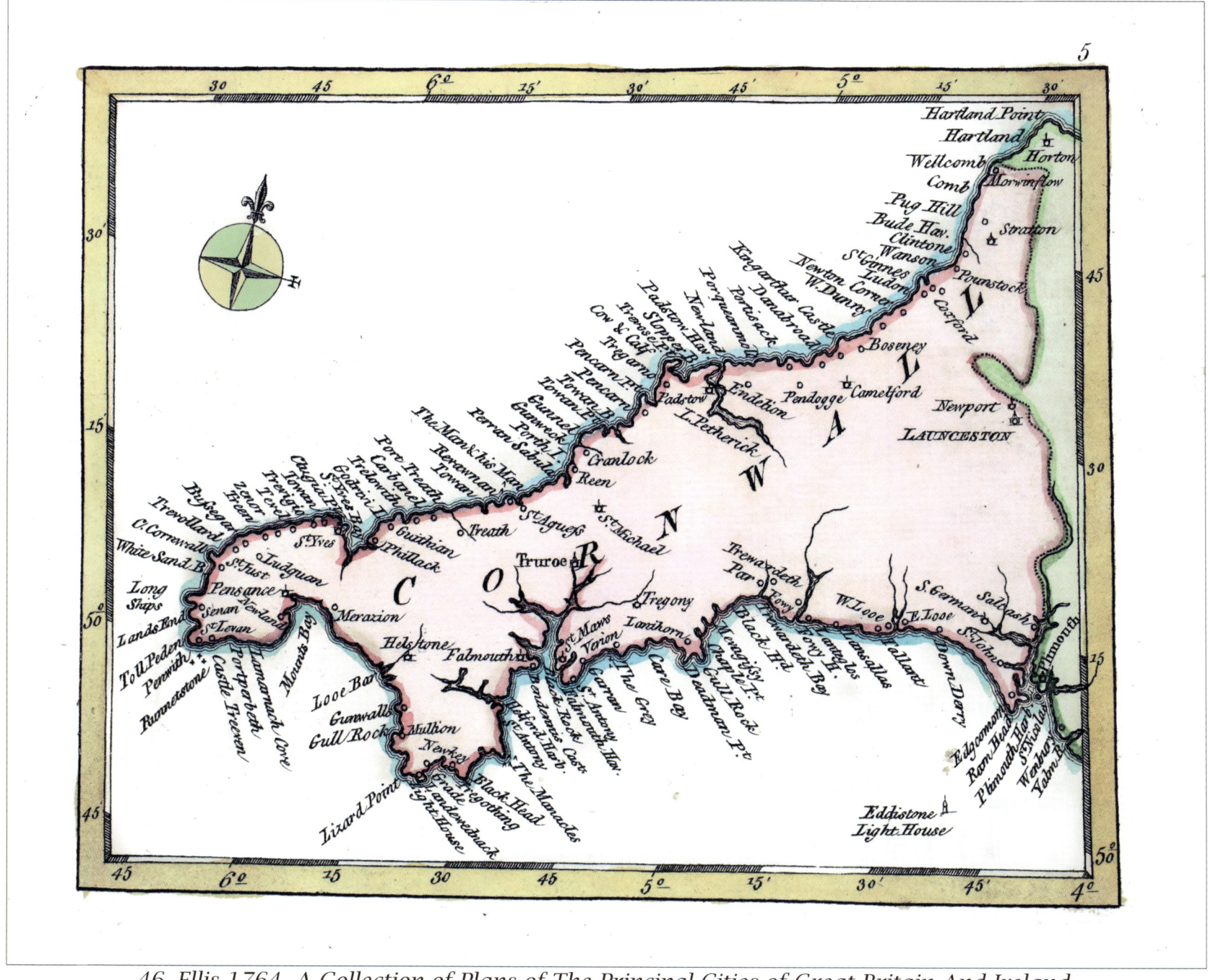

46. Ellis 1764 A Collection of Plans of The Principal Cities of Great Britain And Ireland.

47. DE LA ROCHETTE, LOUIS STANISLAS D'ARCY 1765

Eng. De La Rochette, Pub Ellis
(235 x 197)

D'Arcy De La Rochette (1731-1802) was a French map maker and engraver. He acquired the surname D'Arcy through marriage, sometime around the 1780s: many French references refer to him as D'Arcy De La Rochette. He may have been born in the UK of French Protestant émigrés that escaped France following the Revocation of the Edict of Nantes in 1685. In terms of his professional life, he is often associated with William Faden, with whom he produced several maps and sea charts.

Joseph Ellis published his 'New English Atlas' in 1765 – it is a collection of 54 engraved maps performed by several different engravers. Ellis's name appears on most of them, with some exceptions: William Palmer signed six maps: Buckinghamshire, Herefordshire, Huntingdonshire, Kent and Warwickshire. William Fowler's name is on the Worcestershire map. There are a considerable number unsigned and left as '…by the best authorities'. The atlas was altered the following year, with at least six variants, though thankfully the Cornwall map remains the same throughout. In all volumes, only one map, Cornwall, is signed by De La Rochette, who uniquely excluded a compass rose.

The Cornwall map (plate 11, outside the margin top right) is a fairly decorative map, with title piece in decorative cartouche, very similar in style to the work of Thomas Kitchin. Although it claims to be 'drawn from an actual survey by De La Rochette', it seems to be closely copied from Kitchin's (#39) map, even down to the misspelling of 'Newland' for Newlyn. One remarkable feature is the use of hachures in showing hills, and there is a good display of information, and an inset of a 'Supplement for the Isles of Scilly', together with a brief note concerning the loss of *HMS Association*, in 1707 (see appendices for details). Note also that the island off the coast at Looe is named 'Looe Island'. The map is set onto the page in the same manner as Kitchin's – grid north is straight up the page, although there is no compass rose. 5° West of longitude is, as Kitchin's 1749 map (#39) is, 19' too far east.

In comparison to the almost identical De La Rochette map used by Hatchett (#49), these differences should be noted: the Ellis version contains a map which is not coupled to a map of Devon below– it has a footnote detailing: 'Printed for Robt Sayer in Fleet St. and Carington Bowles in St. Paul's Churchyard'. The cartouche contains the imprint 'By De La Rochette' and suspended from either side of the cartouche are a chain of 'fruit', above the cartouche is a singular large leaf or piece of driftwood. The text of 'British Channel' below Looe is not in italics. There is no shield of the Arms of Launceston. The title for the inset of the Isles of Scilly is set lower on the page. The top-most piece of 'Stratton' extends into the top border, Cape Cornwall is labelled in full and the Devon-Cornwall / Tamar divergencies are shown.

1765   *The New English Atlas being the completest sett of Modern Maps of England and Wales…On fifty-four plates, Published by Robert Sayer and Carington Bowles.*

1766   *Ellis's English Atlas: Or, a Compleat Chorography of England and Wales: in Fifty Maps. Containing More Particulars Than Any Other Collection of the Same Kind … Engraved By, and Under the Direction Of, J. Ellis, Printed for Robert Sayer at the Golden Buck near Serjeants Inn in Fleet Street and Carington Bowles next to the Chapter House in St. Paul's Churchyard, London. Reprints:*

1768   *Published by R. Sayer, T. Jefferys and A. Dury,*
       1773: Published by R. Sayer,

1777   *Published R. Sayer and J. Bennett,*

1786   *Published by Carington Bowles,*

1790   *Published by R. Sayer,*

1790   *Published for Carington Bowles,*

1796   *Published by R. Sayer.*

1766   *Ellis's English Atlas: Or, A Compleat Chorography of England and Wales in 54 maps. Engraved by and under the direction of Joseph Ellis. Printed for Robert Sayer at the Golden Buck near Serjeants Inn in Fleet Street and Carington Bowles next to the Chapter House in St. Paul's Churchyard, London.*
      Reprints: 1768: Published by Carington Bowles.

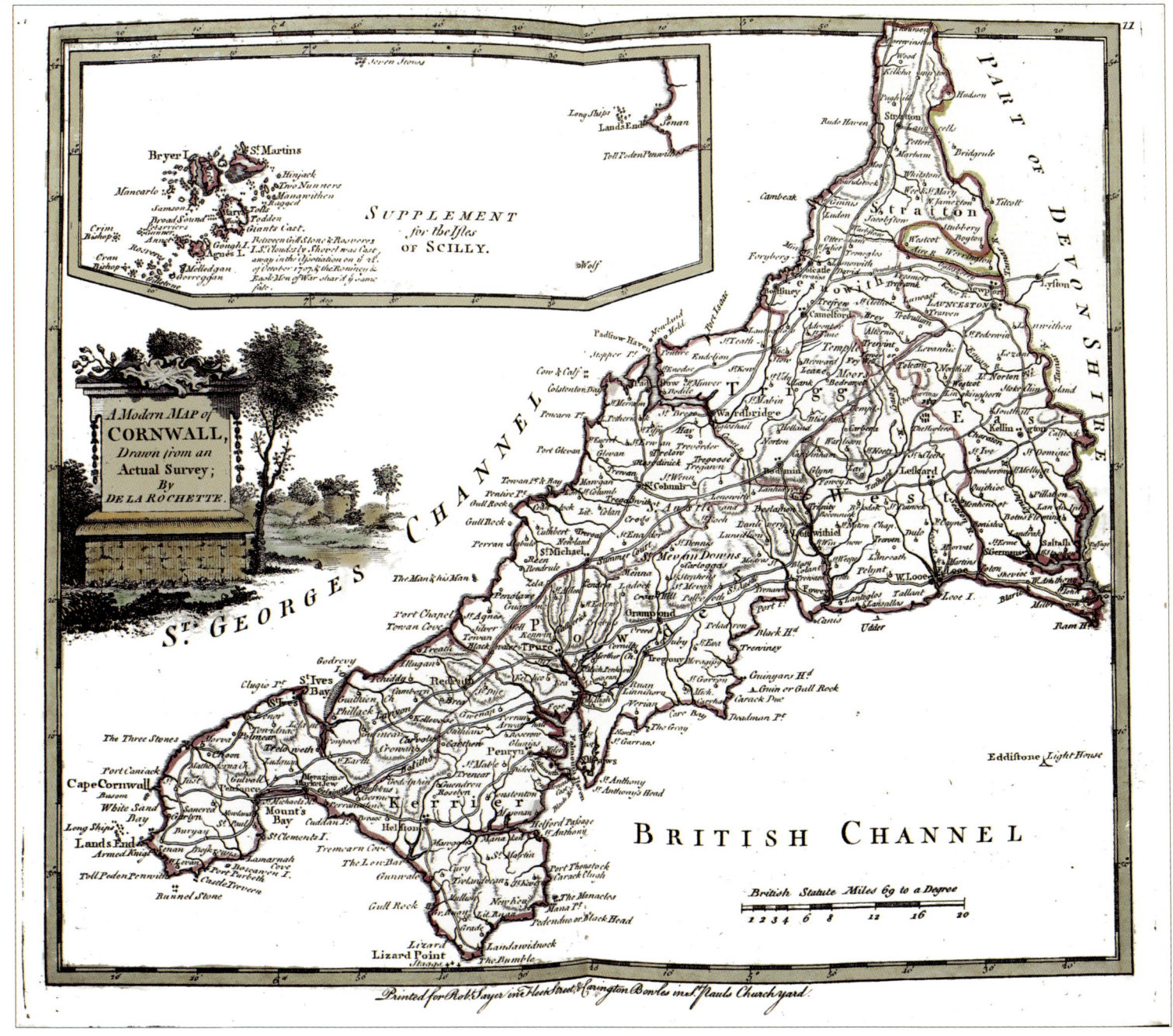

47. De La Rochette 1766 Ellis's English Atlas... J. Ellis, London

48. TOVEY (Jnr), ABRAHAM & GINVER, NICHOLAS 1779

1779 Eng. Uncertain, Pub Sayer & Bennett (625 x 489)
1794 Eng. Uncertain, Pub Laurie & Whittle (625 x 489)
A NEW SEA CHART OF THE ISLANDS OF SCILLY

Abraham Tovey senior died in 1759, the Cornwall Records Office has his will (AP/T/2795). In 1978 a hitherto unknown chart of the Isles of Scilly by Nicholas Ginver came to light (BL ADD MSS 60393), dated 1731. The Ginver chart was never published and was a working update of the Collins chart (#23). The identification of Nicholas Ginver is still something of a mystery, though there are two Scillonian male burial records of this name alive in 1731. Of these, the younger Ginver (died 1754), held the position of Comptroller and Surveyor of Customs, and would appear to be the more likely candidate. With these dates, it is reasonable to presume that Tovey senior, as well as both Ginver senior (died 1736) and junior, were known to each other, but all were dead well before the publication of this chart, in 1779.

Tovey senior had four sons, one of whom was named Abraham (1720-1781). It now seems that it is Tovey junior who published the 1779 chart, with an acknowledgement to the late Nicholas Ginver.

The new chart of 1779 was included in the 'Complete Channel Pilot' by Sayer and Bennett, but the shape of the islands is very similar to the shape used in the Collins chart of 1693 (#23). Nevertheless, there are new features in the chart; the soundings given by Tovey and Ginver are more numerous than those of Collins, and the inclusion of five silhouette views of the islands from various directions must have been a considerable aid to navigation. A small vignette of St. Agnes lighthouse is included at the lower edge of the chart, similar to a small view inserted on Robert Sayer's re-issue of Gerard Van Keulan's chart of 1736 (#32). St. Martin's Flats and Tresco Flats, the areas of sand and mud exposed at low water, are more extensive and of a different shape on the Tovey and Ginver chart, possibly because there had been a cycle of tidal and weather conditions which favoured the growth of sandbanks and mudflats in the 80-odd years since Collins carried out his survey. It is known that the sea level is rising slowly and submerging the Islands at a rate of some four feet every 500 years, so that the accumulation of sand and mud is a temporary feature, very much dependent on the vagaries of wind and weather for the effect it may have on the landscape, and naturally enough the mudflats are very different today.

At Porth Hellick Bay, on the east side of St. Mary's Island, is the legend 'Here the body of Sir Cloudesley Shovell was thrown up and buried; but afterwards taken up by the Purser of the Arundel'. Wrecks were regarded as a source of income by the islanders, and there were many instances of deliberate wrecking, (i.e. luring vessels to their doom by displaying misleading lights on-shore.), both in the Isles of Scilly and along the north coast of Cornwall. It is not surprising, therefore, to hear that a local woman who found the Admiral's body took from it a valuable ring, apparently having bitten off the finger to do so. Having learned that the body was that of an English Admiral, however, she returned the ring to his widow and received a pension for life.

1779 Complete Channel Pilot, by Robert Sayer and John Bennett, London. Reprints: Many reprints during the period 1779 to 1783, when the atlas was being 'assembled'.
1794 Upon the death of Sayer, his business was acquired by Robert Laurie and James Whittle. They re-issued the Channel Pilot with their imprint on the charts.

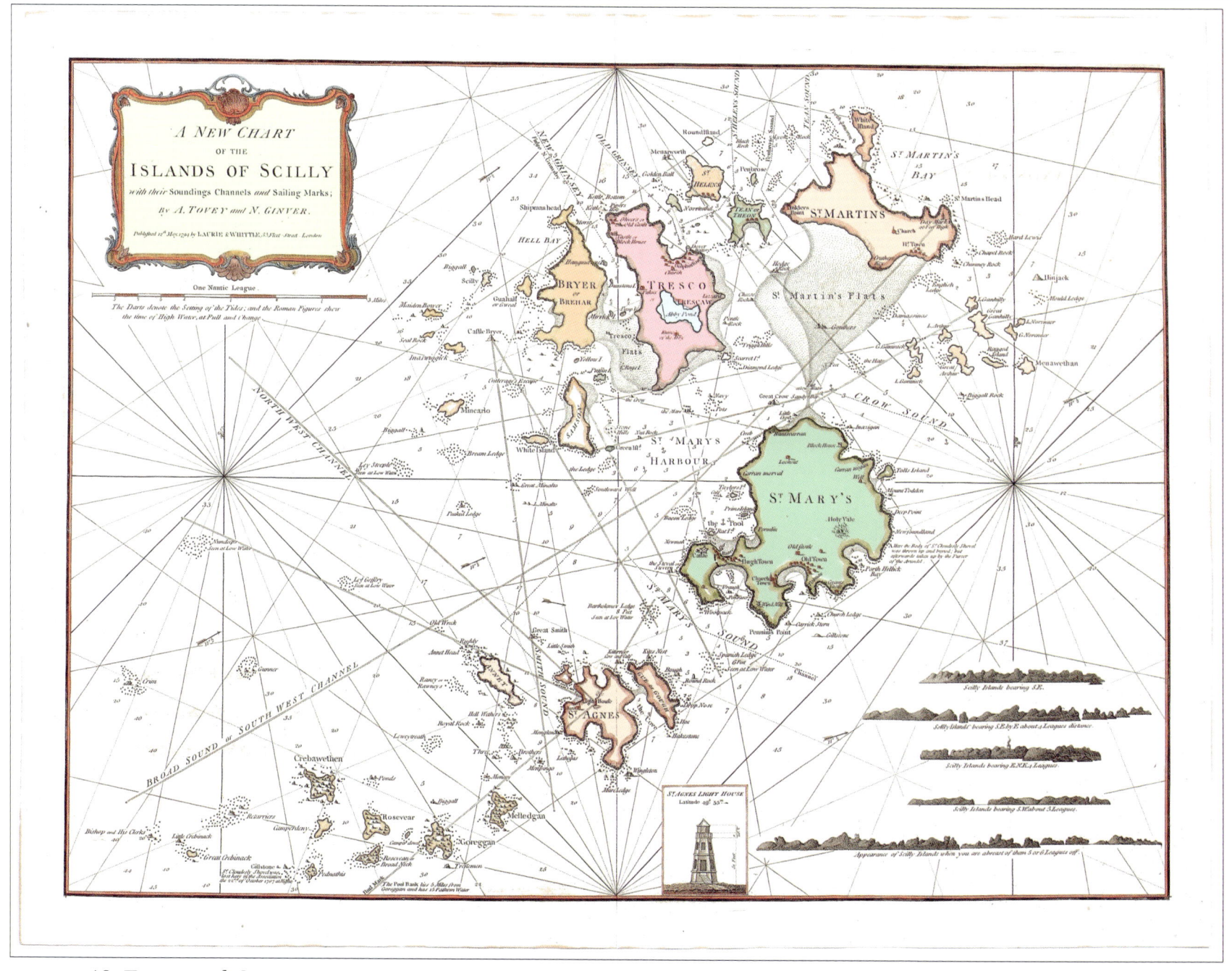

48. Tovey and Ginver 1794   Complete Channel Pilot, Published by Laurie & Whittle. 53 Fleet Street London.

49. "WALPOOLE, GEORGE" & HATCHETT, THOMAS 1784

Eng. Hatchett, Pub. Hogg

(215 x 345)

'The New British Traveller' was produced by Walpoole and published by Alexander Hogg from 1783/4 in 60 weekly parts – these separate pages could be collected and bound later. Hodson (Vol. III, p108) suggests that George Augustus Walpoole may in fact be a pseudonym of Hogg's, (one of several aliases that may have been some form of running joke between himself and rival John Cooke). Both men were notorious part-work publishers not beyond almost anything to turn a profit.

The De La Rochette map (#47) can be used as a cross reference to the following later versions. The Hogg/Walpoole version first appears in a 1784 issue of 'The New British Traveller' and is coupled with Devon below it. The whole page contains scroll work top and bottom, and within the top scroll is the title 'Engraved for Walpoole's New and Complete BRITISH TRAVELLER'. Within the Cornwall cartouche, centre left, is the title 'A Modern Map of CORNWALL, drawn from an original survey by DE LA ROCHETTE'. In the scroll work at the base, below the Devon map, is the sub-title 'Published by ALEX^R HOGG at the King's Arms, N° 16 PATERNOSTER ROW'. The detail surrounding the cartouche, while like #47, is different enough for it to be called a different engraving. The differences extend beyond this into the map body itself as well.

Hatchett's redition of what is evidently De La Rochette's map, with some additional elements taken from Kitchin and Bowen, is a nice, effective and pleasing little map despite the publication shennigans. The map appears reduced in comparison with the De La Rochette map. This gives the impression of the map being more detailed, in fact it is not; there are a few missing towns, Egloshayle near Wadebridge being an obvious example. Much of what differentiates this map from its predecessor lie in the surrounding embellishments. The two maps in their earliest, shield-less states (ignoring the scrollwork on the Walpoole map) are very similar. It is the decoration around the cartouche that differentiates them. The piece of driftwood atop of the

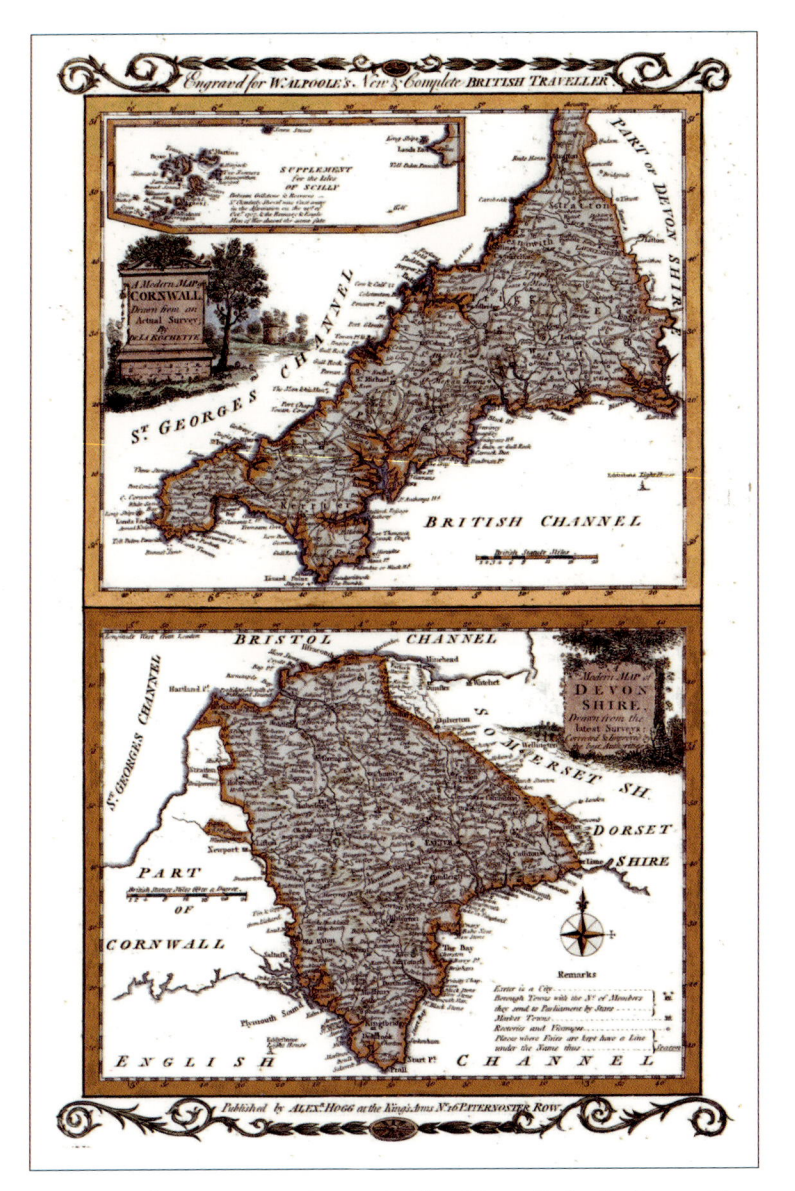

49. Hatchett 1784 State 1 The New British Traveller

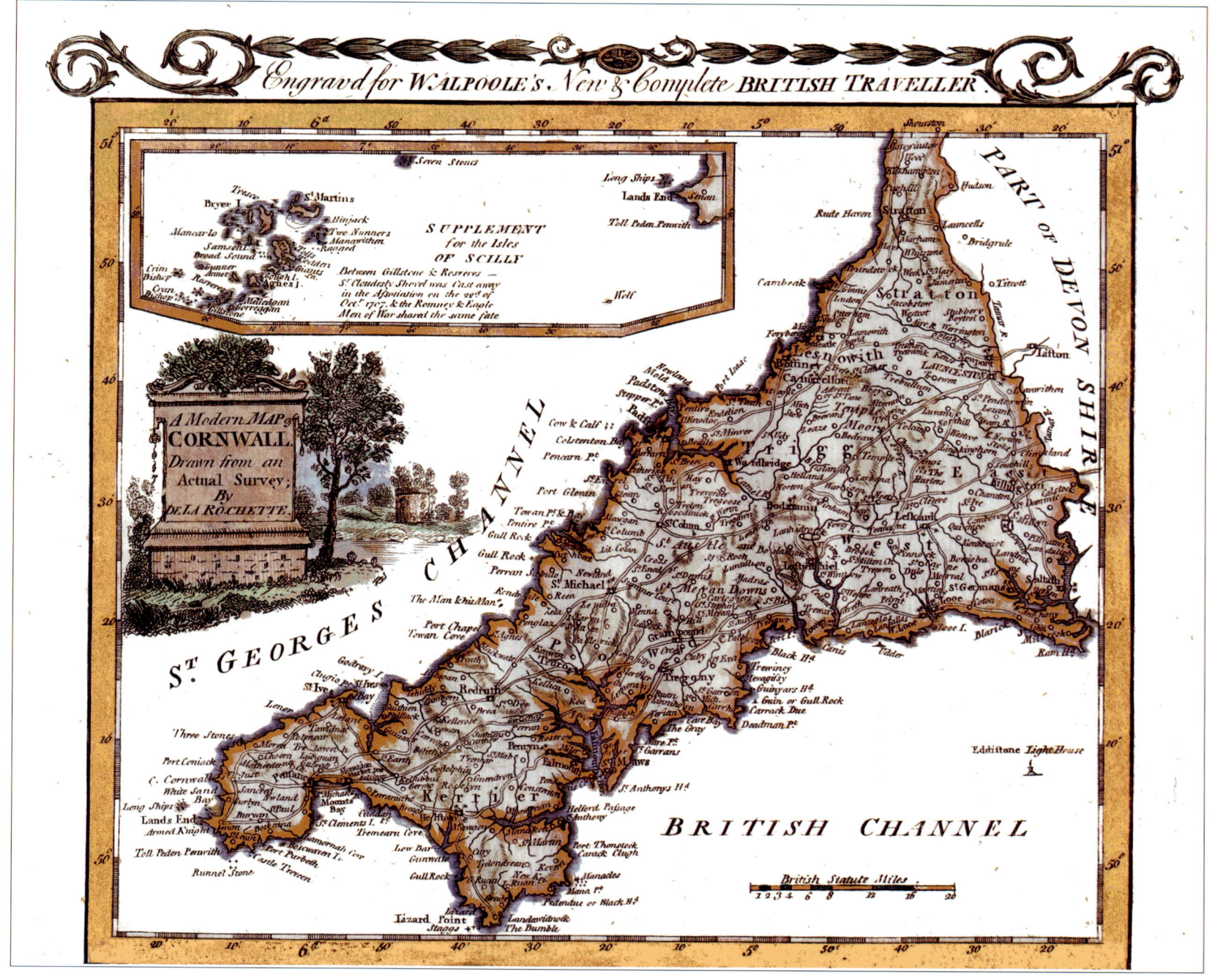

49.1 Hatchett 1784 State 1 The New British Traveller, detail

Antique Maps of Cornwall and the Isles of Scilly

monumental stone has been replaced by a more generic piece of foliage. On either side of the stone are two chains of "fruit"; on the Walpoole version, the right side has been reduced to one segment. To the far right of the background is a solitary tree, on the Walpoole version, this has two clumps of foliage. Italics have been used for the British Channel label, the St. George's Channel label is further from the edge of the cartouche background and curves around it more steeply accentuating an illusion of horizontal compression. The mileage scale is still 0 - 20 British Statute Miles, but the remainder of the label (69 to a degree) has been excluded from the Cornwall map, it is there on the Devon map. On the map itself, the missing Devon enclave north of Launceston on the west side of the Tamar as well as the smaller other enclaves and the missing top-most section of the Stratton Hundred are significant geographical errors. Finally, a careful inspection of the longitude grid used in the Isles of Scilly inset reveals that Hatchett has mistakenly added five minutes between 5° 20' and 5° 30' to the bottom border compared to the top.

It is not until the 3rd state that Hatchett's name appears bottom right of the Devon map (while the scroll work is removed). There are no changes to the maps themselves and we must assume that Hatchett is the original engraver of all three states. Hodson (Vol III p 114) suggest the late addition of Hatchett's name may have been to add weight or authority in order to bolster sales.

The title within the top scroll work is at odds with the title of the volume; this instability of maps with respect to their volumes is a feature of Hogg's publishing approach and makes tying maps to the volumes from whence they came difficult - especially where the maps are detached.

A later (1784) published state (2?) contains the following: the counties are still coupled; scrolls and titles as previously; 'British Channel' in italicised capitals, as previously; shields added (Cornwall - Launceston, Devon - Exeter); De La Rochette's name erased from cartouche, which is otherwise the same.

State 3: All scroll work and top title removed; sub title ('Published by ALEX^R HOGG... &c.') remains; Devon and Cornwall still coupled tight against each others' border; Hatchett added as engraver below right of Devon map.

From State 1 onwards, the Cornwall map is a reproduction of the De La Rochette map (#47) with the changes already discussed. Hogg muddies the waters quite effectively by mixing the plates over and over within the same 1784 publication. It is more than likely that several slight altertions were conducted between 1784 and the next real edition in ~1792. Hodson (Vol III p105) attempts to unravel Hogg's business methodology but concludes by quoting the Victorian reviewer, C.H. Timperley ('Encyclopaedia of literary and typographical anecdote', London, 1842): '...None of these puffers equalled Hogg'.

Hogg produced a final edition re-titled 'The New and Complete English Traveller' in 1794, no changes to the Cornwall map are known. William Hugh Dalton is quite possibly another of Hogg's inventions.

1784 *State 1: Loose sheet or proof? Scroll work, De La Rochette, No shields.*

1784 *State 2: New British Traveller: Or, A Complete Modern Universal Display of Great Britain and Ireland...by George A Walpoole (&c.), Published by Alex. Hogg at the Kings Arms No. 16 Paternoster Row, London. (The full title rambles on for many lines). The first edition published by Walpoole has shields added, (Launceston's below the town of Looe, Exeter's to the right of the compass). At the same time, the name De La Rochette is erased from the Cornwall cartouche.*

1784? *State 3: Scroll work above and below the pair of maps is erased, and the engraver Hatchett's name appears under the Devon map. (Without the pair on one page, this is not possible to determine).*

1792 *The New British Traveller... Pub. Alex. Hogg as previously. This and the 1793 edition are inferred dates, the Cornwall map is state 3.*

1793 *The New British Traveller... Pub. Alex Hogg. Some examples show Cornwall in state 3, while others are state 2 - an example of Hogg's preparedness to use whatever maps fell to hand.*

1794 *The New and Complete English Traveller: Or, a New Historical Survey and Modern Description of England and Wales (as before, the title rambles on for several lines) by William Hugh Dalton, Pub. Alex. Hogg at the Kings Arms No. 16 Paternoster Row, London.*

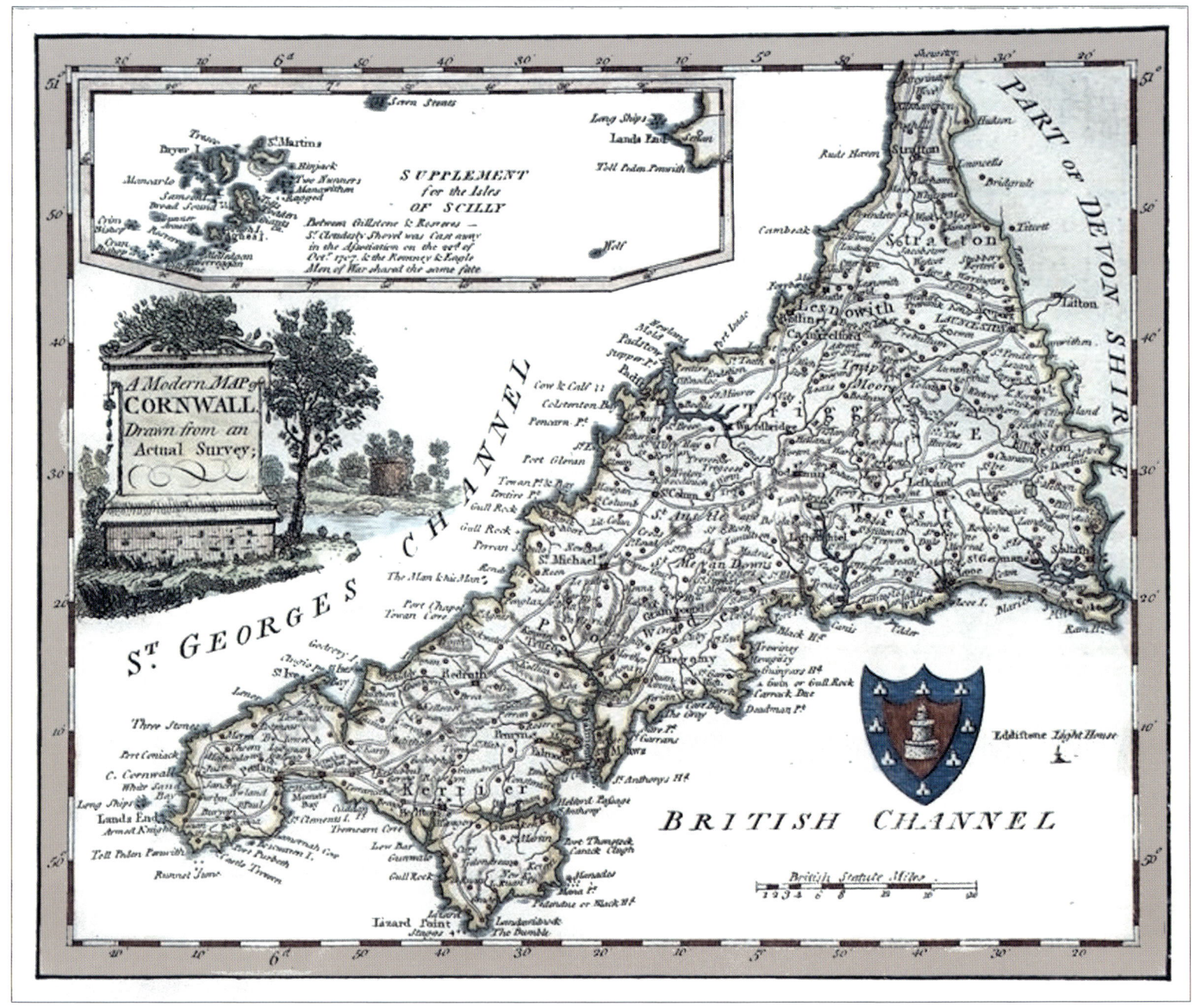

49.2 Hatchett 1784 State 3 The New British Traveller

50. CARY, JOHN 1787, 1789, 1790 & 1809

1787 NEW AND CORRECT ENGLISH ATLAS
Eng. Cary, Pub. Cary (248 x 197)

John Cary (1755-1835) was one of the most enterprising map-makers and publishers to flourish at the end of the 18th, and beginning of the 19th, centuries, and has been described as 'the most representative, able and prolific of English cartographers'. The annual award offered by the Royal Society of Arts for accurate maps of English counties, on the now familiar 'One Inch' scale, had encouraged new survey work throughout the whole country, but the large-scale maps were unsuitable for everyday use. Cary therefore issued a small county atlas which combined clarity, cheapness and convenience.

Cary was born in Corsley, on the Somerset-Wiltshire border, on 23 February 1755, and baptised in early March. The Cary family were prominent Church people. A relative, possibly John's father, George, was church warden of the parish. John had three brothers: George, Francis and William, all born in the same parish. John Cary's will, written in 1833 and proved in 1835 (PROB11/1851/501-550), runs to several pages and details, at length, his wishes in ensuring the care of his family and servants. Evidently the labour of engraving had taken its toll on Cary – he was blind and only made his mark on the will. Hodson (Vol. III, p173) mentions that Cary found himself on the end of several failing enterprises, early in his career. This appears to have been rectified with later better fortune – his sons, George and John, follow him into the business and are left a freehold apiece and a leasehold jointly of properties on the Strand; Cary's daughter, Mary Ann, received a sum of £6000.

Cary's output was nothing short of prolific. From 1783 he produced work based at 188 Strand, and his 'Survey of the Great Post Roads between London and Falmouth', in 1784, surveyed by Aaron Arrowsmith, established Cary as a renowned road book specialist. The sections dealing with Cornwall, plates 24 – 30 and 45 – 49, contain two routes into Cornwall which split at Exeter. The southern route commences with a road map of Plymouth and Rame Head. Arrowsmith has included the names of several Cornish landowners, including that of Lord Camelford at Boconnoc. On plate 27, Arrowsmith notes the presence of an obelisk erected by Camelford to his uncle, Lt Gen. Sir Richard Littleton, KB., in 1771. The northern route, which is shown in Cary's later 'Traveller's Companion' series, splits at Exeter and follows what is now the A30 via Launceston, Bodmin and Mitchell and re-joins the southern route at plate 29. The detail on the northern route is sparse, though the topography, with some indications of uphill/downhill, and streams are shown. The new (built 1750) and now famous Jamaica Inn of Daphne du Maurier fame is shown, possibly for the first time.

At least 18 major works of Cary's appeared from 1783 to 1822, with some, such as his 'New Itinerary', being reissued eleven times. It is not possible to illustrate all his Cornwall maps here, however, a selection has been included.

1787 NEW AND CORRECT ENGLISH ATLAS
Eng. Cary, Pub. Cary
(248 x 197)

The 1787 map of Cornwall in the 'New and Correct English Atlas' is finely engraved, accurate and informative, and, not surprisingly, the atlas in which it appeared ran to more than 16 editions. In line with many other publications of this type, Cary's atlas was published in twelve parts, the first six appearing monthly, the final six slightly less regularly, though it was completed by early 1789. The content of each issue is known by the advertisements placed in several newspapers (Hodson, Vol. III, p177). Cornwall appears in issue VIII, published in July 1788; (the map itself is dated September 1787). The critique in the December 1789 edition of the 'English Review' concluded: *'The neatness of the engraving is highly to be commended as, besides its general pleasing effect, it renders these maps less fatiguing to the eye than those of a much larger scale which are executed, as maps too commonly are, in a slovenly manner'*.

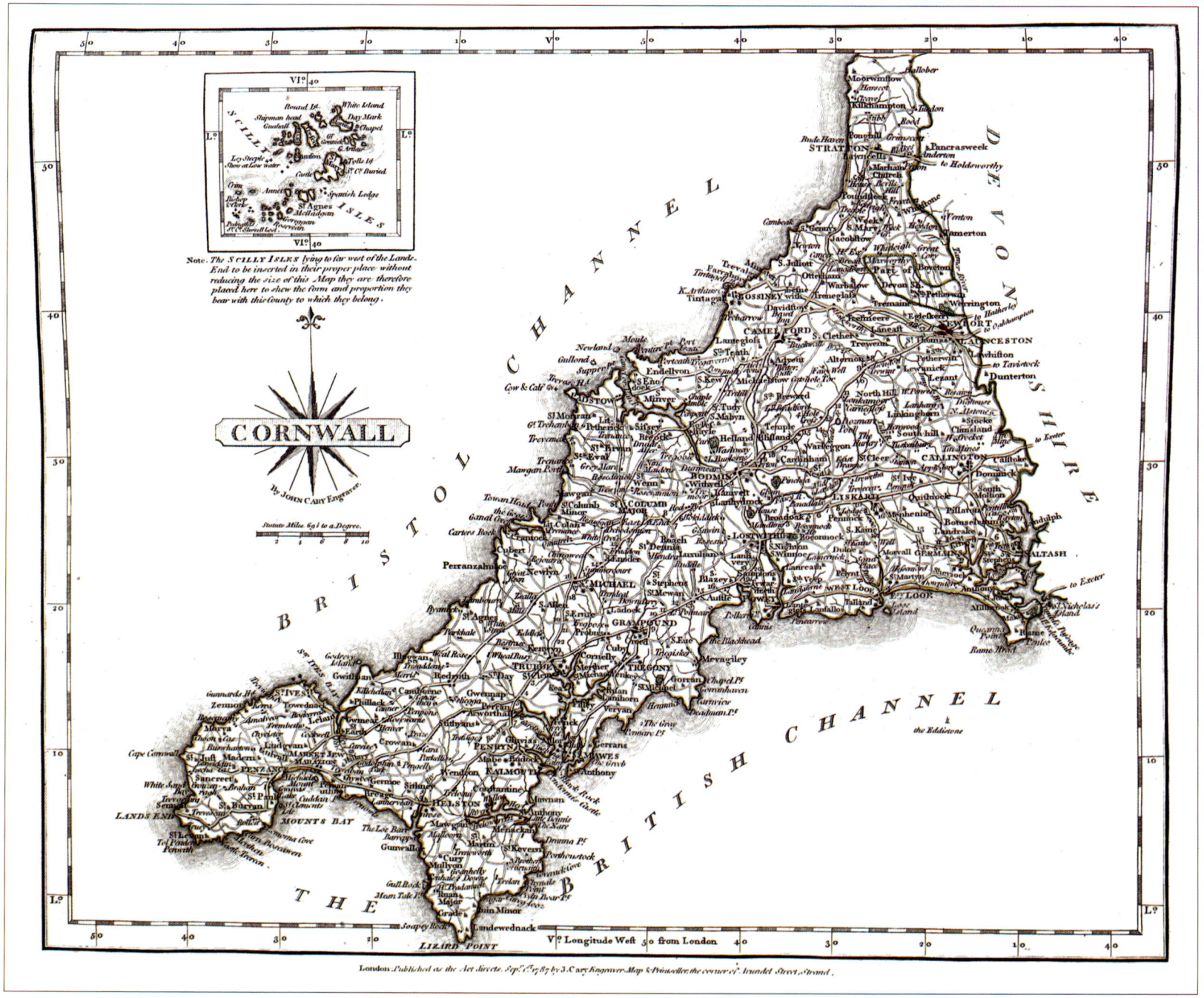

50. Cary 1787 New and Correct English Atlas, London.

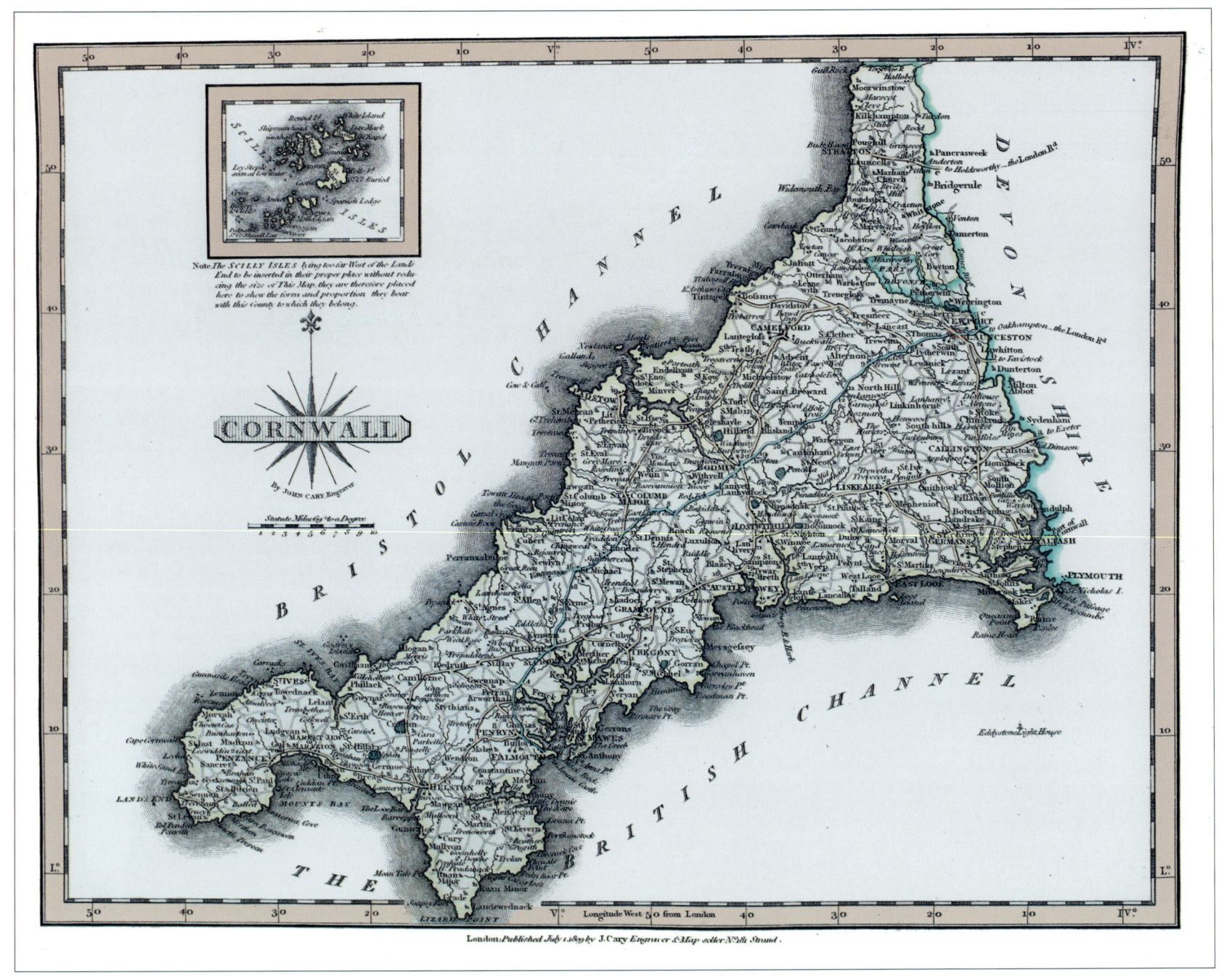

50.1 Cary 1809 New and Correct English Atlas, London.

The Cornwall map is devoid of ornament, except for the hachured panel bearing the name of the county, which passes through a 'star' compass rose at the left centre. Within the map are some slightly older names, such as 'Madern' (Madron), and it is odd that Newlyn, near Penzance, is missing entirely. There are no symbols for highlands at all, though some of the more notable tors are named. At the top left is a 'Scilly Isles' inset with a brief note concerning Sir Cloudesly's fate. Cary's imprint is given below the title. The section of Devon on the west bank of the Tamar in Rame is shown, but the reciprocal piece opposite Saltash is not. Some, but not all, of the county's country parks are shown encircled in a picket-fence, a style used since Saxton. At the foot of the map is the imprint 'London, published as the Act directs, Sept 1st 1787 by J. Cary, Engraver & Print-seller, the corner of Arundel Street, Strand'.

The 1793 issue of the 'New and Correct English Atlas' was published at about the same time as the removal to No. 181 Strand and remained on sale for sixteen years. The Cornwall map is readily identified by the inscription at the foot of the map: 'London, Publish'd Jany 1 1793 by J Cary Engraver and Map-seller, Strand'. From other analyses done for other counties and summarised by Hodson (Vol. III, pp189-198), it is likely other amendments are present on the Cornwall map.

Cary has made quite a few alterations to the grade of roads throughout the county, and for the most part these are down-grades from the previous (1787) map. The two largest changes are the route from Redruth to Penzance and St. Hillary to Perranaworthal, both of which are downgraded - there are at least nine others. The up-grades are far fewer, and these are marked with a heavier line on one side – there are about five, amongst which the roads to St. Agnes and Redruth from Truro are the most prominent. Another addition to the 1793 edition is the alphabetic labels that have been added to the roads exiting the county, (excluding ferry routes such as Cremyll – Stonehouse at Plymouth), from south to north. The first of these is the road over the Tamar, east of Callington (A). The purpose of these is to allow the reader to align roads as one traverses from one county to the next.

The 2nd edition, in 1809, contained re-engraved maps, Cornwall included. There are some changes from the 1793 version to this 1809 edition. The general layout of the map is identical, with the Scilly Isles in the upper centre, an explanation of their location below this and the compass rose below that. Some of the place names have been updated, including 'Madron', near Penzance. Newlyn, nearby, is still missing. In several cases where the old style 'f' had been previously used, Cary now uses the more modern 's' (e.g. 'Morwenstow' in Stratton, 'Blisland' and 'Egloshayle' both near Bodmin &c.). There are some added place names, the most evident being 'Fowey R. and Harb' and 'Widemouth Bay' in Stratton, to name but two. Most of the minor rivers, such as the Bude, Fowey, Lynner, Seaton, Lerryn and Allen &c., have now been named.

A considerable alteration has been performed on the 1809 map with respect to the Camel, which empties into the sea at Padstow: on Cary's 1787 'Atlas' map, as well as on all three 'Traveller's Companion' maps, it is shown passing through Camelford, flowing south-south-west and becoming a tributary of the Fowey, just north of Lostwithiel, at Glym. The source of this error appears to be entirely Cary's; none of the preceding maps indicate any confusion over the course of the river. Gasgoyne (#25), Kitchin (#39) and Martyn (#40) very clearly show the correct course. *

Cary continues to modify and alter the grades of the roads. From the 1793 edition to the 1806 edition there are only a few changes, the largest is the upgrade of a route from Redruth, via Camborne, to Helston. The section of Cornwall on the Devon side opposite Saltash has been added, however, missing from the 1809 edition and the 1789 'Britannia' map is the Tamar Navigation canal (see Smith #58). At the foot of the map is the imprint 'London: Published July 1 1809 by J. Cary Engraver & Map seller N°181 Strand'.

1787 *Cary's New and Correct English Atlas, London. Reprints: 1787, 1793 New imprint (3 issues), 1804, 2nd Ed 1809, 1812, 1818, 1821, 1823, 1825, 1826, 1827, 1831.*

1863 *Lithographic transfer. New title Cruchley's County Atlas of England and Wales, by G. F. Cruchley, London. Repub. 1864, 1868, 1875. 1863 New title Cruchley's Travelling County Atlas of England and Wales, by same author.*

1789 BRITANNIA (GOUGH)
Eng. Cary, Pub. Gough (508 x 394)

In 1789 Cary produced a new set of maps to illustrate Richard Gough's translation of William Camden's 'Britannia'. The maps were drawn by E. Noble and engraved by Cary, and again the map is finely engraved and brilliantly executed, impressive for the workmanship rather than decorative qualities. In order to better fit the volume, Cary has set the county over as with many previous cartographers, compass east-west aligns with the 50° North line, but the 5° West line has been rotated a few degrees west of parallel with north-south. The Scilly Islands are shown in a scroll cartouche just above Penwith, without any indication where the archipelago is with respect to the mainland. Even now the death and burial of Sir Cloudesley Shovell continues to be marked. The Hundreds are marked with dashed lines and named within the map, and the towns' returning MPs are shown using the now familiar twin 'palm trees' first used by Morden some 90 years previously. The map is crammed with many details of towns, villages and farms/hamlets. Topographically, there is nothing shown of highlands, save one or two where space permitted – the county is generally presented as if perfectly flat. To do otherwise would have severely compromised the sheer number of places Cary has been able to fit into the map. Curiously, Plymouth, although the major port of the adjacent county and one of the largest towns of Devon, is not shown.

Opposite Saltash on the Devon side of the Tamar and shown more clearly on Cary's later 1809 'New English Atlas' map, lies a sliver of Cornwall in Devon. This was known as Riverside or Saltash Passage. The existence of this was noted by the Reform Commission in 1832, and this section was given to Devon in 1844. It was finally incorporated into the Devon parish of St. Budeaux in 1895.

On the Cornish side of the Tamar, on the Rame peninsula, lies another administrative curiosity – the parish of Maker had been, since Saxon times, part of Devon. This included the Mt Edgcumbe estate that faces Plymouth, as far as Kingsand. It also included the eastern side of St. John's, to the shore at St. John's Lake. These were transferred to Devon in 1844. A section in the appendices discusses these enclaves further.

The 1789 edition can easily be distinguished by the details below the title top left, which read 'A Map of Cornwall from the best Authorities'. Below this is a bar and below that the simple imprint 'Engraved by J. Cary' with no further information. John Stockdale re-published 'Britannia' in 1805, and added, between the bar and Cary's imprint, this line: 'Published by John Stockdale Piccadilly 26th, March 1805'. The Tamar Navigation canal has also been added to the 1805 edition.

Stockdale published Cary's 'British Atlas' the same year, using these final versions of the 'Britannia' maps; as far as is known, the Cornwall map is unchanged.

1789 *Britannia, by William Camden, translated by Richard Gough, T. Payne and G. G. J. & J. Robinson, London. 2nd Edition: 1805 by John Stockdale, Piccadilly. Reprints: 1806 & 1808.*
1805 *Cary's New British Atlas, Pub. John Stockdale, Piccadilly. Reprinted 1809.*

*The Camel and Allen flow into the Bristol Channel at Padstow. The Allen joins the Camel south of Egloshayle, making the principal system river the Camel. Cary's mistake on the 1787 map above is carried forwards by 45% of the subsequent maps here, with the error either being that the Camel is shown joining the Fowey, or that Camelford is shown on the Allen, or variations around these two geographic themes. As we have seen before, once an error creeps onto a map, it acquires a life of its own and, in the case of the Fowey-Camel-Allen connexion, endured up to Davies's map of 1831 (#81).

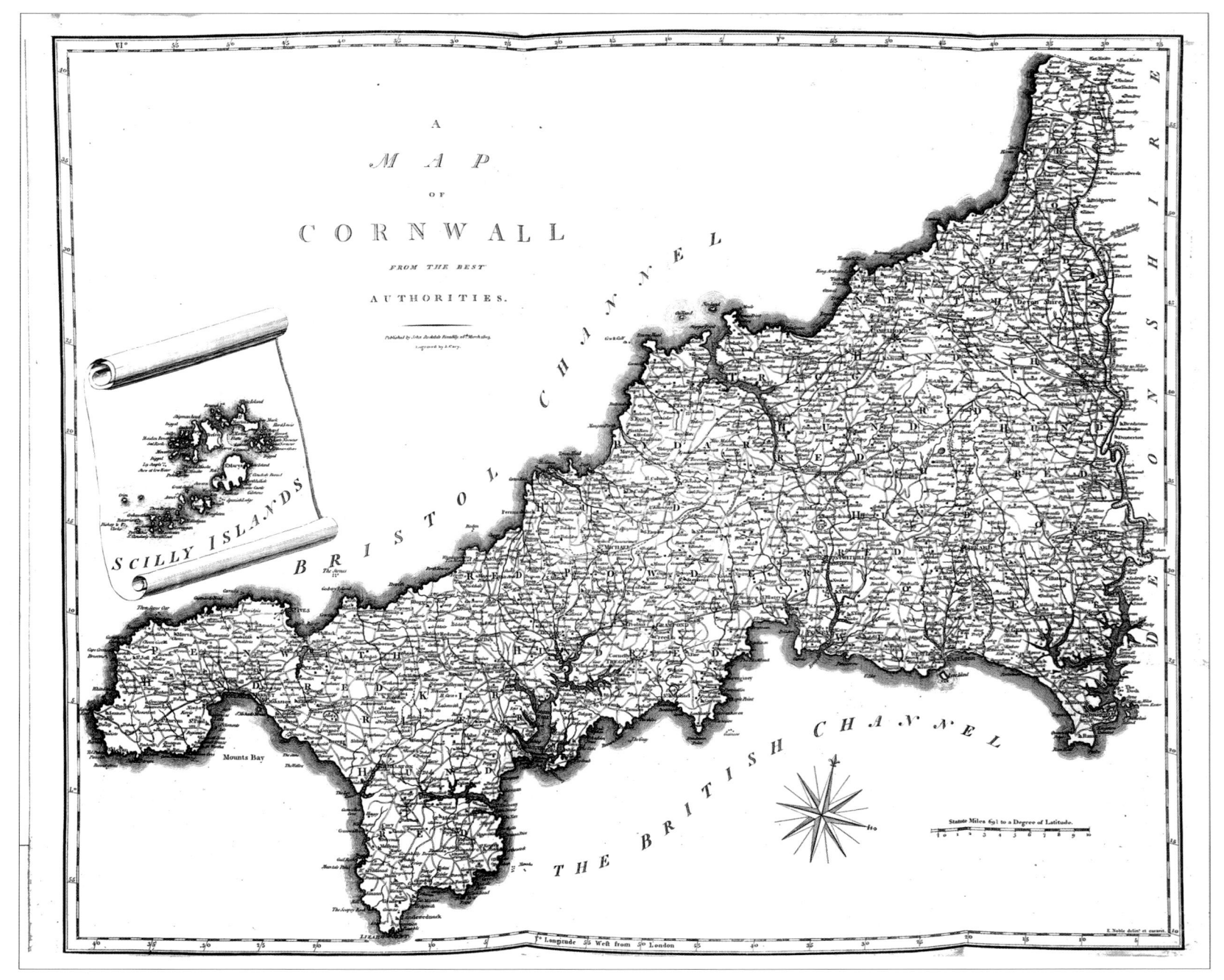

50.2 Cary 1805 Britannia, by William Camden, translated by Richard Gough, Published by Stockdale

50.3 Cary 1790, Traveller's Companion. London

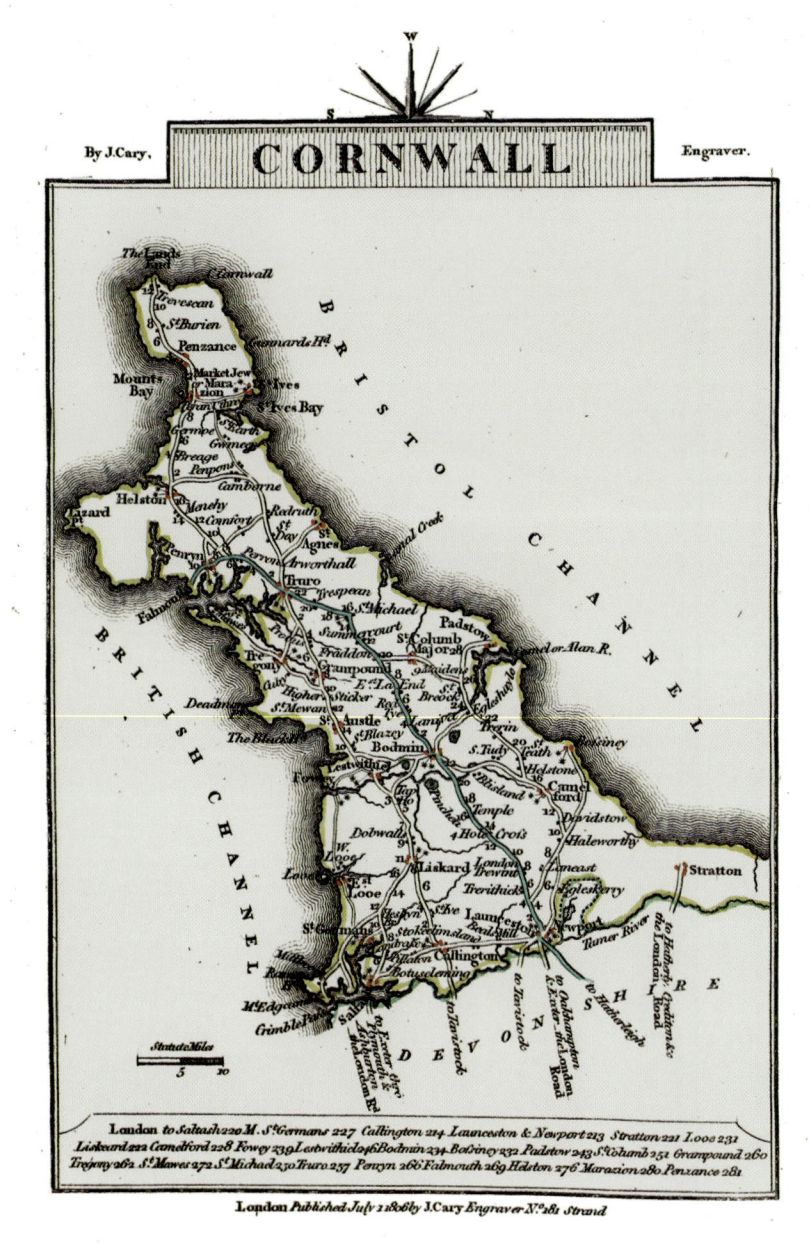

50.4 Cary 1806, Traveller's Companion. London

1790 CARY'S TRAVELLING COMPANION
Eng. Cary, Pub. Cary (89 x 114)

Cary's 'Travelling Companion' was first produced in 1790 as a road guide of the turnpike roads emanating from London to the rest of England and Wales. This was done with an index of every notable town throughout the kingdom, with their market days. On the maps themselves, Cary has marked borough and market towns, returning MPs and, at the foot of the map, a brief listing of towns and their distances from London. The 1790 map of Cornwall is shown with west at the top. The main roads entering the county are labelled 'a'-'e' and the incremental mileage between towns is shown. The 1806 edition of the maps is evidently re-cut, since there are many additions and changes to this plate. The two are easily distinguished by the imprint at the foot of the map. The road network, in the intervening years, appears to have expanded, with many new roads now shown – there are several additional towns added to the map, with some now engraved on an arc, instead of horizontally. This edition also features a mail coach route running through the county from Launceston, via Truro, to Falmouth, coloured in blue.

The third variant of this map was first produced in 1822 and may have been a consequence of a fire destroying the older plates. This version has continued to orient the map so that east is at the foot of the map. However, all the text on the new plate has been rotated 90° clockwise. At the base of the map is the imprint of Cary's sons, George and John, and the address at 86 St. James's Street. The Carys have added some new detail - the country park at Tehiddy, near Redruth, and the presumably still under construction Bude canal are two such examples. The incorrect course of the Camel is still shown, despite having been corrected in a prior publication, (Cary's 1809 'New English Atlas', above).

There are many interim variants to the principal editions, which possibly contain further corrections, amendments and other alterations. Batten and Bennett's 'Printed Maps of Devon' cites many changes to that county, and it is likely that a similar number of alterations to the Cornwall maps exist.

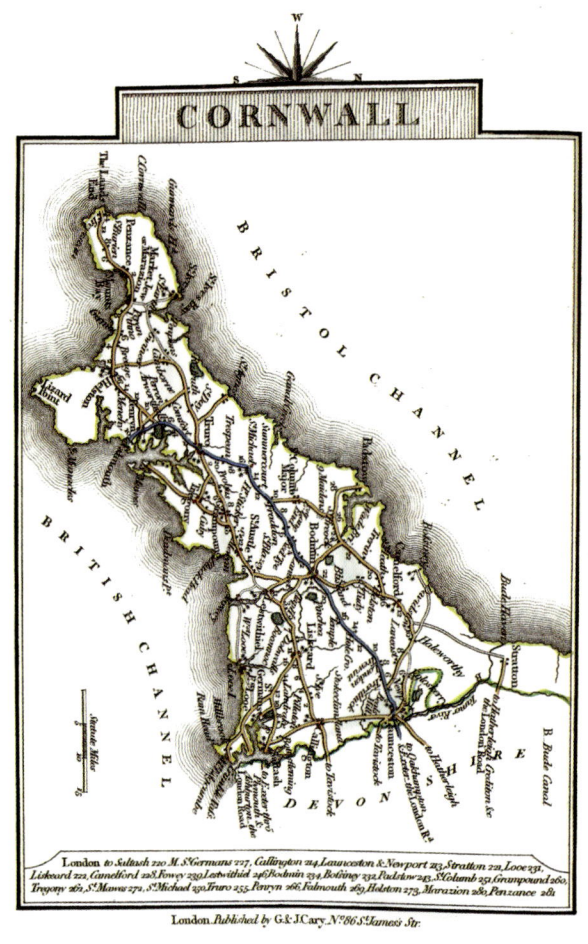

50.5 Cary 1822, Traveller's Companion. London.

1790   *Cary's Traveller's Companion, London. Reprinted 1791, New imprint 1792, 1796, 1797, 1798, 1801, 1804.*
1806   *2nd Edition, reprinted 1810, 1812, 1814, 1817, 1819, 1821.*
1822   *3rd Edition, G & J Cary 86 St. James's Str., London. Reprinted 1824, 1826, 1828, 1835.*
1862   *Retitled Cruchley's Railroad Companion to England and Wales, Lithographic transfer by G. F. Cruchley, Map Seller and Globe maker, 81, Fleet Street, London.*

1809 NEW ENGLISH ATLAS
Eng. Cary, Pub. Cary (521 x 406)

Perhaps the finest of all Cary's series of maps appeared in his 'New English Atlas', of 1809. As maps were completed they were issued between 1801 and 1809; the Cornwall map is dated 1806. The whole atlas is beautifully engraved, on a larger scale than had been used in the earlier maps by Cary, the scale of the Cornwall map being about 4½ miles to 1 inch. The quality of the workmanship and the accuracy of the mapping puts it in the top rank of 19th century cartography.

At some time near the end of the 1700s, Cary must have realised that the 'New and Correct English Atlas' plates were wearing out. The last edition of that atlas in 1809 was done using new plates; between those and the previous 1793 edition the atlas would remain in circulation in one form or another until at least 1875. The 'New English Atlas', at almost twice the scale of the old atlas, competed directly with Smith's New English Atlas (#58) and little else before the Ordnance Survey maps that arrived, county by county, from 1805. It is not as commonly found as the older atlas, perhaps a function of a shorter shelf life.

A simple title, 'A New Map of Cornwall. Divided into Hundreds…by John Cary Engraver 1806', is set into a circular cartouche top left. Below this is a square inset of the Scilly Isles, graduated with latitude and longitude, and a note in explanation of placement. A scale of 0 - 12 miles, in a hachured lozenge, is drawn below a simple compass rose south of Looe. The sea area around the immediate coastline is shaded in tight horizontal lines, which slightly obscures the coastal detailing. The divisions of the county Hundreds have been brought up into prominence, in comparison with the previous 'Britannia' and 'New and Correct Atlas' versions.

The line of 5° West seems to be something of a movable target. The 2nd edition of the 'New and Correct Atlas' (which had not altered the latitude/longitude grid from the 1st edition) and this map were published within three years of each other. Both used London (presumed to be St. Paul's) as the zero meridian, yet the 5° West line has shifted in the 'New English Atlas' 6 miles west, bisecting the Lizard peninsula at Carrick Lûz, to Treguth, near Penhale Point, on the north Cornish coast. Rather inconsistently, the modernisations made on the 1806 map from the 1787 map with respect to the long 'f' have reverted – Pancrasweek, in north Devon has become 'Pancrafweek' together with several Cornish villages that had been overlooked.

Although the 'Britannia' map is not as easy to read, the road structure from it is used almost verbatim on this 1809 map, with some 'tidying up' of some routes that seemed to end in the middle of nowhere, the road south-east from St. Day to Cusgarne is one of several examples. The interim map by Smith (#58) is very similar, but it appears Cary used his own preceding maps as a base for the 1809 map. The inscription at the base of the map reads 'London: Published by J. Cary, Engraver & Map seller No. 181 Strand. Nov 1st 1806'.

A modified version of the atlas plates was used by William Smith (1769-1839) to produce the first geological county maps of England. However, Cornwall was not included in the series of 21 counties, and it would not be until De la Beche's map of 1839 (#68) that this would be rectified.

In 1844 George F. Crutchley bought Cary's plates, and from 1850 issued lithographic transfer copies of both the 'New and Correct Atlas', and this, the 'New English Atlas', for the next 40 years.

1809 Cary's New English Atlas, London. Reprints: 1811, 1818, 1820, 1821, 1824, 1825, 1826, 1828, 1831, 1834, 1842.

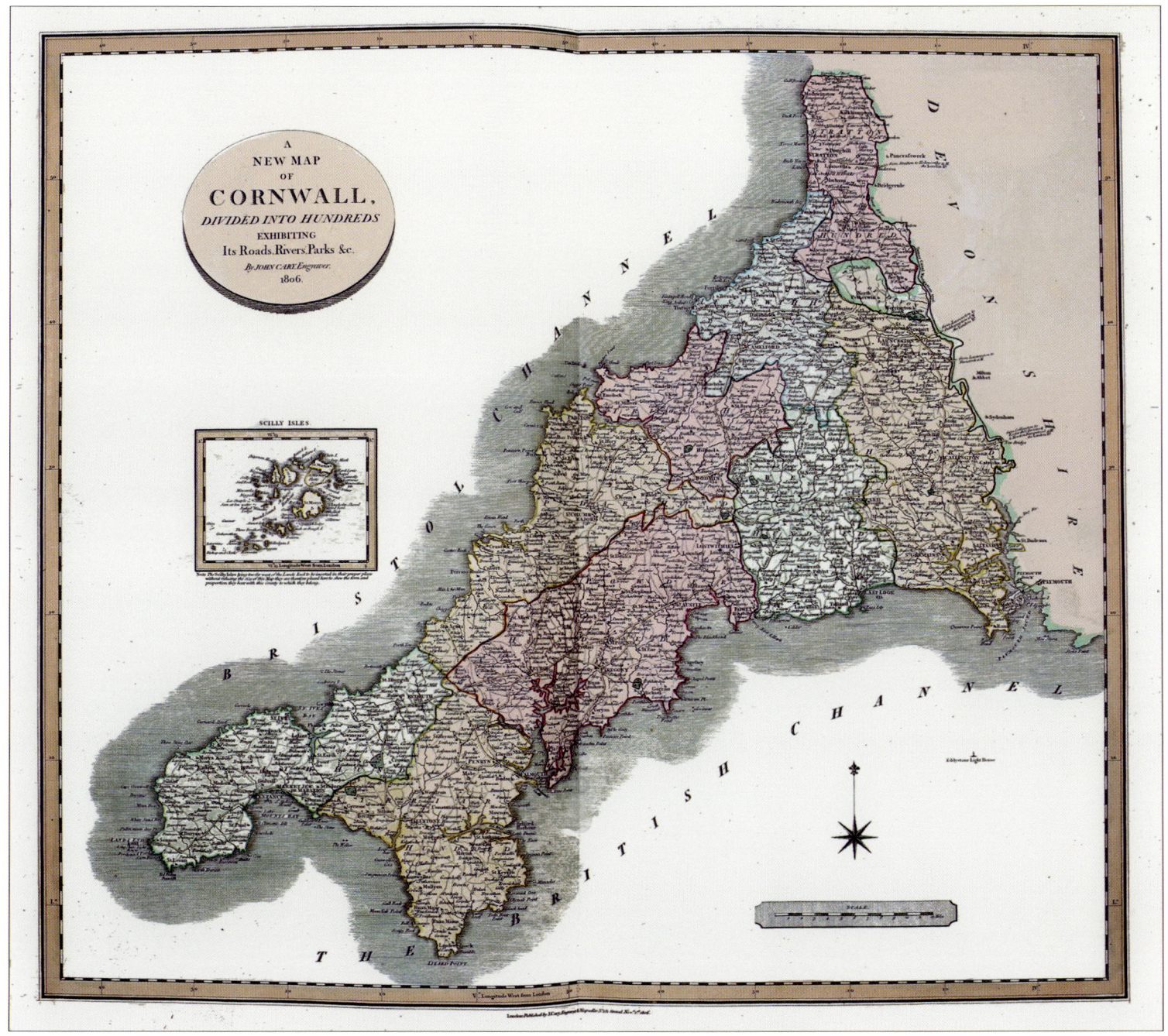

50.6 Cary 1809 New English Atlas. London.

51. MURRAY, JOHN & LODGE, JOHN 1788

Eng. Lodge, Pub. Murray
(279 x 229)

John Lodge (c.1735-1796) was a Merchant Taylor and engraver who worked from premises at 45 Shoe Lane, near Fleet Street, London. He was employed by The Political Magazine from 1780 to 1790, as well as working for other publications of the time. Lodge was apprenticed by Thomas Jefferys in 1750, suggesting a birth date around 1735. He apprenticed his son, also John (b 1771), as an engraver into the Merchant Taylors in 1785. His death was mentioned in the 'European Magazine' and 'London Review' of April 1796; his will (PROB11/1274/185) was written in 1794 and proved on 31 May 1796, leaving his estate, such as it was, to his wife, Ann.

John MacMurray, a former Royal Marines officer, bought a bookselling business at 32 Fleet Street, in about 1768, dropped the 'Mac' and built a thriving business. The list of published authors from this house is remarkable: Jane Austen, Lord Byron and Charles Darwin, to name but three. In 2003, after seven generations, the company became part of Hodder Headline, and the Murray archive was bought by the National Library of Scotland, in 2005, for £31m.

The Cornwall map is simply titled 'A New map of Cornwall, from the best Authorities', with an inset 'Supplement for the Isles of Scilly'. It is quite well produced and informative, showing latitude and longitude, as well as the usual detail. It is not particularly remarkable for either original work or decorative appearance.

There are several items suggesting influence from previous maps. In the inset of the Isles of Scilly is a short paragraph concerning the loss of HMS Association – this is a verbatim copy of the same text used by De La Rochette in 1766 (#47) and thereby Hatchett in 1784 (#49). Additionally, the shape of the border encompassing the Isles of Scilly is identical to that of these predecessors. As has been seen elsewhere, there are several tell-tale omissions/inclusions that, once set onto a map, tend to linger, and Lodge's map is no different. 'Newland' in lieu of Newlyn, near Penzance, and also in place of Newlyn East, near Mitchell, 'Matherderna' is used in place of Madron, near Penzance, (all on De La Rochette). 'Drunkard' is still being used in north Cornwall (missing from Hatchett); it becomes 'Hallworthy', though not until after the turn of the century. As with De La Rochette, but not Hatchett, the top-most part of 'Stratton' has spilled over the top border and the enclaves that criss-cross the Tamar are all shown. The content of the map is not wholly De La Rochette or Hatchett. However, all these place name errors appear in Kitchin's 1769 map (#39), and, as suggested previously, these errors may stem from Gasgoyne (#25).

For the last time on a map, Lodge's reproduction of De La Rochette's 1766 map shows a route across Mount's Bay from Marazion to Penzance as well as another route overland. This is discussed further in the appendices.

At top right appears 'Political Mag. Jan^y. '88'; below the map is the imprint 'Published as the Act directs, Jany 31st 1788 by J. Murray, No. 32, Fleet St.'. These two items were erased in the reprint produced in 1795.

1788 *The Political Magazine, &c., by J. Murray, London. Reprint: 1795.*

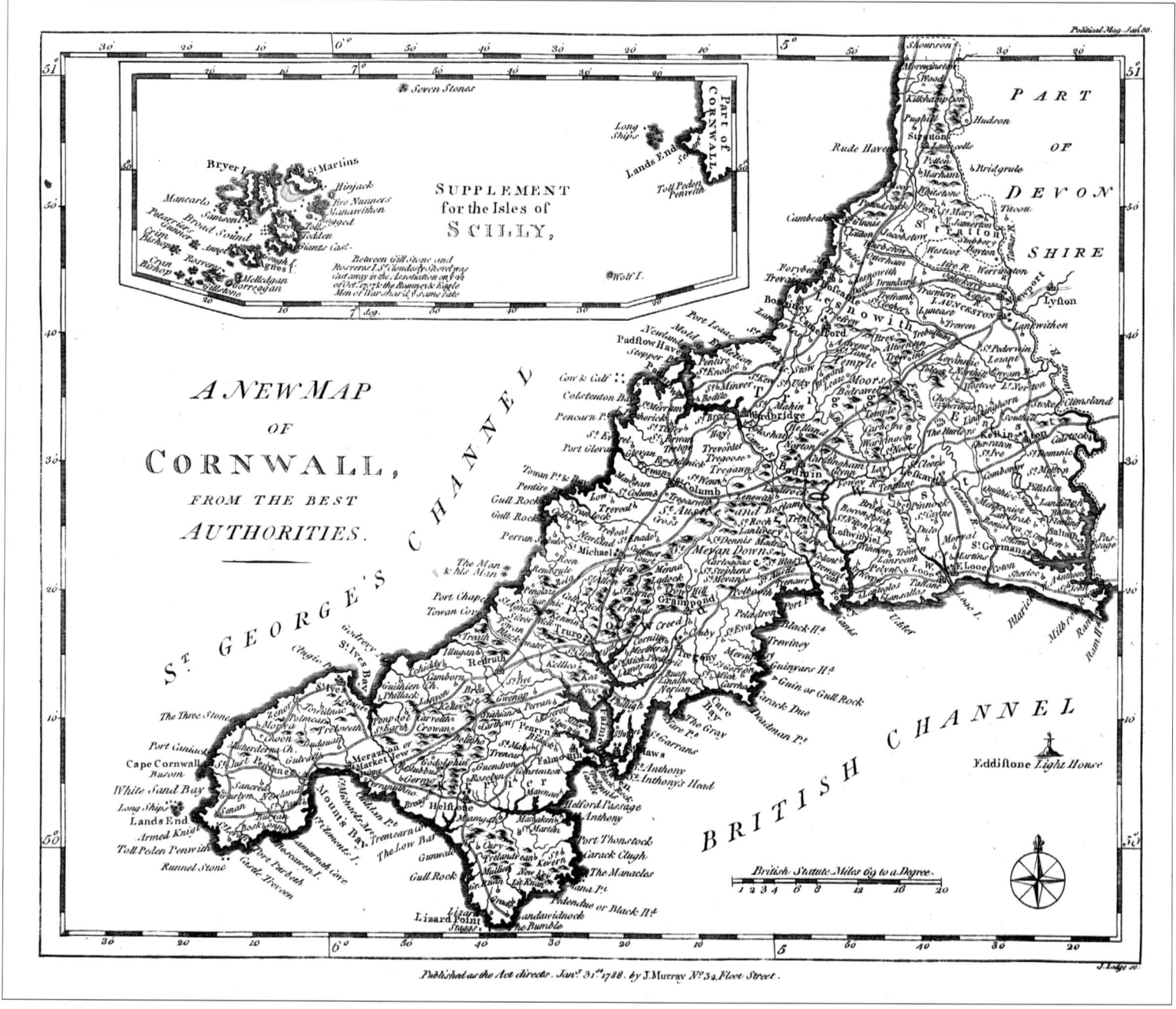

51. Lodge 1788 *The Political Magazine, &c., by J. Murray, London*

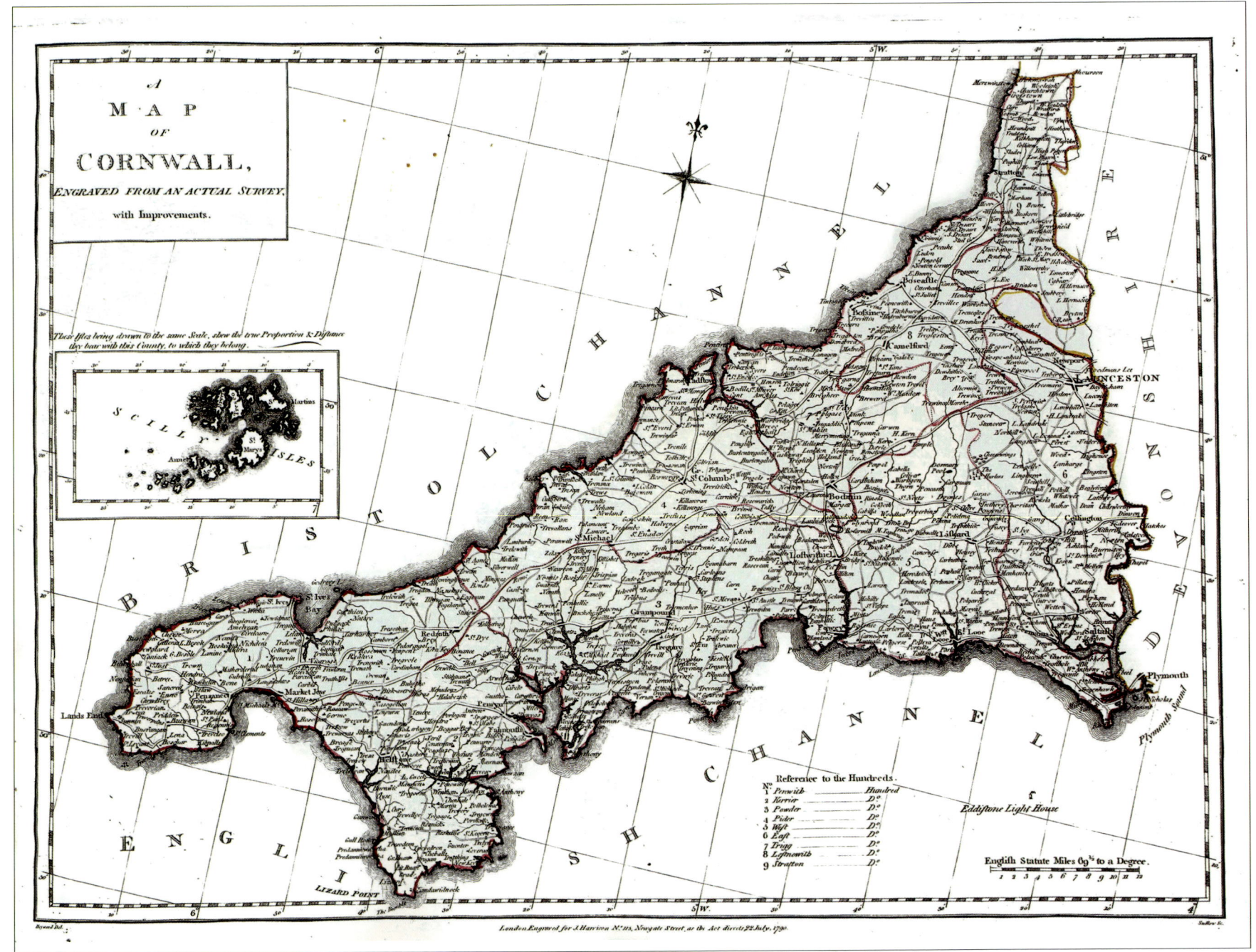

52. Sudlow 1791 Maps of the English Counties, by John Harrison

Antique Maps of Cornwall and the Isles of Scilly

52. HARRISON, JOHN & SUDLOW, EDWARD 1790

Eng. Sudlow, Pub. Harrison
(445 x 318)

John Harrison was a printer and publisher based at 115 Newgate Street, London, from the late 1700s to his death, in 1815. This map was drawn by James Haywood and very finely engraved by Edward Sudlow, in 1790. This, along with other county maps, was incorporated by Harrison into his accompanying atlas to Rev. Nicholas Tindal's translation of 'The History of England', written originally by Paul Rapin de Thoryas, in French, ('Histoire d'Angleterre', published in ten volumes, from 1724 to 1727). Tindal's translation ran to 13 volumes, which he published from 1727.

Edward Sudlow (1761 -?) was born in Manchester and moved to London before 1785. He married Lucy de la Motte, the daughter of the late Robert de la Motte, a fan maker of the parish of St. Clement Danes, in February that year. From this, Sudlow entered, by marriage, into the world of engraved illustrations mounted onto ladies' fans and became a specialist in this trade. By the middle of the 1700s, a fan was essential for the lady about town, and demand was brisk. With this came an evolution in style and content, with some, such as George Bickham junior (#42), supplying amusing and slightly tongue-in-cheek moral messages. Sudlow's Fan Warehouse at 191, The Strand records the Sudlows as engravers / fan makers in the 1790 Electoral Roll and thereafter. The output of Sudlow fans at the end of the 1700s quite possibly eclipsed his cartographic engraving.

In 1791 Harrison published his Maps of the English Counties, reusing the maps from 'The History'. 'A Map of Cornwall engraved from an actual survey with improvements' contains elements redolent of Gasgoyne, the 1701 Morden and thereby Moll. Sudlow's map is more detailed, though lacks much of the coastal detail included in Morden's map. The map is still canted over a few degrees more than Morden's, so the Devon border is parallel with the right margin.

An inset of the Isles of Scilly is present on the left margin, with a brief note explaining where they belong relative to Land's End. Longitude is shown from London and, in common with several of the maps of this period, it is shown 20' too far east. The scale is given also in line with maps at the time – 69½ English Statute miles to a degree (of latitude). Numbers 1-9 on the map refer to the Hundreds, with a table of them below Fowey. At the foot of the map is the inscription 'London, Engraved for J. Harrison, N⁰· 115 Newgate St, as the Act directs, 22 July 1790'.

1791   *Maps of the English Counties, by John Harrison, London. Reprinted 1792.*

53. AIKIN, JOHN & JOHNSON, JOSEPH 1790

Eng. Unknown, Pub. Johnson
(191 x 114)

Dr. John Aikin (1747-1822) was born at Kibworth, in Leicestershire, but moved soon thereafter to Warrington. After studying medicine at Edinburgh and surgery in London, he settled into medical practice in Great Yarmouth in 1784. His published political and religious opinions quickly set him apart from his more conventional friends and clients and he found his career prospects in the town compromised.

In 1792 he moved to the more anonymous Hackney, where he was able to continue medicine, until he suffered a stroke in 1796. He was forced to give up his medical career and the house in Broad Street, Hackney. The family moved to the cleaner air of Stoke Newington. Here Aikin extended his writing interests, covering a wide variety of subjects, until his death in December 1822.

Joseph Johnson was a publisher of a wide variety of topics, associate of a number of radical thinkers of the time and proponent of 'new ideas'. His contribution to children's literature started in the 1770s, and it may have been through his publication of Aikin's sister, Anna Laetitia Barbauld's 'Lessons for Children', in 1778, that Aikin and Johnson became acquainted.

Aikin's 'England Delineated', published in 1788, must have been done while he was still in Great Yarmouth, and contained no maps. This was rectified in the second edition, in 1790. The footnote to the title indicates that the book is for the 'use of young persons', and the simplicity of the maps is thus explained. In common with other books of the time, Aikin divided the countries of England and Wales into groups, from the north southwards, dealing with Wales last. Cornwall falls into the south-western group, with 'Devonshire' and 'Somersetshire'. Maps for the second edition were simply appended to the end of the book in the same order as they appear in the text; there are no page numbers, nor plate numbers to the maps. Cornwall appears as the 42nd map.

The Cornwall map is simply titled, with no cartouche. The major rivers are drawn and named, and a limited number of coastal features are shown, along with the main towns. The border with Devon is drawn and labelled. There is no scale, border or any other embellishments. It is a simple and pleasant little map.

1788 *England Delineated. Or, A Geographical Description of Every County in England and Wales. Printed for J. Johnson, St. Paul's Church-yard by T. Bensley, Bolt Court, Fleet St. London. Second Edition 1790, Reprints: 1795, 1800, 1803, 1809 & 1818 (No maps).*

CORNWALL.

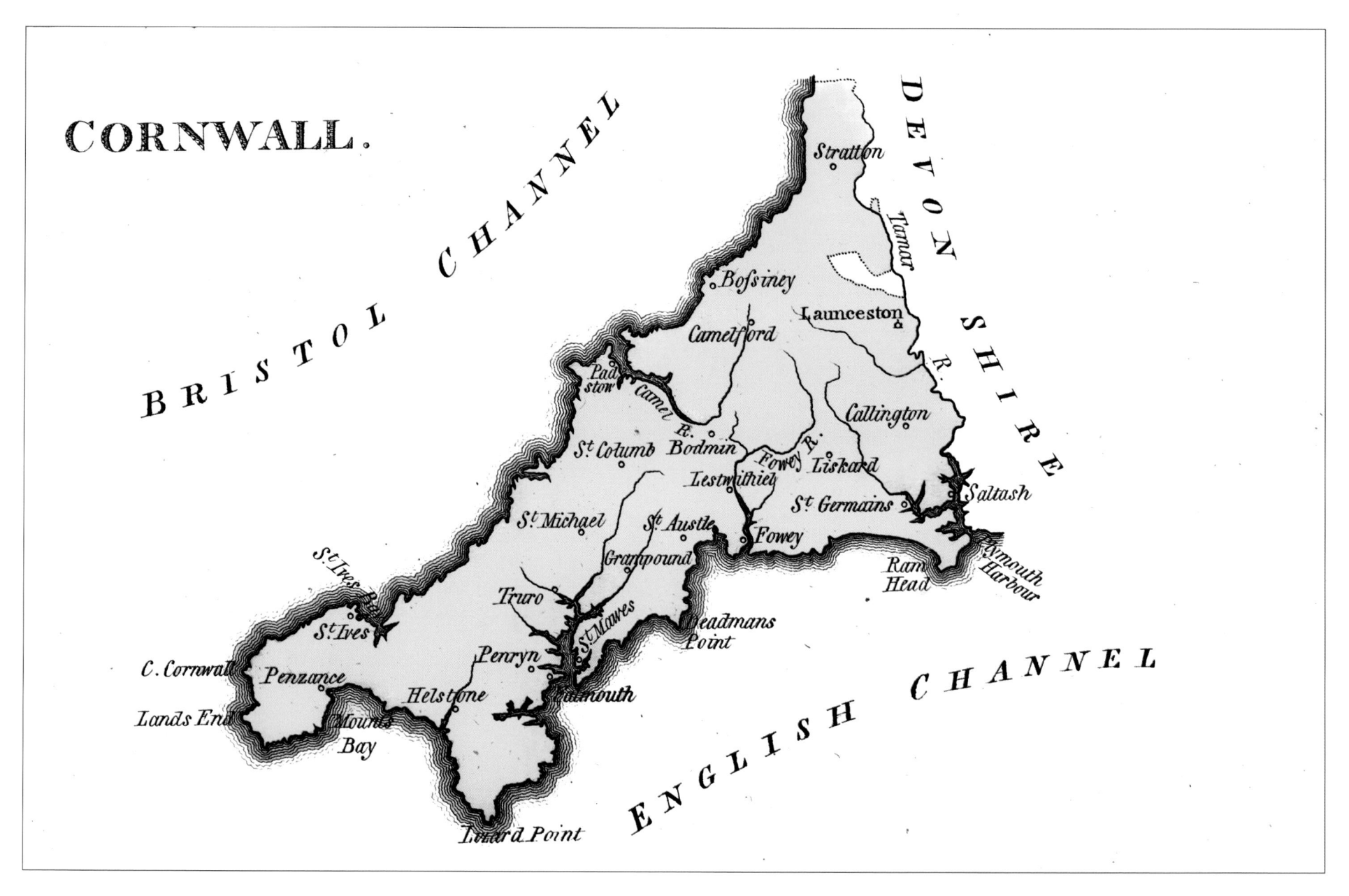

53. Johnson 1790 England Delineated. Or, A Geographical Description of Every County...

54. BAKER, BENJAMIN 1791

Eng. Baker, Pub. Bent 1791, Darton & Harvey 1804, Laurie and Whittle 1806, Whittle and Laurie 1816.
(216 x 171)

Benjamin Baker (1767-1841) was an engraver based in Islington. Trade cards from the period place him at 32 High Street, Islington, and the Electoral Rolls of 1795 show him working from Lower Street, also in Islington. He married Charlotte Barnard in 1791 and had four daughters and three sons. The sons all followed him into the Ordnance Survey. His will, drawn up in 1828, shows he owned stock in the Stationer's Company and planned to use this to provide for his widow and unmarried children (PROB11/1948/451-500). Baker worked in Islington for 15 years before his appointment to the newly established Ordnance Survey as their principal engraver, in 1804 (#68).

This is the second set of maps to be published in 'The Universal Magazine' between 1791 and 1797. Bowen and Kitchin's map had appeared in the first series in 1747-66 (#30). The Cornwall map, along with others, was incorporated into the atlas published by Robert Laurie and James Whittle in 1806. This was titled 'Laurie and Whittle's New and Improved English Atlas' and was more akin to Camden's 'Britannia' in adding details per county with maps inserted in the appropriate places. Laurie retired and was replaced by his son, Richard Holmes Laurie, who took over in 1816 and published the same atlas, without the text inserts, with his own name alongside that of his father's partner, Richard Whittle, in 1816. At least one further edition was published in 1846.

The 1791 map opposite is a clear, uncluttered map. The cartouche of Cornwall appears with Baker's title below it. There is an inset of 'The Isles of Scilly', which the map notes are 'Bearing W by S from the Land's End, Distant 11¼ leagues or 39 miles' (this is to the Eastern Isles); the distance to Hugh Town is closer to 44 miles. On the main and insert maps, longitude is drawn from London, (taken to be the dome of St. Paul's Cathedral). Baker has placed his 5° West line about 2' west of today's position (from Greenwich). His placement of the Isles of Scilly is nonetheless 18 miles too far west.

The 1806 edition contains several alterations. A compass rose has been added behind the Cornwall cartouche, almost obliterating Baker's inscription. The main map is still set in the same position with respect to the 5° West line, even though Baker has set it to Greenwich - in other words, he has not moved it the 5' that this shift would entail. The line of 50° North has been shifted 2' northwards and now cuts the Lizard to the north of Gull Rock (Mullion Island). Baker's original placement was closer to being correct. The content of the map has been extensively expanded. There are an additional 32 place names added to the coastal areas alone: Tintagel Head, Longships lighthouse (first built in 1795) and Runnel Stone. as well as many, many others. The Country Parks, while marked previously, are now labelled. Three new roads have been added to the new edition: Redruth to Penryn, Tregony to Probus and a western 'bypass' of Lostwithiel. Several of the pre-existing minor roads have been upgraded to main roads. 'Love I' has been corrected to 'Looe I', which must be considered an improvement. On the Isles of Scilly, the inset and positioning of the islands are identical to the 1791 map; however, the grid of latitude and longitude has been altered, and the lighthouse on St. Agnes has also been labelled. The label between the islands and Land's End has had the '...Distant 11¼ leagues or 39 miles' erased. Baker's revised placement of Hugh Town is within a couple of minutes of today's co-ordinates from Greenwich.

1791	The Universal Magazine of Knowledge and Pleasure, Volume LXXXIX, August, pages 121-123, by William Bent, London.
1804	Maps of the Several Counties and shires in England, by Darton and Harvey, London.
1806	Laurie and Whittle's New and Improved English Atlas. 1807, 1816, 1821 (Laurie only).
1816	New and Improved English Atlas, by James Whittle and Richard Holmes Laurie, London.

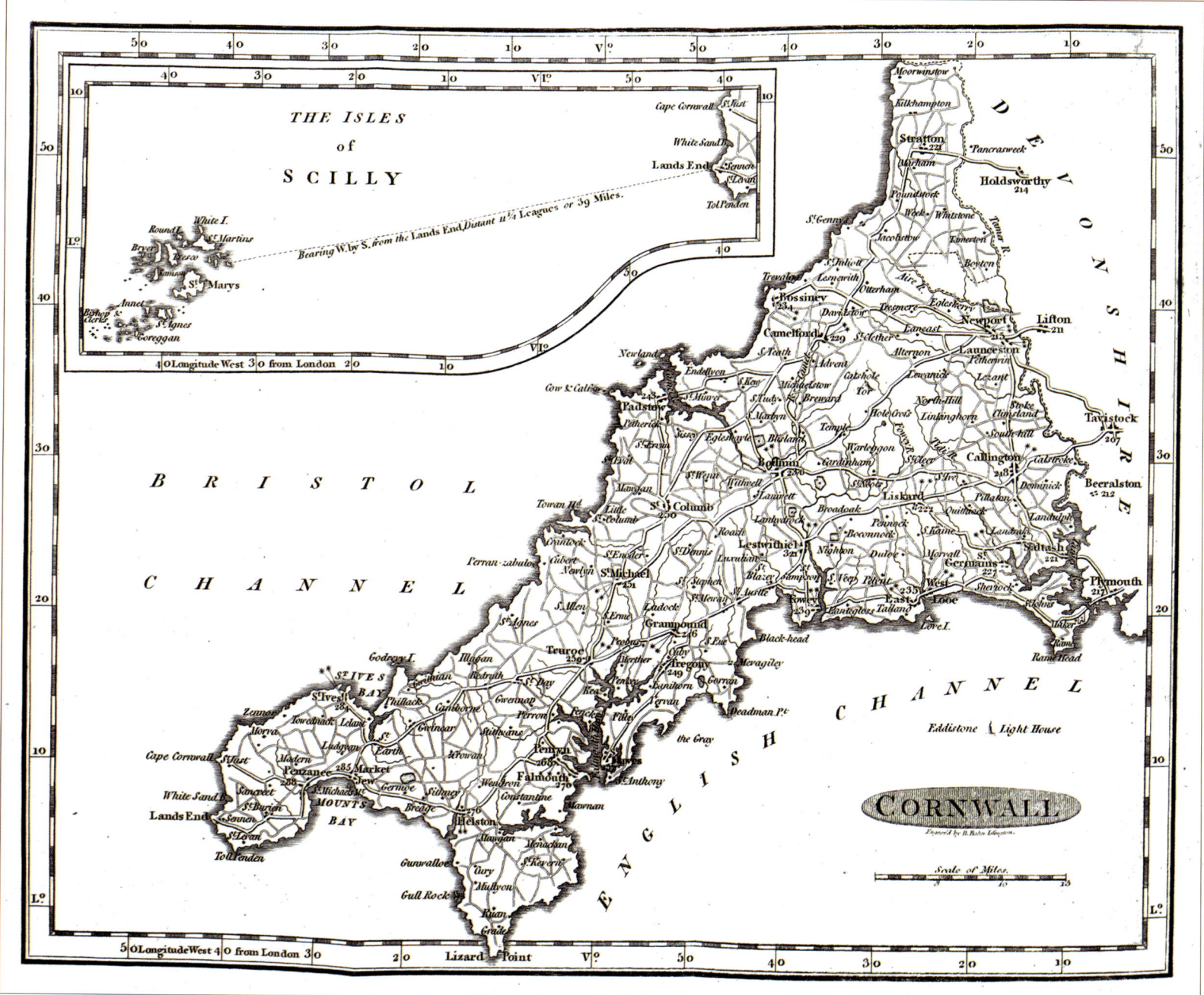

54. Baker 1791 The Universal Magazine of Knowledge and Pleasure. Vol LXXXiX

55. TUNNICLIFF, WILLIAM 1791

Eng. Tunnicliff, Pub. Collins and Crowder and Trueman
(527 x 476)

Tunnicliff first appears in 1786, with the publication of a series of three county maps: Staffordshire, Cheshire and Lancashire. These were originally sold separately but were combined into one volume the following year and titled 'A Topographic Survey of the counties of Stafford, Chester and Lancaster'. In the style of several preceding works (e.g. Blome (#18) and Martyn (#40)), Tunnicliff sought financial patronage from the local nobility in exchange for featuring these families; several pages are set aside per county for their coats of arms – with quite a few anticipatory blanks included. His next publication was to cover a further three counties, those of Somerset, Gloucestershire and Worcestershire. This was completed in 1789 and the two sets were combined into one six-county publication.

The only clue as to Tunnicliff's location is at the end of his address to the subscriber/reader, where he indicates home being Yarlett, near Stone, in Staffordshire. Yarlet Hall, to the north of the village, is now a public school. In Lewis's 'Topographical Dictionary' of 1845, it is listed as a 590-acre estate belonging to John Tunnicliffe, a Liverpool corn merchant. One might suppose that William was a scion of the same family, who embarked on a career as a surveyor.

His final publication was to survey the western counties of Hampshire, Wiltshire, Dorset, Somerset, Devon and Cornwall in 1791. A general map of the whole region was produced, together with separate maps of the six counties.

The map of Cornwall is one such map of the south-western counties and appears to be partly based on the maps produced by Thomas Martyn (#40), supplemented by original survey work carried out by Tunnicliff. The map is clearly engraved and is well drawn but shows little advance on the map-making techniques of the period, although supplementary detail in the text of the atlas includes a travelling index of roads, with details of distances, fairs and inns.

The map itself is quite featureless - no symbols for highlands or hills are present, and the number of towns and villages is light for the size of the map. Market towns, villages and 'Gentlemen's Seats' are shown, as too are turnpike roads. An inset shows the Isles of Scilly, along with brief details of the HMS Association and Shovell's fate, the event evidently still notable. Latitude and longitude (with no origin, St. Paul's is assumed) are marked on the borders, and the directions are shown by means of a simple compass rose. The map is correctly oriented, so the county runs to the southwest.

There are placement, as well as transcription, errors - Madren (Madron) has moved quite a few miles west of its true location, to Sancreed, while Zennor has become 'Lennor'. Helston is incorrectly shown open to the sea, and the roads show a certain artistic interpretation. Overall, the map's outline is fair, though it must be said the content is restrained and not as complete as recent predecessors such as Sudlow.

1791 *A Topographical Survey of the Counties of Hants, Wilts, Dorset, Somerset, Devon and Cornwall commonly known as the Western Circuit, by William Tunnicliff, B. C. Collins in Salisbury, S. Crowder in London and Trueman & Son in Exeter.*

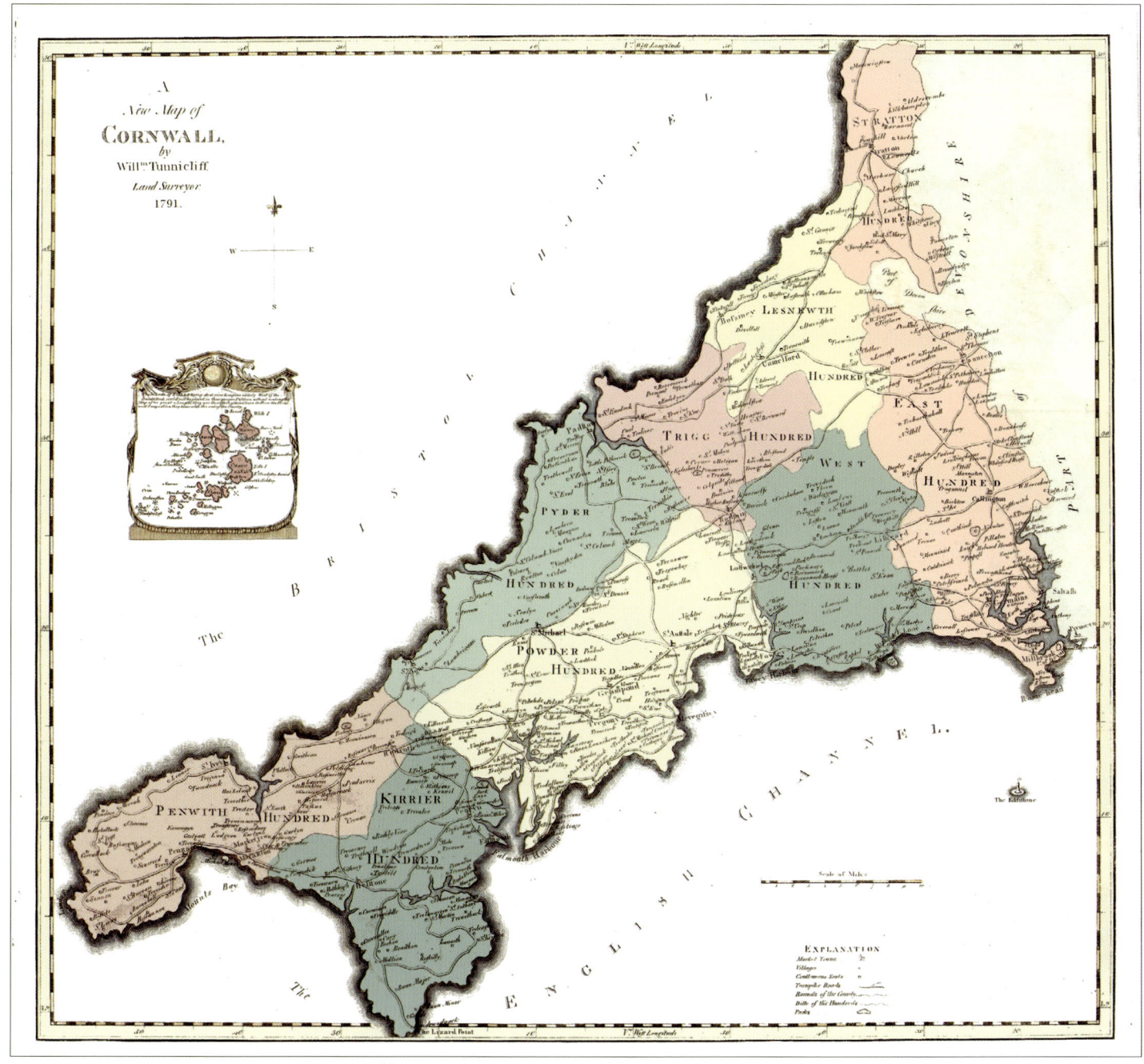

55. Tunnicliff 1791 A Topographical Survey of the Counties...

56. SPENCE, GRAEME 1792

Eng: Unknown, Pub HM Hydrographical Office
(978 x 660)

Spence (1758-1822) was born in Orkney and apprenticed to his cousin, Lt Murdoch Mackenzie RN, into Maritime Surveying in 1773; this would have finished seven years later (1780). Spence is recorded assisting in several works, during this apprenticeship, in the surveys of Plymouth, Falmouth and Torbay. He continued as Assistant Surveyor to Mackenzie until 1788, when both were released from the Admiralty. Spence was then briefly engaged by Trinity House, before returning to the Admiralty as a civilian to survey the Isles of Scilly from 1789 to 1793. This would become the first official survey since that of Collins (#23), since Ginver's survey of 1731 has to be considered 'unofficial' in this context. Spence died in London in 1822; his will was written September 1821 and proved 4 September 1822 (PROB11/1661).

In the process of his work at the Admiralty, Spence produced a number of charts and reports, most of which remained the property of the United Kingdom Hydrographic Office and were never published in the public domain. His 'Survey of the Isles of Scilly' appears to be an exception. This was preceded by an internal (unpublished) chart termed 'A Maritime Survey of Scilly', drawn at about the same scale as the later 'Survey of the Isles of Scilly'. This chart, illustrated, is dated 1792, and at the foot of it is the publisher's imprint 'Hydrographical Office, Published according to Act of Parliament June 27th 1810 by Capt. Hurd RN, Hydrographer to the Admiralty'. It is notable that this chart contains no reference to either latitude or longitude, despite being a 'maritime chart'. One could speculate that the sanitisation of the chart for public consumption was done due to the sensitivity of the information that accurate positioning by co-ordinates would give to the enemy. By inference, this may explain Collins' erasure of similar information from his main chart of Scilly (#23).

Identifying the Spence chart is quite straight-forward: it is clearly titled lower left 'A Survey of the Scilly Isles by Graeme Spence 1792, Variation 24° 45'W'. Set around the edges of the chart are 23 views from offshore onto various aspects of the islands, together with brief annotations, compass bearings &c.; (considering a magnetic declination of over 24° West, these become crucially important). The grid and alpha-numeric annotations present on the chart illustrated are later additions which have been added by a chart owner for private use.

It is the detail of the islands and the immediate area that sets Spence's chart/map apart from Collins (#23) and Ginver (1731). While it is true that Spence was surveying at the behest of the Admiralty, he has not passed up the opportunity of augmenting the terrestrial parts of the map as well. The detail covering the islands themselves is finely done, with roads, tracks, field boundaries &c. all shown for the first time. There is a differentiation of low-lying coastal areas, compared to the rockier cliffs, and the extent of tidal flats and sand bars offshore is much more detailed and extensive than any of the foregoing charts (Collins (#23), Ginver (1731), Van Keulen (#32) and, importantly, Tovey and Ginver (#43) which, while dated 1794, must be in fact based on data perhaps 50+ years older). By reference, it is worth inspecting the extent of the Abbey Pond and its larger neighbour, the Great Pool, to the north-west. Collins shows only the former, as a simple outline with no mention of the adjacent St. Nicholas's Abbey ruins – these would later become the site of the world-famous Abbey Gardens originally created by Augustus Smith from c.1834. Both Ginver (1731) and Van Keulen (1735) show a larger pond, but there is still no indication of the larger Great Pool that, by Spence's time, 60 years later, has expanded to the north-west, with an outflow to the sea south of New Grimsby, and is marked as 31ft deep. Spence shows both the Great Pool and Abbey Pool as connected entities, with a bridge between them. Today they are separate pools.

A second amended edition of the chart was published in 1858 by J. D. Potter, Agent for the Admiralty Charts. This can be distinguished by an addition to the chart under the mileage scale below Spence's title, detailing tidal heights.

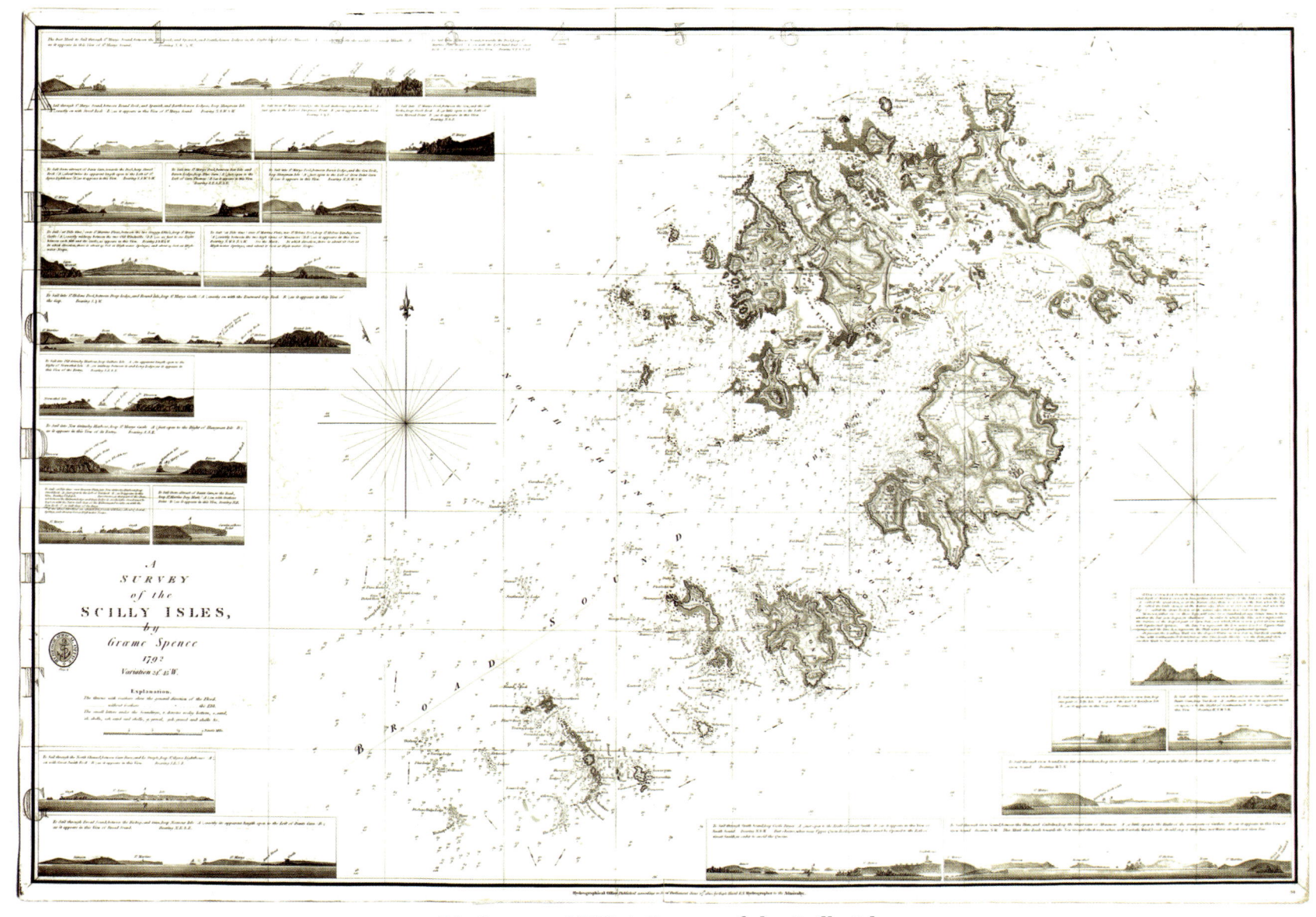

56. Spence, 1792 A Survey of the Scilly Isles

1810   A Survey of the Scilly Isles, Pub. Hydrographic Office.
1812   A Geographical and Nautical Description of Scilly, with ... Sailing Directions... Tide Tables ... [with] two charts taken ... in the years 1790, 1791, 1792, by Graeme Spence, Maritime Surveyor to the Lordships.
1858   2nd Edition with some amendments. Pub. J. D. Potter, London.

57. FAIRBURN, JOHN & ROWE, ROBERT 1798

Eng. Rowe, Pub. Fairburn
(58 x 89)

There are, in fact, at least three John Fairburns. Fairburn the father (c.1750-1832), son (1787-1854) and grandson (1811-1843). Fairburn senior owned a bookshop at 146 Minories, between The Tower of London and Aldgate. He opened a second shop on Ludgate Broadway in 1811, and it seems that this new address was used by Fairburn junior as a publication address as well as the Minories address. The business moved from 146 to 110 Minories, at some point in the 1820s, and it is from this address that son and grandson Fairburn produce the later work. It seems logical to assume that Fairburn senior produced the cartographic output discussed, in view of the dates of publication. Other publications from the Fairburn house featured a wide-ranging selection, often exposing the fates of the underdog, the socially disadvantaged or just simply unfortunate. John Fairburn (1787-1854) left a will (PROB11/2202/178) detailing an extensive portfolio of properties, both in London and in Gloucestershire.

In 1795, (according to the watermark only, as it is otherwise undated), Fairburn senior produced an atlas of 24 roundels, titled 'A Map of the World'. Some English counties are included, (not Cornwall, unfortunately). They are imprinted 'Published by John Fairburn, No. 146 Minories'. A later edition (watermarked 1795 also) was produced which expanded the counties to 14, still excluding Cornwall. The engraver of all these maps is unknown, and the atlas itself is a scarce item.

In 1798 Fairburn produced a card game, with a set of county maps engraved by Robert Rowe (based on John Cary's 1789 work (#50)) entitled 'The Game of English Geography Being a Sett of County Maps on cards, with rules for playing'.

Each county is on a separate playing card, with an extra card for Anglesey. The purpose of the game was to identify the adjacent county to the one in your hand. The principal town in each county is given in Roman capitals, with a note of its distance from London.

The Cornwall map is oriented with Devon at the foot of the card (set in portrait format), with north to the right. The border comprises tight parallel lines perpendicular to the edge, with the title within this. Only principal towns and rivers are marked, along with the major roads. The second reprint, done later the same year, adds some further roads, as well as numbers denoting the adjacent counties - in the case of Cornwall, this is somewhat moot.

In 1811 Robert Rowe collaborated with Joseph Allen to engrave an almost identical set of cards, again based on Cary's 1789 (#50) maps, called 'Allen's English Atlas'; these are slightly larger, at 63mm x 93mm. The Cornwall map is still oriented with the Devon border at the base, and the scale is shown bottom left. Under the title is the inscription 'Pub. by J Allen 3 Hampden Str, Sommer's town 1811'. The border is a decorative foliate with a panel at the base bearing the mark 'Also by R. Rowe, No. 19 Bedford Str, Bedford Row, London'. A second edition, in 1813, has the date removed from the top panel and a short county description in place of Rowe's inscription at the base.

1798 *The Game of English Geography, by John Fairburn, London. Reprinted 1798 with added detail, including figures indicating adjacent counties.*

57. Rowe 1798 The Game of English Geography

SECTION FOUR:

58. SMITH, CHARLES 1801
59. WILKES, JOHN & NEELE, SAMUEL 1802
60. DUGDALE, JAMES & NEELE, SAMUEL 1814
61. LYSONS BROS & NEELE, SAMUEL 1814
62. PINNOCK, WILLIAM & NEELE, SAMUEL 1820
63. BUTTERS, ROBERT 1803
64. LUFFMAN, JOHN 1803
65. COLE, GEORGE & ROPER, JOHN 1805
66. CAPPER, BENJAMIN & COOPER, HENRY 1808
67. WALLIS, JAMES 1812, 1812 (x2), 1820
68. BAKER, BENJAMIN & ORDNANCE SURVEY 1813
69. ROWE, ROBERT 1816
70. LANGLEY, EDWARD & BELCH, WILLIAM 1817
71. CRABB, THOMAS 1819
72. LEIGH, SAMUEL & HALL, SIDNEY 1820
73. DIX, THOMAS & DARTON, WILLIAM 1821
74. SMITH, CHARLES & GARDNER, WILLIAM ROBERT 1822
75. PERROT, ARISTIDE-MICHEL & MIGNARET, Mme 1824
76. GREENWOOD, C & J 1827 and 1829
77. TEESDALE, HENRY 1830
78. MURRAY, T. LAURIE & HOARE & REEVES 1830
79. LEWIS, SAMUEL & STARLING, THOMAS 1831
80. COBBETT, WILLIAM 1832
81. FISHER, HENRY & DAVIES, BENJAMIN REES 1832
82. DUNCAN, JAMES & EBDEN, WILLIAM 1811
83. BELL, JAMES & SCOTT, ROBERT 1833-4
84. PIGOT, JAMES & Co. 1830
85. PINNOCK, WILLIAM & ARCHER, JOSHUA 1833
86. MOULE, THOMAS 1836
87. DUGDALE, THOMAS & ARCHER, JOSHUA 1842

Section Four
The Nineteenth Century

58. SMITH, CHARLES 1801

Eng. Jones and Smith, Pub. Smith
(470 x 406)

Smith's 'New English Atlas' appeared in 1804, though all the maps in it, except Wales, had been engraved by Edward Jones and Benjamin Smith of Pentonville in 1801. The atlas is a superb piece of work, very similar to the 'New English Atlas' by John Cary, which was probably inspired by the work of Smith. The accuracy of the maps and the presentation of a vast quantity of reliable information places the work of both Smith and Cary on a par with the Ordnance Survey maps which began to appear at about the same time (Kent 1801, Essex 1805). It is the first English atlas to use Greenwich as the prime meridian (see side note).

The scale of Smith's map of Cornwall is about ¼ inch to 1 mile, and, apart from a few variations in the spelling of place names, the work might pass for a map of the present day. The map was usually issued coloured by hand - turnpike roads in red, parks in dark green and each Hundred completely covered in a wash of pale green, pink or yellow ochre - while its border was outlined in a stronger tone of appropriate hue. The border is divided into degrees of latitude and longitude, a further sub-division into minutes being made along the inner edge of the border.

One other particularly interesting feature of Smith's map of Cornwall is the representation of the 'Proposed Tamar Navigation' on the Devon side of the Tamar, running from the 'New Bridge' above Calstock, up as far as Tamarton. Evidently this originally referred to the projected Bude-Tamar Navigation envisaged by Edmund Leach in 1774. The original Act (14 George III Cap 53, 24 May 1774) proposed a canal or cut from Bude to Calstock, about 5 miles downstream of the tidal limit of the Tamar. The whole project was ambitious: a rise from sea level at Bude of 240ft (73m), followed by a similar drop to Calstock over an overland distance of 28 miles. The linear length of the entire construction would be 81 miles. The 1774 Act allowed only ten years for completion, and it evidently stalled. A new and shorter initiative, to reach Launceston from Bude, on the north coast, was started in 1819 and completed in 1826.

In the meantime, an amended proposal to the original, called the Tamar Manure Navigation Act, was passed in 1796 with the intention of constructing a canal to bring shell-sand and seaweed manure into the inland areas. The route started above Morwellham Quay, on the Devon bank, running on that bank northwards. In fact, a 500-yard bypass of the weir at Gunnislake (at the tidal limit) was completed, extending the navigable river by only 3 miles. The project was abandoned in 1808, due probably in part to objections to the route by the 6th Duke of Bedford, through whose land, near Milton Abbot, part of the canal would pass.

One of the advantages of viewing a number of maps of the same area together is seeing the evolution of a feature such as (in this case) Hayle Causeway. The lowest bridging point of the river Hayle is the 15th century bridge at St. Erth. Maps from Norden onwards have clearly shown this bridge connecting the two halves of Penwith (the other bridge is at Relubbus). With the development of Hayle, St. Ives and Penzance, this crossing point was quite a detour and a shorter route developed racing the tides across the flats of the estuary. It was not without dangers and there were several drownings. Smith's map is the first to show a crossing downstream of St Erth that, in 1825, becomes the road causeway from Hayle in the East to Grigg's Quay in the West. The Greenwood's map of 1827 (#76) shows the completed road over the estuary.

1804 Smith's New English Atlas, by C. Smith, London. 2nd Edition 1808, 3rd Edition 1818, 1821, 1827, 1828, 1832, 1834, 1839, 1841, 1844, 1864 New imprint Smith & Son 63, Charing Cross.

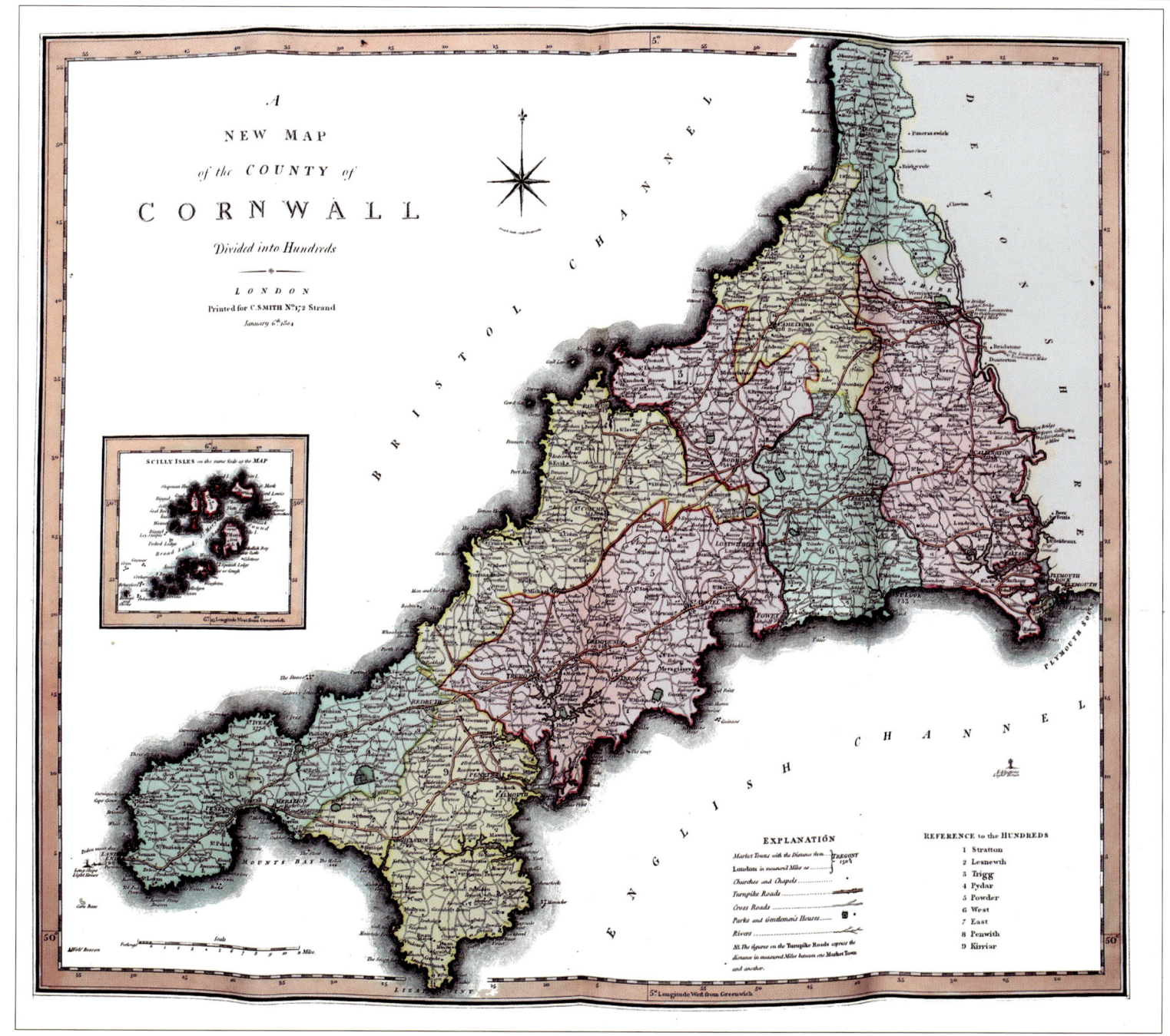

58. Smith 1804 Smith's New English Atlas. C. Smith, London.

THE GREENWICH MERIDIAN, RAILWAYS & DECLINATION

Prior to the establishment of a prime meridian at Greenwich, map makers had used a multitude of reference meridians. Nautical charts needed longitude earlier than terrestrial maps, so it is not surprising to see longitude appearing on charts first. The 1494 Treaty of Tordesillas is possibly the earliest division of the globe into two meridians, which defined the exploration areas for the Spanish and Portuguese; the line itself was 370 leagues west of the Cape Verde Islands, with the Spanish taking the western 'hemisphere' and the Portuguese the eastern 'hemisphere'. (Spanish nautical leagues, at the time, were a rather flexible unit of measure, and we have not attempted to convert them). Three island groups played a role in the early attempts to find a prime meridian: the Cape Verde Islands, the Canaries and the Azores.

Gerard Mercator constructed his first world map in 1538 and prompted by Ptolomy's 'Geographica' (1477), he drew his prime meridian through the Canary Islands. His later globe, in 1541, used Fuerteventura, and notably shows the magnetic north pole, (later called *Rupe Nigra*, or black rock). Columbus's navigators had noted the variation in compass north and magnetic north 100 years previously, which led Mercator to adopt the idea of a meridian where there would be zero magnetic (agonic) declination. Mercator thought the Cape Verde Islands were unaffected by declination, while others claimed the Azores enjoyed similar status. Mercator's 1569 World Map had to shunt the various islands about, to align the Azores and Cape Verde Islands and place an agonic meridian straight through them. In fact, the agonic meridians are not a simple north-south division of the earth into two hemispheres.

Willem Janzoon Blaeu (#10) produced his two-sheet world map in 1604 using Corvo (western-most island of the Azores) as a prime meridian, but, as insurance, included the Lizard as a supplementary meridian. However, by 1619 he had moved his prime to the Peak of Tenerife (3720m), on the Canary island of Santa Cruz, because '*utpote a sexagenis leucis conspicuus*' - it was visible from 60 leagues and provided a navigational reference. Working the maths back from an elevation of 3720m suggests the peak is visible from 220km.

From the 1500s to the 1800s some 25 different prime meridians were in use globally, including St. Pauls, the Lizard and Greenwich, as well as foreign centres such as Paris, Amsterdam, Toledo and Washington DC. Norden (#6) had concluded that using magnetic north instead of grid north created too many problems in the mapping of the counties. The chart here shows why this is so, and why it was avoided.

The Royal Observatory at Greenwich was founded by Charles II, in 1675. Sir Christopher Wren, formerly professor of Astronomy at Oxford and now architect of the re-built London after the 1666 fire, was given charge of the endeavour. He selected the ruins of Greenwich Castle (built in 1433), which was on Royal Parks' ground and in an elevated position: Flamsteed House, (named for John Flamsteed, 1st Astronomer Royal), was built on the old foundations and became the Royal Observatory.

Edmond Halley (2nd AR) established a prime meridian there in 1721. This was corrected several times by James Bradley (3rd AR), and it was Bradley's meridian established in 1750 that was (and still is) used by the Ordnance Survey as the Zero Meridian. In 1851 this was refined using the Airy Transit Circle telescope, designed by George Biddell Airy (7th AR).

The history of quite how Greenwich was selected as the world's prime meridian is complex and not, as one might think, inevitable. What follows is a summary, which is not intended to be a full explanation. Withers' 2017 analysis supplies a fuller story.

Following three International Geographic Congresses, in Antwerp (1871), Paris (1875) and Venice (1881), the principle of a standard Prime Meridian at Greenwich was gaining favour. The International Meridian Conference held in Washington, USA in October 1884 was attended by delegates from around the world, and, a month later, the conference drew up seven resolutions that really were world changers. Principal among these was a common meridian at Greenwich, with that meridian defining where west and east began and ended. This would define where, on the earth's surface, a global day started and ended, and therefore where midnight and midday started.

The selection of Greenwich appears to have been entirely serendipitous; while London was sitting on an agonic meridian in

166 *Antique Maps of Cornwall and the Isles of Scilly*

the mid 1600s, this might have been a co-incidence. Other competing locations for a prime meridian had been proposed, each with a geographic rationale, but all had disadvantages that Greenwich had already overcome. To an extent, one could argue that the use of St. Paul's had embedded itself in English cartography since Morden's maps, and the transition to Greenwich 200 years later was a refinement. Smith's 1804 atlas is a clear declaration of intent and was ahead of the non-binding recommendation of Greenwich prime by international authorities by 80 years. The railways of Britain had followed suit in the 1840s, again pre-empting the 1884 International Conference. One of the principal arguments for Greenwich was that Britain's marine fleet made up about 30% of the world's total in the late 1800s; its trade, commerce and naval reach was governed by reference to a meridian that had risen to dominance by virtue of sheer numbers. Of the world's shipped tonnage, 72% used Greenwich: more people already depended upon it than any other alternative.

Referring briefly to Morden (#20), Bowen (#30) and Kitchin & Jefferys (#41), there is 20 minutes difference between the centre of Cornwall and London marked on the top border of each map. Time across the kingdom was kept locally; travellers were obliged to alter their (carriage) clocks or watches to local time as they progressed, by referring to the town clock, sun dial or almanacs published for the purpose. The Bristol Corn Exchange building, built in 1822, added a second minute hand to the clock before 1852 to show both 'local' Bristol time (GMT minus 10 minutes) and GMT. The city adopted GMT fully in September 1852, but the clock still tells two times, even today.

The electronic telegraph was the product of evolving inventions by various scientists from the late 1700s. William Cooke and Charles Wheatstone commercialised their patented telegraph system in 1837, this was installed on the Great Western Railway in 1838 and GWR standardised its timetables in 1840. George Biddell Airey, the 7th Astronomer Royal, proposed the standardisation of time to Greenwich for the whole railway system; he had seen the master and slave clocks built by Charles Shepherd, at the Great Exhibition of 1851, and requested of Shepherd a design for his proposal. Shepherd's master clock, or Normal Clock, sent electronic pulses to slave clocks, one of which, the Shepherd Gate Clock, can still be seen at Greenwich, with its 24-hour face. This same signal was sent to London Bridge Station and the Central Telegraph Station of the Electrical Time Company, in Founder's Hall on Lothbury, behind the Bank of England. From there, a signal was sent daily to each station, allowing the distant station to set its clocks to GMT. The Statutes (Definition of Time) Act unified the whole of Great Britain to GMT in 1880 (Withers 2017 p130).

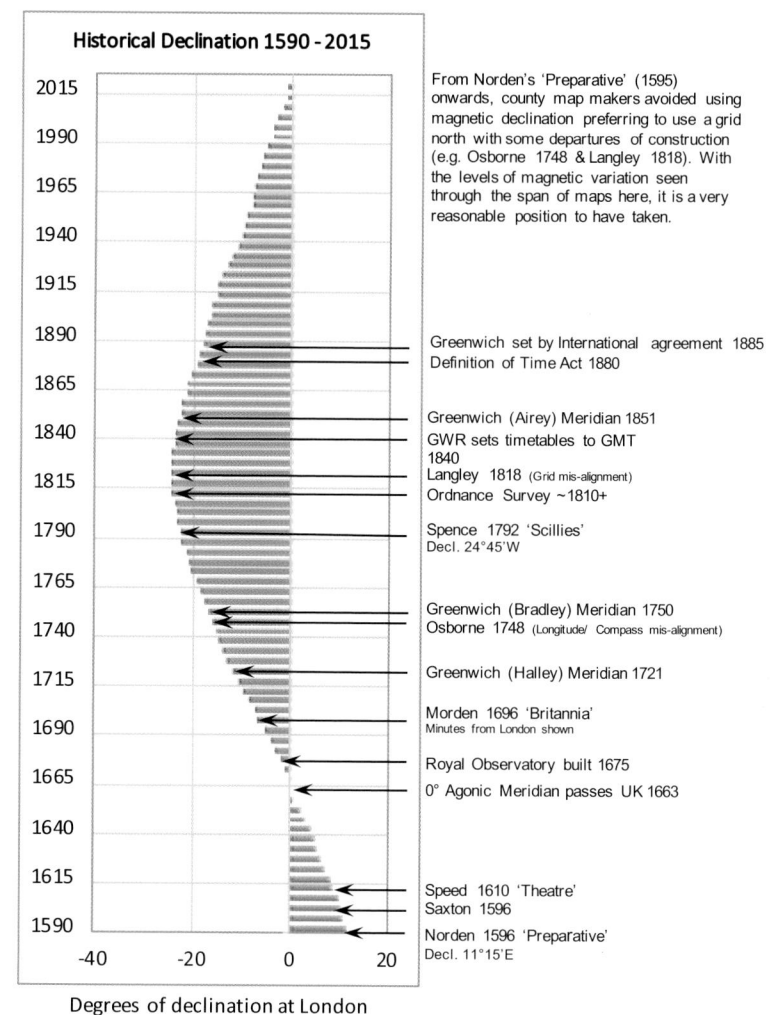

Historical Declination 1590 - 2015

From Norden's 'Preparative' (1595) onwards, county map makers avoided using magnetic declination preferring to use a grid north with some departures of construction (e.g. Osborne 1748 & Langley 1818). With the levels of magnetic variation seen through the span of maps here, it is a very reasonable position to have taken.

Greenwich set by International agreement 1885
Definition of Time Act 1880

Greenwich (Airey) Meridian 1851
GWR sets timetables to GMT 1840
Langley 1818 (Grid mis-alignment)
Ordnance Survey ~1810+

Spence 1792 'Scillies'
Decl. 24°45'W

Greenwich (Bradley) Meridian 1750
Osborne 1748 (Longitude/ Compass mis-alignment)

Greenwich (Halley) Meridian 1721

Morden 1696 'Britannia'
Minutes from London shown

Royal Observatory built 1675
0° Agonic Meridian passes UK 1663

Speed 1610 'Theatre'
Saxton 1596
Norden 1596 'Preparative'
Decl. 11°15'E

Degrees of declination at London
Negative (West), Positive (East)

Antique Maps of Cornwall and the Isles of Scilly

59. WILKES, JOHN & NEELE, SAMUEL 1802

Eng. Neele, Pub. Wilkes
(178 x 222)

John Wilkes (1750-1810) was a printer, bookseller and publisher. The 'Encyclopaedia Londinensis' was 'compiled, digested and arranged' and then published between 1801 and 1828, over 24 volumes. Cornwall was engraved in 1802 and published in Volume V pp213-215 in 1810. The map was clearly engraved by Samuel J. Neele (1758-1824); it is signed bottom right as 'Neele sculp Strand' and is titled at the base 'Cornwall, Published, as the Act derives, May 20th 1802 by J Wilkes'.

Samuel John Neele* was born in July 1758, in Stepney, and is noted as a prolific engraver. From about 1785 he established himself at 352, Strand, in London, where he is recorded on the Electoral Rolls until his death in May 1824. An entry in Wakefield's 'Merchant and Tradesman General Directory' of 1790 registers him as an engraver. He married Mary Chapman, of Frome, in Somerset, in August 1787, and had possibly six children, at least two of whom were boys - James and Josiah. Neele's acumen and skill made him a very successful man. At the proving of his will (PROB11/1690/501-550), it is evident that he was the owner of several London properties, including 352, Strand, and bequeathed a sum of £6500 to his children to be held in securities. James and Josiah took over their father's business around 1818, becoming notable engravers in their own right. Their engraving for the Greenwood's famous map of London in 1827 is, perhaps, their most well-known.

The map of Cornwall bears a striking resemblance to the Baker map of 1791: the Baker map is oriented correctly, and Neele has simply rotated it through 90° and shifted all the text, as well making it one of two maps here with west at the foot of the map (Butters (#63)). There are some differences - Neele/Wilkes has omitted the annotation denoting the returning MPs from the county, shown since Morden's 1720 map and resembling a pair of palm trees. There are some slight variations in spelling though in general most have survived the transcription. The inset of the Isles of Scilly is set bottom left and indicated as being 39 miles from Land's End - this is copied from Baker.

1810-28 Encyclopaedia Londinensis, Or Universal Dictionary Compiled, Digested and Arranged by John Wilkes of Milland House, Sussex. Printed by J. Alland West Smithfield, London.

* Three of Neele's productions are shown here (# 59, #60 and #61).

59. Neele, 1810-28 Wilkes Encyclopaedia Londinensis

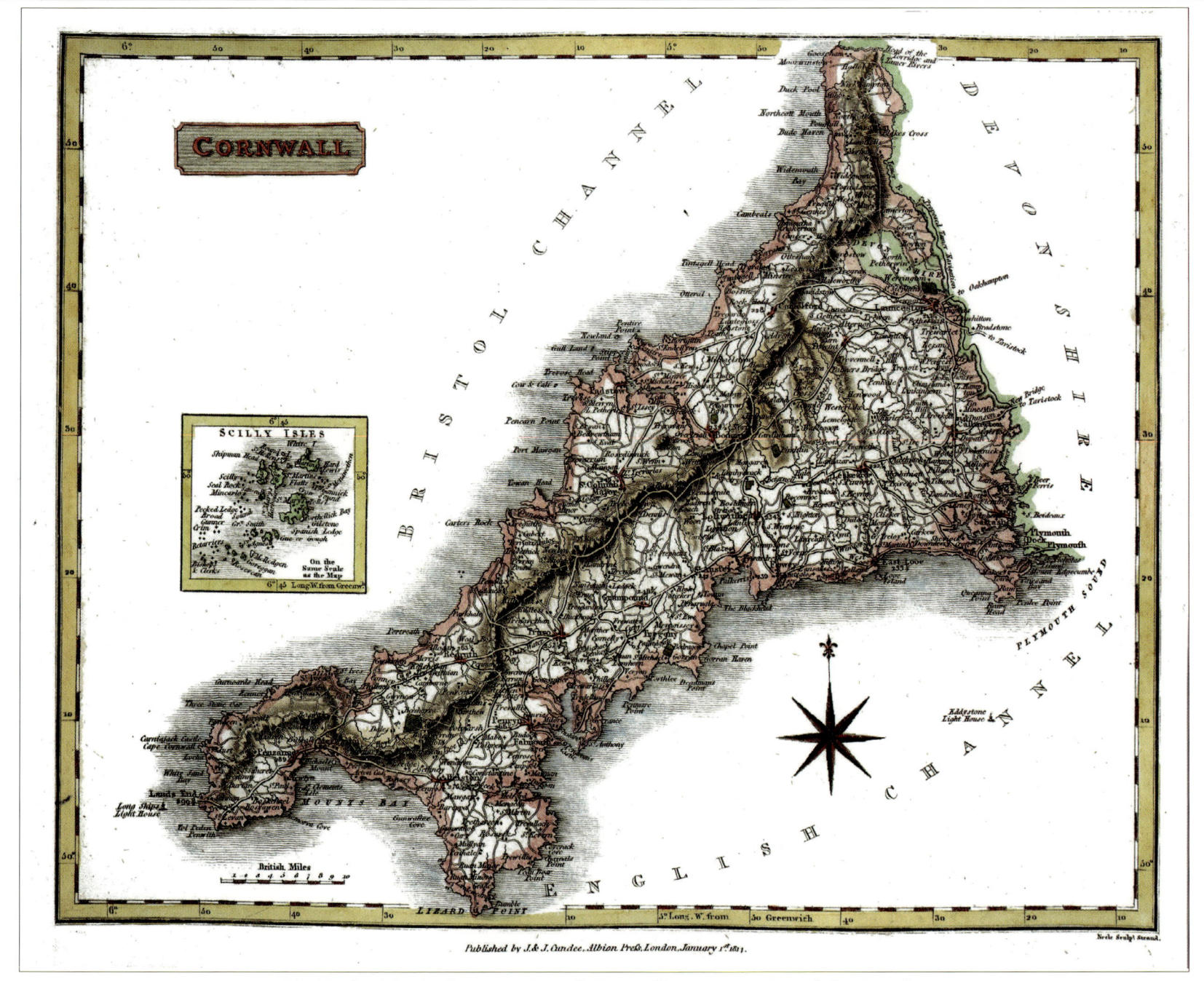

60. Neele 1814 *The New British Traveller*, James Dugdale, London

60. DUGDALE, JAMES & NEELE, SAMUEL 1814

Eng, Neele, Pub J. Cundee
(178 x 222)

Neele contributed many maps to numerous publications. The 'New British Traveller' was started in 1812 by James Dugdale LLD, in four volumes. (Cornwall appears in Volume 1; the map is dated 1 January 1814). This travel book started life under the auspices of Alex Hogg (#49), and the elaborate title leads one to suspect that the otherwise elusive Dugdale might be yet another of Hogg's aliases.

Dugdale's 'New British Traveller' was obtained by James Cundee (1771-1831) around 1811 and expanded. By 1814 James was joined by his brother, John (1776-1842), and Neele was commissioned to engrave new maps. The Cundees' publishing house was dissolved in October 1812 ('London Gazette' Issue 17011 - this was finalised in May 1815) and taken over by J. Robins & Co.; later versions (1818 onwards) bear that imprint.

The map of Cornwall is curious since, while it bears Neele's name, it is radically different from another 1814 map also produced by him for the Lysons brothers (#61).

Of note here is a seam of highlands running the length of the county, from Stratton to Land's End. The depiction is odd at first; however, a closer inspection reveals that the line of 'highlands' bisects the county north-west to south-east and defines the drainage watersheds of the rivers and streams of the county, with very few exceptions. This is later copied by Darton (#73), Gardner (#74), Migneret (#75) and Davies (#81). Major and minor roads are shown, as too are the private county parks. The Scilly Isles are shown inset with longitude from Greenwich. The 5° West line is 8' too far east, in line with most of the other maps of the day. Taking this into account, Neele's placement of Land's End is within a minute of today's position west of Greenwich. His placement of Hugh Town, on the Isles of Scilly, (with the 8' offset) is still 18' too far west, or 13 miles. Running from Newbridge, near Callington on the Tamar, to Tamarton, Neele has marked the Proposed Tamar Navigation canal, which had been abandoned as a viable project six years previously.

1812-14 The New British Traveller; Or, a Modern Panorama of England and Wales... (the full title runs for several lines), by James Dugdale, Pub. James Cundee, London.
1815 The New British Traveller, by James Dugdale, Pub. J. &J. Cundee, London. Repub. 1819 with separate title pages for each publisher (Cundee and Robins).
1818 New Imprint: Pub. J. Robins & Co., Albion Press, London.

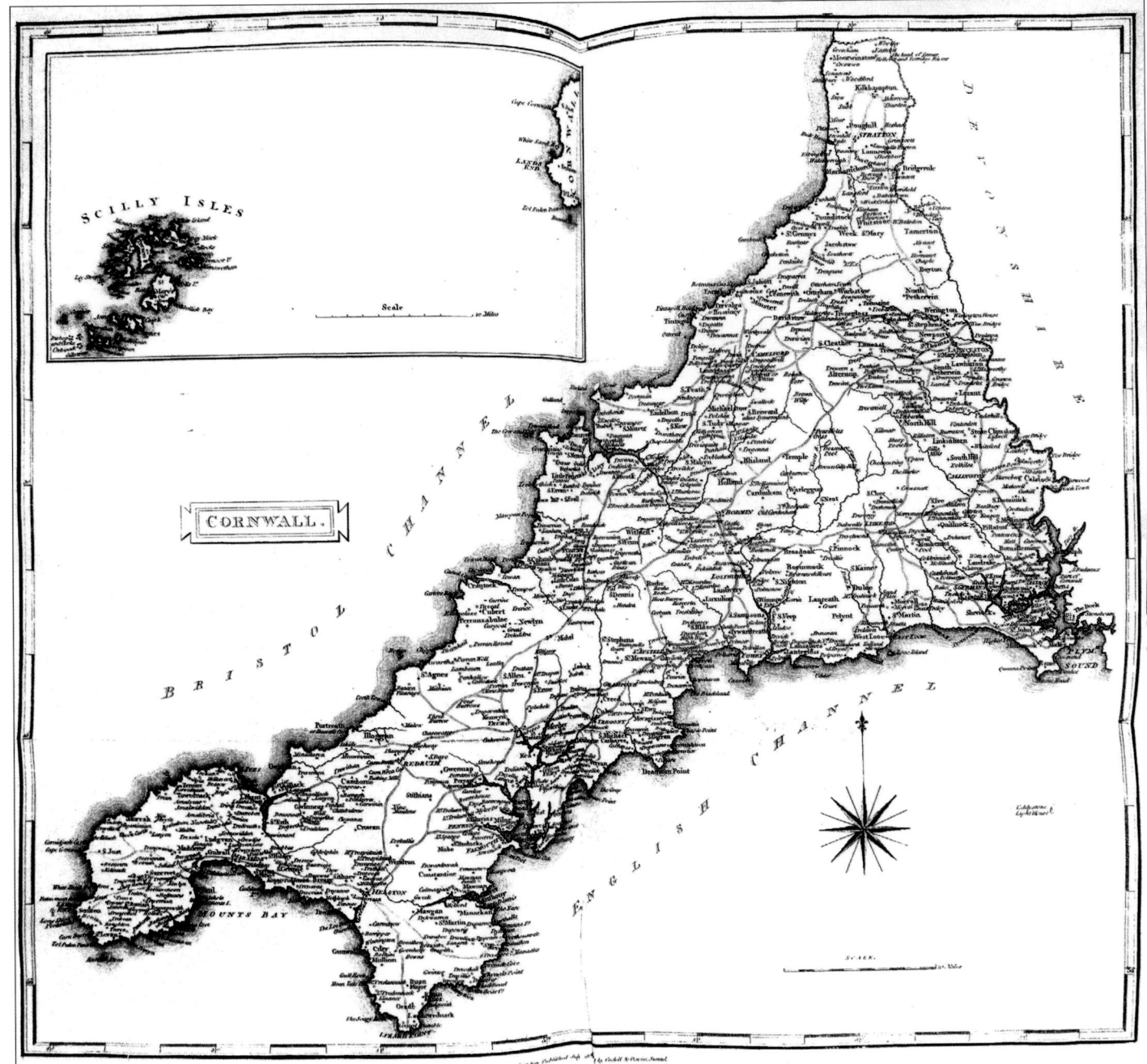

61. Neele 1814 Lysons Magna Britannia being a concise topographical account of the several counties of Great Britain.

61. LYSONS BROTHERS & NEELE, SAMUEL 1814

Eng. Neele, Pub. Cadell & Davies
(470 x 430)

The Rev. Daniel Lysons (1762-1834) was an English antiquarian and topographer. He attended St. Mary Hall, Oxford, graduating with an MA in 1785 and initially followed his father into the clergy. Upon moving to Putney, his attention was drawn to the topography of the area, publishing his major oeuvre 'The Environs of London, being an Historical Account of the Towns, Villages and Hamlets within twelve miles of that Capital' in 1792.

Samuel Lysons (1763-1819), younger brother of Daniel, went straight into law from grammar school. He was introduced to George III in 1796 and was appointed Keeper of the Records in the Tower of London in 1803. His greatest work '*Reliquiæ Britannico-Romanæ*' was a 25-year labour covering Roman mosaics of Britain, published in 1813-1815 and making him (still) an authority on the subject. According to his DNB entry (Volume 12 p362), only 50 copies were produced, selling for £48 6s each.

Daniel and Samuel embarked upon an updated improvement on Camden's 'Britannia' in 1806. In total, only six volumes of 'Magna Britannia' were produced, containing nine county maps: Volume 1: Bedfordshire, Berkshire and Buckinghamshire (1806), Volume 2: Cambridgeshire (1808) and Palatine of Chester (1810), Volume 3: Cornwall (1814), Volume 4: Cumberland (1816), Volume 5: Derbyshire (1817) and Volume 6: Devon (1822). Samuel Lysons died following the publication of the Derbyshire volume, and Daniel completed Devon alone, though he credits his late brother in the Devon frontispiece.

'Volume The Third' entirely devotes itself to Cornwall and runs to 250 pages of data and 390 pages of text. Within the text are a total of 37 engraved illustrations, ranging in subject, of many views and sketches drawn by Samuel Lysons. Some are engraved by Letitia Byrne (1779-1849), while others were etched by Joseph Farington RA (1747-1821) – many of which are very evocative renditions of some of the county's major sights, such as Mount's Bay, the Cheesewring and Tintagel &c. The remaining engravings are of other traditional points of interest covered by previous authors such as Norden and Borlase. There are two sketch maps, within the book, of the harbours at Falmouth and Fowey, copied from an anonymous map produced about 1540 which is still with the British Library. Ahead of the frontispiece is the only full map of the county.

When the Lysons map is compared with a contemporary Neele map (#60), it is interesting to note the differences. The map itself is there in support of the text of the book, and as such is drawn to contain elements of the book and little else – some of the antiquities mentioned in the book are shown, for instance, but no hills or highlands are drawn. The road system shown is simplified, with several major routes missing, e.g. Penzance to Angarrack, and a non-existent road from Helston to Redruth has been added. Major conurbations such as Truro and Penzance are drawn with a cluster of blocks indicating several houses. Smaller church-towns are marked with a cross, while hamlets are shown with a simple circle. Some houses or estates of note are separately marked and named. The aborted Tamar Navigation canal (1808) is not shown on the Lysons map, though from the text, the omission appears intended.

The foot of the map is marked 'London Pub July 18 1814 by Cadell and Davies, Strand'. To the right of this is the simple engraver's mark: 'Neele at 369 Strand'.

1814 *Magna Britannia being a concise topographical account of the several counties of Great Britain, by Rev. Daniel Lysons AM, FRS, FA, LS and Samuel Lysons FRS, FAS. Volume the Third containing Cornwall. T. Cadell and W Davies, London.*

62. PINNOCK, WILIAM & NEELE, SAMUEL 1819

Eng. S.J. Neele, Pub. Geo B. Whittaker 1819, G. & W. B. Whittaker 1823-25
(160 x 130)

William Pinnock (1782-1843) was born in Alton, Hampshire and became a school-master. He moved into the trade of bookseller and author while still in Alton. In 1811 he moved to Newbury and set up a co-partnership of booksellers with William Vincent and Samuel Maunder. In April 1816 this partnership was declared bankrupt ('London Gazette', Issue 17125, p656). Pinnock and Maunder moved to 267 Strand, London, and set up a new partnership, with T. Bensley (see Aikin #53). This was wound up in November 1820.

Pinnock's bibliographic output always was on the educational side, and the 83 issues of 'Catechisms' were a major success. It was later collected into one volume, called 'The Juvenile Cyclopaedia' in 1839. Other successes included an abridgement of Goldsmith's 'Histories of England' in 1825. This led Pinnock to over-extend himself financially into ventures beyond his experience: he attempted to corner the London veneer market for pianos &c. and was forced to sell his copyrights to George Whittaker in an attempt to shore up his finances.

The 'History and Topography of England and Wales' was published in 1819, and engraved by (Samuel John) Neele & Son, 352 Strand, London. This version lacks the explanation key that is added to the 1820 'History and Topography of Cornwall' that forms part of the 83-part 'Catechisms' series.

The 'Travellers Pocket Atlas' was published by Pinnock and Maunder the same year, using the same maps. George Whittaker subsequently republished both works, bearing at the foot of the map the imprint 'Published G. & W. B. Whittaker, Ave Maria Lane, 1821'. The engraver's imprint bottom right 'Neele & Son, 352 Strand' was retained also.

The Cornwall map is highly simplified, with no topographic elements other than river courses shown. A key top left contains an explanation of the features included on the map, though this only extends to conurbations, country seats and roads. Unlisted but shown are many dots denoting the locations of mines, which are noted directly onto the map. The roads shown are marked with the incremental mileage, with the full mileage from London shown encircled. From the map, there are tracts of the county apparently devoid of any human impact – West Penwith, Stratton and Lizard are particularly affected.

The main roads through the county have shifted in emphasis. The main route here enters Cornwall from Okehampton to Launceston, and then describes what in time will become the main A30 as far as Truro, before ending in Falmouth, indicating the town's increased importance as a Packet and Naval port.

1819 *Pinnock's History and Topography of England and Wales Volume I. Published by Geo B. Whittaker, London. Reprinted 1825.*
1820 *The Travellers Pocket Atlas, Pinnock & Maunder, London. Republished 1823.*
1820 *Pinnock's County Histories: The History and Topography of Cornwall. Pub G. & W. B. Whittaker, London. New imprint: Published by G. & W. B. Whittaker, Ave Maria Lane, 1821.*

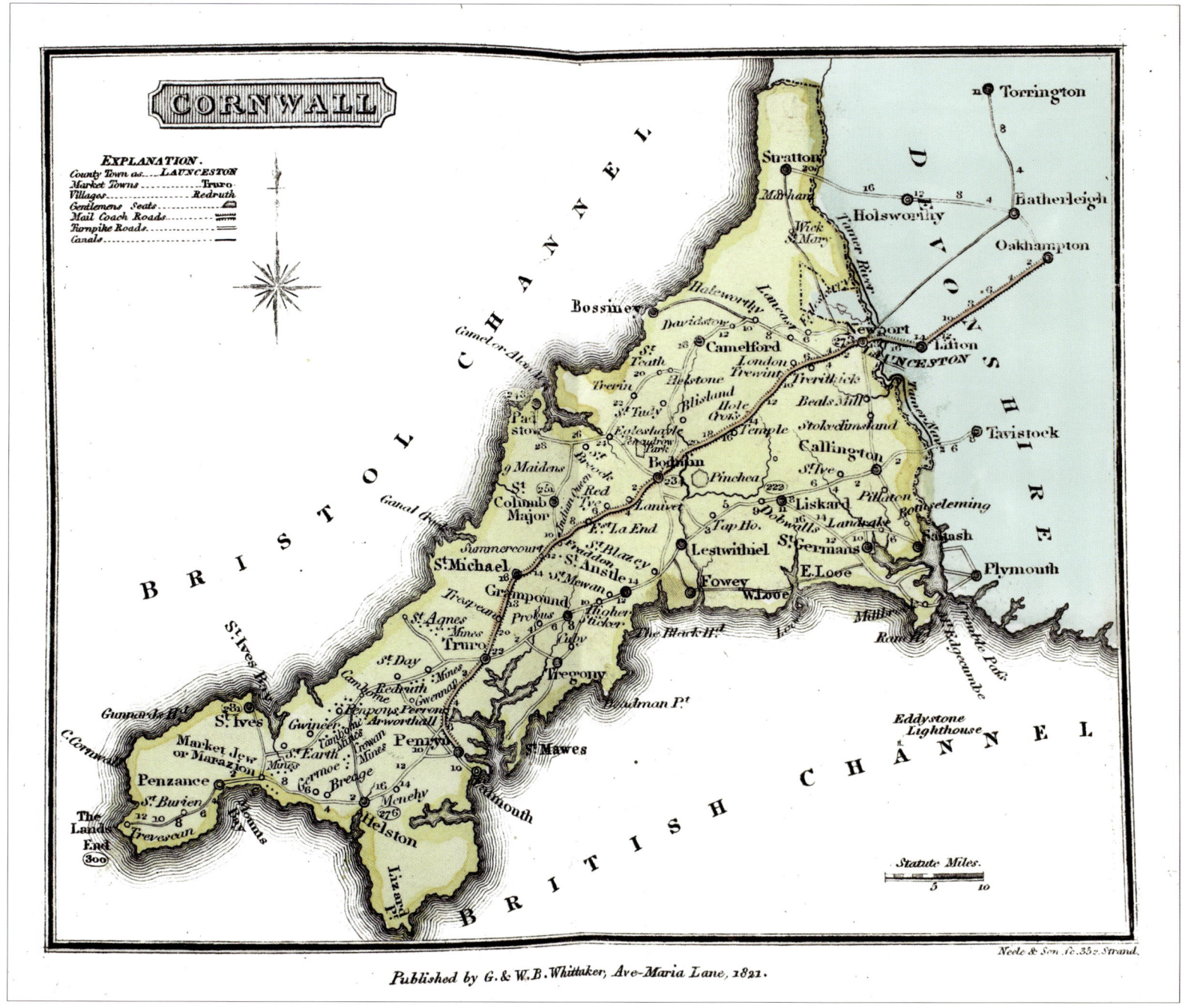

62. Neele 1821 Pinnock's History and Topography of Cornwall

63. BUTTERS, ROBERT 1803

Eng. Green ?, Pub. Butters, later Green

(89 x 119)

    Robert Butters (1748-1821) was a Fleet Street printer/publisher who occupied premises on Fleet Street in the 1780s, and later in Fetter Lane. He lived in Poppins Court and Lane Side, near Fleet Street, for much of the early 1800s. Butters acquired the licence to print and publish the Old Bailey Sessions papers from 1805 to 1816.

    In 1803 Butters published 'An Atlas of England' (the author is unknown). This is a series of 41 miniature maps, with the whole of England as the frontispiece and 40 of the English counties in loose alphabetical order – Cornwall is 7th in this series. These are collectively referred to as the 'Upside-down series'. Overall, the maps are loosely based on Cary's 1789 (#50) publication, though with the restricted size, details are lacking or erroneously placed. The engraver of all these maps is uncertain - William Green is a possibility.

    The Cornwall map is presented with Land's End at the foot of the page, along with the title. There is a scale of 0-15 miles, but no other embellishments. There are some odd omissions – Launceston, for instance, is unmarked and may have been substituted for Newport, slightly to the north. The island at Looe is shown as 'Love I', (the source of this error appears to be Baker (#54)), while Saltash is spelled 'Callash'. The second (1805) edition added a compass rose to some maps - though not on the Cornwall map.

1803 *An Atlas of England, Printed and sold by R. Butters. No. 22 Fetter Lane, Fleet Street, London. Reprinted 1805.*

1803 *Picture of England, by William Green, Pub John Hatchard, London. Reprinted 1804.*

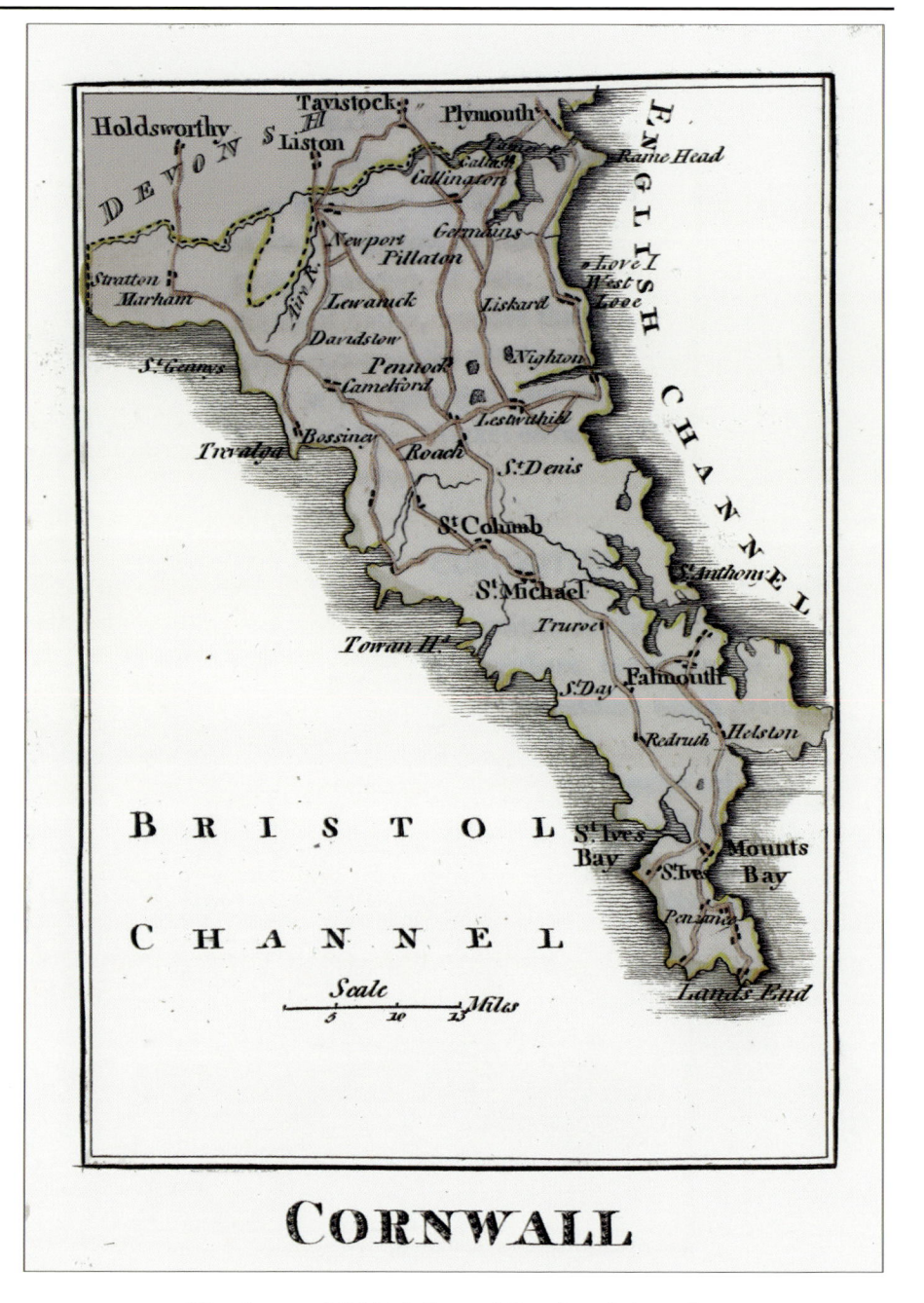

63. Green 1803 Atlas of England, London

64. LUFFMAN, JOHN 1803

Eng. Luffman, Pub. Luffman, Lackington, Allen & Co.
59mm Diameter

John Luffman (1751 – ?), son of Richard and Margaret Luffman, was apprenticed to John Bayley, of Old Fish Street, a brother of The Worshipful Company of Goldsmiths, to be an engraver in February 1766. This would have lasted seven years, to 1773. He married Ann Armstrong, of Whitechapel, in 1774 and had three daughters and two sons.

He worked from several addresses through the late 1780s and into the 1800s. During this period, he produced publications covering a variety of subject matter. Some, like the 'Map of the Western Pyrenees', in 1813, and the 'Seat of War between France and Russia…', in 1807, were geographic. Others, such as the more philosophical 'Passions and their effects…', in 1792, or his engraved song titled 'The Ministers', in 1800, show a range of ability.

In 1803 Luffman engraved, printed and published 'A New Pocket Atlas and Geography of England and Wales'. The 54 small, circular county maps are very unusual. Each map was engraved with a text of topographical information below it. The style of the maps lent itself well to the specialisation of the goldsmith: the creation of work onto a circular surface, such as rings, cane-tops &c. Additionally, one might consider these compact maps with succinct texts suitable for young minds – this was part of a burgeoning move towards educating children.

Cornwall is plate No. 6. In the 1803 version, the number is some 8mm above the top of the roundel. The second edition, of the same year, moved this to be almost flush with the top border. Around the border, at the top, is the simple title 'Cornwall'. At '3 o'clock' is marked the details of the County town, Launceston, and its distance from London (214 miles). At the base is a scale of 0-20 miles and, finally, at '9 o'clock' are the details of the MPs returned to Parliament (44). The map itself is a simple outline, with major towns, roads and the county boundary shown.

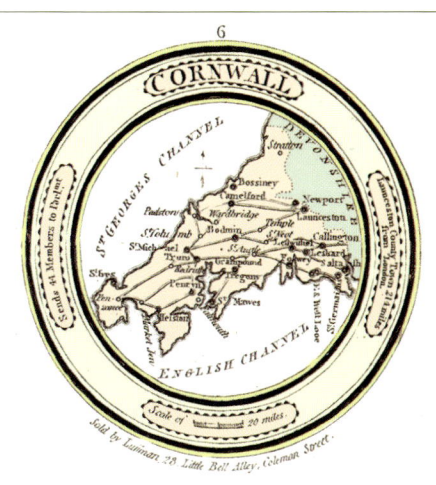

64. Luffman 1803 A New Pocket Atlas and geography of England and Wales

1803   New pocket atlas and geography of England and Wales. 28 Little Bell Alley, Coleman St., London. John Luffman, Lackington, Allen & Co.
1803   Plate number moved.
1806   New pocket atlas and geography of England and Wales, by Lackington, Allen & Co. Plate number removed.

65. COLE, GEORGE AND ROPER, JOHN 1805

Eng. Roper, Pub. Vernor, Hood & Sharp 1810, Baldwin 1816, Nightingale 1816, Dugdale, Tallis & Co 1835, Darton & Co & Collins Bros 1858.

(232 x 183)

George Cole was an artist and cartographer, and John Roper an engraver. They collaborated to produce 'The British Atlas', published in 1810. The atlas comprised the maps and town plans drawn by Cole and others and engraved by Roper, to accompany Britton and Brayley's 'The Beauties of England and Wales'. This was a topographic work published in parts, with the maps usually separate. The Cornwall map is dated 1805 and was probably available from that date. The map is canted over, as with previous maps, and in the top left is an insert of the Isles of Scilly. To the right of this is an extensive legend of symbols &c. used in the map. Below Land's End is an alphabetical list of the Hundreds, numbered 1-9. The map contains a wealth of roads, including turnpikes and mail coach roads, as well as minor roads. Mining, by this stage, had become important, and this is reflected by the annotation of copper, as well as copper/tin mines. The Stannary Towns of Penzance, Helston, Truro, Lostwithiel and Launceston are also marked.

'Stannary' derives from the Latin '*Stannum*', or tin, and thus Sn is the chemical symbol for tin. In Devon and Cornwall, a Stannary Charter was granted by King John in 1201, to confer tinners' rights to search for the metal. This was refined in respect to Cornwall by Edward I, in 1305, and expanded powers to Stannary Courts to settle legal disputes. All tin produced in Cornwall was to be sent to the five Stannary towns, (initially these were Lostwithiel, Bodmin, Liskeard, Truro and Helston), to be taxed – this is termed 'Coinage'. The word derives from the French '*coin*' meaning a corner. The assay would cut a corner off the tin or copper ingot and assay its purity – this process became known as 'Coinage', and thereby the modern word 'coin'.

This is the first map here to show the numerous tin and copper mines in the county – these are denoted by hollow circles for tin, filled circles for copper and open squares for combined tin/copper. There are some other mines working other metals, such as lead, silver and cobalt. One odd inclusion on the map is a line running from Ruan Minor, on the east side of the Lizard, to St. Agnes, on the north Cornish coast. This is clearly marked 'Great Cross Course' and appears on later maps as well (Wallis and Langley). This is discussed further in the appendices.

Finally, the construction of longitude and latitude on the map is very odd. While the lines themselves are not drawn, they are counted off on the borders. However, one is at odds with the other. Roper's line of 5° West is correctly parallel with compass north (but is about 5' too far east), but the lines of latitude do not intersect longitude correctly – there is a 5° rotation counter clockwise, so the two do not intersect at 90°.

All the maps were reissued several times in the following years, in different volumes, until 1858.

1810   *The British Atlas, by Vernor, Hood and Sharp, London.*
1816   *Reprinted (Pub. Baldwin, Cradock & Joy, London).*
1816   *Reprinted in: English Topography, by the Rev. J. Nightingale, London. 1827 Plate number (8) added top left, all detail outside borders removed.*
1835   *Reprinted in: Curiosities of Great Britain, or England and Wales Delineated, by Thomas Dugdale, Tallis & Co., London.*
1858   *Reprinted in: Collins' Railway and Pedestrian Atlas of England, Darton & Co. and Collins brothers.*

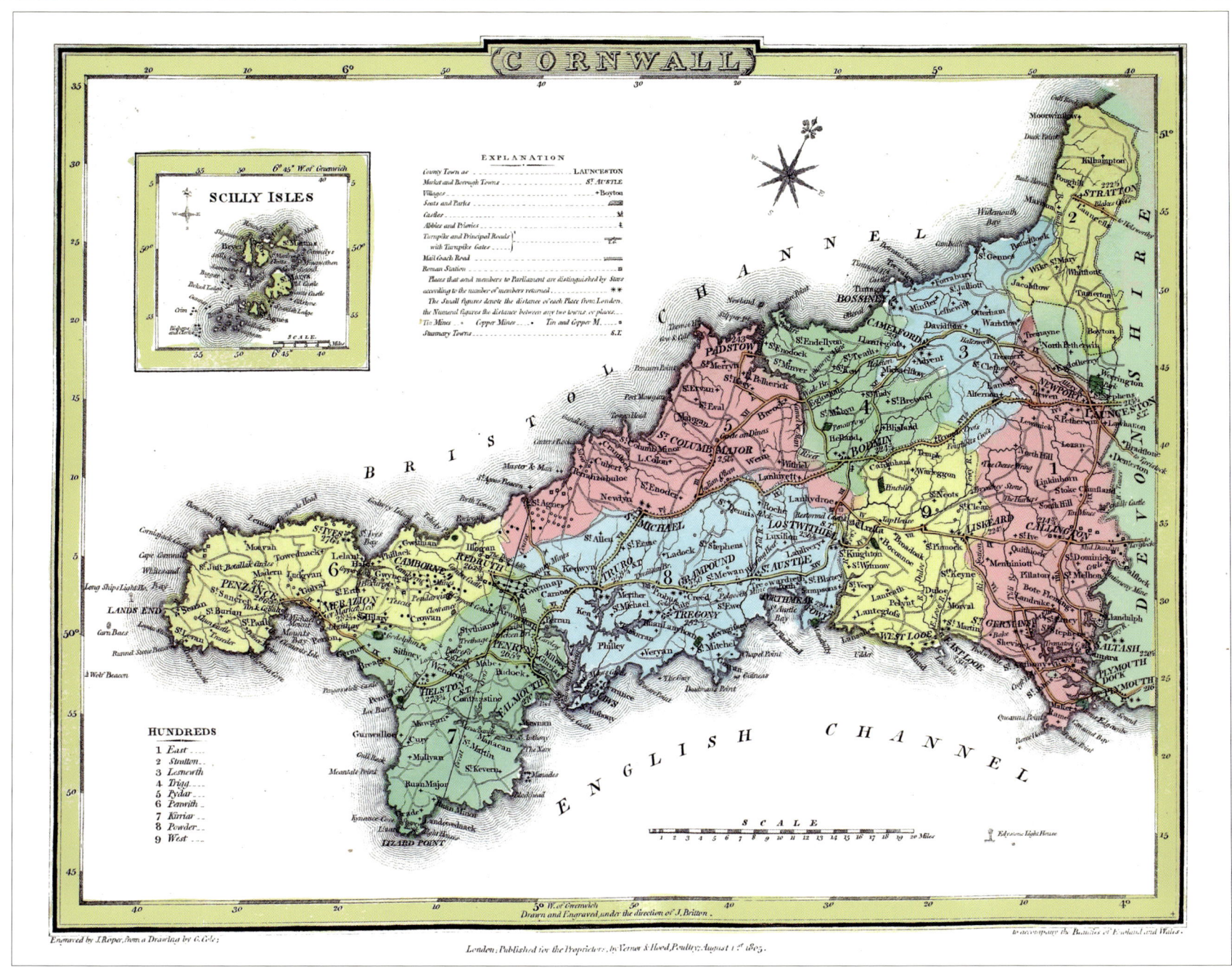

65. Cole & Roper 1805 *The British Atlas*, Vernor, Hood and Sharp, London.

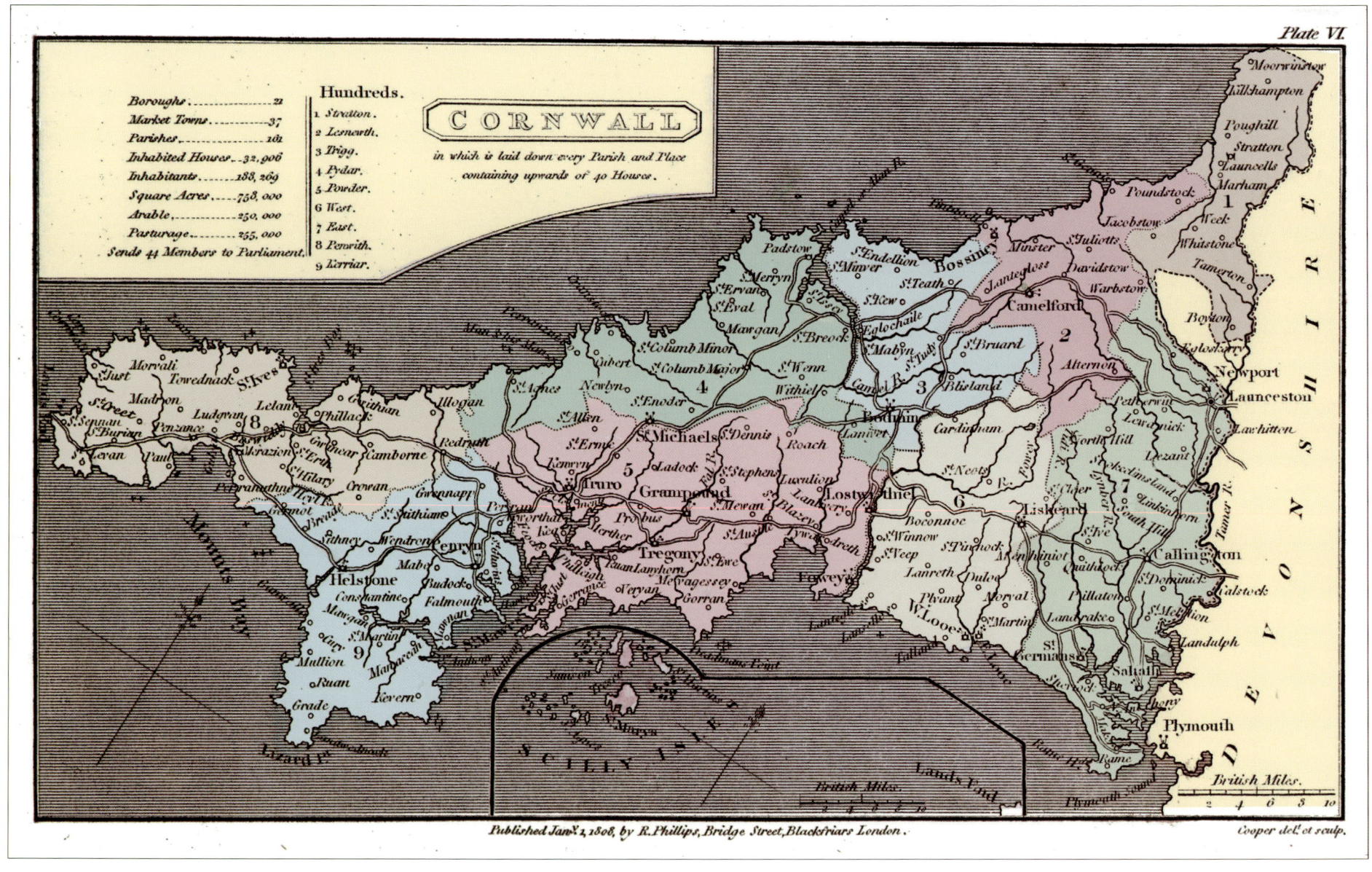

66. Cooper 1808 A Topographical Dictionary of the United Kingdom

66. CAPPER, BENJAMIN & COOPER, HENRY 1808

Eng. Cooper, Pub. Phillips 1807, 1808. Whittaker 1824.
(190 x 120)

Benjamin Pitts Capper (1761-1850) was Chief Clerk at the Aliens Department, under the Secretary of State's Office. Of possibly greater interest was his role in the arrest and deportation of General Gourgaud in 1818. Baron Gaspard Gourgaud had saved Napoleon's life, twice, and negotiated his asylum, after Waterloo, with the British. He accompanied Napoleon to St. Helena but was allowed to come to the UK in 1818. A letter from him to Marie Louise (Napoleon's second wife) led the UK authorities to conclude that Gourgaud was an undesirable and should be removed: Capper led the arrest with some zeal, on 14 November 1818. ('Parliamentary Debates', Hansard Volume 39 p1356).

Capper produced only one cartographic publication: 'A Topographical Dictionary', containing 47 maps of the counties of the United Kingdom. In this, the Cornwall map is printed in landscape, with the plate number (VI) marked top right. The entire sea area is engraved in narrow horizontal lines, with the Isles of Scilly set as an inset below Looe. At the foot of the map bottom right is the brief mark 'Cooper del^t et sculp'. The whole county is rotated clockwise beyond the point that would be needed to align the Devon border with the right margin - this gives the effect of the county pointing north of due west. In the top left is a simple cartouche titling the county in a double border. Alongside this is a list of statistics of the county, as well as a numerical list of Hundreds in east to west order (Stratton to Kerrier), with the corresponding number on the map. The Hundreds are shown on the map denoted by a dotted line. No topographical elements are shown, save the rivers and towns of over 40 houses. A simple compass points correctly to grid north, though there are no lines of latitude or longitude marked.

Even at this late stage of Cornish mapping, there are some departures of spelling - 'St. Creet' makes its first appearance (Sancreed) and Morvah is shown as 'Morvali'. Scattered about the coast are '+' symbols indicating rocky hazards. St. Michael's Mount, while drawn, is unlabelled. The major roads through the county are drawn, and show the changing relevance of routes now, compared to e.g. Ogilby (#19). St. Mawes, opposite Falmouth, is incorrectly shown as being of greater importance by the size of the script.

1807 *Published Aug 1, 1807 by R. Phillips, Bridge St, Blackfriars, London.*

1808 *A Topographical Dictionary of the United Kingdom, published by Richard Phillips, Bridge St, Blackfriars, London. Reprinted by Longman, Hurst, Rees, Orme and Brown, London 1813. Both these editions were deleted.*

1824 *New imprint by George Whittaker, 13 Ave Maria Lane, London. Reissued 1825, 1826, 1829, and 1839.*

67. WALLIS, JAMES 1812 (x2), 1820

1812 WALLIS'S NEW POCKET EDITION.
Eng. Wallis, Pub. Wallis 1812, Martin 1816, Simpkin and Marshall 1818-19, Lewis 1819-35.

In the ten years between 1810 and 1820, James Wallis was involved in the engraving and production of three separate county atlases. Wallis's 'New Pocket Edition of the English counties' or 'Traveller's Companion' was the first of these. Published c.1812, it is similar in several ways to Cary's 'Traveller's Companion' of 1789 (#50). Wallis reissued the atlas in 1814, and subsequently P. Martin and then William Lewis used the maps under their own imprints in the following years, up to 1836.

The Cornwall map is plate No. 5 and bears the subtitle 'London Published by J Wallis, Engraver. Berwick St, Soho and sold by Davies and Eldridge, Essex'. North is to the right, with the Devon border at the foot of the map. At the top of the map is a simple title within the border, with vertical lines behind the title. Both latitude and longitude are shown from Greenwich, though 5° West is about 8' too far east. Within the map itself are marked the major and minor towns; the distances from London are included for the major towns. The coach and turnpike roads are shown, along with separate symbols for tin and copper mines. Towns returning MPs are marked with a pair of stars attached, though he does not explain this in a key. The map is simple but quite balanced.

1812   *Wallis's New Pocket Edition of the English counties or Traveller's Companion*, by J. Wallis, London. Reprinted: 1814.
1816   *Martin's New Traveller's guide*, London, Published by P. Martin No. 198 Oxford Street.
1818-19   *Martin's Sportsman's Almanac for 1818 (and 1819)*, Simpkin and Marshall, London, 1818, 1819.
1819   *Lewis's New Traveller's Guide*, W. Lewis, London, 1819, 1821, 1824, 1825, 1827.
1835   *Lewis's New Traveller's Guide and Panorama of England and Wales*, W. Lewis, London, Reprinted 1836.

1812 WALLIS'S NEW BRITISH ATLAS
Eng. Wallis, Pub. Wallis also separately S.A. Oddy
(200 x 270)

In the same year that he produced his Traveller's Companion, James Wallis was also working on another atlas: Wallis's New British Atlas appeared in 1813. The title page is dated 1812 and the maps are dated 1812 or 1813. It was reissued the same year with a different title: A New and Improved County Atlas.

The Cornwall map (overleaf) is a rotated copy of the Roper map of 1805 - Wallis has oriented the map correctly with north up the page. Both the Lizard in the far south and Stratton in the north spill over the border. The detail of the map is less dense than the Roper map, however the Great Cross Course is still shown as an unlabelled line. The title cartouche, top left bears Wallis's imprint below the compass rose that is set behind it. Below the border is the publisher's mark 'London, Published by S.A. Oddy 1812'. Note that the labelling of longitude along the bottom border has reversed the minutes so they increment up from left to right.

1812   *A New and Improved County Atlas. Wallis's New British Atlas*, Pub J.Wallis, London. *Wallis's New British Atlas*, Pub S.A. Oddy, London, Reprinted as *Wallis's Second and Superior British Atlas*, James Wallis, London, 1814, 1816.
1819   *Ellis's New and Correct Atlas of England and Wales*, G. Ellis, London.

1820 THE PANORAMA
Eng. Wallis, Pub. WH Reid
(100 x 67)

Wallis's third county atlas, 'The Panorama: or Traveller's Instructive Guide Through England and Wales', was published by W H Reid and appeared in 1820. The atlas contained 53 hand coloured maps. Following each map were several pages of information about the county including principal towns, fairs, principal seats, parks, members of parliament &c.

The Cornwall map is 100mm x 67mm, almost the same size as the Crabb map of 1819 (#71). There is nothing on the Cornwall map indicating the engraver or publisher, though eight other maps in the atlas contain plate numbers, while 20 others contain a publisher's imprint (J. Wallis & C. Hinton). None contain both plate number and imprint.

The title of the map is set in a lozenge top left, with a note indicating Mail Coach Roads below it. Below this is a very simple compass, pointing up the page, and the map is set correctly onto the page. The top of Stratton Hundred is clipped off the top of the map. In the sea area south of Looe is a simple scale of 0 – 20 miles, and at the base of the map the longitude is indicated from London. Within the body of the map itself, Wallis has included main roads through the county, as well as separately showing the mail route from Launceston to Penryn. Although there are similarities to the Crabb map, there are some notable differences. While Crabb has marked both Marazion <u>and</u> Market Jew, Wallis more correctly uses Marazion only. He has included St Austle (sic), whereas Crabb has missed it completely. Neither has included Newlyn, near Penzance, though this is a common omission. To the south of Rame Head, Wallis has shown the Eddystone Lighthouse; Crabb has not. C. Hinton, whose name appears on the imprint of the atlas, shared an address with Thomas Crabb at 1, Ivy Lane, off Paternoster Row, which may go some way towards explaining the similarities.

1820   *The Panorama: or Traveller's Instructive Guide Through England and Wales*, London, by W. H. Reid, Charing Cross. Reprinted: 1820.

1825   *The Panorama of England and Wales.* Pub. Orlando Hodgson & Co., 10 Newgate St., London.

1825   *The Panorama of England and Wales.* Pub. William Cole, 10 Newgate Street, London.

67. Wallis 1812 New Pocket Edition of the English counties

Antique Maps of Cornwall and the Isles of Scilly

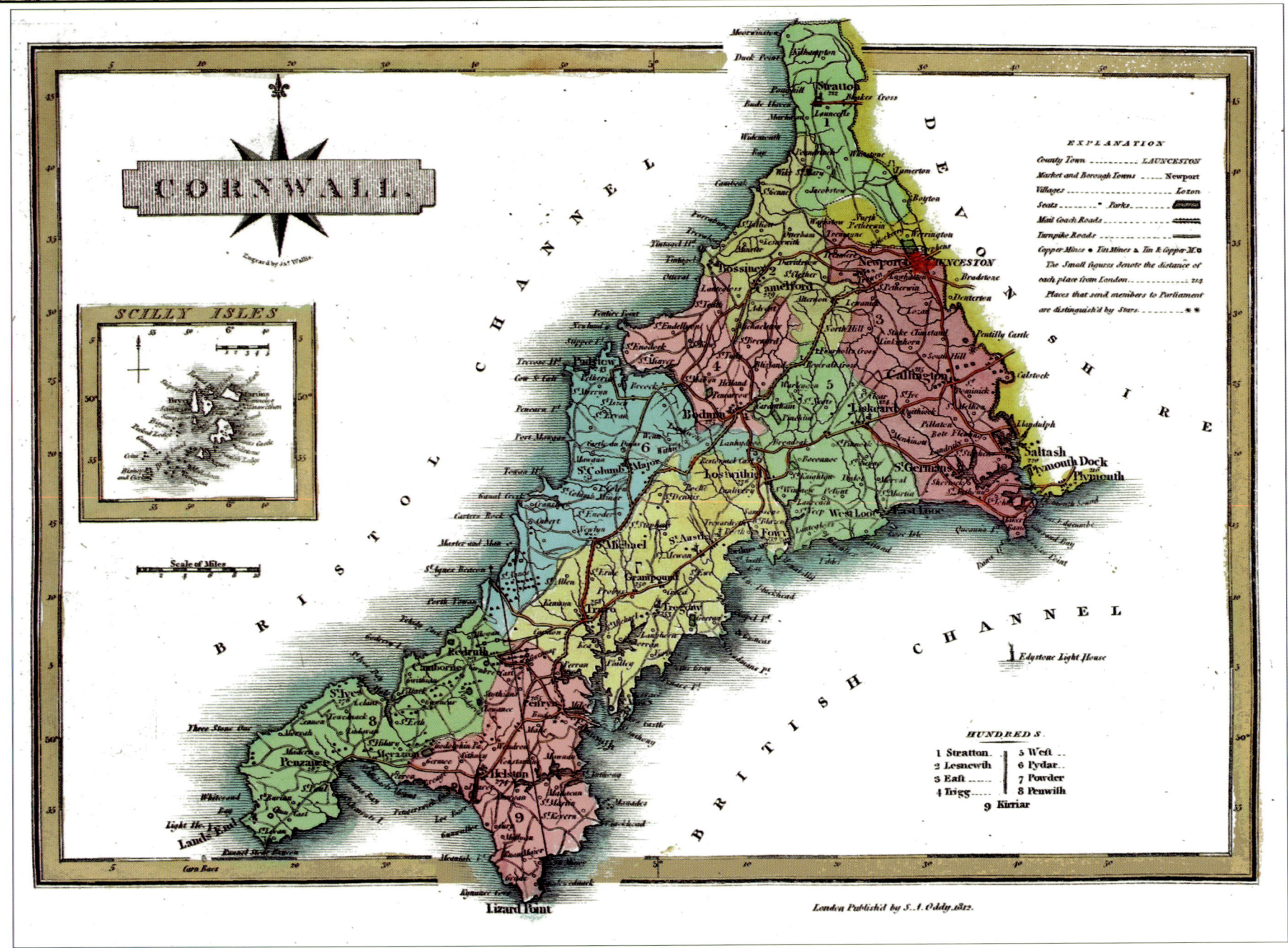

67.1 Wallis 1812 A New and Improved County Atlas

68. BAKER, BENJAMIN & ORDNANCE SURVEY 1813

Eng. Baker, Pub. Ordnance Survey
(660 x 914)

Benjamin Baker (1766-1824) (see also #54) was appointed the principal engraver to the Ordnance Survey in 1804. Baker led a team of engravers while working for the OS, though it is his name that appears on all the Cornwall sheets.

The Ordnance Survey grew out of the need for good maps covering the highlands of Scotland following the Jacobite rising (which ended in 1746 at Culloden). By 1791 the Board of Ordnance had received the newer Ramsden theodolite and work started on mapping southern Great Britain- the earliest maps of Kent (published privately in 1801) and Essex appeared (1805).

The Ordnance Survey county map of Cornwall was published in 1813. There are draft 'Ordnance Survey Drawings' of numerous areas of Cornwall from 1806 to 1810 that pre-date the publication of the final version. These were done by draughtsmen ahead of the final version and included Robert Dawson (Bodmin 1805, Redruth 1809 and Helston 1811), Henry Stevens (Camelford, 1805), John Hewitt (Land's End 1809) and Charles Budgen (Grampound, 1811), all of whom worked under the direction of Major General William Mudge, Royal Artillery, FRS, born in Plymouth in 1762.

The following sheets cover Cornwall and Devon:
Sheet 24 Plymouth to Looe, Pub. 1809 (price 7/6)
Sheet 25 Dartmoor to Launceston, Pub. 1809 (price 14s)
Sheet 26 Bideford to Stratton, Pub. 1809 (price 14s)
Sheet 27 Barnstable Bay. Sheet 28 Lundy Island (both 5s)
Sheet 29 Bude Bay, Pub. 1813 (price 5s)
Sheet 30 Padstow, Lostwithiel and St. Columb, Pub. 1813 (10s)
Sheet 31 St. Austell, Truro and Helston, Pub. 1813 (Price 10s)
Sheet 32 The Lizard, Pub. 1813 (Price 5s)
Sheet 33 St. Ives and Penzance, Pub. 1813 (Price 6/6)

In each case, the maps are notated with the sheet number in Latin top right. The placement of the numerals varies with each sheet, with most of the Cornwall/Devon sheets having the numeral outside the piano-key style border. Sheets 24, 25 and 26 have the numerals overprinting the border. None of the maps are titled on the sheets themselves, and on all sheets is a note identifying Benjamin Baker as the engraver and Ebenezer Bourne as the scriptwriter - though not always in the same place. Outside the border top left the price of the sheet is given - this seems to have varied possibly as a function of the complexity of the map. the Bude, Lizard and Lundy sheets are 5 shillings and 95% water! Not all copies appear to include this printed price.

The maps crossed county borders, so there are sections of Cornwall contained in maps that are predominately Devon. The maps are printed in eight sections per sheet, cut and mounted on linen. These were folded into a book-like box. At the base of each map is the imprint: 'Sold by Jas Gardener, Agent for the Sale of the Ordnance Maps, 163 Regent Street, London'. These were collated into a 1 inch to 1 mile map of the whole county in 1813.

In 1835 Henry De la Beche completed a geological map of Devon using the OS maps as a base. William Smith had used Cary's 1794 2nd Edition of his 'New and Correct Atlas of England and Wales' (#50) to produce the first geological map, in 1815 - 'A delineation of the Strata of England and Wales with a part of Scotland'.

The Geological Survey of Great Britain was formed in 1835, with De la Beche as its director. Following the success of the Devon map, he was invited to carry out a survey of Cornwall. This resulted in the first publication of the 'Geological Survey of Great Britain', in 1839. This contained a report with sections and plans, as well as the folded map of west Somerset, Devon and Cornwall superimposed on the OS map.

1813   *Part IID: Containing All of Devon (including eastern parts of Cornwall, Plates 20 - 27). Boxed.*
1813   *Part III: Containing the western part of Cornwall, plates 29, 30, 31, 32 and 33. Boxed.*
1836   *Report of the Geology of Cornwall, Devon and West Somerset. Henry De la Beche FRS &c. Pub. by Longman, Orme. Green & Longmans.*

69. ROWE, ROBERT 1816

Eng. Rowe, Pub. Rowe 1816, Teesdale & Co 1829-42, Collins 1849-55, W.S. Orr
(420 x 350)

The English Atlas was published in 1816, with 46 maps by Robert Rowe, an engraver and publisher of many maps, including two sets of playing cards with John Fairburn (#57) and later with Joseph Allen. After the first two editions of the original atlas under Rowe's own imprint, it was revised and reissued several times from 1829 to 1842 by Henry Teesdale & Co., with a new imprint.

Robert Rowe (1775-1843) is recorded in the Electoral Rolls as resident near Bedford Row, Holborn (Bedford St. and later 36 John St.) until his death in 1843. His will refers to his estate in Stogursey, in Somerset, where, in the church of St. Andrew, is a Rowe family tomb. There is a familial connection here yet to be proven (PROB11/1978 Volume 6).

Perhaps by co-incidence, Rowe engraved and produced a very rare board game using the map of Somerset as a base, in 1805. There are similarities between this map and the Cornwall opposite, especially the construction of the compass rose.

Rowe's title, 'A New Map of the County of Cornwall divided into Hundreds, by R. Rowe', is set in a double bordered oval cartouche, with no further decoration. Below the title, within the two borders, is the inscription 'London; Printed for R. Rowe, No 19 Bedford Street, Bedford Row, Jany 1 1813'. A simple compass is also placed top centre, with north up. (The county orientation has been set correctly). Below the title is a summary of the returning MPs to Parliament (eleven) and a scale of English miles. Below this is a bordered inset of the Isles of Scilly with an explanation of their offset to the county itself. The Hundreds are marked and summarised in an alphabetic list, to the south of Looe. Finally, in the bottom right is a table of explanation of features contained within the map.

Rowe's plates were acquired by Henry Teesdale around 1829 and were extensively altered (see #77). The changes in the 'New British Atlas' and 'British Gazetteer' will be detailed here. For details on the 'New Travelling Atlas', refer to Teesdale's section (#77).

1816	*The English Atlas*, by R. Rowe, London. Reprinted 1819.
1829	*New British Atlas* Acquired by Henry Teesdale, retitled and corrected to the year 1829, to 1830, to 1831. In 1829, oval title cartouche removed, replaced with simple title 'Cornwall' see Teesdale (#77). Explanation table (1) starts with Market towns and adds line 'The stars prefixed to the towns denote the number of Members return'd to Parliament', Foot of the map bears the imprint 'London, Published by Henry Teesdale & Co 302 Holborn'.
1831	Railway lines added: Looe to Liskeard, Truro to Port Towan and mineral lines around the Redruth area. Bude to Launceston canal added. Reference to Rail Roads added below list of Hundreds. The entire canal from Calstock to Bude is shown despite the lower Tamar section from Calstock to Tamerton having been aborted in 1808.
1832	Retitled as 'Improved Edition of New British Atlas' and has north-eastern and south-western Divisions added. Explanation panel (1) removes 'The stars prefixed...' and adds 'Railways', deletes Rail Roads from below Hundreds. Adds number of MPs (14) below Cornwall title. Corrected to 1835 (plate number 11 added). Final revision 1842 London, Henry Teesdale & Co.
1849	*New British Atlas*. Acquired by Henry George Collins. Retitled again. Added foliate decoration (1) to border corners and mid edge. Foliate 1 identifiable by double spike pointing inwards at 50° 03'. 'Cornwall' title encased in lozenge. Imprint 'London. Published for the Proprietors, by H. G. Collins, 22 Paternoster Row'.
1852	*The British Gazetteer* retitled by B. Clark. Added floral decoration above title lozenge. Foliate décor in corners and mid border still present. Explanation panel (2) now commences with county divisions (bottom right) and is much expanded. Railway lines (and planned) expanded including main line from Plymouth added. Base inscription 'London, Published for the Proprietors by H. G. Collins, 22 Paternoster Row'. 1852(1): Alternate floral décor (2) used in corners and mid border, identifiable by single spike facing inwards at 50° 03'. British Gazetteer can be found with either Explanation tables 1 or 2 and with either décor 1 or 2.

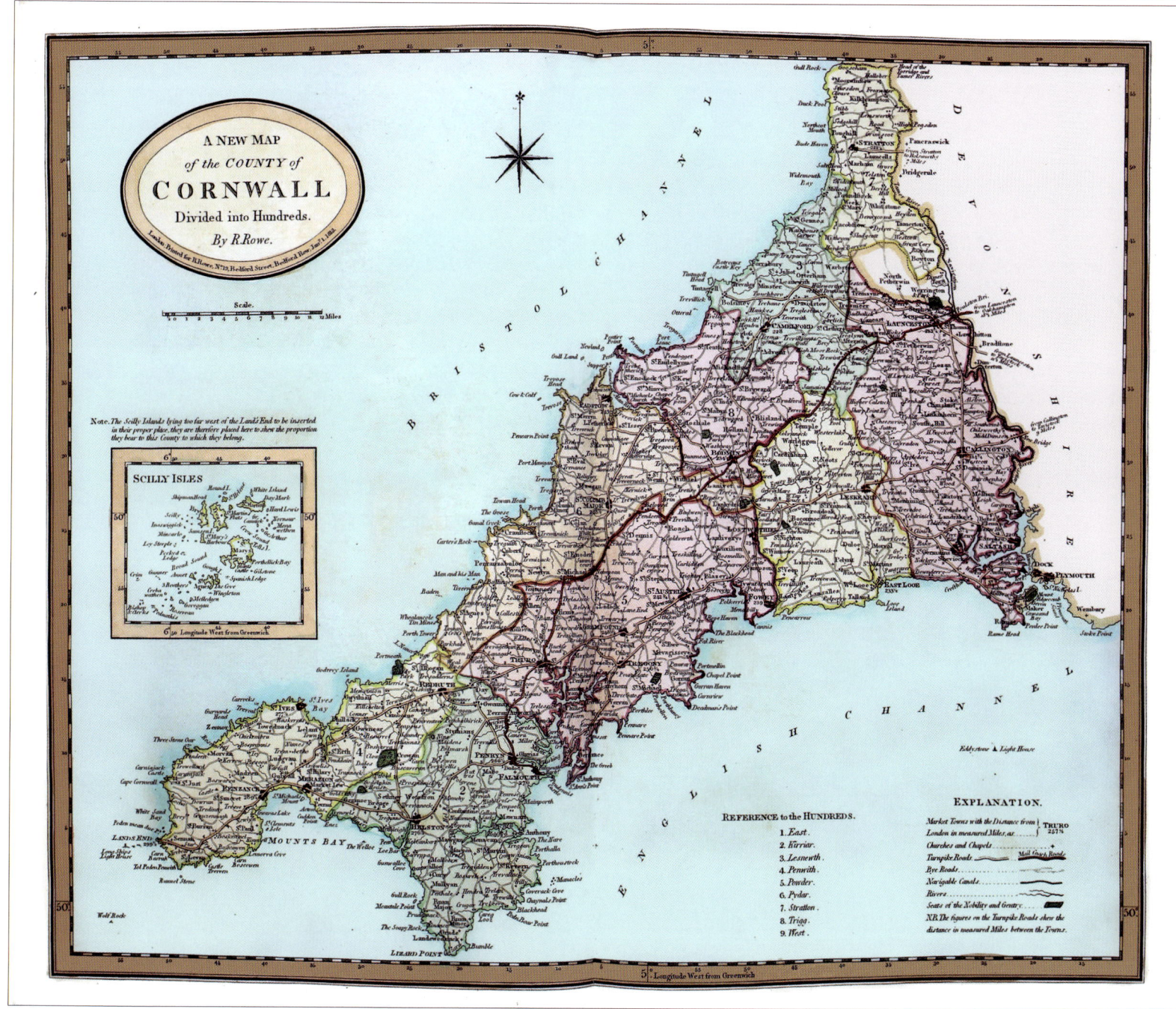

69. Rowe 1816 The English Atlas

70. LANGLEY, EDWARD & BELCH, WILLIAM 1817

Eng. possibly Belch, Pub. Langley & Belch
(248 x 165)

Edward Langley (fl.1780-1835) produced a wide range of printed material from children's drawing books, on traditional subjects such as horses, shipping and faces, to more weighty items such as his illustration of the London Custom House in 1780. He ran his business from 173 High Street, Borough, London – this is imprinted at the foot of the maps he produced in association with William Belch (apprenticed to William Darton senior in 1788), with whom he collaborated from 1807 to 1819. Together, they produced the 'New County Atlas' in 1818, though some of the county maps are dated up to two years earlier. The company declared itself bankrupt in October 1819, ('London Gazette' Issue 22861).

Belch continued producing work from High Street, Borough. The pitiful story of Chunee the Elephant was played out in the spring of 1826. Exeter Change, on The Strand, contained, amongst a host of other trades, a menagerie. This included a wide variety of animals, including Chunee, an Indian elephant. The elephant's handlers lost control of Chunee and, in brief, decided to have the animal destroyed. What followed descended into a slaughter and provoked public consternation. Within a month the Zoological Society of London was founded and the menagerie closed. Copies of William Belch's engraving of the event are available even today.

Langley and Belch, prior to the 'New County Atlas', had produced other maps; perhaps the best known was their 'New Map of London' produced in 1812. None of the maps, however, contains an engraver's name or other identifying mark.

The Cornwall map is one of a series issued in colour, somewhat restrained in style, but nonetheless pleasant for that. Refer to the Roper (#65) and Wallis (#67) - this is a reset copy of them. There is a lively view of St. Michael's Mount in the top left centre, and a small inset of the Scilly Isles at bottom left. The map is divided into the Hundreds with an alphabetic key top centre. Below Fowey is an explanation of the various elements of the map, including distances from London, mines and returning MPs. In line with several previous maps, Langley and Belch have included the Great Cross Course, a line from Ruan Minor, on the Lizard, to St. Agnes, on the north coast. This is discussed in the appendices.

As has been done elsewhere, the map has been canted over to fit the Devon border along right margin of the page. To do this the county has to be rotated about 22° clockwise. The compass rose below Plymouth continues to point up the page and not northwards. Compounding this, latitude and longitude are drawn incorrectly square to the page.

At the base of the map under the border is the imprint 'Printed and Published by Langley & Belch. No. 173 High Street, Borough, London. Aug 3rd 1817'.

1818   *Langley's New County Atlas of England and Wales. Published by Langley and Belch, London. Reprint: 1820 by Pinnock and Maunder. Reprinted 1820.*

1821   *Republished by G. & W. B. Whittaker, Reprinted 1823, 1825.*

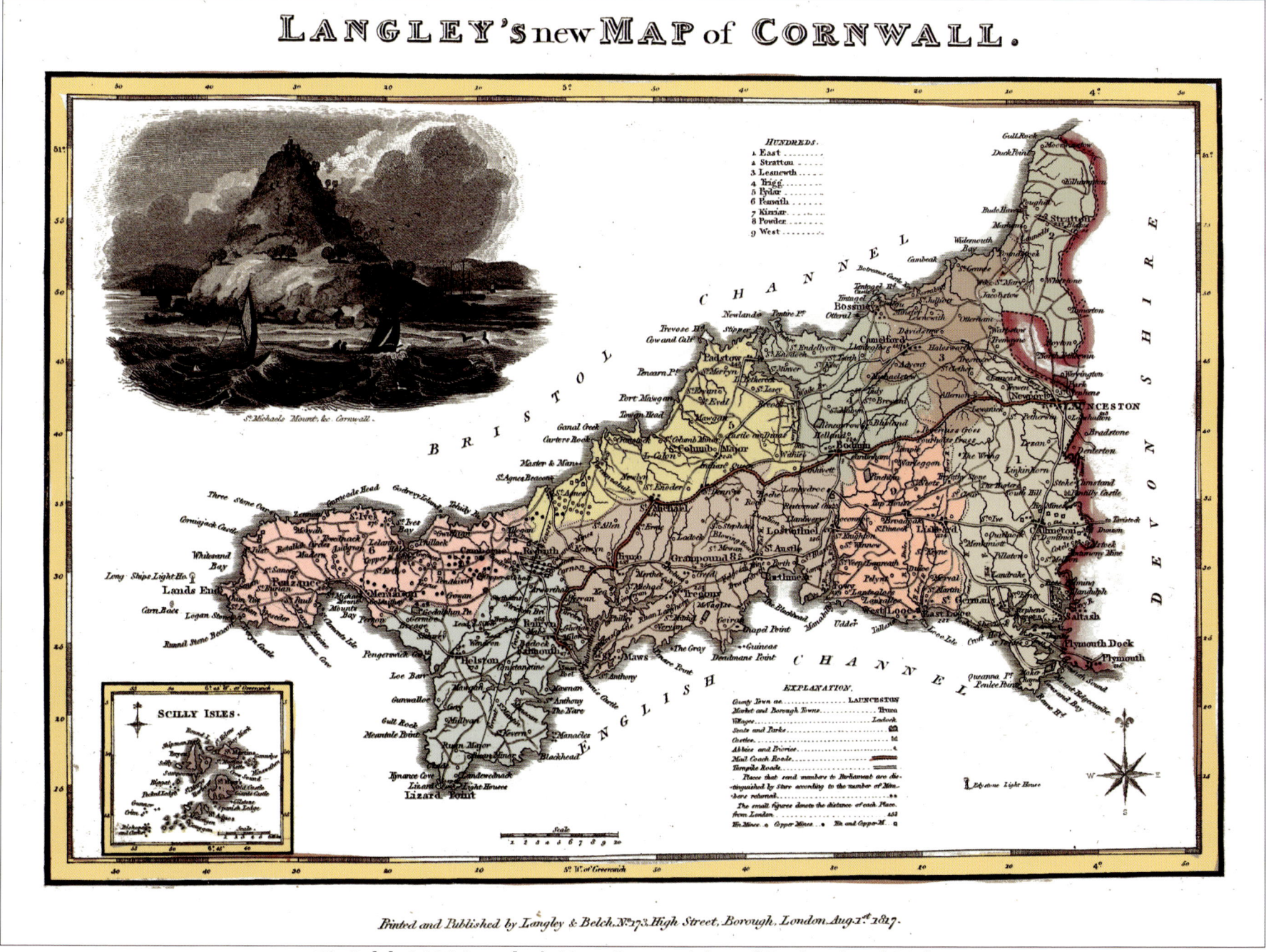

70. Belch 1818 Langley's New County Atlas of England and Wales.

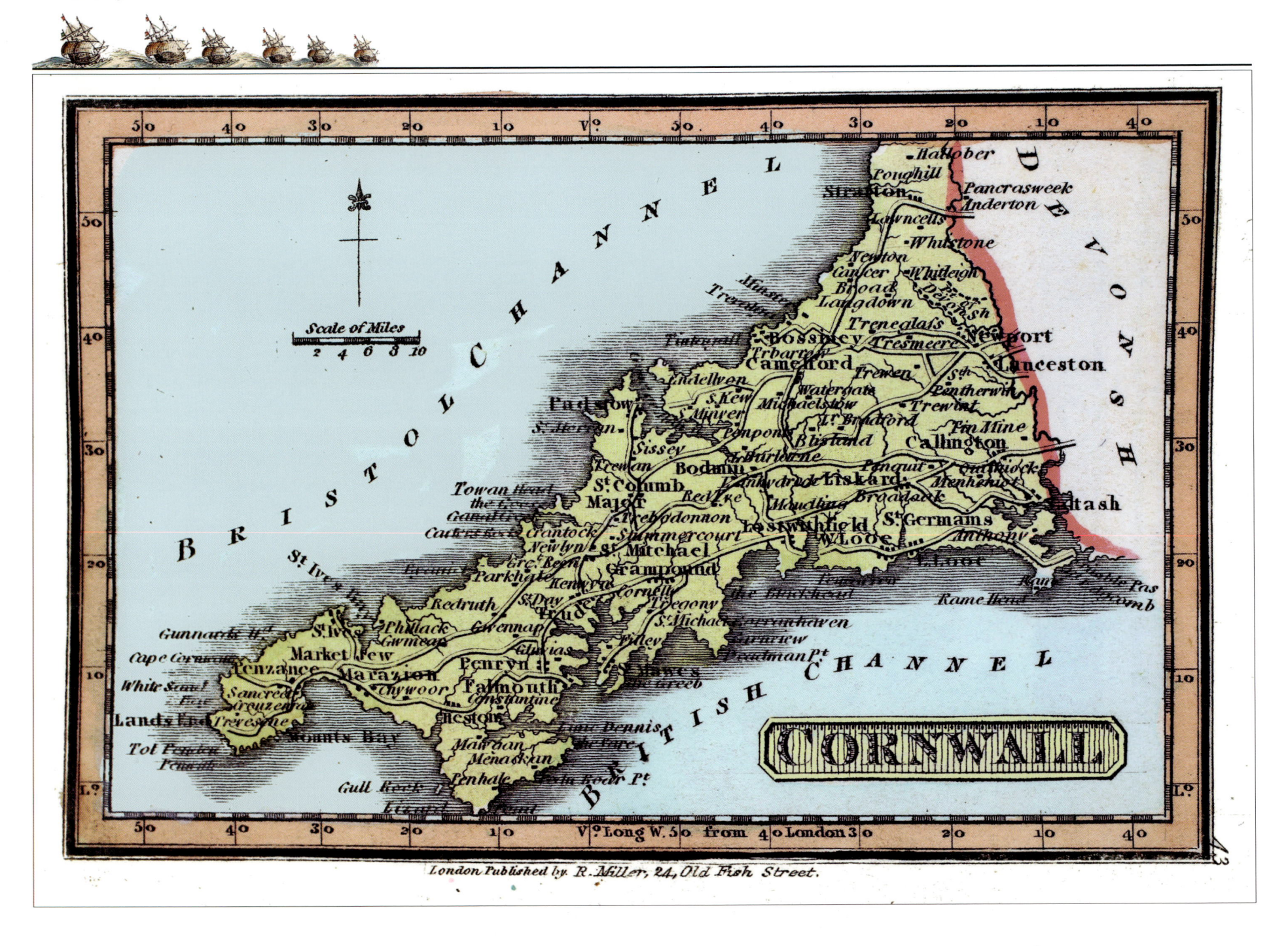

71. Crabb 1820/1 Miller's New Miniature Atlas, Pub Robert Miller, 24 Old Fish Street, London

71. CRABB, THOMAS 1819

Eng. Crabb, Pub. Crabb, then Miller
(105 x 70) PLAYING CARDS

Thomas Crabb (1790-1819) was born on 26 June 1790, in the parish of Christchurch, Surrey. He was apprenticed by Ovenden & Co. into the Company of Middlesex Engravers on 11 March 1806, and married Mary Deborah Bailey in 1810. Together, they produced two boys, Thomas (born in John Street, off Blackfriars Rd in 1814) and Alexander (born at Ivy Lane, Paternoster Row in 1818). Neither went into the printing/engraving trade, preferring instead music. Thomas Crabb died in August 1819 and his will was proved the following year, where he mentions most members of his immediate family, as well as his father-in-law, Thornton Bailey (PROB 11/1625/52). From this we see Thomas had a somewhat brief career as an engraver, cut short by some physical illness that he knew might kill him: his will starts '...Engraver, bookseller and printer being weak of body but of sound mind...'. The will was drawn up on 19 July 1819, less than a month before his death, aged 29.

Crabb engraved a series of county playing cards in 1819; these carry the imprint 'Published by T. Crabb, 15, John Street, Blackfriars Road' at the base of the card. These were re-issued in 1820 by Robert Miller, who altered the imprint to 'London, Published by R. Miller, 24 Old Fish Street'. This is now, in part, Distaff Lane, south-east of St. Paul's Cathedral. The imprint was altered later, in 1822, by William Darton junior, who changed it to 'William Darton 58, Holborn Hill'. They are considered as being based on the Cary maps of 1789 (#50).

Darton's business partner, Rev. Samuel Clark (1810–1875), created the pseudonym Reuben Ramble. His 'The Travels through the counties of England...' is a children's geography text book with maps and views of each county. The Reuben version of the Cornwall map is a bordered map with longitude from London marked. The major towns and other points of interest are shown, though without any note of topography. The railway is marked.

Surrounding the map are four views of Cornwall, including St. Michael's Mount, the Cheesewring (in a stylised agricultural view), a tin mine (Botallack is mentioned in the following two pages of text) and, oddly, the Eddystone lighthouse (always considered as part of Devon).

The Crabb map is small, and a little compressed horizontally. The only embellishment is a simple compass straight up the page, with the county correctly oriented. Crabb has marked off degrees and minutes of latitude and longitude correctly, from London (St. Paul's). Some errors in transcription have occurred, with 'Loswithfield', 'Lauceston' and 'Trude' being the most evident. Market Jew and Marazion are marked as two separate places, and St. Michael's Mount is missing altogether, as too is Newlyn, near Penzance. The original Crabb pack was organised with no suits or numbers to them. When Miller acquired the cards, he compiled them into a miniature atlas and ordered the maps into an odd sequence, that generally runs out from London northwards and counter-clockwise, before ending in Wales. Cornwall is No. 43 (plate number on its side, bottom right).

1819   *Set of playing cards, by Thomas Crabb, London.*
1820/1 *Set of playing cards, Pub. Robert Miller, 24 Old Fish Street, London.*
1820/1 *Miller's New miniature atlas, containing a complete set of county maps, Pub. Robert Miller, London.*
1822/3 *Set of playing cards, Pub. William Darton, London.*
1822/3 *Darton's New miniature atlas, containing a complete set of county maps.*
1845   *Ruben Ramble's Travels through the counties of England, Pub. William Darton & Samuel Clark, London. Repub. 1850 by Darton & Co., London.*

72. LEIGH, SAMUEL & HALL, SIDNEY 1820
Eng. Hall, Pub Leigh
(80 x 130)

Sidney Hall (1788-1831) was a cartographer, apprenticed by George Neele, possibly father of Samuel Neele (#59), before working for the Arrowsmith Company as an engraver from 1817. He later went to work for himself before teaming up with Samuel Leigh, who published one cartographic work: 'Leigh's New Pocket Atlas'. This was sold with or without maps and can be often found bound with 'Leigh's New Pocket Road-book of England and Wales'. Following Samuel Leigh's death in 1831, the business was continued by his widow, whose imprint appears as M. A. Leigh.

Hall's map of Cornwall is engraved 'Sid^y Hall Scuplt' bottom right. (The map is drawn in landscape into the atlas that is oriented in portrait format). Leigh's imprint appears bottom left: 'Pub by S. Leigh, 18 Strand', with the plate number '6' top right. The map is oriented with north facing directly up the page, with a scale of 0-30 English miles shown. Major and minor towns are shown, with the distances from London indicated on the main towns, (Penzance is 287 miles, Launceston 214 - both are within 3% of today's shortest distances). With the restricted size of the map, there is a limit to the detail, though with some surprising exclusions and inclusions: Newlyn is, for instance, missing. The hamlet of Guildford has appeared near the missing St. Erth, and its inclusion here is curious - it appears on Gasgoyne's map (#25), Kitchin's map (#39) and the first OS map (#68) and would become notable later for the viaduct constructed over the valley for the railway in the 1850s. On the OS map, it is marked as a collection of houses on a crossroads, and of little importance. Hall's reasons for including it are unclear, beyond prior precedence. Some of the larger private parks have been included, such as Clowance and Godolphin. Only two major roads (Launceston-Truro and Plymouth-Truro, and then a combined route from Truro to Falmouth) are shown; given the date of the map, this is surprising, as no roads west of Truro are deemed 'major routes'.

The fact that Hall's name continued to appear as co-publisher into the 1850s was finally resolved by Laurence Worms in 2013. Sidney Hall married Selina Price, from Radnorshire, in Wales. Selina may have had some training herself, or directed others using a slightly altered imprint - following her husband's death, in 1831, the imprint changed slightly, from 'Sid^y Hall' to 'S Hall', and there was a slight change in the style.

1820	Samuel Leigh 'Leigh's New Pocket Atlas of England and Wales', published by Samuel Leigh, printed by W. Clowes, London.
1826	Second edition
1831	Third edition
1833	Fourth edition, Published by M.A. Leigh 421 Strand.
1835	Fifth edition
1837	Sixth edition, Hall's name removed
1839	Seventh edition
1840	Eighth edition
1842	Ninth edition, Retitled Leigh's New Pocket Atlas of England and Wales, New Edition. London G. Biggs, successor to Leigh & Son, Strand.

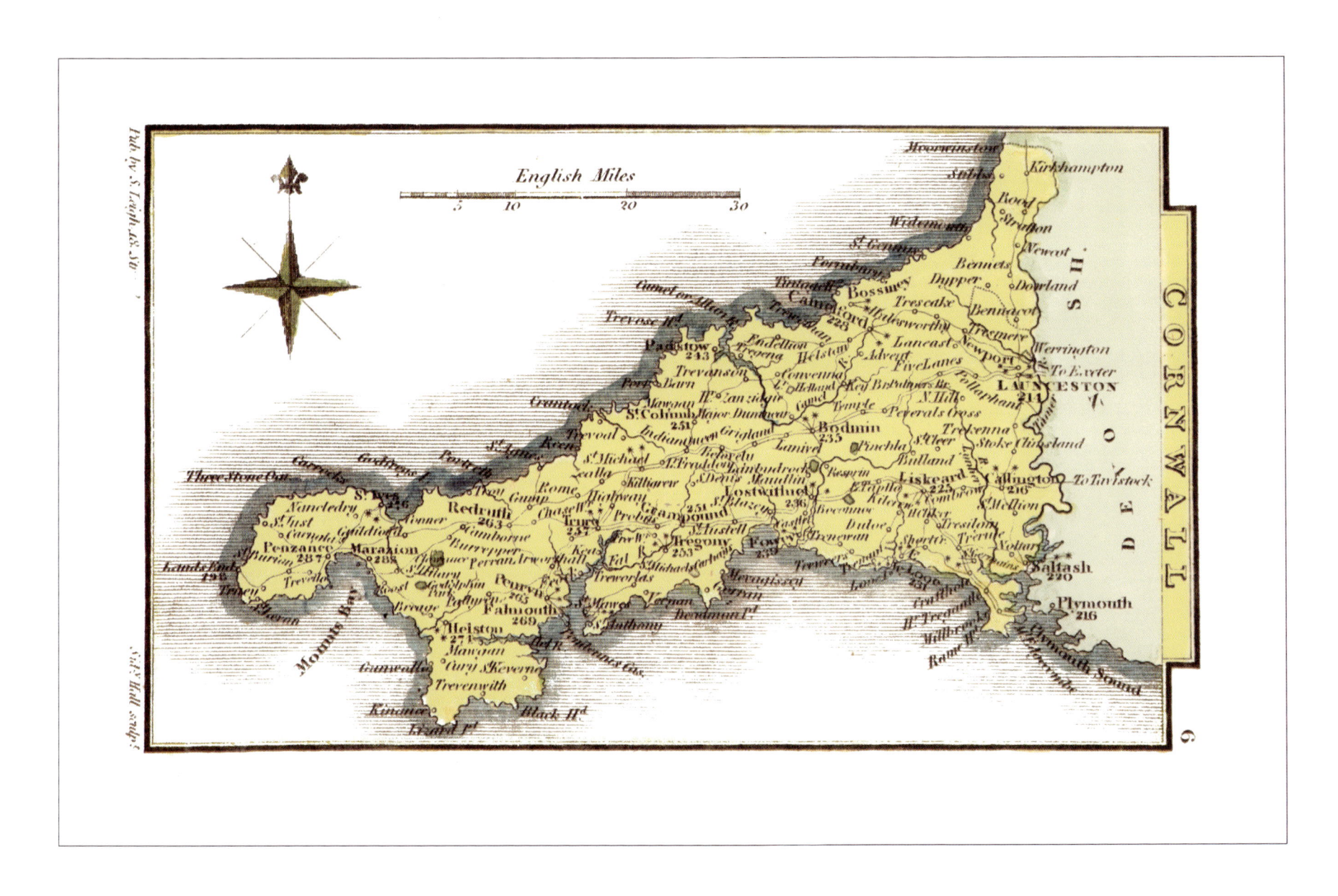

72. Hall 1820 Leigh's New Pocket Atlas of England and Wales

73. DIX, THOMAS & DARTON, WILLIAM 1821

Delineated Dix, Eng. Darton Snr, Pub. Darton Jnr 1821, Dix & Darton 1822-1833, Darton & Son 1835-77
(429 x 351)

Thomas Dix (1770-1813) was an Usher (junior master) at Oundle School, before becoming Master of North Walsham Classical, Commercial and Naval Academy. The 'Norfolk Chronicle' of 11 January 1806 carried a general article about the Academy and mentioned the newly published treatise by Mr. Dix on the 'Construction and Copying of geographical maps' for 3s. The 'Eclectic Review' (Volume II pt. 1), of the same year, was complimentary, after a thorough review and critique: 'On the whole we strongly recommend the use of this small treatise to every student and teacher of geography'. In fact, Dix had already published on Land Surveying in 1799 while at Oundle, and would produce his Juvenile Atlas in 1811, published by William Darton senior.

The Oundle School archive mentions Dix and notes his untimely death in 1813. His family story is one of tragic events, one after another. He married Susannah Castell in 1804 and they had five children: Susannah, Thomas 1, Thomas 2, William 1 and William 2. None of the children would live to see their 2nd birthdays.

Dix died suddenly, at the age of only 43, on 31 May 1813, following the death of his infant son, William 2, less than a week earlier. The two were buried on 5 June 1813; the 'Norfolk Chronicle' of the same day recorded the news.

Dix started the 'Complete Atlas', drawing the 42 maps, but died before it was finished. William Darton senior (1755-1819) was an engraver and publisher of children's books of some note. While it is likely that Darton senior published the 'Juvenile Atlas', it seems less likely that he undertook the 'Complete Atlas', at least to final production - his son, William Darton junior (1781-1854), is a more likely candidate.

Darton junior worked at 40 Holborn Hill until 1808; he moved to number 58 thereafter and completed the atlas in 1822. There are several counties that pre-date this publication date, including Cornwall. After this there are several re-issues. The 1833 issue of Cornwall was completed with the Parliamentary divisions, along with the Hundreds.

This is a beautifully engraved coloured map, on a scale of 1 inch to about 5½ miles; the information given on the map seems to have been culled from various sources. An inset of the Scilly Isles is included, as too is a view of the Cheesewring, on Bodmin Moor: this is a naturally eroded stack of seven granite slabs totalling 32ft (9.7m) in height and gives the map a certain decorative quality. Note the raised line of hills running through the county - see Gardner (#74) and Migneret (#75).

The early copies of the maps were issued loose, as separate linen-backed sheets, before being later bound as a complete atlas. The linen copies are highly sought and rare items.

1821   *A New Map of the County of Cornwall divided into Hundreds in 12 sections mounted on linen. Note the circular cartouche bottom centre bearing Thomas Dix's name only, published by W. Darton Junr, 58 Holborn Hill, London.*

1822   *A Complete Atlas of the English Counties, by Dix & Darton, London.*

1830   *Folding map, published 23 July 1830.*

1833   *Circular title removed and reworded 'Cornwall, Divided into Hundreds AND THE Parliamentary Divisions'. Reissued in 1835 and 1838 by William Darton and Son as The Counties of England, London. New imprint 1839 and 1844, 1852 and 1877.*

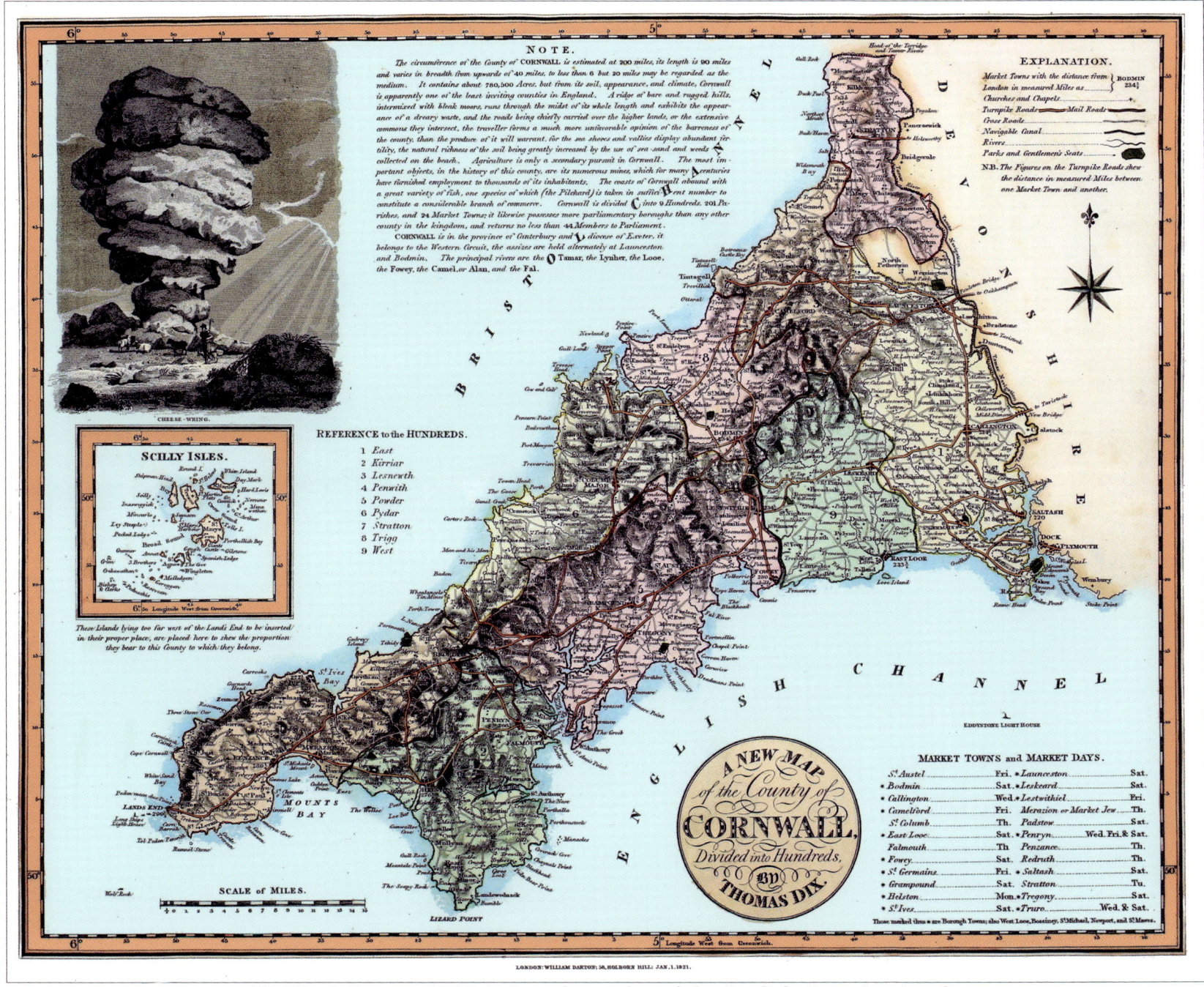

73. Dix & Darton 1822 A Complete Atlas of the English Counties, London

74. SMITH, CHARLES & GARDNER, WILLIAM ROBERT 1822

Eng. Gardener, Pub Smith
(205 x 230)

Smith was a very successful publisher, engraver and map seller. In 1822 he published a reduced version of his 'New English Atlas', which was first published in 1801 (#58). He became Map Seller Extraordinary to HRH the Prince of Wales and produced several other notable cartographic works, including a road book (1826), maps of London (1803) and Bristol (1829), and plans of rivers and canals. Charles Smith (fl1799-1855) moved into the production of globes and grew, by the mid 1830s, a highly successful business. Of his four children, William came into the business, in about 1827, and inherited his father's stock of plates, globes, tools &c., as well as £2400 as part of the will proved in March 1855 (PROB11/2209-251-300). The other children and grandchildren benefited from the will with property in Greenwich and Southampton, as well as gifts of money. William took over the business from 1852 and continued to produce globes of varying diameters, as well as continuing the publication of the atlases under the name Smith & Son. The company was originally based at 172 Strand, moving at some time before 1850 to 63 Charing Cross Road. Smith & Son globes are still highly desirable items which sell easily into four figures and beyond.

The 'New English Atlas' contained 44 maps. Some (including Cornwall) were engraved by W. R. Gardner, with others by John Pickett.

William Robert Gardner lived in Carmarthen St, off Fitzroy Sq. (this is now University Street). In October 1823, he was robbed of a 5s (25p) handkerchief - the two teenage culprits, George Thrush, 16, and Isaac Barrow, 18, were found guilty and transported to Australia for life in 1824 ('Proc Old Bailey' t18231022-84). The force of law might have affected Gardner's later decision after August 1829, when he was declared bankrupt ('London Gazette' Issue 18671). The story has further twists: Gardner had been forging bills for many years previously (estimated to be in the region of £10,000), but fled to the USA, avoiding his inevitable arrest, leaving a wife and children, never to be heard of again. ('Stamford Mercury', 29 Sept 1829).

The Cornwall map is correctly oriented, with a chain of hills running through the county from Stratton all the way to Land's End - this has been discussed in Dugdale's section (#60). There are many roads marked, with their significance given by width and colour: the main coach route through the county from Okehampton via Truro to Falmouth is shown in blue, with other main routes are shown with no real differentiation in status. The route from Penzance to Pendeen, for instance, is shown as having the same status as that from Truro to Redruth. The principal towns are shown with their mileage from London. The distance from London to Land's End, via Redruth, is noted to be 290 miles. Above Penwith is an insert of the Isles of Scilly with no embellishment. A fairly simple compass rose fills the sea to the south of Looe, while the island off the town is named 'Looe Island'. Overall, the map is good and well detailed, though maps of this period are becoming very similar, with few distinguishing themselves as exceptional to the norm. Railways were added to the final edition of the atlas in 1844.

1822   *Smith's New English Atlas being a reduction of his large folio atlas, C. Smith, London.*
Reprints: 1828, 1828 (1829), 1828 (1830), 1833 (1834) and 1844.

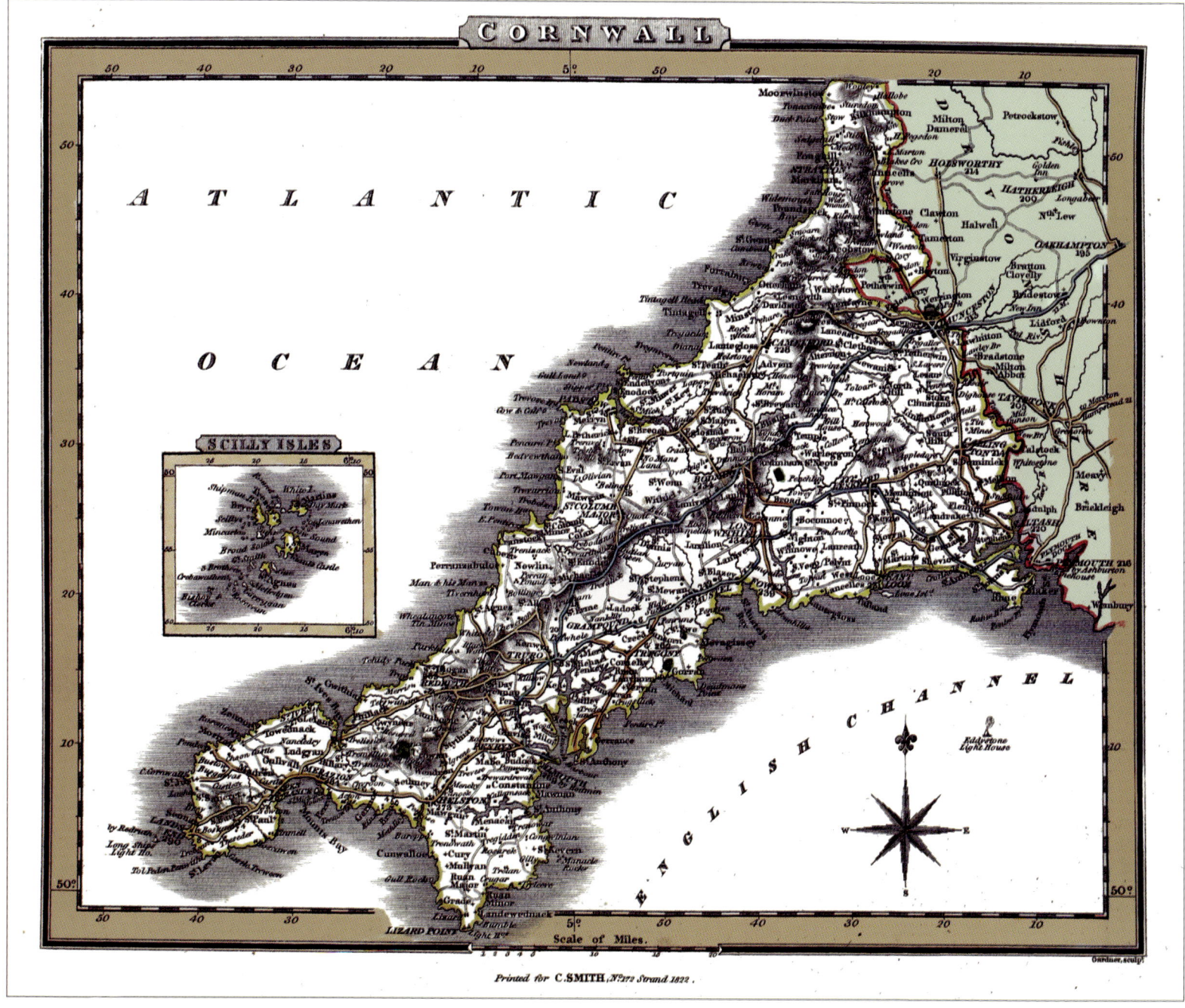

74. Gardner 1822 Smith's New English Atlas

Antique Maps of Cornwall and the Isles of Scilly

75. PERROT, ARISTIDE-MICHEL & MIGNERET, Mme 1824

Eng. Migneret/Thierry, Pub Depping
(70 x 110)

This very small, but delightfully curious, map by the French geographer Aristide-Michel Perrot (1793-1879) appeared in '*L'Angleterre ou Description Historique et Topographique*', a geographical work by Georges-Bernard Depping (1784-1853). Depping was born in Münster, Germany moved to Paris in 1803 and became a French citizen. '*L'Angleterre*' is a miniature atlas in six volumes, containing a total of 59 maps and 16 views engraved by Me/Mme Migneret. Through the six volumes' maps there are variations in both Perrot's and Migneret's imprints, most of which are signed 'A. M. Perrot 1823' (52/59) and 'Me Migneret' (42/59).

Perrot published a volume of French departmental maps, the '*Atlas Portatif du Royaume de France...*', in 1823, and if these are viewed alongside the British maps they bear a striking resemblance, with the notable exception that they are engraved by Émile Théophile Blanchard.

Cornwall (uniquely amongst the English counties), along with all the Welsh counties, is signed 'A. M. Perrot del' and 'Me Migneret Sc' and is undated. Migneret is recorded elsewhere as 'Mme' on five English, two Scottish and eight Irish maps. Given the obvious gender implied by the imprint, this is not the better-known Adrien-Jacques Antoine Migneret, as is often reported.

The Migneret publishing house was founded by Mathieu Migneret (1743-1814) at 22, rue du Dragon in Paris, amid the French Revolution. His wife, Barbe-Félicité (née) Brisset, took over the business briefly, before passing it to their son, Nicolas Migneret, in 1817. There are three possibilities: Mme Migneret is the widow of Mathieu, the wife of Nicolas or the wife of Adrien-Jacques.

Mme Migneret's other work is often of a zoological nature – her illustrations in '*Histoire Naturelle du Genre Humain*' by J. J. Virey, Paris 1824, bear an identical imprint; the 'Orang-Outang' is particularly fine.

Only ten of the maps bear an imprint referring to Thierry, (Cornwall is not one of them). The Thierry brothers were engravers, based at rue des Mathurins-St-Jacques, in Paris, during the early 1800s, and specialised in map engraving. There are, therefore, a number of hands in the execution of these miniature maps and the text supporting them. We can consider G.-B. Depping the author of the texts, and Perrot the geographer, whose maps may have been engraved by Thierry. We can also consider the supporting embellishments to have been engraved, to a specified design, by Blanchard for the 1823 production, and by Migneret for the 1824 atlas.

The map of Cornwall (*Cornouaille*) is between pages 80 and 81, in tome V of 1824. The map occupies around half of the engraving and has little detail. On some copies of the map there is a reference (T4) in the top left of the plate indicating the tome number. Two things arise from this: the presence or absence of the Tn mark appears to be inconsistent, with some maps bearing the mark and others not, within the same volume. Also, in the case of Cornwall, the T4 suggests it should be in Volume IV, when it is in fact in Volume V. It may be possible that the layout of the volumes was changed, with Volume IV now comprising the counties of Middlesex and Surrey. The map of Surrey is in Volume V.

There is a 17-page section devoted to Cornwall, which in general is a re-write of many previous authors: 'A chain of sterile granite hills traverse the county, trees only grow in valleys and sheltered ravines, it rains in quantity and winds blow with violence'. Hardly the Cornish Riviera! Almost half of the written section describes the Isles of Scilly in some detail and describes the islanders in laudable terms: '...*un peuple actif, courageux, très intelligent, et d'une fort constitution; peuple qui doit à ses dispositions naturelles qu'a l'éducation, et mène dans cet petit archipel une vie assez heureuse.*'

Of the map itself, the principal towns are named, larger rivers included and the hills are hachured, although these are shown as a single, continuous range from Stratton to Penzance. The Scilly Isles and Eddystone lighthouse are also indicated. Above and below the map are decorative indications of the produce and features of the county, including fishing nets and an attractive seashore with rocks, starfish, an eel and part of an anchor. The sea is entirely shaded, and to the south of the county it is simply named 'MANCHE' – French for the English Channel. Despite its size and lack of general cartographic usability, it is a pleasing little piece and of increasing interest.

1824 *L'Angleterre ou Description Historique et Topographique du Royaume Uni de la Grande Bretagne, par M. G.-B. Depping, Paris. Chez Etienne Ledoux, rue Guenegaud No. 9. 1828: Second Edition, 1835: Third Edition.*
1828 *New Imprint: Longue Rue des Dominicains, Bruxelles. L. J. Brohez.*

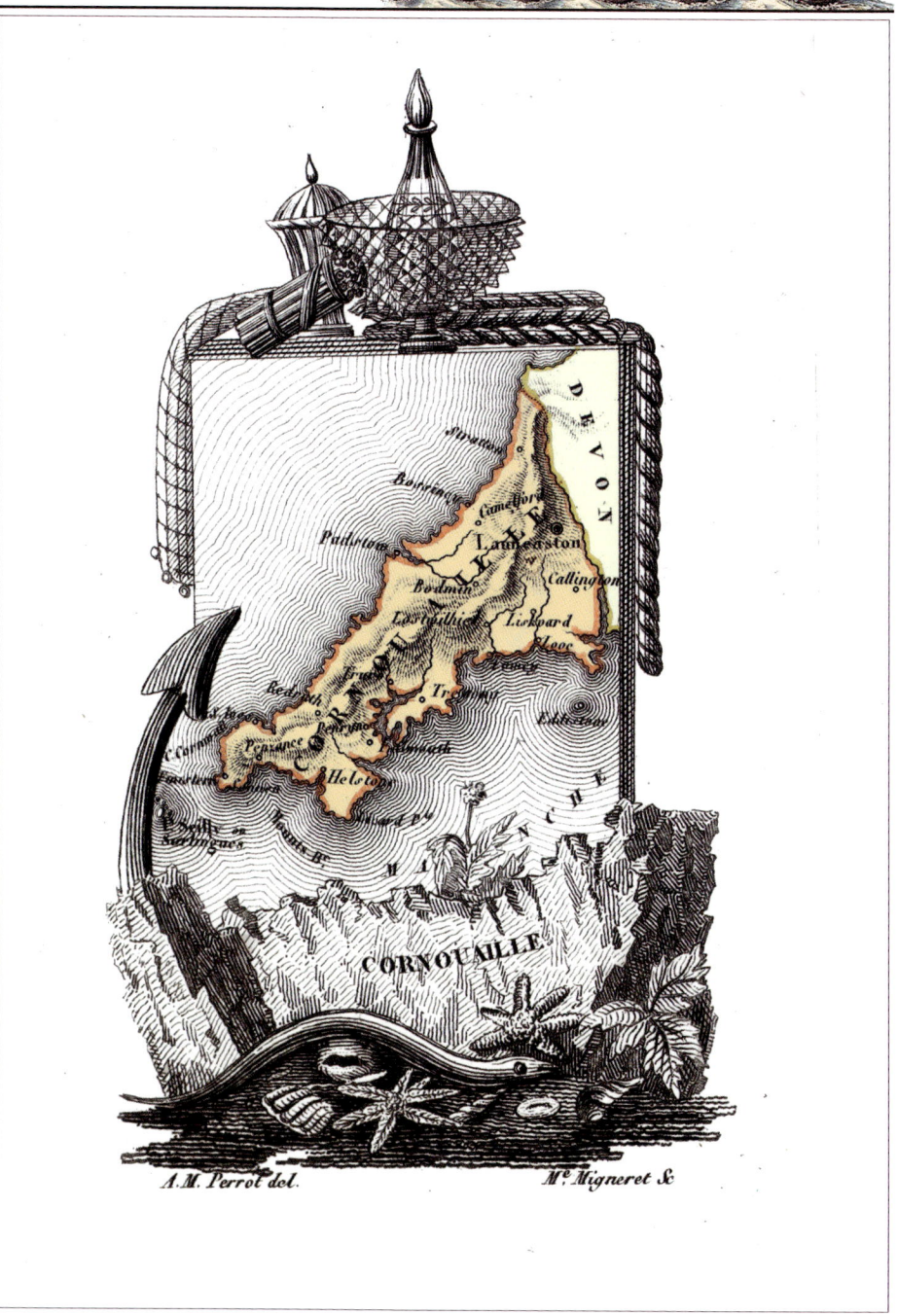

75. Migneret 1824 L'Angleterre ou Description Historique...

Antique Maps of Cornwall and the Isles of Scilly

76. GREENWOOD, CHRISTOPHER & JAMES   1827 & 1829

Eng. Dower, Pub. Greenwood & Greenwood
1827 (1778 x 1740), 1829 (673 x 552)

Christopher and James Greenwood surveyed 36 of the English counties between 1817 and 1833. They published their maps on the scale of 1 inch to 1 mile, in many cases anticipating the Ordnance Survey, which was covering the country systematically at that time, and undoubtedly rivalling the O.S. maps in accuracy and clarity of engraving.

Their first map of Cornwall was published on 1 September 1827 and consisted of six sheets that were sometimes mounted in sections to be packed in a leather case. Copies were available coloured or plain, but unfortunately very few copies have survived to the present day in good condition. Several features of the map reflect the contemporaneous changes in the geography of Cornwall. The first two railway lines are shown, one running from Crofthandy and the Poldice Mines at St. Day to the north coast at Portreath, and the other from Wheal Butter, at Pennance, to Lower Devoran, on a branch of the Fal estuary; both railways were concerned with the transportation of tin and copper from the rich mining area east of Redruth. The new causeway and bridge across the Hayle estuary (misspelled 'Payle' on the map) appears for the first time on a map, having been built in 1825 under the Turnpike Act; prior to this, all traffic had to cross the bridge at St. Erth, and it is interesting to note that in Elizabethan times trading ships had used St. Erth as a port. The silting up of the Hayle Estuary was accelerated by the rapid expansion of the tin mining industry, much of the silt being washed down by streams used in the traditional tin-washing methods of extraction. West of the River Tamar is shown the Bude and Launceston Canal, and the island at Looe bears the legend 'St. George's or Looe Island'; both these features occur in Pigot's map (#84), so that it would appear that Pigot copied some of his information from Greenwood's map. Another point is the sub-division of the Hundreds into smaller units of administration, much the same in extent as the areas in use today, with further sub-division into parishes.

In the lower right corner is a large vignette of St. Michael's Mount, measuring 380mm by 254mm, a beautifully engraved view from the east, which shows that there were fewer trees clothing the slopes of the mount in the early 19th century. Other noteworthy features are the hachures used in representing relief, and an inset of the Isles of Scilly (241mm x 290mm) on which longitude west of Greenwich is marked.

1829   *Greenwood & Compy's Atlas of England and Wales - Part First. London.*

In 1834 the Greenwoods published their 'Atlas of the Counties of England', the culmination of a series in which the county maps had been issued, in sets of eleven or twelve at a time, in four parts of the complete atlas from 1829 to 1834. The map of Cornwall, engraved by J. Dower in 1829, was issued in Part 1 of the atlas, in the same year. All the county maps in the Greenwood atlas were drawn on the same scale (1 inch to about 3 miles), and the work is a magnificent example of improved techniques and scientific approaches to the art of map-making. The Cornwall map is a reduced scale version of the 1-inch map of 1827, and though the vignette view of St. Michael's Mount and the slightly ornate lettering of the title-piece add some decorative value, in truth the map can stand on its cartographical merits alone.

1834   *Atlas of the Counties of England from Actual Surveys made from the Years 1817 to 1833, by C. & J. Greenwood. Published by the proprietors Greenwood & Co. Burleigh Street, Strand, London. Engraved by J. & C. Walker. Published 1 April 1834. Reprinted 1834.*

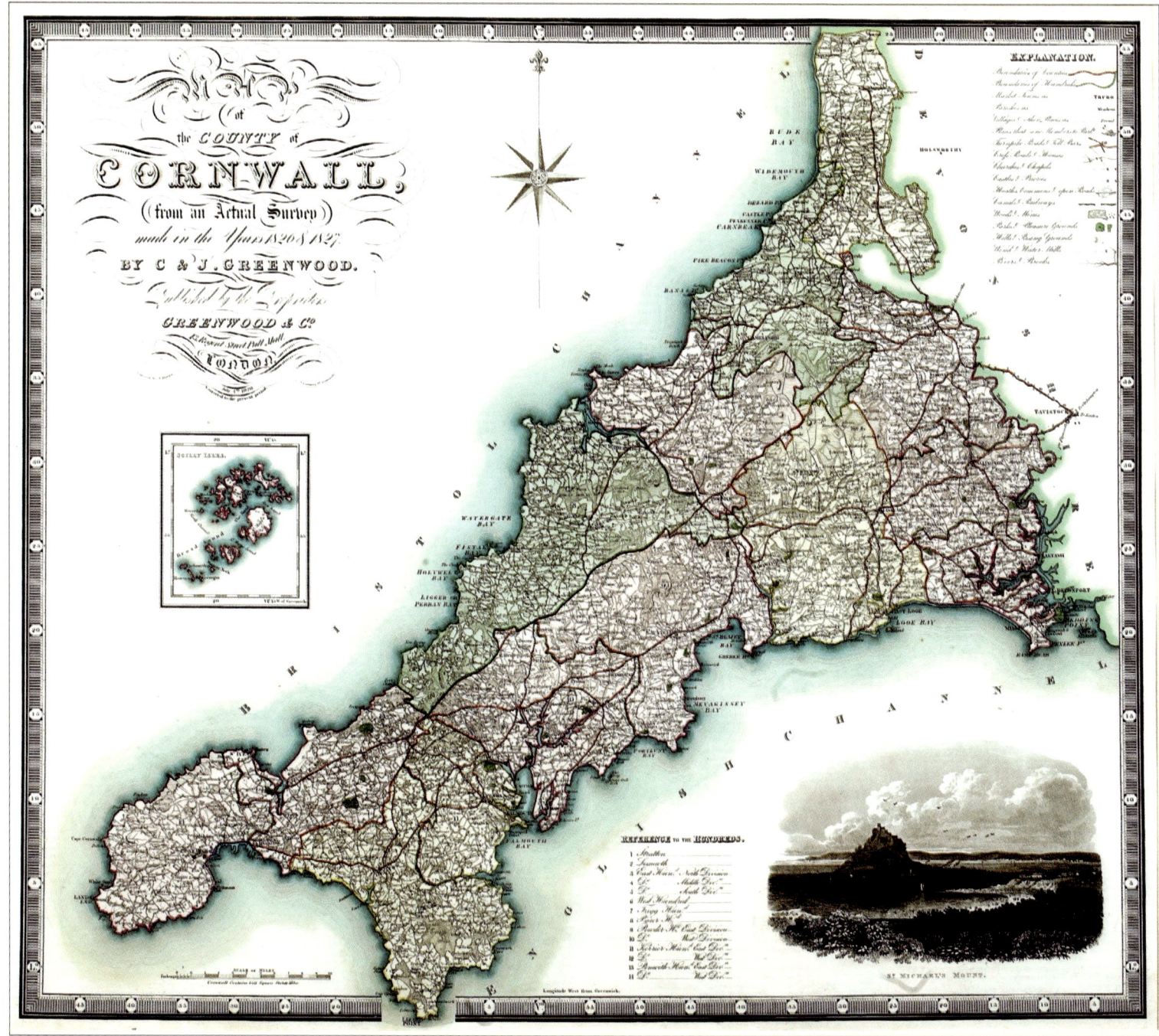

76. Greenwood 1829 Atlas of the Counties of England.

77. TEESDALE, HENRY 1830

Eng. Rowe/Teesdale, Pub. Teesdale 1829-43, HG Collins 1848-50, Orr 1852, Haywood 1858-82
(419 x 343)

Henry Teesdale (1776-1856) was a publisher and elected to the Royal Geographic Society in 1830. He went into partnership with John Jordan and William Colling Hobson as Henry Teesdale & Co., based at 302 High Holborn while living at 39 Cross Street in Islington, but dissolved the company in November 1832. Teesdale re-appears as a publisher in his own right, based at Brunswick Row near Queen's Square from the late 1830s to at least 1850. Teesdale's acquisition of Rowe's plates and issue of the 'New British Atlas' in 1829, and the later 'British Gazetteer' in 1852, have been already discussed (#69). Teesdale's version of the Rowe map is shown here, along with Haywood's 1868 version in his 'Travelling Atlas'.

The 'New Travelling Atlas' appeared in 1830 and will be detailed here with the later derivations. The 'Travelling Atlas' may be differentiated from the similar 'New British Atlas' by the piano-key border, though this was removed and replaced with a triple line border around 1848. The single issue by Orr, in 1852, retained the triple border, but the plates went to Haywood by 1858, who re-instated the piano-key border. Haywood continued publishing the maps under the title 'The Travelling Atlas' and briefly 'The Tourist's Atlas' into the 1880s. The illustration opposite is from the New British Atlas.

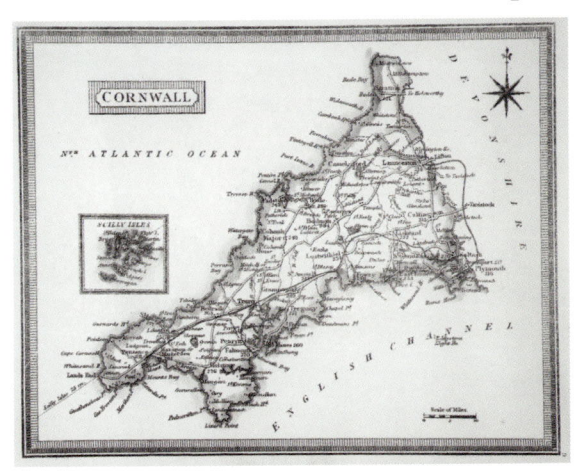

77.1 Teesdale/Haywood 1868

The Travelling Atlas

The late Haywood version (this page) is quite underwhelming in comparison with the previous maps, either by Teesdale or Rowe. The embellishments outside the map are simple and functional. The title is enclosed in a lozenge set inside a rectangle which is vertically shaded. The piano-key border is unmarked by latitude or longitude. Within the map itself, the distribution of place names is uncluttered to the point of being conservative. Even this late, Market Jew (Marazion) continues to be shown, Newlyn, however, is still missing. Only major roads are marked, as too are the main line railways – the branch lines to St. Ives and Looe &c. are not shown. The Bude – Launceston canal is shown, but unlabelled. There is no publisher's imprint at the base of the map here. At the far right is a plate number (9), printed sideways.

1830   *A New Travelling Atlas Revised and corrected to the year 1830, by Henry Teesdale & Co. London. Reprints: 1843 (...Revised and corrected to the year 1843).*

1848   *The Travelling Atlas...Revised and corrected to the present time. New imprint 'Published for the Proprietors by H. G. Collins, 22, Paternoster Row' London – border and lozenge surrounding title removed. Reprinted 1848, 1850.*

1852   *The Travelling Atlas of England and Wales, New imprint London. (Published for the proprietors) by W. S. Orr & Co., 2 Amen Corner, Paternoster Row, London.*

1858   *The Travelling Atlas of England and Wales Imprint: Printed and published by J. Haywood, 170 Deansgate, Manchester. Piano key border and lozenge reinstated. Penzance to Truro railway line added Reprinted 1860.*

1865   *The Tourist's Atlas of England and Wales New Imprint: PRINTED & PUBLISHED BY JOHN HAYWOOD, 143 DEANSGATE & 3 BRAZENOSE ST, MANCHESTER. Pub. Manchester: John Haywood. London: Simpkin, Marshall & Co. Plate number 9 added.*

1868   *The Travelling Atlas of England and Wales. No imprint at the base of the map. Pub. Manchester: John Haywood, London Simpkin, Marshall & Co.*

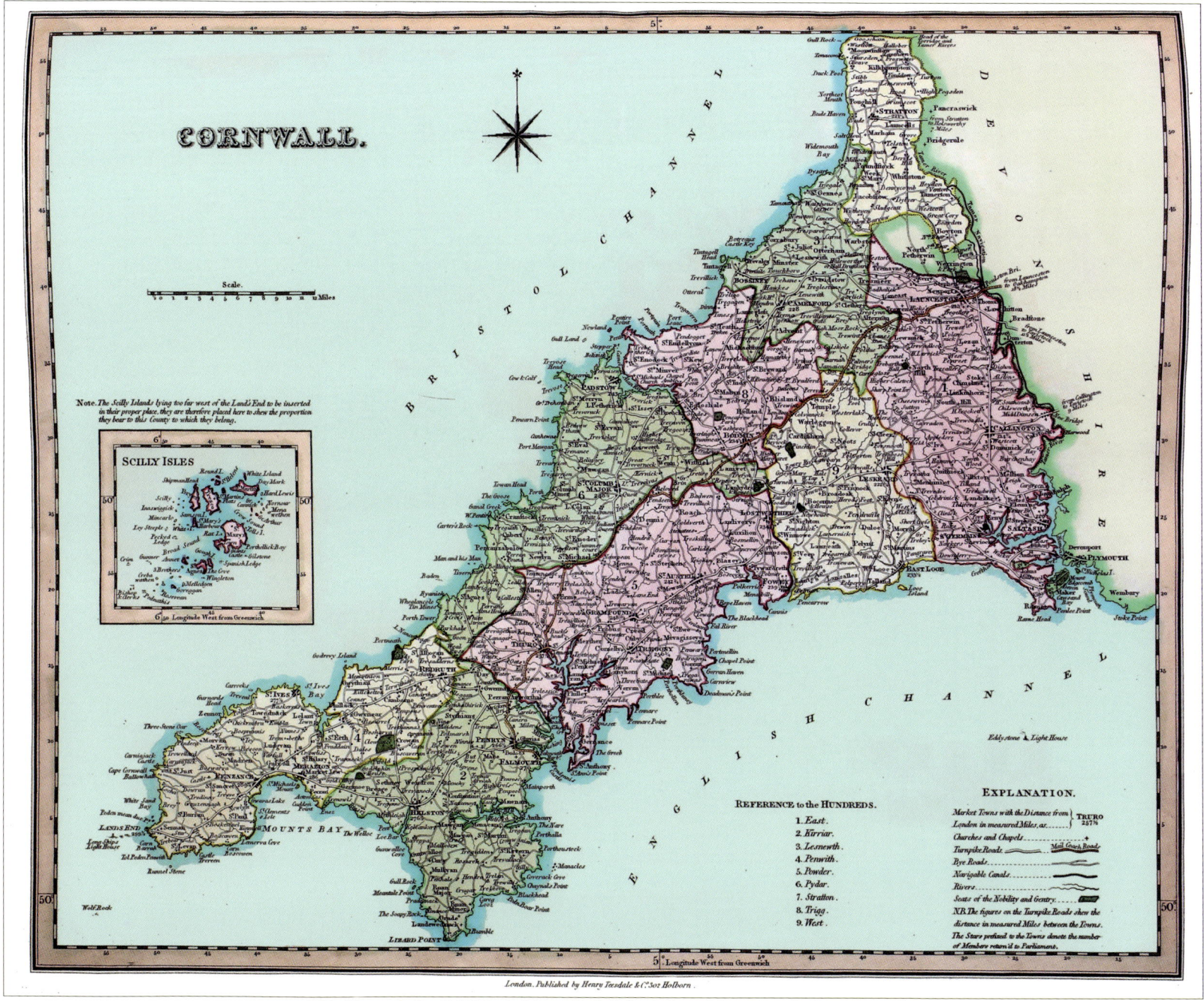

77. Teesdale 1830 A New British Atlas, New and Corrected

78. MURRAY, T. LAURIE & HOARE & REEVES 1830

Eng. Hoare & Reeves, Pub. Murray
(457 x 367)

T. Laurie Murray was a publisher, surveyor and early Fellow of the Royal Geographic Society, in London, from 1830 to 1832. His 'Atlas of the English Counties' was published in 1830, based on those maps of the Ordnance Survey. As far as can be determined, Murray had no connection with the Board of Ordnance. This was a huge governmental body that had existed since Tudor times. Amongst its many other arms, it was given the task of overseeing the new Ordnance Survey. Murray's slightly flamboyant title is considered now to be a little hyperbolic. The maps bear some similarity to John Cary's larger maps, and while they may have been copied from Ebden's maps of 1828 (#82), they are devoid of decoration.

Joseph Hoare (c.1810 -?) and James Reeves (1801-1868) operated from 15 Warwick Court, Holborn, as Hoare & Reeves. Several examples of their trade cards, as well as other work, can easily be found (Ebden #82). The Warwick Court address is mentioned in a 'London Gazette' announcement (Issue 23575, p159) of 1870, where the death of James Reeves, in 1868, precipitates the winding up of the Hoare & Reeves partnership, which had endured since before 1830. Following this, the company swaps names, becoming Reeves (son, also James) & Hoare (son, James), and enters the fledgling photographic business while continuing operating from the same address. They built one of the early examples of a 6x6 format camera, supplied photographic material and offered portraitures. The company exhibited at the Royal Photographic Society Exhibition of 1878.

The map is titled 'Cornwall', without a border or cartouche in the sea south of Looe. Under the bottom margin is the inscription 'London. Published May 1st 1830 by T. L. Murray, 19 Adam St, Adelphi'; the bottom right corner is marked 'Hoare and Reeves sculpt'. There are no other identifying marks on the map and the rear is plain. At the top left is an inset of the Isles of Scilly in a border marked off with latitude and longitude. Below the Isles of Scilly inset is a list of explanations, or key to the map (roads, canals, market towns &c.). The Hundreds are listed in alphabetical order, from East (1) to West (9). For the size of this map, the labelling of elements in the county is sparse – Newlyn, for instance, is missing, as too is St. Michael's Mount. Some attempt to illustrate highlands has been made, though it does appear to resemble escarpments rather than granite.

Although the title of the atlas includes 'Rail-roads', these are absent from the map's explanation list and from the map – suggesting that passenger rail-roads were the intent, not ore-carriers. The distances from London to the principal towns are shown.

1830   *An Atlas of the English Counties... Exhibiting the whole of the Inland Navigat'n Rail Roads, &c. Projected on the basis of the Trigonometrical Survey by Order of the Honble. The Board of Ordnance. Under the Superintendence of T L Murray, London. Reprints: 1831. The 1832 reprint shows the Parliamentary Divisions that would come into effect with the 1832 Reform Act.*

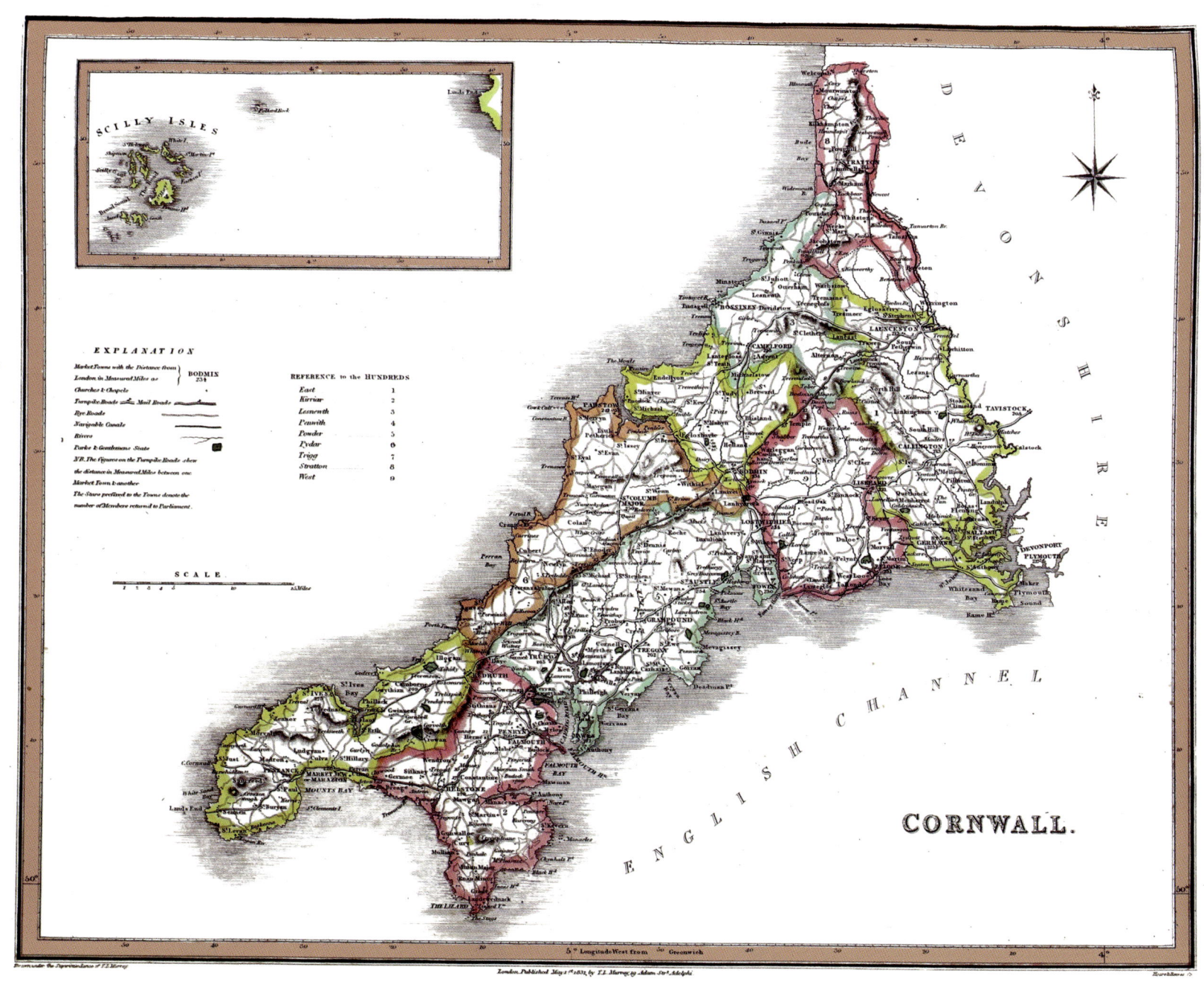

78. Hoare & Reeves 1831 An Atlas of the English Counties

79. CREIGHTON, ROBERT & STARLING, THOMAS 1831

Eng. Starling, Pub. Lewis
(235 x 175)

Samuel Lewis (1782-1865) published his 'Topographical Dictionary of England' in seven editions, from 1831 to 1848/9, the last edition being in four volumes and an atlas. He also produced companion versions of Scotland (1846), Wales (1833, 1844 and 1849) and Ireland (1846). The England edition included maps of the whole country, the counties of England, Guernsey, Jersey, Man and a plan of London. This was a huge task, not undertaken since Camden's 1586 work; gathering the information took six years and was achieved by sending 2000 questionnaires to every parish priest in the kingdom. The final work attracted the less scrupulous, and Archibald Fullerton was sued in 1839 for copyright piracy (#83).

Thomas Starling (1796-1850) was an engraver based in Camden Street, in Islington though his work can be traced initially to Clark's Place, and later Wilmington Square, both in Islington. He is perhaps best known for his 'Family Cabinet Atlas', of 1830, but was producing work as early as 1822. Starling's work appears to be concentrated into the 1820s and 1830s; little is known of him later than this. He declared himself bankrupt in 1825 ('London Gazette' 18099, p100). A co-partnership with Walter Charles Venning, based in Wilmington Square, was dissolved in 1837 ('London Gazette' 19524, p1899).

The map of Cornwall was drawn by Robert Creighton and engraved by Thomas Starling, and some of the other counties were engraved by J. & C. Walker. Starling's work can be differentiated by the capitalisation of his 'SCALE OF MILES'. It is correctly oriented, with north pointing up the page and 5° West correctly placed. There is an insert of the Scilly Islands in a square border top left; below this is a nice compass rose. The title of 'Cornwall' is in the lower right, above a scale of 0-50 miles. In the version illustrated, the highest points in the county are selectively drawn as clear tops with hachured lines radiating around them, though the primary purpose of the map is to illustrate the new divisions that were set following the Great Reform Act of 1832. This divided Cornwall into two Divisions - Eastern and Western. Within these Divisions were a total of 14 Unions; these are listed on the map to the left of the compass and are Eastern Division 1-9 and Western Division 10-14.

1831 *Topographical Dictionary of England in four volumes, Published by S. Lewis and Co, 87 Aldergate Street, London. Second Edition 1833 (places of election and polling stations added to the top of the map).*

1835 *Third Edition: Supplementary volume added 'View of the Representative History of England', 4th Ed. 1840, Eastern and Western Divisions. The Constituency towns are shown. It is a Political map designed to inform of one subject.*

1842 *Fifth Edition retitled 'An Atlas, comprising maps of the several counties...', unchanged from 4th Ed. 6th Ed. 1845 & 7th Ed. 1849: Unchanged. S. Lewis & Co, 87 Hatton Garden, London.*

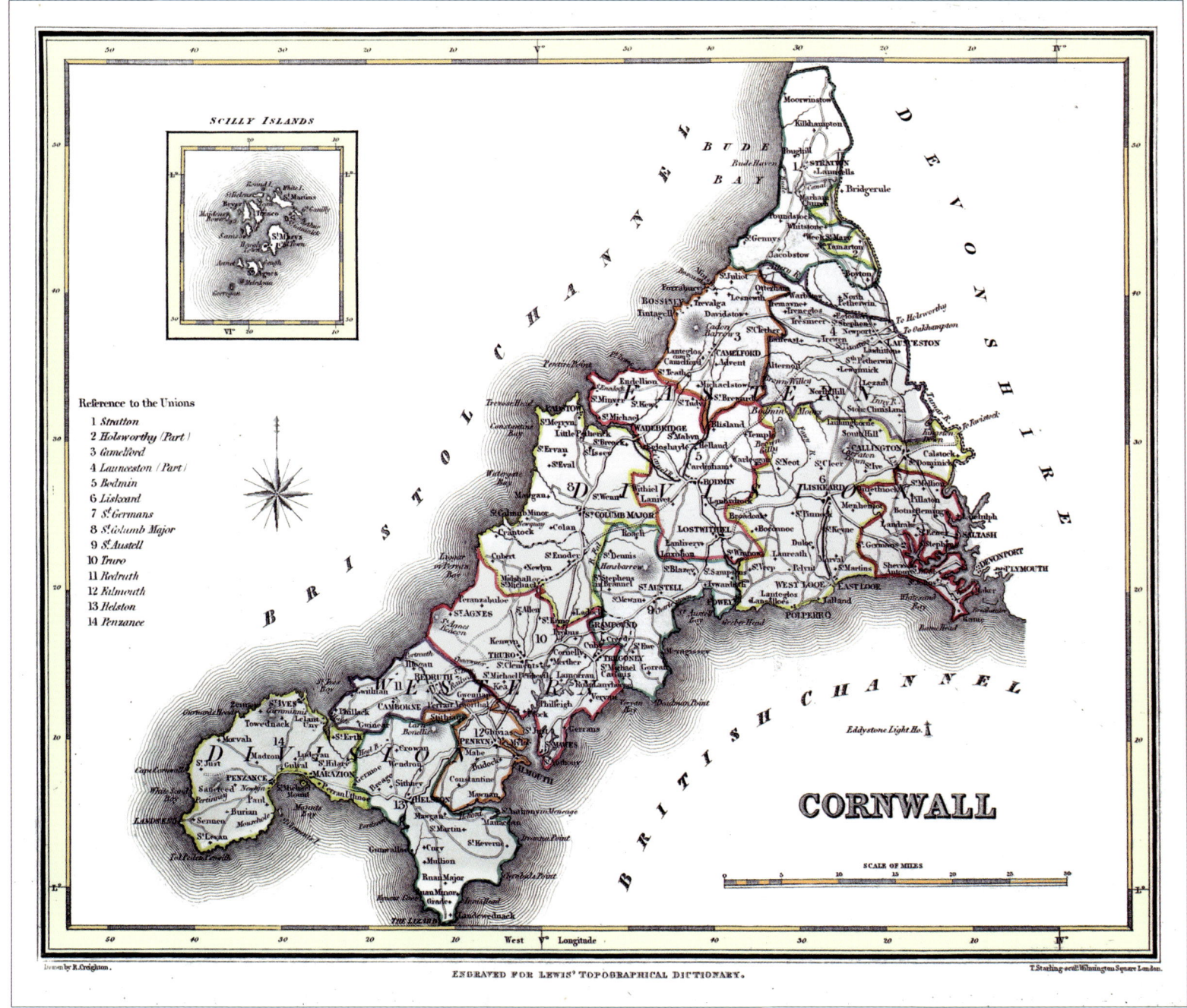

79. Starling 1840 (A) Topographical Dictionary of England in four volumes

80. COBBETT, WILLIAM 1832

Eng. Unknown, Pub. Cobbett
(189 x 246)

81. FISHER, HENRY & DAVIES, BENJAMIN REES 1832

Eng Davies, Pub. Fisher & Co
(195 x 237)

William Cobbett (1763-1835) published his 'Geographical Dictionary of England and Wales' in 1832, evidently in reaction to the Reform Bill of the same year. His better claim to fame could be the initiation of publication of Parliamentary debates, later taken over by the Hansard brothers after whom the records are named. The dictionary is of more importance than the very basic outline maps of the counties, none of which are of any cartographical significance. Cornwall is presented in alphabetical order, following an 84-page index and the preceding five counties, and is facing page 41. It is projected rather more like the Kintyre peninsula than anything else and is a curious map indeed.

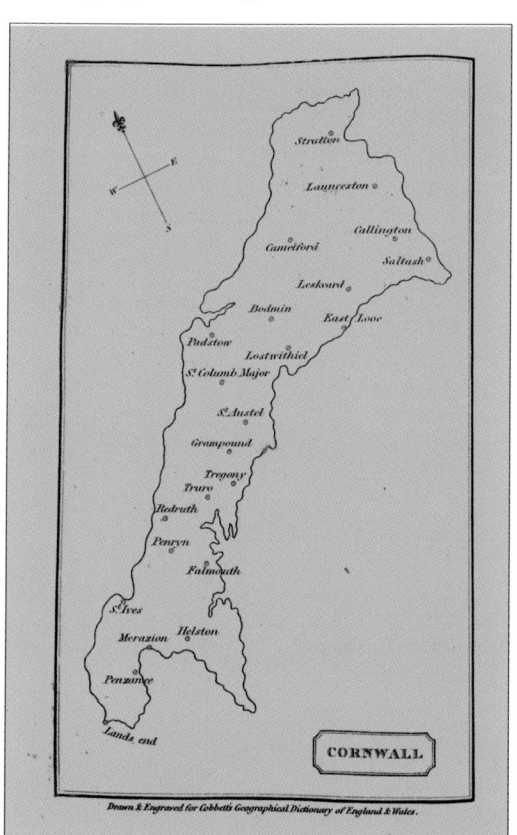

1832   Geographical Directory, written and published by Wm Cobbett. Printed by Mills, Jowet and Mills, Bolt Court, Fleet Street, London.

80. Cobbett 1832 Geographical Directory

Henry Fisher and Son were publishers at the Caxton Press, in Martin-le-Grand, London. In 1832 they published two maps to complement a topographical work entitled 'Devon and Cornwall Illustrated'. This started as a monthly installation, with the volumes covering Devon and Cornwall being produced separately. They are now found sometimes bound into one volume. The Cornwall map appears to have been engraved by Benjamin Rees Davies (fl.1811-1872), though there are parallel dated copies of the identical map engraved by J. & C. Walker.

B. R. Davies was born in Holborn and apprenticed under John Lodge (#51). He was an early proponent of engraving onto steel, a medium that yielded delicate and detailed work. From 1848, he became associated with Edward Stanford (1827-1904) - Stanfords continues to this day as one of the most eminent cartographic publishers in the world.

The Cornwall map is almost square. The top-most section of Stratton has been clipped off the main map and appears as an inset set within north Devon. (No other map has this variant). Through the length of the county is a chain of enhanced hills running from Stratton to Land's End. In the top left is an imposing engraving of the Cheesewring, on Bodmin Moor, with a reduced scale man at its foot intended for dramatic effect. Below this is a well annotated inset of the Scilly Isles, with the offset from Greenwich. The general map of Cornwall is shown with towns, roads and country parks. Below Looe is a simple compass rose and mileage scale. Latitude and longitude are marked off inside a border. The overall map is a clean and effective production.

1832   Devon and Cornwall Illustrated, by H. Fisher, Son & Co. Reprinted 1835, 1840, 1844, 1849.

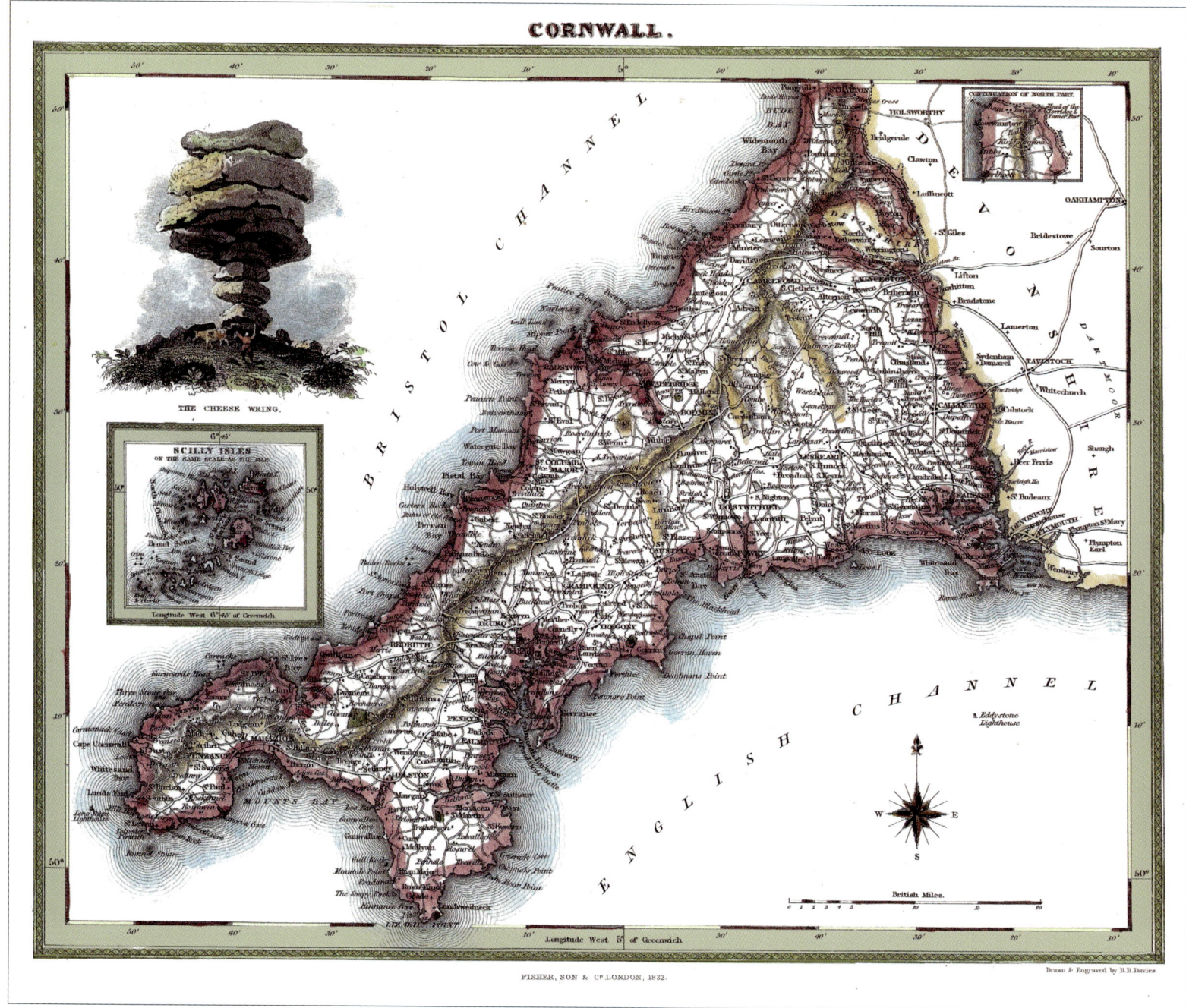

81. Davies 1832 Devon and Cornwall Illustrated

82. DUNCAN, JAMES & EBDEN, WILLIAM 1833

Eng. Hoare & Reeves, Pub Duncan
(436 x 350)

William Ebden was an English draughtsman and cartographer whose fine maps are rare in their first states, but commoner in later versions when published in these atlases by James Duncan. Some of these maps are thought to be the source of the Murray atlas (#77). In addition to these atlases, Ebden contributed to other atlases over the same period: Laurie and Whittle, Darton & Son, M. J. Godwin & Co. and possibly others.

It is possible that this map, as with others, predates the 'New English Atlas' of 1833. Ebden was active at least as early as the 1810s, though little else has been found about him.

The 'Complete County Atlas' was published in 1835 by James Duncan, using maps that had been re-worked and now engraved by Hoare and Reeves. Duncan worked from 37 Paternoster Row, though is recorded in the 1835/37 electoral rolls as a Liveryman 'Felt-Maker'.

The map is well detailed, with the Isles of Scilly shown in a rectangular insert in the top left of the map. Below this is a rather ornate title with decorative scroll work surrounding it. This is given as 'New Map of the County of Cornwall, divided into Hundreds containing the District Divisions and other Local Arrangements effected by the Reform Bill'. Each line of the title is done in a different script.

Of interest on the map opposite is the Launceston - Victoria Railway line. This has been somewhat heavily drawn onto the map as a (proposed) line from Launceston to the north Cornwall coast, near St. Ginnys. The original prospectus and map for the railway had been drawn up in 1831 by Roger Hopkins (1775-1847), a Welsh civil engineer who had worked on the Plymouth and Dartmoor railway (1821-23), the Wadebridge - Wenfordbridge and Bodmin railway (1831-34), as well as other projects in South Wales. An Act of 28 July 1836 allowed for the construction of a line from St. Ginnys, south of Bude, to Launceston. The 'Victoria' part of the title derives from a plan to re-name Tremoutha Haven to Port Victoria. Neither the port nor the railway was built.

The division of the county into Western and Eastern parts was done cutting Pydar and Powder Hundreds in two - a line can be seen added later to the map, from Deadman Point on the south coast, north-west to the north coast, near Crantock. The map has ignored the part of Devon that lies to the west of the Tamar, north of Launceston.

The square inset of the Scilly Isles is shown top left along with the Pollard Rock, this is one of the Seven Stones. It was first shown in lieu of the Seven Stones by Reeves (#78). They appear on several earlier maps and charts: reference the charts of Willem Blaeu (#10) back in 1608 which clearly shows the Seven Stones as a navigational hazard. Even in recent times the dangers of this reef continue - the Torrey Canyon disaster of 1967 remains seared in childhood memories of beach trips, glutinous tar and dead marine life; it remains the largest oil spill in UK waters.

Ebden's construction of longitude around the Scilly Isles' inset is curious - both along the top and bottom margins is inscribed 4° (West of Greenwich) at a mid point between Land's End and the archipelago. This should be 6° West.

The foot of the map is inscribed with James Duncan's name and Paternoster address; to the far right is the mark of the engravers, Hoare and Reeves.

1833 *A New English Atlas, Pub. James Duncan, 1833.*
1835 *A Complete County Atlas of England & Wales, Pub. James Duncan. Repub. 1837, 1838, 1840, 1845.*

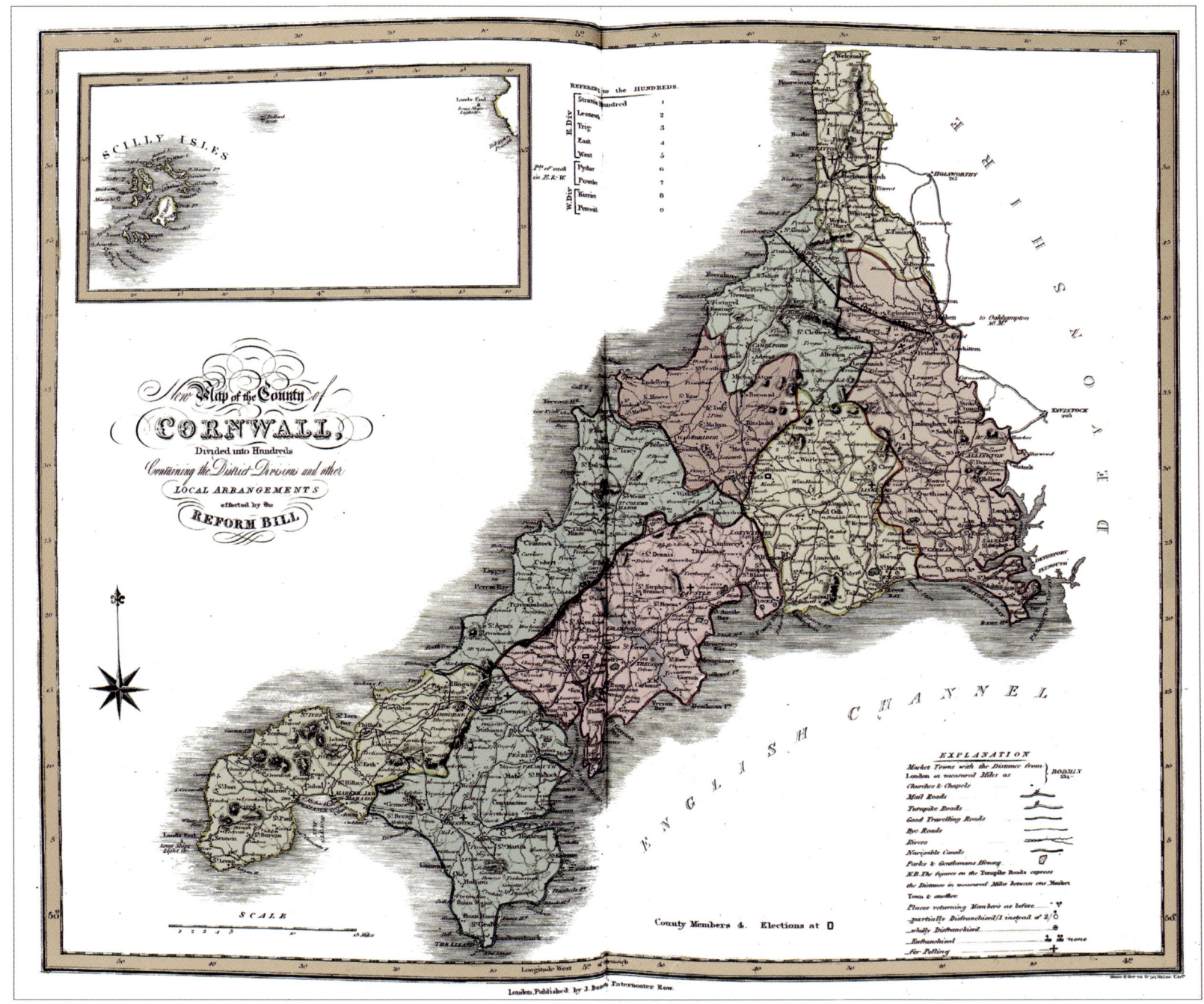

82. Hoare & Reeves 1835, A Complete County Atlas of England & Wales

83. BELL, JAMES & SCOTT, ROBERT 1833-4

Eng. Scott, Pub Fullerton
(239 x 191)

James Bell (1769-1833) struggled with asthma all his life, and after a somewhat precarious start, found himself tutoring Latin and Greek to Glaswegian university students. His writing career started in 1816, with geographic contributions to a popular work called 'Glasgow Geography'. He followed this with several other Glasgow oriented publications through the 1820s, before starting work on a publication called the 'New and Comprehensive Gazetteer'. This was completed in four volumes in two books, published posthumously.

Archibald Fullerton (?1780 – before 1838) established a firm of engravers and publishing in the early 1830s in Glasgow, having previously been in partnership with William Sommerville and John Blackie in Edinburgh. This expanded over the following five or so years, to London, Edinburgh and Dublin. Fullerton senior adopted an approach that set him sailing close to the laws of copyright. In 1839 Archibald's son, John Archibald, was the defendant opposite plaintiffs Samuel Lewis and George Pringle, publishers of 'Lewis's Topographic Dictionary of England and Wales' (#79), charged with copyright piracy. In fact, it was James Bell, (both Bell and Fullerton senior were, by now, dead), who was the culprit in the plagiarising of a large quantity of text from the Lewis publication. Lord Langdale MR, sitting in judgement, concluded that copyright had been infracted and issued an injunction against John Fullerton restraining him from any further printing, publication or distribution. (Reports of cases... 'Courts of Law' Volume 2, 1839. Pub. 1840, Halsted & Voorhies, New York).

Cornwall appears in Volume 2. This small map is another good example of the high quality of engraving on steel, an art that characterises the 19th century particularly. The map of Cornwall was engraved by R. Scott (1777-1841) and may be identified by the vignette view of Launceston Castle, and the imprint of 'Archd. Fullerton and Co., Glasgow', the publishers, at the base of the map.

The reprint, done in 1840, with several re-issues of Fullerton's 'Parliamentary Gazetteer', covered four volumes, with Cornwall appearing in the first volume pp500-505. The text has been lightly re-worked, presumably considering the court case. Fullerton's map (between p500 and p501) is unchanged from the earlier gazetteer, however, the 'Comprehensive Gazetteer' has the map as a fold-out between p90 and p91.

1833-4 A New and Comprehensive Gazetteer of England and Wales, by James Bell, Published by A. Fullerton & Co., 34 Hutcheson St, Glasgow and 31 South Bridge, Edinburgh. Reprints: 1836.
1840 Fullerton's Parliamentary Gazetteer, A. Fullerton & Co., Stead's Place, Leith Walk, Edinburgh and 106 Newgate Street, London. Reprinted 1843, 1845, 1846, 1848 and 1851.

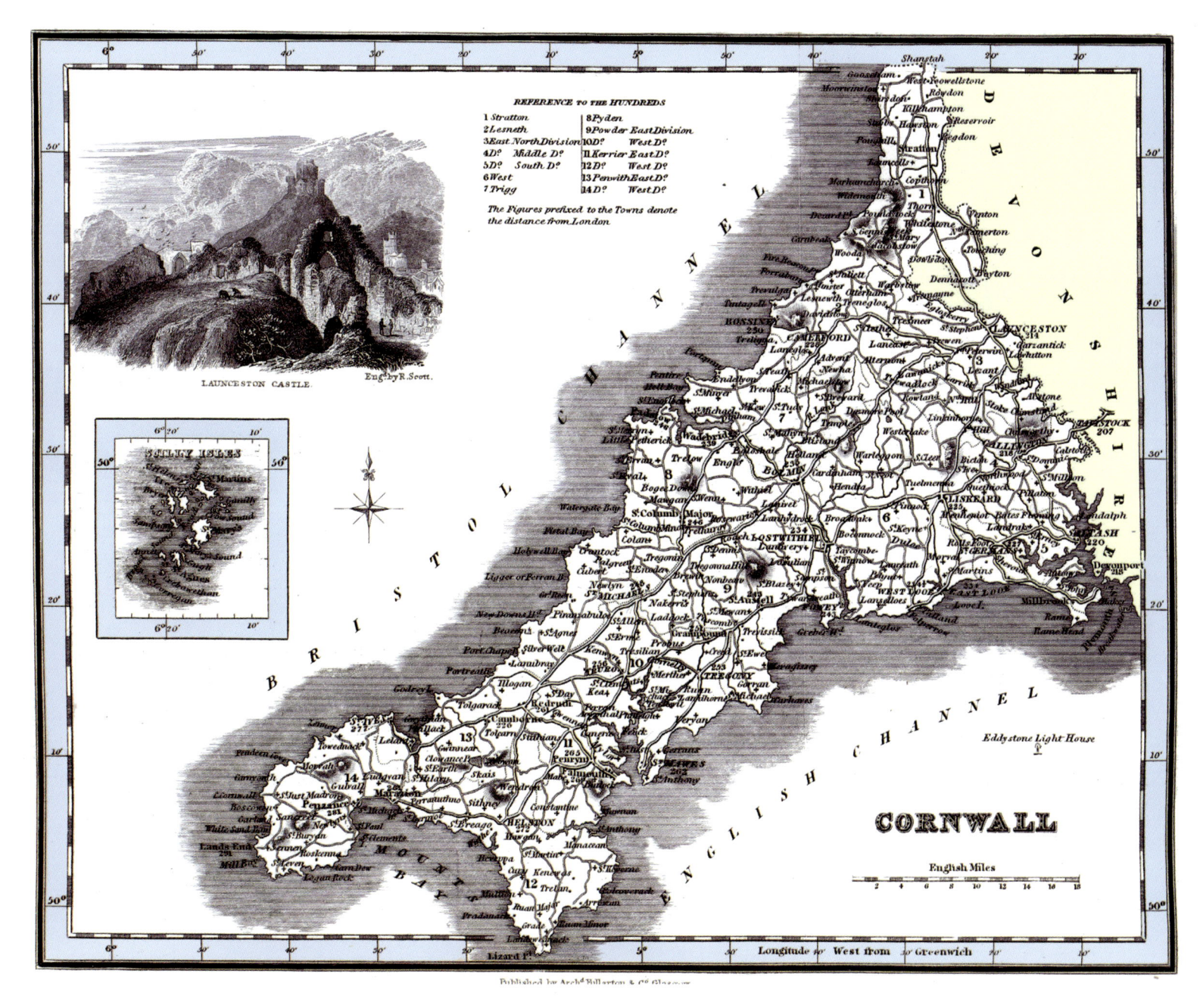

83. Scott, *A New and Comprehensive Gazetteer of England and Wales*, by James Bell, London

84. PIGOT, JAMES & Co 1830

Eng Pigot & Son, Pub Pigot & Co
(343 x 216)

James Pigot (1769 -1843) was a printer/publisher, born in Macclesfield. By the age of 25 he was engraving onto copper, in Manchester. His son, James junior, was born in 1798. Pigot senior published his 'Manchester and Salford Directory' in 1811. The first edition of the 'Commercial Directory' of 1814 was published anonymously, but by 1818 it shows him as publisher with R. & W. Dean (also printers). Sometime before 1828 Pigot & Son started trading at 16 Fountain St., Manchester, but the company was dissolved by mutual consent in February 1839. At the same time, and possibly in parallel, Pigot & Co., a partnership between Pigot senior, Charles Elkins and Isaac Slater evolved possibly as early as 1833, but with the death of Elkins, in 1835, the company was taken over by Pigot senior and Slater. Pigot junior ceased professional trade with his father in 1839, possibly due to health reasons, and died at the age of 43 in 1841. Pigot senior died two years later, leaving Slater to run the business using his own, and Pigot's name, variously.

The Cornwall map is an elegant, medium-sized map, finely engraved on steel and full of accurate information that is presented with great clarity, despite the crowding. The atlas was usually issued with the maps, lightly coloured by hand, and, in the more expensive versions, the delightful vignette of St. Mary's Church, Truro was coloured, too. The map appears to have been copied partly from Cary's 1809 Atlas and partly from Greenwood's maps (#75), and was published in Pigot's 'Commercial Directories', as well as in atlases.

Two interesting points emerge in this map: firstly, Pigot marks the 'Bude Canal' from Bude to Launceston to the Cornwall side of the Tamar, in contrast with Smith (#58) and Cary (#50), whose maps show the 'Proposed Tamar Navigation' on the Devon side of the river. Secondly, the island at Looe is marked 'St. George's Island'; the only other early appearances of this title for Looe Island are in the Norden map of 1728 (#6) and the Greenwood maps (#75).

1829   *Pigot & Co.'s British Atlas of the Counties of England, London & Manchester.*

1830   *Pigot & Co.'s British Atlas of the Counties of England, Address changes: 17 Basing Lane, London and 18 Fountain St, Manchester. Reprints 1831.*

1830   *Pigot and Co.'s National Commercial Dictionary, London & Manchester.*

1839   *Pigot & Co.'s British Atlas of the Counties of England, Address changes: 59 Fleet St, London and 18 Fountain St, Manchester. Reprints 1840, 1843.*

1846   *I. Slater's New British Atlas. Published by I. Slater, Fleet Street, London and Fountain St, Manchester. Reprints 1847, 1848, 1855, 1857.*

1850   *I. Slater's (Late Pigot & Co.) Royal National and Commercial Directory and Topography, by Isaac Slater, Manchester and London. Reprints 1851, 1852.*

The 'Pocket Atlas, Topography and gazetteer of England... Illustrated by maps of the English counties and vignettes of cathedrals &c.' was produced fortnightly, from late 1838. Cornwall is issue #9, probably published early in 1839. The imprint at the base of the map is shown as 'Published by Pigot & Co., London and Manchester', while the engraver's mark at bottom right confusingly is 'Pigot & Son, Engravers Manchr'.

The Cornwall map here is smaller than (100mm x 160mm), and a slight variation on, the 1830 map - the vignette of St. Mary's Truro has been removed and the Isles of Scilly inset moved into its place. The compass rose has moved from below Looe to below Penwith and is simplified. The key explaining the Hundreds set above Padstow has been removed, as too have the dotted lines on the map. The Explanation key is reduced in detail.

1839   *A Pocket Atlas...Pub. Pigot & Co., London & Manchester. Reprinted as 'A Pocket Topography and Gazetteer of England in 1841 and 1850, Pub. Pigot & Co., in London, Longman & Co. and Sherwood & Co., in Paternoster Row, Simpkin & Marshall, Stationer's Court, London and Pigot & Slater, Fountain St., Manchester.*

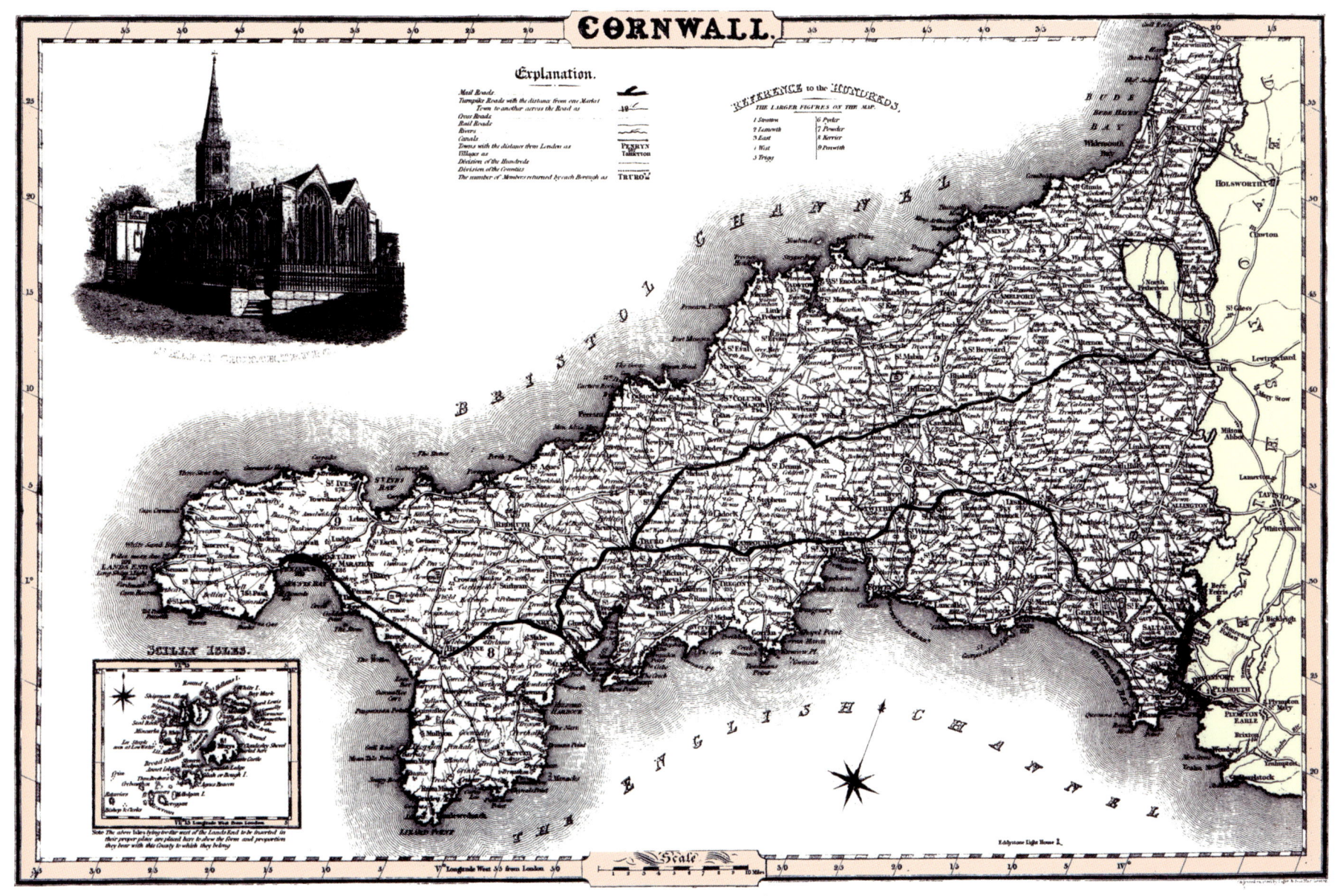

84. Pigot & Co. 1831 British Atlas of the Counties of England

85. PINNOCK, WILLIAM & ARCHER, JOSHUA 1833

1833 Eng. Archer, Pub Edwards

(248 x 191)

William Pinnock had worked with Maunder and Neele to produce his 'County Catechisms' in 1819 (#62). The 'Guide to Knowledge' appeared in 1833-34, with the maps engraved by Joshua Archer and 'Sidney' Hall. (Note: Hall had died in 1831, and his work was taken over by his wife, Selina (see #71)). The Cornwall map is engraved by Joshua Archer. The Guide was issued in monthly parts, with Cornwall appearing in March 1833. The map is plate XLVI and presented in rotated landscape format with the Devon border at the top of the page. What sets this series of maps apart from most others is that it is a woodblock print where the detail has been carved into the block, resulting in white (inkless) detail on a black inked ground. Within the same volumes are several well executed 'star maps' of the various constellations, also engraved by Archer, which are far better suited to this white on black approach.

Joshua Archer (1792-1863) was born in Barnstable, in Devon. He married Jane Jones and had two boys, Alfred and John. A trade card of 1839 shows him as an engraver based at 2 Southampton Terrace - this would continue to be the family home until his death. Prior to this, he found himself in front of the Court for Relief of Insolvent Debtors in 1834, where his address is shown per that inscribed on the map - 100 Drummond St., Euston Sq., London ('London Gazette' Issue 19225). He was discharged in 1845 (Issue 20493).

The map of Cornwall is notable, as are the others, only for its presentation. Of itself, it is not particularly impressive: there is a host of spelling errors, e.g. 'Lamorno', 'Zennon', 'Merazion' and 'Sancret'. St. Michael's Mount and Newlyn are unmarked. The major and minor roads are shown, though with the engraving method are rather too prominent. Of the preceding maps, it bears closest similarity with Langley's, though to give Archer some credit, he has correctly oriented the map with respect to north and drawn the 5° West line of longitude in the right place. In the sea to the north of St. Ives is an inset of the Scilly

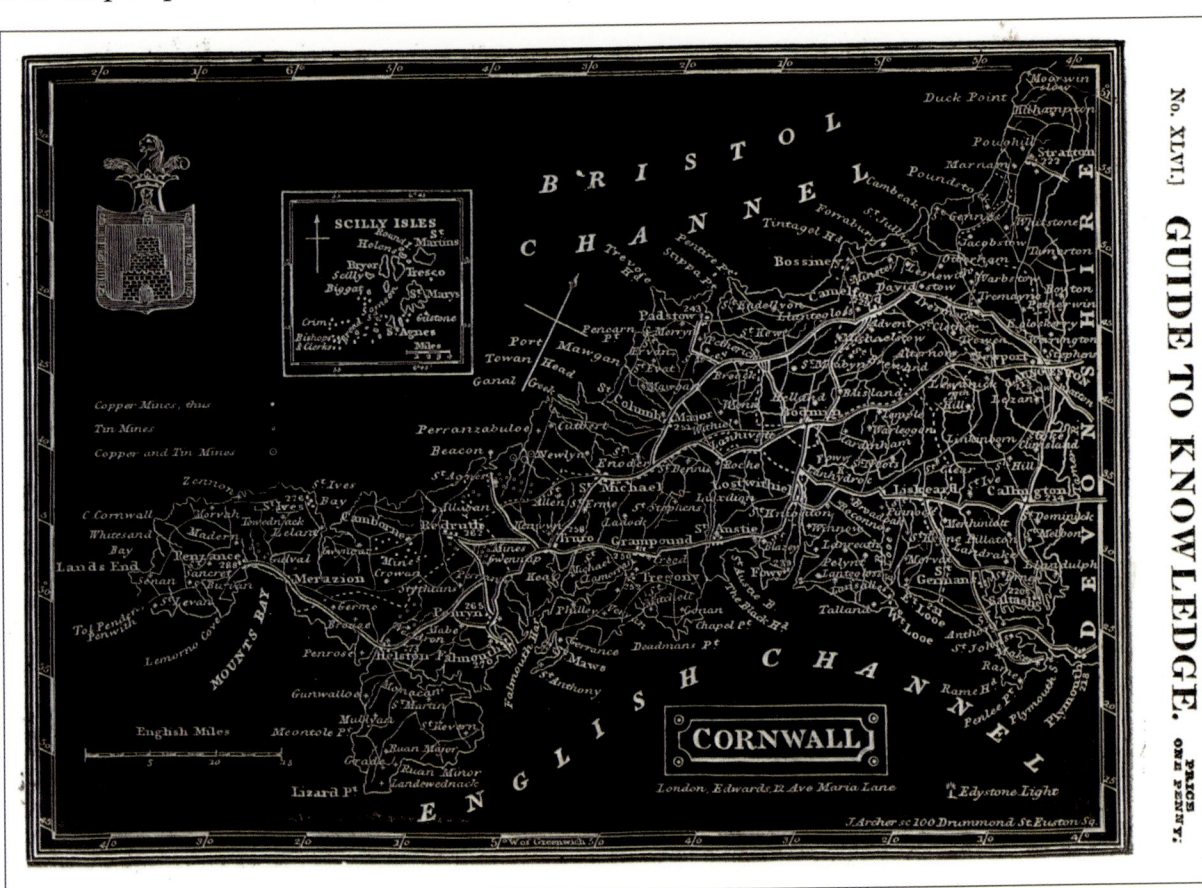

85. Archer 1833 Pinnock The Guide to Knowledge

Isles, with a shield of the arms of Launceston to the left.

Below this is a brief key indicating the presence of mines: tin, copper and combined mines. Below Looe is a simple rectangular cartouche bearing the title 'Cornwall', with the imprint of William Edwards below: 'London, Edwards, 12 Ave Maria Lane'. Some light changes were made from 1838 (see below), but the detail on the map is unchanged. The lithographic transfers produce a print that is less sharp in detail.

1833 *The Guide to Knowledge, Edited by W. Pinnock, Pub. William Edwards, Ave Maria Lane, London. Reprinted 1838 with some slight amendments: Grecian Key frame added inside thin double line outer frame, sea area around coasts shaded.*

1844 *Lithographic transfer. Descriptive County Atlas of England and Wales... Edited by William Bayne, Pub. Shepherd & Sutton and Richard Groombridge, London. Cornwall title, cartouche and Edwards imprint removed.*

1844 *Shepherd & Sutton's New Series of Descriptive County Map. Pub. Shepherd & Sutton and Richard Groombridge, London. Added three panels in a floral-style over the top of the map. Centre panel reads 'Shepherd & Sutton's New Series of Descriptive Maps', Panel left 'County of', panel right 'Cornwall'. Title below bottom border 'Historical Sketch of the County of Cornwall'.*

1847 *Lithographic transfer. Johnson's Atlas of England, Manchester, 1847, 1849, 1863. Now printed normally (black on white), Grecian Key frame and thin double line outer frame and Cornwall cartouche below Looe reinstated. Edwards' and Archer's imprint missing.*

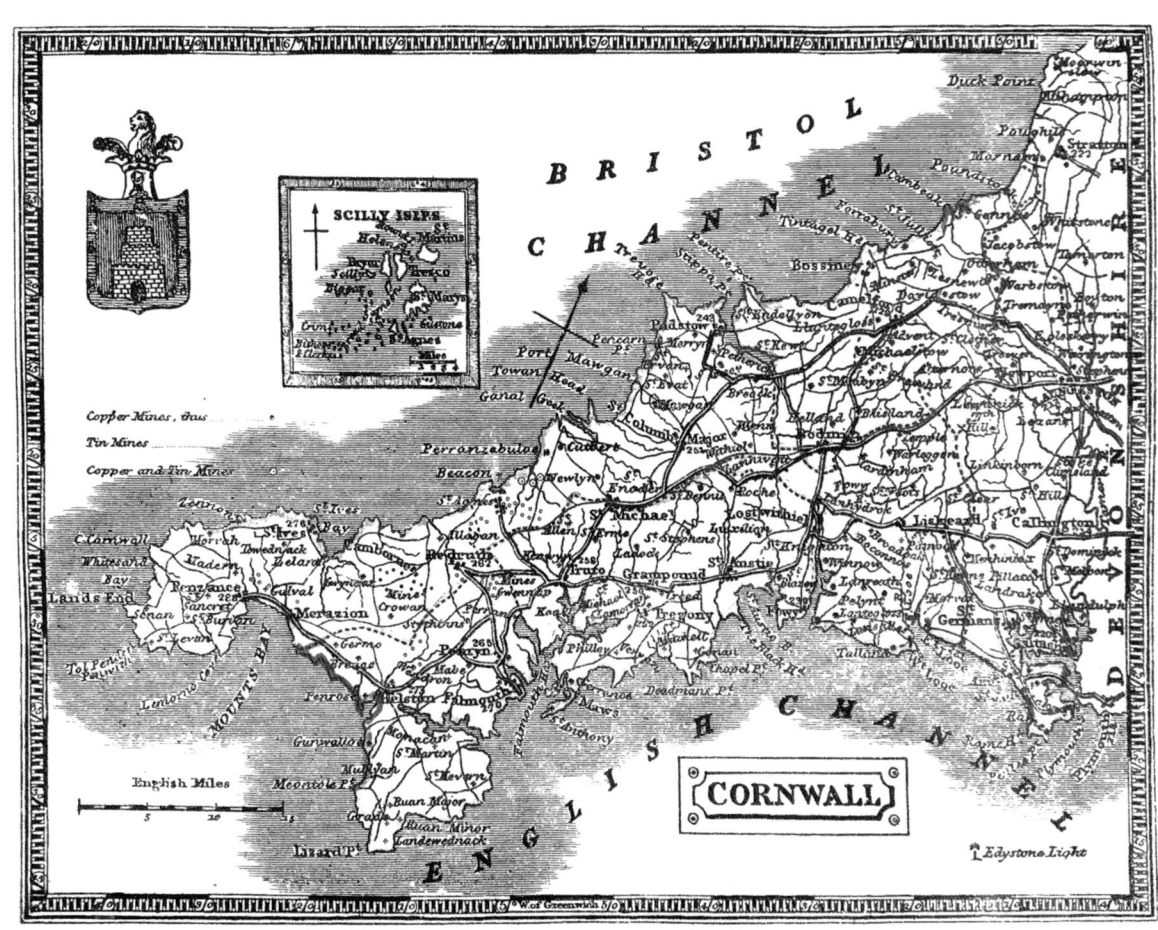

85.1 Archer 1847 Johnson's Atlas of England

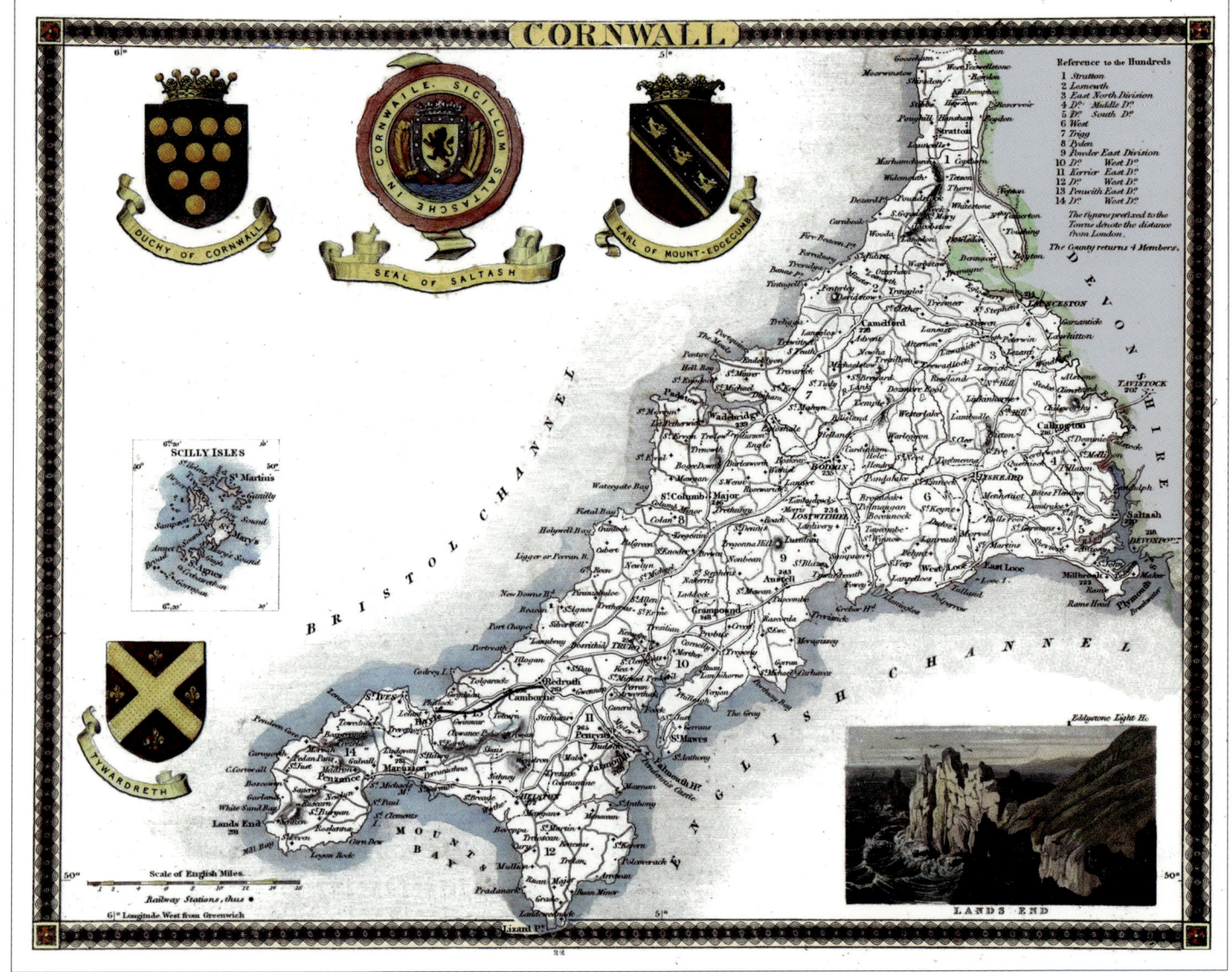

86. Moule 1848 Barclay's Complete and Universal Dictionary (State 7 below)

State	Engrv	Shields	MPs	Plate 22	Rail	Example
1	✓	X	X	X	X	1834 Pamphlet
2	✓	✓	X	X	X	1836 English Counties
3	X	X	X	X	X	1837 County Atlas
4	X	✓	X	X	X	1838 & 1839 English Counties
5	✓	✓	✓	X	X	1838 English Topographer
6	X	✓	✓	✓	X	Pre-1848 Barclay's Dictionary
7	X	✓	✓	✓	✓	Post-1848 Barclay's Dictionary

218   *Antique Maps of Cornwall and the Isles of Scilly*

86. MOULE, THOMAS 1834

Eng. Dower, Pub. Virtue & Kendrick 1834, Virtue 1836-39, Barclay 1841-55
(248 x 191)

Of all the maps of the 19th century, those of Thomas Moule (1784-1851) must surely take pride of place, for their decorative quality. Moule started as a bookseller in Duke St. near Grosvenor Square, in London. This led him into an interest in heraldry, which in turn led to the decorative embellishment of maps. He first published a collection entitled 'Moule's English Counties', in 1834. This was done as a series of pamphlets which formed two volumes, published by George Virtue at 26 Ivy Lane and John Kendrick at 54 Leicester Square. Cornwall appears as No. L (50?), priced at 1s. (or 1/6 coloured). The map of Cornwall contains the engraver's mark at the base of the map: 'Drawn and engraved for MOULE'S ENGLISH COUNTIES by J Dower'; thereafter it is erased. The map is quite plain, with none of the later heraldic embellishments.

'Moule's English Counties Delineated' was published from 1836 to 1839, as a single volume with the maps enclosed. Two alterations were made to the map. Firstly, the familiar shields of the Duchy of Cornwall, Seal of Saltash, Arms of the Earl of Mount Edgecomb (sic) and those of Tywardreath were added in the 1836 version; secondly, in 1838 the engraver's mark was removed. No further alterations were made to the map during the life of the publication to 1839. In 1837 'Moule's County Atlas' was published and contains a mid-step in the evolution of the Cornwall map: both the engraver's inscription and the shields are missing – this is the only state to contain neither marks.

In 1838 'England's Topographer' was published by George Virtue. The Cornwall map used has a few additions, due to the political boundary changes. Below the script detailing the Hundreds (top right) has been added the brief note 'The County returns 4 Members'. On the map itself, a symbol (*) denoting these constituencies has been added, though there are more than four. James Barclay's 'Dictionary' was published from 1842 and can be distinguished from earlier states of the map with the addition of a plate number (22) below the Lizard. Aside from this, the map contains the shields and the MP note, but no engraver's imprint. The final alteration of the map occurs in the 1848 edition of the dictionary, when a short railway line is added between Redruth and the coast, just to the north of Hayle, near Phillack.

George Virtue published what must be a re-publication of David Hume's 'History of England'. The Moule map of Cornwall that is contained in this edition is the same as those seen in Barclay's 'Dictionary', except the map is folded 2/3 of the way down on the landscape edge.

There are six versions of Moule's Cornwall map, depending on the occurrence or absence of the following elements:
1. Engraver's mark at the base of the map
2. Presence of armorial shields
3. Note of returning MPs
4. Plate number (22) at the base of the map below the Lizard
5. Railway line from Redruth to the coast north of Hayle.

1834 *Moule's English Counties, pamphlet version. Pub. G. Virtue, 26 Ivy Lane and John Kendrick, 54 Leicester Sq.*
1836 *The English Counties Delineated, by Thomas Moule. Pub. George Virtue London. Reprints: 1837 & 1839.*
1837 *Moule's County Atlas, Pub. George Virtue, London.*
1838 *England's Topographer. Pub. George Virtue, London.*
1841 *Barclay's Complete and Universal Dictionary. Reprints 1842, 1848, 1850 and 1855. Pub. George Virtue from 1841 to 1855. James Virtue took over his father's business upon George's retirement in 1855.*

87. DUGDALE, THOMAS & ARCHER, JOSHUA 1842

Eng. Archer, Pub. Tallis

(235 x 184)

Thomas Dugdale published a volume called 'Curiosities of Great Britain' in 1835, using maps from Cole and Roper (#65), which by that stage were over 30 years old. This was followed by a more ambitious treatise called 'Curiosities of Great Britain, England and Wales Delineated', which ran to eleven volumes from 1842. The maps were drawn by Joshua Archer, who also engraved the Cornwall map. Thomas Dugdale, like his namesake James (#60), presents something of an enigma - he is well known as an antiquarian in association with William Burnett, yet almost nothing beyond this- no addresses, electoral roll registrations &c. are known. A far more notorious Thomas Dugdale was gaoled in 1847 for selling obscene material, but this is unlikely to be the same person.

The publisher Lucinda Tallis (née Chance) married John Tallis in 1814, and they produced two children, Lucinda (1816-1880) and John (1817-1876), both born in Worcestershire, and possibly a third, Frederick, born in London (1822-1902). John and Lucinda established a book-selling business based at 21 Warwick Sq. while living at 12 Chadwell St, Pentonville, which Lucinda continued with her daughter and grandson, Charles, until her death in 1880. Up to about 1842, Lucinda senior worked with her son, John, and it is her name we see as publisher until this date. In about 1842 John went into a partnership with Frederick which lasted until 1849, when it was dissolved ('London Gazette' Issue 21069). John then set up a company called John Tallis & Co., from about 1851 to 1854. From this, John Tallis would become a well-known publisher of cartographic material; his 'Illustrated World Atlas', produced for the 1851 Great Exhibition, set Tallis on the world stage and marked possibly the last of the truly decorative maps.

The Cornwall map shown is inscribed lower right 'Drawn and Engraved by J. Archer', and bottom centre 'Engraved for Dugdales, England and Wales. Delineated'. Top right is marked (plate) '8'. Longitude is given from Greenwich and has Penzance correctly placed at 5° 31' West. The map is included here as an illustration of the industrialisation of Cornwall due to its burgeoning tin and copper industries.

Archer's map shows several railway routes that had been, or soon would be, constructed in the mid Cornwall area. All these lines were for industrial use: taking ore from the mines from Wendron near Helston and Gwennap, to Portreath and Hayle on the north coast. Later routes were added to access the port at Devoran on the Fal. Other lines were constructed to support the China clay industry, from St. Austell to Pentewan, and to transport sea sand inland from Wadebridge to Bodmin - this route also carried passengers.

Archer has corrected several of the spelling errors that were present in the previous map, and somewhat reduced the density of place names. There are several notable omissions - Newlyn and St. Michael's Mount, for instance. The Hundreds are listed above the inset for the Scilly Isles, in a generally east to west order.

Overall the map has started to resemble much of what one sees today with the obvious exception of more recent man-made additions. It has become a utilitarian map for reference rather than one of decorative quality.

1842   *Curiosities of Great Britain, England and Wales Delineated, by Thomas Dugdale Antiquarian Assisted by William Burnett...Vol 1. Pub. Lucinda Tallis, London. Republished same year without Dugdale imprint, New imprint 1850 (twice).*

1842   *The Universal English Dictionary..., by Rev. J. Barclay. J. &F. Tallis London and Glasgow, Repub. 1850. 1850 Barclay's Universal Dictionary, by Rev. J. Barclay. Pub. John Tallis & Co., London and New York.*

1850   *Modern and Popular Geography Vol 1, by William Goldsmith. Pub. J. & F. Tallis, London, Edinburgh and Dublin.*

1858   *Dugdale's England and Wales Delineated, Ed E. L. Blanchard, Pub. Lucinda Tallis, London.*

1860   *(Tallis's) Topographic Dictionary of England and Wales Vol 1, Pub. L. Tallis, London.*

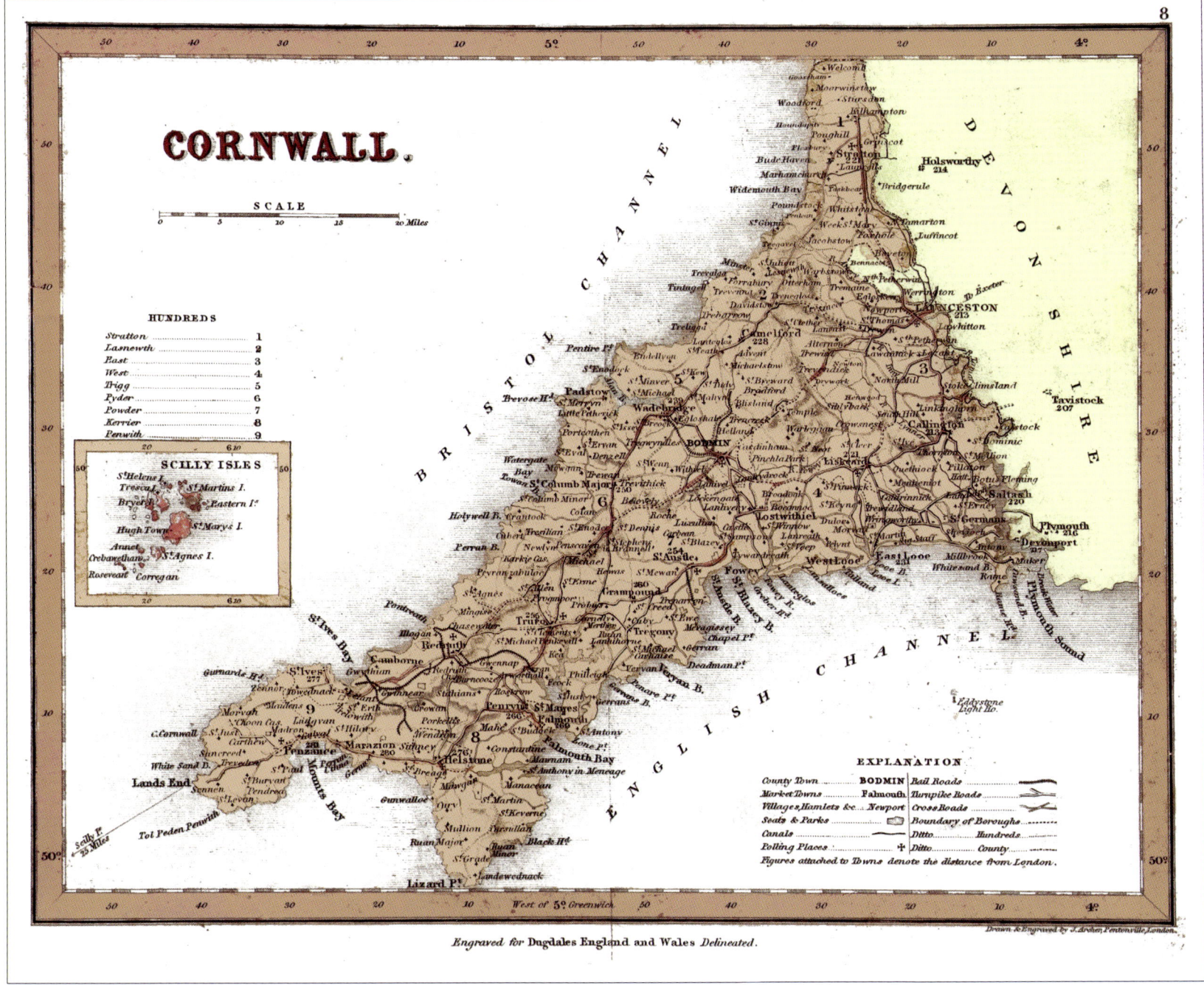

87. Archer 1858 Dugdale's England and Wales Delineated.

SECTION FIVE:
1. CORNISH PLACE NAMES
2. MOUNT'S BAY AND THE ROAD TO PENZANCE
3. THE GREAT CROSS COURSE
4. DUNHEVED CASTLE
5. SIR CLOUDESLEY SHOVELL AND THE ASSOCIATION
6. THE DEVON BORDER
7. LATITUDE AND LONGITUDE
8. THE SAXTON - NORDEN - KIP SEQUENCE
9. SUPER GROUPS
10. SURVEYOR/ENGRAVER/PUBLISHER CROSS-INDEX
11. REFERENCES
12. INDEX

Section Five
Appendices

APPENDICES

The following are some short notes concerning some aspects of the maps of Cornwall that affect more than one map. Some of these are unique to Cornwall, others are of a wider nature.

1. Cornish Place-names

Crossing the Tamar, one is immediately hit with the sense of being 'abroad'. The sign on the A30 at Dunheved bridge, on the Tamar, welcomes you in Cornish and English with 'Kernow a'gas dynergh', 'Welcome to Cornwall'. Many of the towns and villages in the county bear bi-lingual sign posts and it is evident one has stepped over more than a river. It is thought that 80% of the place names in Cornwall are derived from Cornish, and some of these are well over a thousand years old; indeed, the Cornish for St. Michael's Mount, near Penzance (Cara Couze in clouze) ' seems to describe a geography that is far older. By the mid 1600s Cornish as a language was on the decline in the county, yet most place names had Cornish origins and presented some problems for the surveyors as they made their way through the county. The language barrier led to several mis-translations that, once on the record, stayed there for many (hundreds of) years. Some are simple spelling alternatives, such as 'Newland' for 'Newlyn', near Penzance. Two other persistent examples occur throughout many of these Cornish maps: Market Jew and Hall Drunkard.

To the east of Penzance lies the town of Marazion, opposite St. Michael's Mount. On maps, from the earliest examples through into the mid 1700s, it is referred to as 'Market Jew'. The derivation of this stems from the Cornish name 'Marghas Yow' meaning 'Thursday (or Small) Market'. This corrupted into 'Market Jew' and, with the incorrect assumption that there was some religious connotation, became 'Mara-Zion' (my hyphen).

Hall Drunkard was in north-east Cornwall, near Davidstow. It is now known as 'Hallworthy'. The derivation stems from two original places: Halworgy and Hal-Dronket (both recorded in 1439). The former translates as hal (marsh in Cornish) + personal name - Gorgi becoming 'Marsh of Gorgi', thus Halworgy. The latter is a similar transition: Hal, added to this is tron-groes, or Hal-Troen-groes. This translates as 'Marsh of a wooded promontory', and becomes Hal-Dronket, and finally Hall Drunkard.

Cornwall, like Wales and other Celtic/Gaelic countries, provides a rich history of place names that describe the immediate environment, from which one can understand the geography that leads to the name. Cornish names usually contain two parts: the prefix gives an initial indication of what the place is notable for, the suffix describes this in better detail - colour is often used, such as Baldhu: Bal - mine, Dhu - black.

Craig Weatherhill's book 'Place Names in Cornwall and Scilly' provides further reading on this subject.

Richard Carew wrote his 'Survey of Cornwall' in 1602 - in it he supplies the old rhyme in aid of identifying Cornishmen:

'By Tre-, Pol-, and Pen-, Ye may know the Cornishmen'

Table 1: Some Cornish place name roots

Cornish Root	Examples
Bos or bod - Home or dwelling	Boscaswell, Bodrifty, Bossiney
Car or Ker or Cayr - Enclosed farmstead or fort	Carlyon, Carharrack, Carveth
Enys - Island or isolated place	Enys Dodman, Enniscaven, Ennisworgy
Hen - Old or ancient	Hendra
Lan - Sacred enclosure	Lanner, Lanhydrock, Lanvean, Launceston
Maen or men - Stone or rock	Men-An-Tol, Maen Scryfa, Maen Dhu Point
Nans - valley	Nancealverne, Nancledra, Nanjizal
Pen - a headland	Penzance, Penhale, Penberth, Pendeen
Pol - Pool, lake or well	Polperro, Polzeath, Poldhu
Porth - Bay, port or harbour	Porthleven, Porthcurno, Porthgwarra, Porthennis
Tre or Tref - Settlement - often a farm.	Trevose, Trengwainton, Trewellard, Tregony
Ty or Chy - House (Often of higher status)	Tywardreath, Chysauster
Venton - Spring	Ventonleague, Ventongimps, Ventonwyn, Ventongassic

2. Mount's Bay and roads to Penzance

The construction of maps from earliest times may have had several reasons, not least of which is a desire to understand where things are - the maps here do this with varying levels of accuracy and thereby success. Navigational charts are probably the ultimate expression of this need, for lives depended on it. The ownership of maps became the mark of an educated man - they were used as decorative wall hangings like tapestries or other works of art as an expression of someone who had 'arrived'. Notwithstanding the propensity for copying previous maps, the maps of Cornwall occupy a unique place in British cartography - they contain a coastline that occupies about 90% of the county's perimeter, making it easy to see how changes in the coastline have evolved. An advantage here is that coastlines visibly change over the course of human timespans, and if the maps are diligently recorded and updated, the maps will show this.

The Cornish term for St. Michael's Mount is 'Cara Couze in clouze', or 'Brown Rock in the wood'. Around the base of the Mount, especially on the eastern side, can be found petrified wood and, after severe storms, stumps of ancient trees are exposed. These trees are thought to be between 4000 and 6000 years old – after the last ice age. Since then, sea level has flooded the area around the foot of St. Michael's Mount, entombing the trees in the process. Evidently the area continued to be near sea level, or at least poorly drained and swampy marshes developed, which are still there today.

At the turn of the 1600s, surveys were conducted by Christopher Saxton and John Norden. When the two maps were drawn up, and ignoring some differences in overall geometry, the coast between Penzance and Market Jew (aka Marazion) shows an area drained by some six or so rivers/streams. Norden goes further by showing a large sandy area extending across the whole area. The next time the area was surveyed, rather than copied, might have been as late at 1675, with Ogilby's road map. The section covering this segment is contained on plate 28, and shows the road running cross country through Market Jew, past St. Michael's Mount, and clearly crosses a causeway from there to Penzance. The next reliable survey we get is Joel Gasgoyne's map of 1700. This quite clearly shows the road east of

Extract from Norden's Penwith map (drawn ~1598)

ANTIQUE MAPS OF CORNWALL AND THE ISLES OF SCILLY

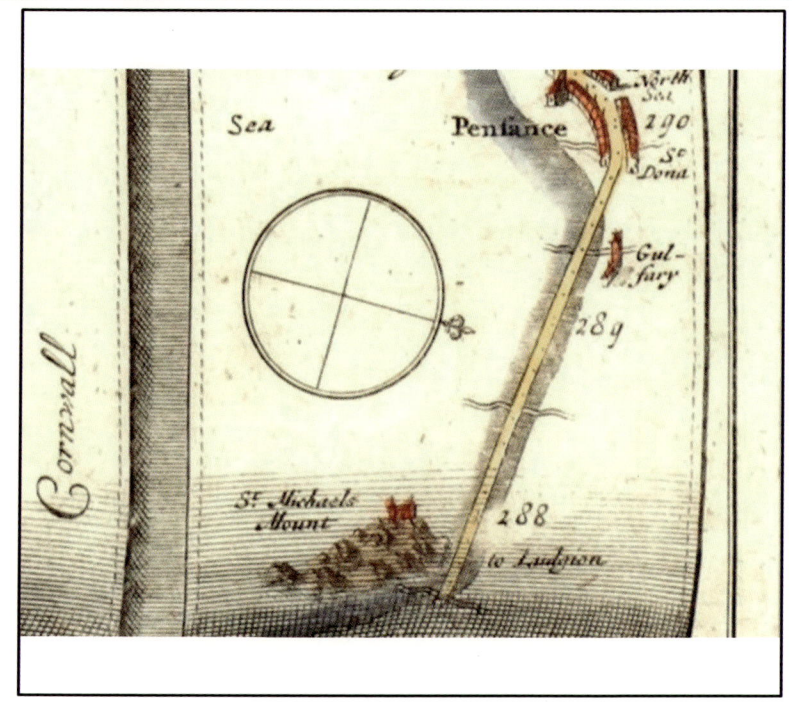

Extract from Ogilby's 1675 Britannia (plate 28)

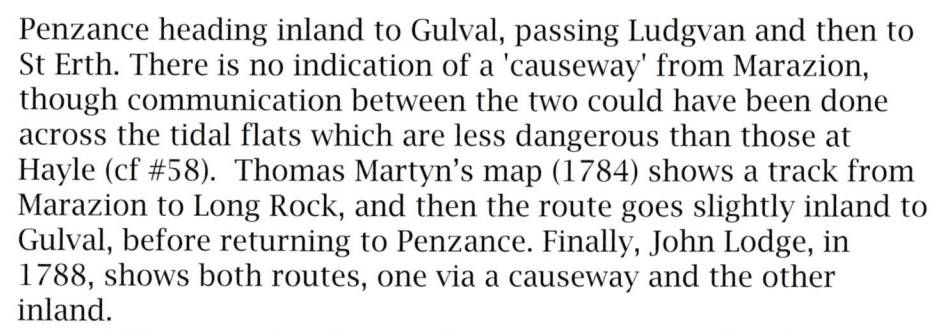

Extract from Lodge's 1788 Cornwall

Penzance heading inland to Gulval, passing Ludgvan and then to St Erth. There is no indication of a 'causeway' from Marazion, though communication between the two could have been done across the tidal flats which are less dangerous than those at Hayle (cf #58). Thomas Martyn's map (1784) shows a track from Marazion to Long Rock, and then the route goes slightly inland to Gulval, before returning to Penzance. Finally, John Lodge, in 1788, shows both routes, one via a causeway and the other inland.

    What is evident here is that Saxton and Norden drew a section of West Penwith that was swamp, with many streams/ rivers draining into it. In front of this, on the seaward side, was a stretch of beach that might have extended right across the area from Penzance to Marazion. Neither map notes any woodland or forest, though Norden goes as far as to suggest this may have been the fabled land of Lyonesse...The area has, from Norden's time to Ogilby's, silted up, and the rivers become less evident; a storm beach has formed, facilitating the construction of a causeway across the head of the bay. This, in due time, was consolidated and possibly increased in elevation. By the time of the construction of the passenger-carrying railway linking Penzance to the rest of the world, in the late 1800s, this bank was a permanent feature and remains so today. The area behind this causeway/bank continued to be brackish, especially at the eastern end, though this is steadily being encroached upon by out-of-town shopping facilities and other commercial enterprises.

This demonstrates that these maps were not just decorative, they endeavoured to portray the county as accurately as time, technology and men were able. It is easy to regard these maps, especially the more embellished ones, as pieces of art – and to an extent they are, but their underlying purpose was to inform.

3. The Great Cross Course

Cornish tin and copper mining rose to international importance by the end of the 1700s and early 1800s. Map producers at the time were naturally keen to show how this industry impacted the land, and several maps were produced over this period to illustrate the mines of Cornwall. The first map to show the location of the burgeoning mining industry was Simpson's map of 1744. The mines were placed in the general areas of Redruth/Camborne, St. Agnes, St. Ives/Lelant and between Helston and Falmouth. By the time of the three maps under discussion - those of Cole & Roper (1805), Wallis (1812) and Langley (1817) - the number of mines had increased, as too had their geographic spread. What marks these maps apart is the inclusion of a line marked '(The) Great Cross Course', from a point on the Lizard near Ruan Minor, and on a bearing of about 350°, to the north coast at St. Agnes. The reason for its inclusion initially on Cole & Roper's map is as unclear as it is curious. Nowhere on the map, nor elsewhere in the textless publication from whence it came ('The British Atlas' of 1810), is there an explanation of the line.

Cornwall and Devon have surface exposures of granite which are of Carboniferous age - these are about 270-300 million years old. There are five main bodies of granite - Land's End, Carnmenellis near Redruth, St. Austell, Bodmin and Dartmoor. Smaller exposures at Godolphin and Carn Brea (which may be part of the larger Carnmenellis granite to its south) are also found, and, offshore, the Scilly Isles and Haig Fras. Associated with most of these granites, and generally either to the sides or on top, are extensive mineralised zones that have been exploited for perhaps 4000 years - these contain primarily tin and copper,

Detail of Cole & Roper's British Atlas 1805

though there is a host of other less extensive metal minerals too, (black lines on the sketch map below). These mineralised zones are generally aligned with the trend of the granites, i.e. east-north-east to west-south-west. Following the emplacement of these zones are faulted zones that run perpendicular to them, with displacements both vertically and horizontally. These are known as Cross Courses (Blue lines) and are common throughout the area.

The line that has been drawn on the Cole & Roper map et seq. represents the Great Cross Course that divides the mining area of Camborne and Redruth - to be fair, the map represents the general idea of the location of the Cross Course fault, in fact it is further west and oriented about 300°. It does not, however, extend onto the Lizard, as shown.

Obviously, the map makers considered it of sufficient interest to include - from a mining perspective, it is, but not as much as the lodes running at near right angles to it.

SW England Granites, associated lodes and cross courses

Blue - Cross Course faults
Green Roper's Cross Course
Surface granites
1 Penwith
2 Carnmenellis & Carn Brea
3 Godolphin
4 St Austell
5 Bodmin
6 Dartmoor

Antique Maps of Cornwall and the Isles of Scilly

4. Dunheved Castle

During John Norden's survey of Cornwall between 1580 and 1598, he sketched a view of the ruins of the ancient castle at Launceston, called Dunheved.

Dunheved Castle was built following the Battle of Hastings by William the Conqueror's half-brother, Robert de Mortain, Earl of Cornwall. It was a classic motte and bailey construction, placed at Launceston to protect and defend a narrow route into Cornwall along the Kensey river. The original structure was re-enforced in stone and updated by a later Earl of Cornwall, Richard, son of King John. Richard's son, Edmund, inherited the castle in 1272, but moved the Cornish capital to Lostwithiel. This precipitated the castle's slow demise and by the mid 1300s it was little more than a ruin.

The hand drawn view of Dunheved by John Norden was reproduced by John Pine when he engraved illustrations, as well as the maps, in 1728. The original and rendition are reasonably similar, so we can use the Pine version as a base. The motte is shown on the right of the sketch, surrounded at its base with a wall. To the left is an enclosed walled area with two fortified entrances, while inside, according to Norden, are a decayed chapel and the town assizes, (by Norden's time, the structure was serving as the county gaol).

William Kip produced an enhanced and expanded version of this in the 1607 edition of 'Britannia'. This is unlabelled, but shows the walled town extending both around the motte and to the left. The detail is exceptional and includes a depiction of what one assumes is St. Stephen's Church, on a hill in the background.

John Speed's map of Cornwall in 1610 also contains an engraving of the same view, though he has simplified it and added labels to the various parts. From this is it is possible to orientate all the sketches - The South Gate and St. Magdalene are to the east of the motte, with St. Stephen's in the background. The mountains of Cornwall are less imposing. Nonetheless, one can say the Norden sketch and the later derivatives are from the vantage point of Windmill Hill, to the south-east of the castle.

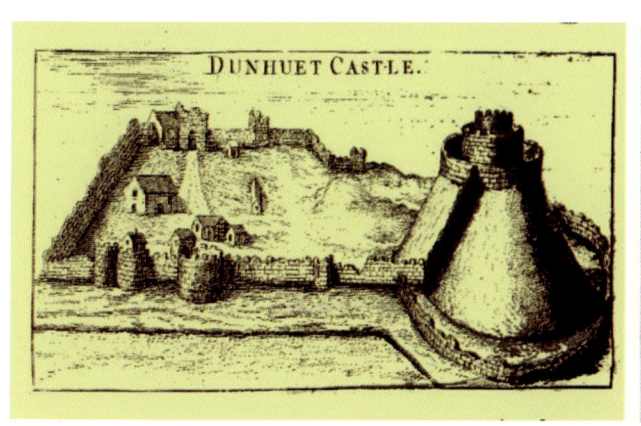

From left to right:

1. Pine's engraving of Norden's field sketch (1728/~1598)   2. Kip 1607   3. Speed 1610

5. Sir Cloudesley Shovell and HMS Association

On 22 October 1707 at about 8pm, the wood hull of HMS Association ran up against the uncompromising, jagged granite top of the Gilstone rock in the far western rocks of Scilly and initiated one of the largest Naval disasters in British maritime history. Sir Cloudesley Shovell had been commanding the British fleet engaged in the inconclusive siege of Toulon, in the Mediterranean, and was en route home to Portsmouth. They had crossed the Bay of Biscay in storms and were in the Western Approaches with no real idea where they were. A meeting amongst the captains of the 15 ships disagreed about their location, with most considering themselves off the coast of Brittany, near Ushant. In fact, they were about 100 miles further north and approaching the Isles of Scilly, three hours after sunset with a low waxing moon behind them, in a storm, with no lights to warn of their impending doom. Four ships of the line smashed into the Gilstone and were lost. Between 1450 and 2000 men drowned, Shovell amongst them. The disaster precipitated the urgent rush to determine a reliable method of calculating longitude and led to the Longitude Act of 1714. It took until 1759, and several attempts by John Harrison, to perfect a marine chronometer that would enable the accurate calculation of longitude over extended periods at sea.

A cross-section of the archipelago from the south-west, near the Gilstone, to north-east of St. Martins, illustrates in stark relief the dangers seafarers faced when approaching the Scillies' shores. Near the Gilstone, site of HMS Association's demise, the seafloor rises from over 80m (44 fathoms) depth to sea level in as little as 600 metres.

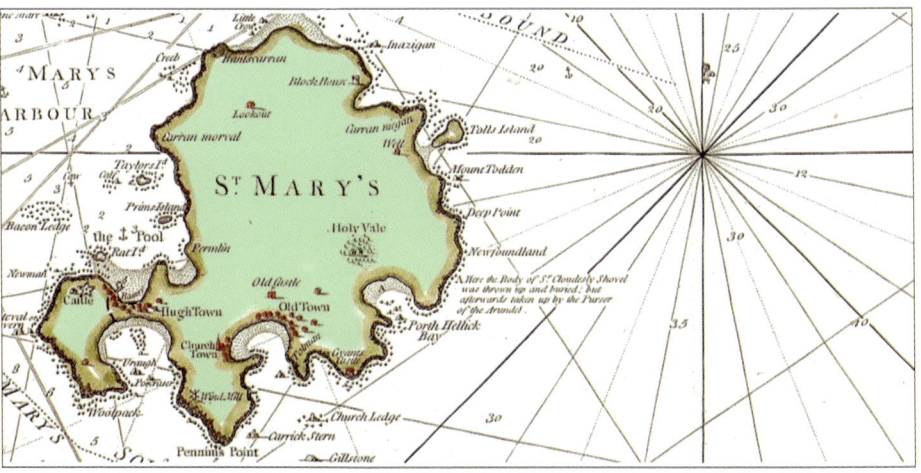

The death of Sir Cloudesley Shovell.
Tovey & Ginver's Isles of Scilly - almost 90 years later

Collins's 'Coastal Pilot' offered this warning: *'To Sail in at the south west Channel, which is the best of the two, you must Sail in between the Bishop and the Crim, which are the two westernmost Rocks of Scilly, and are a good height above the water, then steer in north east by east, keeping the Islands of Great Gannelly and Great Gannick open and shut of St. Mary's Island, as you may see in the Draught of the Islands of Scilly, [Chart] 20, and with this Mark you run in amongst many Rocks very terrible to behold, and the Marks difficult to be known; therefore, I advise none to Sail in here without a Pilot from the Island.'*

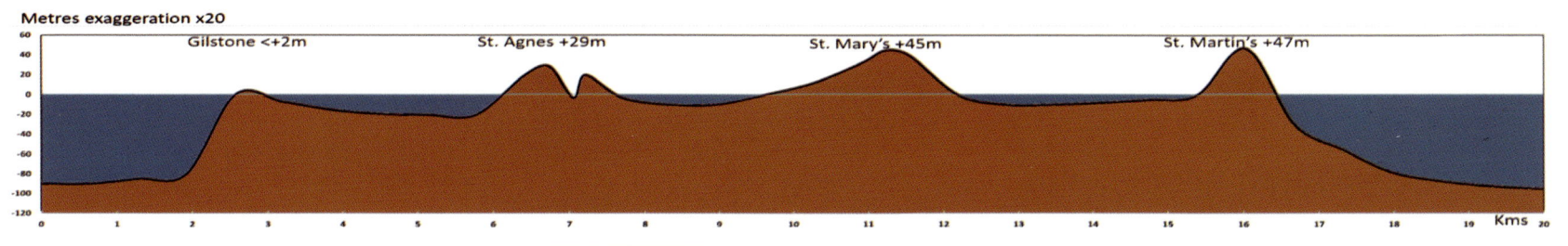

Bathymetric cross section of the Scilly Isles from SW to NE

Antique Maps of Cornwall and the Isles of Scilly

6. The Border with England

The border of Cornwall with Devon has, since the earliest maps, been the Tamar for most of its course. The source of the river is, according to the OS, on Woolley Moor, about 3½ miles from the north Cornish coast. From the source of the Tamar, the final leg of the county boundary strikes west and picks up the course of the Marsland River to the north coast. Although Saxton shows this border running more northwards than west, he clearly shows the border passing between Morwenstow, on the Cornish side, and Welcombe, on the Devon side - i.e. along the course of the Marsland stream. From its source, the Tamar flows south to the English Channel at Plymouth. There are several points during this journey where the river and the border separate, which are recorded by Saxton and later maps - Kip does not show any of these small enclaves. These older separations were for the most part rectified during the 1844 Counties (Detached Parts) Act. There are six such diversions from the river's course:

Dexbeer (Devon, west of Tamar). Shown by Saxton as 'Desboro' and by the 1809 OS as 'Dexbrough'. This is a very small (less than 1sq mile) segment of the Devonian parish of Pancrasweek, which falls on the west side of the Tamar and remains to this day as part of Devon.

Bridgerule (Devon, west of Tamar and 1.6sq miles), transferred to Devon in the 1844 Counties Parts Act. The village of Bridgerule straddles the Tamar, with a little more than 50% on the east bank of the Tamar. Norden records this village as belonging to both counties - none of the other large maps mention it.

East and West Venton (Cornwall, east of the Tamar). This 1.6sq mile section of North Tamerton parish was transferred to Cornwall under the same Act in 1844. Not marked by any map until Gasgoyne.

North Petherwin and Werrington (Devon, west of Tamar). This segment is by far the largest (19sq miles) and forms the very evident section seen on all the Cornish maps here as part of Devon, across the Tamar to the north of Launceston. These two parishes were returned to Devon in 1966. This section is shown throughout all the maps here.

Saltash Passage (Cornwall, east of Tamar). At less than a square mile, this section of land was noted by Saxton and later map makers - historically, this small section of Cornwall on the Devon side of the Tamar has been part of the estate of Trematon Castle (which included the village of Saltash, the ferry and landing on the Devon bank) since the Norman Conquest. Roger de Valletort sold the castle (village, ferry and enclave in Devon) to Richard Earl of Cornwall in about 1270. Saltash's original Charter of c.1225 was re-drawn in 1381 and re-confirmed nine times to 1774. It predates Plymouth's Charter of 1439 and as such prevented Plymouth's encroachment on the Passage land. It was noted as a geographic anomaly by the 1844 Act, but not formally handed to the Devon parish of St. Budeaux until 1895.

St. John's (Devon, west of Tamar) and Maker (Devon west of Tamar). The ancient manors of St. John and Maker can probably be considered together. Again, following the Norman Conquest, the manor of Maker was divided into two - one held by William I (the Devon part, which faces the sea and Plymouth Sound), and the other held by the de Valletorts. on the north-west side facing inland. The reasoning here was simply to ensure that both sides of the mouth of the Tamar were controlled by Norman forces. In 1844, all the land on the Rame peninsula was allocated to Cornwall.

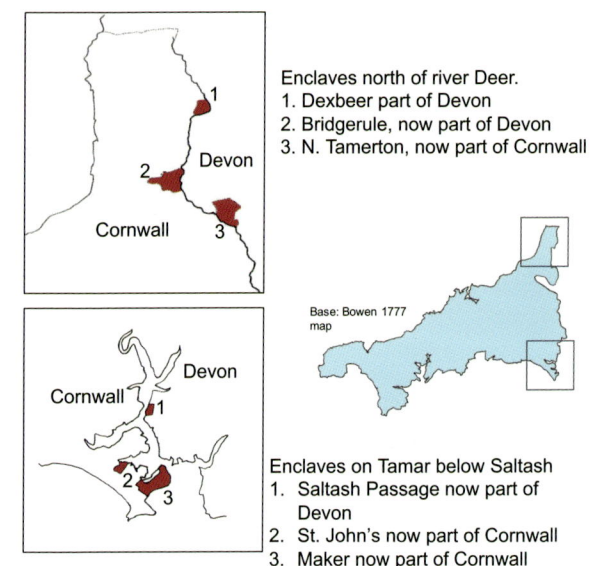

Enclaves north of river Deer.
1. Dexbeer part of Devon
2. Bridgerule, now part of Devon
3. N. Tamerton, now part of Cornwall

Base: Bowen 1777 map

Enclaves on Tamar below Saltash
1. Saltash Passage now part of Devon
2. St. John's now part of Cornwall
3. Maker now part of Cornwall

ANTIQUE MAPS OF CORNWALL AND THE ISLES OF SCILLY

7. Latitude and Longitude

The question of how to project a near spherical object onto a flat plane has troubled map makers since the earliest times, with many attempts to resolve this problem. Latitude was understood by the ancient Greeks, as well as Arabian astrologers, and the Astrolabe, a forerunner of the sextant, was used by Europeans by the 1500s. Latitude, in simple terms, divided the earth horizontally into segments north or south of the equator which, with measurement by Astrolabe or later instruments, could determine the position north (or south) of the equator at midday. Of course, this only solved half the problem – determining longitude proved to be a far trickier problem, and it was not until the late 1700s that it was achieved accurately.

This didn't stop early mathematicians attempting to wrest control of the problem – it was recognised early on that longitude is connected with time. The Sumerians created a number system, based on the base of 60 (Sexegesimal); this enabled them to count to 12 on one hand using the joints of the four fingers. Carrying this 12 over to the other hand and counting five fingers of it gives a total of 60. The length of a day was naturally split into day and night with each cycle set to 12 hours each. Twelve, 24 and 60 are all divisors of 360. In terms of maths, 360 is known as a Highly Composite Number: it has 24 divisors, making it a very flexible number when it comes to dividing it without messy remainders – in mathematical terms, it is an easy number to use and a logical choice for large-scale calculations such as these. By using a chord of equal length to the radius of a circle one obtains a 60° equilateral triangle (Draw a circle of R radius, use this same radius length to mark off from the edge of the circle and you will obtain this triangle). There are six such triangles within the circle, each contains interior angles of 60°. 6 x 60 = 360. Dividing the circumference of the earth into 360 equal units still gives us degrees of latitude and longitude today.

Gerard Mercator's map of 1595 (#8) is the earliest one here to draw longitude and latitude onto the map. He used the Azores as the zero meridian, as was customary into the 1600s. John Bill (#13) added simple lines of latitude and longitude to his 1628 map, and Schenk and Valk added both latitude and longitude onto the Jansson map of 1646 (#17), still using the Azores as the meridian, in 1712 (#28). Morden's 1695 map (#20) in Camden's 'Britannia' is possibly the earliest map to use London as the zero meridian – this was taken as St. Paul's Cathedral until the meridian of 0° at Greenwich was established, in 1884.

Canting of the Cornwall maps to fit them better to a page became a common practice from the earliest maps here. The reason for this is simple: Cornwall isn't page shaped and cartographers were aware of the aesthetics of fitting the county to the page. Faced with a nearly straight boundary with the adjoining county of Devon, the simple solution was to rotate Cornwall about 22° clockwise and fit this up against the right margin. This artistic shortcut led to several problems later. Osborne's 1748 map (#38) and Langley's map of 1817 (#70) are examples of this confusion. The Osborne map has set the Devon border almost parallel with the right margin, with the compass rotated to point to 'grid north'; however, the latitude/longitude grid is completely at odds with the compass. Longitude is set straight up the map, while latitude is drawn about 6° West of perpendicular. On Langley's map he too has set the Devon border parallel with the right margin. This means north should be about 22° to the north-north-east, whereas in fact it is straight up the page. Latitude and longitude are drawn incorrectly grid-wise across the page.

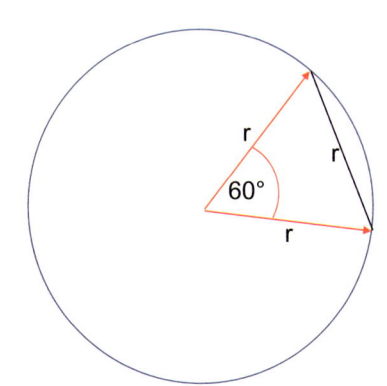

Chord of a Circle

Antique Maps of Cornwall and the Isles of Scilly

We have taken four maps drawn between 1701 and 1784 to illustrate some of the problems that map makers faced before the establishment of reasonably accurate longitude in the 1780s. The English statute mile was defined in 1593 as 1760 yards. All these maps are assumed, in the absence of other information, to be using this mile. The issue of exactly how long a yard was is a completely other story beyond this book.

The maps are: Morden 1701 (#20), Moll 1724 (#31), Bowen 1777 (#30) and Martyn 1784 (#40). Joel Gasgoyne's 1700 map (#25) should be considered as the forerunner to all these maps, for the principal reason that it is the first map to truly reflect the outline of the Lizard, away from the flat-bottomed rendition done by Saxton and continued by Norden-Kip-Speed et seq. Unfortunately, Gasgoyne did not draw longitude lines onto his map and thus can't be used here.

Extracting the miles per degree of latitude and longitude for each of these maps (table 2) strongly suggests that the lines of latitude and longitude were not used as a base for the maps' construction. From today's modern map, a degree of longitude mid-county is 43 Statute miles; a degree of latitude is 69 miles.

Robert Morden drew his 1701 map on a reduced scale from his previous map that was used in the 1695 edition of Camden's 'Britannia'. It is a markedly different map and strongly suggests influence by the intervening Gasgoyne map. Morden supplies a scale of 1 inch to 10 miles, along with ticks along the borders of degrees and minutes of latitude and longitude. From this it is easy to read off the map: 1 degree of latitude is 50 miles

Table 3: Truro and Lizard Co-ordinates

Town	Latitude / Longitude
Truro Now	50° 15'N, 5° 03'W
Truro Moll 1724	50° 03'N, 5°36'W
Lizard Now	49° 57'N, 5°12'W
Lizard Moll 1724	49° 35'N, 5°48'W

Table 2: Latitude and Longitude by map and miles

Map	1° Lat miles	% error	1° Long miles	% error
Morden 1701	50	-27%	37	-16%
Moll 1724	42	-39%	37	-18%
Martyn 1748	65	-6%	42	-4%
Bowen 1764	66	-4%	40	-9%
Baseline Now	69*	0%	43*	0%

and 37 miles of longitude. His degree of latitude is 27% too short; longitude is 16% short. All four of these maps contain similar apparent differences, though with time, there is an improvement towards today's figure.

To re-base all the maps to the same measurements, it is necessary to calculate the latitude and longitude according to the miles / degree used in each map. We have taken as an example the distance from the Lizard to Truro working with today's co-ordinates compared with Moll's data.

From today's Truro co-ordinates (table 3), there are 9' of longitude offset (5° 12' - 5° 03') and 18' of latitude offset (50° 15' - 49° 57'). These minutes need to be translated into miles. One degree of longitude at Cornwall is 43* miles; thus 9' is 6.45 miles. One degree of latitude here is 69* miles, thus 18' is 20.7 miles. Simple trigonometry: $\sqrt{(6.45)^2 + (20.7)^2}$ gives 21.7 miles – the measured distance is about 22 miles.

Herman Moll's map of 1724 constructed a latitude / longitude 1° grid of 42 x 37 miles. Using this as a base and applying the same process, his latitude offset from Truro to the Lizard is 28' (50° 03' - 49° 35') and his longitude is 12' (5° 48' - 5° 36'). Using 42 miles / 1° of latitude, 28' becomes 19.6 miles and 37 miles/1° of longitude becomes 7.4 miles. Applying the same trigonometry: $\sqrt{(7.4)^2 + (19.6)^2}$ gives 20.9 miles. Measuring the same distance off his map yields 21.3 miles. The margin of error in measuring from a copy of the map can stem from many sources; nonetheless, the proof of Moll's accuracy by two methods is a surprising testament to his cartographic ability.

The four maps referred to above were drawn from 1701 to 1784, all featured lines of latitude as well as longitude, and all were wrong compared with the current locations of two reference lines: that of 50° North latitude and 5° West longitude.

Robert Morden's 1701 map is the earliest of these and he has placed 5° West intersecting a line from just west of Deadman Head (Dodman Point today, west of Mevagissey, on the south coast) to Pentire Head (east of the Camel estuary, on the north coast). The true location of 5° West is some 7 miles west of this, at St. Anthony's Head in the south, to Harlyn in the north.

What is curious is that the eastwards error from 5° West gets worse with the subsequent mappers:: Although Thomas Martyn constructs a 1° latitude / longitude grid which is very close to today's size, he puts 5° West 17 miles too far east. Grid and compass north are the same. Both grids are drawn from 'London', which we take to be St. Paul's Cathedral, and not Greenwich. What is puzzling is that Martyn, along with Bowen and, later, Kitchin, construct a longitude grid that is so far east. Martyn drew his map as a stand-alone effort; he didn't have the benefit of mapping the counties from London westwards and might be forgiven for setting his main line of longitude too far east, but Bowen and Kitchin had mapped the entire country.

Latitude is thought to have been understood and mapped earlier than longitude, though it too suffers from erroneous construction. The baseline for Cornwall is 50° North, and this line cuts the tip of the Lizard south of Coverack. The next line of full degrees (51° North) occurs in North Devon, near Clovelly. On Morden's 1701 map he places 50° North slightly north of its correct position, an error of about a mile. However, his 1° of latitude at 50 miles is too small by 27%. The placement of 50° North over the period of the maps under discussion remains more or less in the same place, with the exception of Martyn; the issue is the number of miles allocated to 1°. This steadily increases with time until the production of the Bowen, Martyn et seq. maps, which use a separation of about 69 miles, in line with today's figure.

Four 18th Century maps aligned to their 50°N baselines and rescaled to similar sizes (the actual scale of each map differs)

Map	1° Longitude miles	5°W offset miles	50°N offset miles
Morden 1701	37	7	1.5
Moll 1724	37	15	9
Martyn 1748	42	17	9
Bowen 1764	40	12	4.5

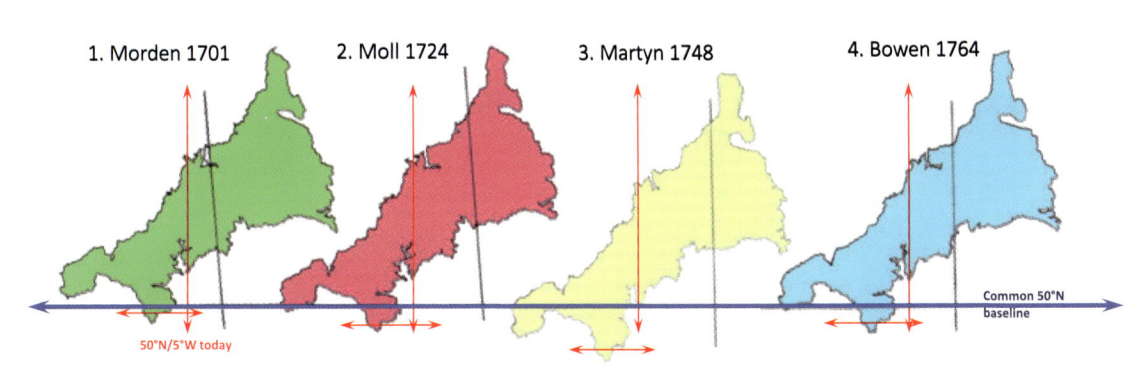

Antique Maps of Cornwall and the Isles of Scilly

8. The Saxton - Norden – Kip sequence

Prior to the discovery of the Norden manuscript maps in Cambridge, the link from Saxton's map to the later maps forced the conclusion that all later maps were derived from Saxton's. The impact of Norden's map on maps of Cornwall post-Saxton, and from Kip onwards, has been hitherto understated.

Looking at the outline of the coast by Saxton, Norden and Kip, it appears that Kip's map bears a closer resemblance to Norden's manuscript map than to Saxton's. There are several inclusions from Norden's main map, as well as the maps of the Hundreds, that support this thesis. The outline of Cornwall by Norden includes several key elements that are not drawn, or are depicted differently, on Saxton's map. Kip almost certainly did not survey the county and thus relied on (or copied) previous work; recall that he was employed by Norden previously.

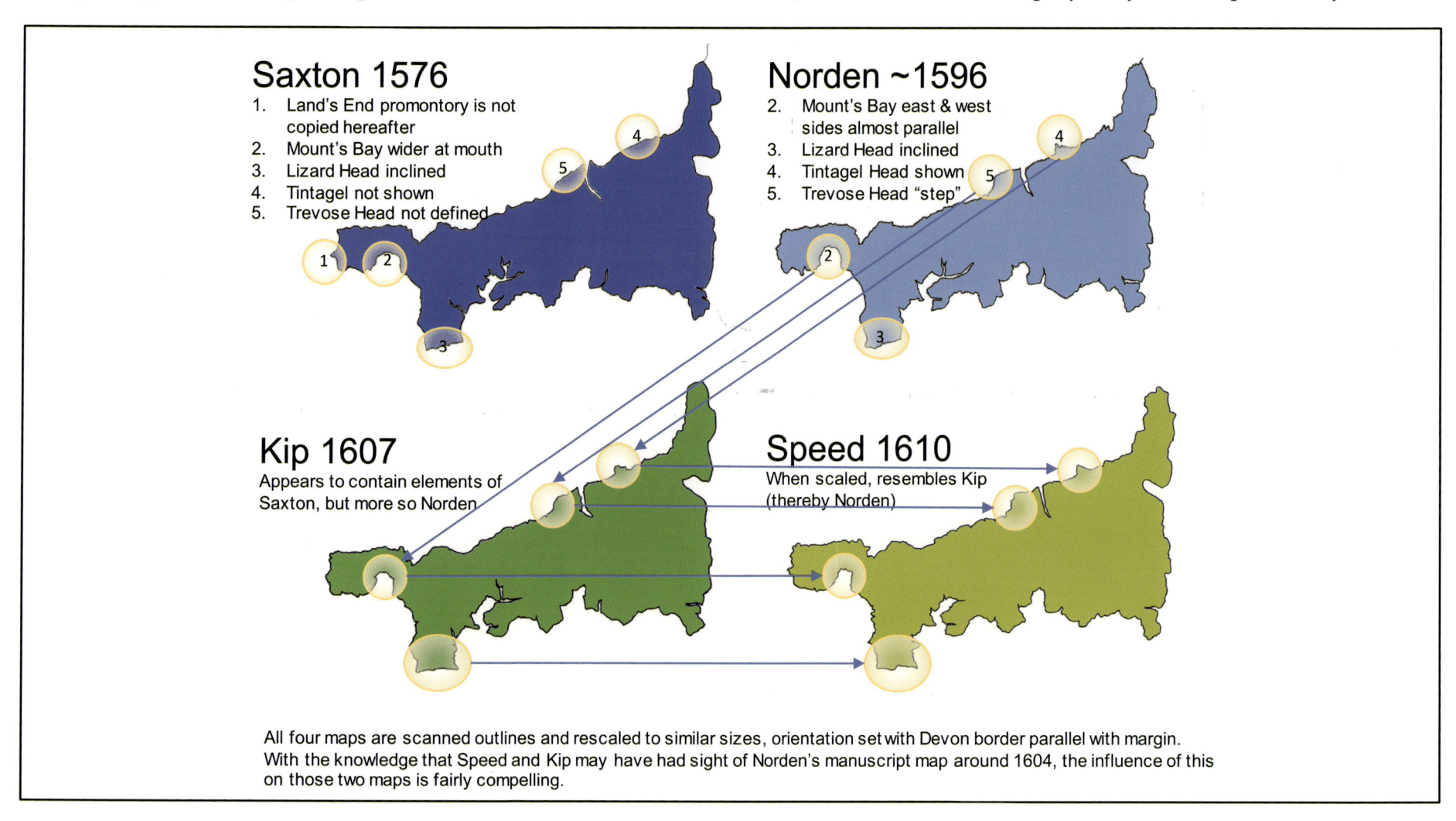

Saxton 1576
1. Land's End promontory is not copied hereafter
2. Mount's Bay wider at mouth
3. Lizard Head inclined
4. Tintagel not shown
5. Trevose Head not defined

Norden ~1596
2. Mount's Bay east & west sides almost parallel
3. Lizard Head inclined
4. Tintagel Head shown
5. Trevose Head "step"

Kip 1607
Appears to contain elements of Saxton, but more so Norden

Speed 1610
When scaled, resembles Kip (thereby Norden)

All four maps are scanned outlines and rescaled to similar sizes, orientation set with Devon border parallel with margin.
With the knowledge that Speed and Kip may have had sight of Norden's manuscript map around 1604, the influence of this on those two maps is fairly compelling.

234

Antique Maps of Cornwall and the Isles of Scilly

The number of place-names in the county has also been used to determine how Kip, who never surveyed the county, was able to augment the number Saxton carried on his 1576 map. In the Penwith Hundred alone, Saxton mentions 58 places. Norden, whom we now know surveyed the county personally, mentions 101 places on his main and Penwith maps combined. Kip mentions 90 places, strongly suggesting he had sight of Norden's survey/maps.

There are sufficient differences to assert that Kip took several elements of Norden's map and included them to those of Saxton; in particular, Mount's Bay, Trevose Head and Tintagel Head, as well as about 40 place names.

Kip includes several labels unused by Saxton:
o   Land's End is marked 'ANTVESTUM BOLERIUM sive VELERIUM Promontorium'
o   The Lizard is marked 'OCRINVAL sive DANMOTORVM Promontorium'
o   The Fal estuary is marked 'CENIOUIS FLU OSTUUM'
o   Lostwithiel is labelled 'UZELA'
o   The mouth of the Tamar is marked 'TAMARI OSTIUM'
o   The sea off the north coast is marked 'MARIS HIBERNICI SIVE VIRGIVIS PARS'

Apart from the last point, none are drawn onto the Norden map but are mentioned within the text of his 'Description of Cornwall', citing Carew (1602). The Latin labels at Land's End, the Lizard and Launceston are, in fact, far older – they can be seen, for instance, on the Ptolemy maps of the early 1400s. They are mentioned in the text of Camden's 'Britannia', which was first published (without maps) in 1586, as well as later. All these labels are later used by Speed, but not until the 1623 edition, Blaeu (1645) but not Jansson a year later, Blome (1673) and Morden (1695). No Latin is used after Morden's 1695 map.

- **SAXTON**
  - Marks a clear promontory at Land's End
  - Shows the entrance to Mount's Bay as a wide mouth narrowing to the north
  - Shows the coast line eastwards to Trevose Head (west of the Camel estuary) as a gentle line SW-NE
  - Omits entirely the headland at Tintagel
  - Shows the base of the Lizard peninsula as a flat bottom running slightly SW-NE

- **NORDEN**
  - Reduces the impact of the Land's End promontory
  - Shows Mount's Bay with the east and west coasts almost parallel – the bay is squarer
  - Shows a clear ramp in the coast as it approaches Trevose Head
  - Includes Tintagel head
  - Draws the Lizard slightly flatter, but is similar to Saxton
  - Uses a 3d shading technique on parts of the south coast

- **KIP & SPEED**
  - Retains the reduced Land's End profile drawn by his predecessors – Saxton & Norden
  - Keeps the narrow parallel sided Mount's Bay drawn by Norden
  - Keeps the ramp onto Trevose Head first drawn by Norden (Omitted by Saxton)
  - Keeps the promontory at Tintagel (Omitted by Saxton)
  - Draws the Lizard square with an inclined base, similar to both Saxton and Norden
  - Retains the 3d style used by Norden

Antique Maps of Cornwall and the Isles of Scilly

9. Super - groups

The outline form of Cornwall remains static through the 1600s, with two camps prevailing: The Saxton et seq. camp on one side, and the Norden et seq. on the other, until Gasgoyne's map of 1700. The Gasgoyne refinement concerns the eastern side of the Lizard, St. Mawes, Dodman Point and Rame Head. From Saxton and Norden on, the Lizard is shown as a flat-bottomed, rectangular peninsula. Gasgoyne refines the eastern side of the Lizard with a small headland from the Lizard Point to Cadgwith, and then a bulge from there around to the mouth of the Helford. All the subsequent maps from then onwards retain this outline and this defines the outline of the county to the modern day.

Based on this new analysis, we think it is possible to suggest a set of three super-groups, each derived from a parent map: those of Saxton, Norden and Gasgoyne.

Of the derivations of the Saxton map, Web, Lea and the last rehashes of the Saxton plate by Willdey, Jefferys and Dicey are not new work, but simply new imprints from the old plate. The playing cards of Bowes, Simmons and Morden are not really of much cartographic significance. The Willem Blaeu map is, in fact, one of the whole of south-west England, including South Wales; the outline of Cornwall in this context is minor. The Van Den Keere and Bill maps contain detail that shows an evolution from Saxton, but neither progresses beyond these issues.

- **SAXTON 1576**
  - BOWES 1590 & 1595
    - SIMMONS 1635
  - VAN DEN KEERE ~1605
    - BILL 1626
  - BLAEU, W 1608
  - WEB 1645
    - LEA 1689
      - WILLDEY 1732
      - JEFFERYS 1749
      - DICEY 1770
  - MORDEN 1676
  - BLOME 1681

- **NORDEN ~1596**
  - KIP 1607
    - SPEED 1610
      - SELLER 1635
      - JENNER 1643
      - BLAEU, J 1645
      - JANSSON 1646
        - NICHOLLS 1712
        - SCHENK & VALK 1714
      - BLOME 1673
      - MORDEN 1695

- **GASGOYNE 1700**
  - MORDEN 1701
    - MOLL 1724
      - BADESLADE 1742
      - ROCQUE 1746
        - DURY 1764
      - OSBORNE 1748
    - BOWEN 1720
    - BOWEN 1748
      - GIBSON 1759
    - KITCHIN 1749 et seq
      - DE LA ROCHETTE 1766
      - WALPOOLE 1784
      - LODGE 1788
      - BAKER 1791
      - CARY 1787
  - SUDLOW 1789
  - MARTYN 1748 et seq

The Norden manuscript map must have been seen by Kip, and, by Speed's own admission, was seen by him also. From Speed's masterpiece we get a number of key maps throughout the 1600s. The Speed, Blaeu and Jansson maps exemplify this as possibly the apex of cartography at this time. Speed revisited his map of 1610 and embellished it further in 1623, with detail that Kip already had introduced (Latin titles for Land's End &c.). The last map within this group, that of Morden, in Gibson's version of Camden's 'Britannia', is an important map, in the sense that it was issued again and again throughout the remaining life of the book. However, when compared with the previous maps, such as that of Blaeu, it is a mediocre effort. His next map, in 1701, is a huge change, but comes on the back of Gasgoyne's.

Joel Gasgoyne produced his map in 1700 at almost 1 inch to 1 mile, he surveyed the county assiduously and re-drew a section that neither Saxton nor Norden had accurately done. The Lizard peninsula is a flat-topped piece of land: geologically, as well as geographically, it is quite different from the rest of Cornwall. Gasgoyne's map (1700) is a huge change from the previous efforts and leads to what can be called the recognisable outline of Cornwall as it is seen today. It is the construction of the coast from the Lizard itself eastwards that is the telling change. The flat-bottomed line has been altered to the curving sweep that characterises the coast from Lizard to Helford, and it is this that marks Gasgoyne as the originator of the modern outline of Cornwall. There are minor changes to other parts of the south coast, perhaps the more interesting is the evolution of

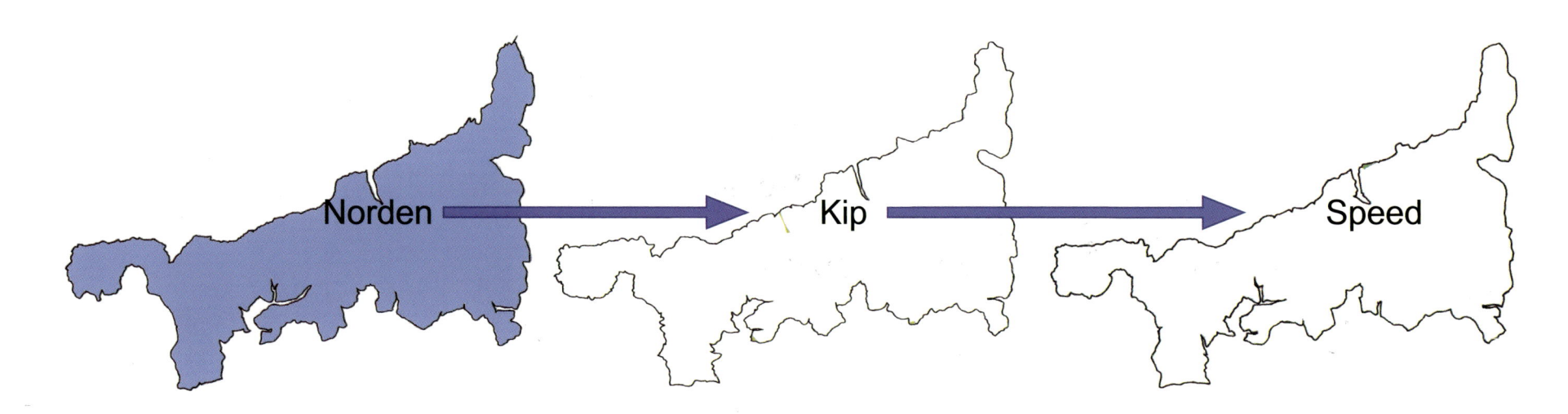

Outlines of Norden, Kip and Speed demonstrate a clear copy/evolution of the coastal outlines, detailed previously.

ANTIQUE MAPS OF CORNWALL AND THE ISLES OF SCILLY

a smoother coastline between Portwinckle and Rame Head. What we see here is a gradual sanding up and evolution of an extended sand bar/beach, like Chesil Beach without the back-lagoon. It is unfortunate that no interim surveys were performed in detail between Norden and Gasgoyne which may have shown when this happened.

Robert Morden's 1701 map, along with Herman Moll's 1724 map, are the direct result of this new survey, and while neither acknowledges Gasgoyne, it is quite evident that there has been a re-setting of the map, and neither Saxton nor Norden's derivatives hold sway any longer. From this point onwards, the outline shape of Cornwall is that of Gasgoyne, but with some light changes. Benjamin Baker mapped the county for the Ordnance Survey at the turn of the 1800s, and with that, the shape of Cornwall is 'fixed'.

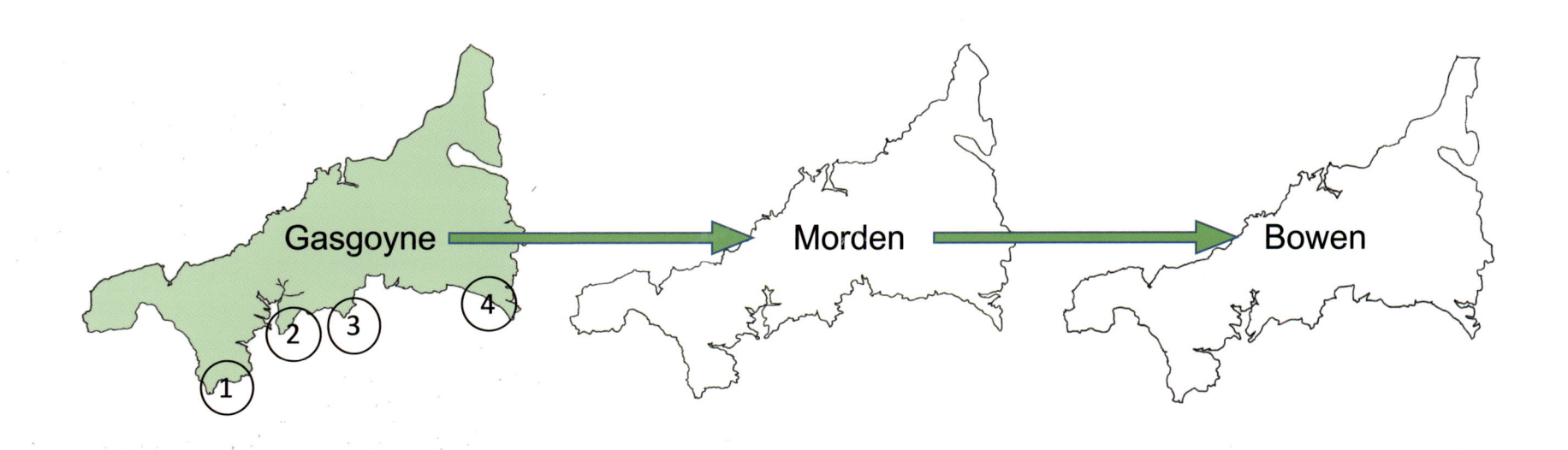

The outline of Cornwall by Gasgoyne, especially the south coast (1. Lizard Point in particular, but also 2. St Mawes, 3. Dodman Point and 4. Rame Head are redrawn also). The later maps of Moll, Bowen, Kitchin, Martyn &c are near identical copies. Compare this to Norden et seq.

238   Antique Maps of Cornwall and the Isles of Scilly

10. Contributing surveyors / engravers / authors / publishers

The maps shown here have, for the most part, come from larger publications; (there are some maps produced as stand-alone productions). Through the 1500s and 1600s, this association is relatively simple - no-one refers to Speed's maps as Hondius's, and we have kept the index of these maps to the person either who drew the original or the engraver. These are highlighted through the following tables, with the following logic:

Contributors through the 1500s and 1600s are ordered by Surveyor or Engraver. In cases where the engraver has altered the original work, such as Lea's alteration of the Saxton map, Lea's name is used. There are occasions where the original surveyor is uncertain or unknown; this becomes more the case later. Later tables covering the 1700s and 1800s, where the inter-relationships become more complex, are indexed by the author or publisher (sometimes this is the same person) of the volume in which the map is found. Therefore, the indexing is done using the author/publisher first, and the engraver second. Again, the individuals are highlighted at each instance.

Two major works of index have been used to cross reference as many of the maps here as possible: Dr. R. A. Skelton's 1970 'County Atlases of the British Isles 1579-1703' and Donald Hodson's 1984-1997 three-volume continuation of Skelton's work, 'County Atlases of the British Isles', Volumes 1-3, covering 1704-1742, 1743-1763 and 1764-1789, respectively. Neither author has included sea charts, road maps (Ogilby for instance) or one-off publications such as those of Gasgoyne or Martyn. Both publications terminate well before the last map here, and in consequence the 19th century is a work in waiting.

INDEX-HEAD	CHAPTER #	1ST DATE	SURVEYOR / DRAWN BY	ENGRAVER	AUTHOR	PUBLISHER	TITLE	SKELTON / HODSON INDEX
SAXTON, CHRISTOPHER	1	1576	SAXTON	TERWOORT	SAXTON	SAXTON	AN ATLAS OF ENGLAND AND WALES	SK-1
WAGENHAER, LUCAS JANSZOON	2	1584	WAGENHAER	DEUTCOM	WAGENHAER	WAGENHAER	SPIEGEL DER ZEEVAERDT	-
De BRY, THEODORE	3	1588	WAGENHAER	DE BRY	ASHLEY	ASHLEY	THE MARINERS' MIRROUR	-
BOWES, WILLIAM	4	1590	BOWES	RYTHER	BOWES	BOWES	ENGLAN: FAMOUS PLAC	SK-2
VAN DEN KEERE, PIETER	5	1605	SAXTON	VAN DEN KEERE	VAN DEN KEERE	CLAESZ	COURNUWALLIA	SK-4
NORDEN, JOHN	6	1728	NORDEN	PINE	NORDEN	BATEMAN	SPECULI BRITANNIAE PARS	-
MERCATOR, GERARD	8	1595	MERCATOR	MERCATOR	MERCATOR	MERCATOR	ATLAS SIVE COSMOGRAPHICAE MEDITATIONS	-
KIP, WILLIAM	9	1607	NORDEN/SAXTON	KIP	CAMDEN	CAMDEN	BRITANNIA	SK-5
BLAEU, WILLEM	10	1608		BLAEU- in house	BLAEU	BLAEU	HET LICHT DER ZEE-VAART	-
SPEED, JOHN	11	1610	SPEED	HONDIUS	SPEED	SUDBURY & HUMBLE	BRITANNIA THE THEATRE OF THE EMPIRE OF GREAT BRITAIN	SK-7
HOLE, WILLIAM	12	1612	HOLE	HOLE	DRAYTON	LOWNES ET AL	POLY-OLBION	SK-8
BILL, JOHN	13	1626		BILL	BILL	BILL	THE ABRIDGEMENT OF CAMDEN'S BRITANNIA	SK-15
VAN LANGEREN, JACOB	14	1635		VAN LANGEREN	SIMMONS	SIMMONS	A DIRECTION FOR THE ENGLISH TRAVILLER	SK-20
WEB, WILLIAM (after SAXTON)	15	1645	SAXTON	WEB	WEB	WEB	THE MAPS OF ALL THE SHIRES IN ENGLAND AND WALES	SK-27
BLAEU, JOHANNES WILLEMSZOON (JAN)	16	1645	BLAEU	BLAEU - in house	BLAEU	G&J BLAEU	THEATRUM ORBIS TERRARUM	SK-28
JANSSON, JAN	17	1646		JANSSON	JANSSON	JANSSON	NOVUS ATLAS	SK-34
BLOME, RICHARD	18	1673	SPEED	LAMB / HOLLAR / PALMER	BLOME	BLOME	BRITANNIA: OR, A GEOGRAPHICAL DESCRIPTION OF THE KINGDOMS	SK-90
BLOME, RICHARD	18	1681	SAXTON	HOLLAR / PALMER	BLOME	BLOME	SPEED'S MAPS EPITOMOMIZ'D	SK-104
BLOME, RICHARD	18	1715	SAXTON	HOLLAR / PALMER	BLOME	TAYLOR	ENGLAND EXACTLY DESCRIBED	DH-139
OGILBY, JOHN	19	1675	OGILBY	OGILBY	OGILBY	OGILBY	BRITANNIA, VOLUME THE FIRST	-
MORDEN, ROBERT	20	1676	MORDEN	MORDEN	MORDEN	MORDEN	THE 52 COUNTRIES	SK-94
MORDEN, ROBERT	20	1695	MORDEN	MORDEN	CAMDEN	CAMDEN	BRITANNIA	SK-117
MORDEN, ROBERT	20	1701	MORDEN	MORDEN	MORDEN	MORDEN ET AL	THE NEW DESCRIPTION AND STATE OF ENGLAND	SK-123
REDMAYNE, WILLIAM	21	1676		REDMAYNE	REDMAYNE	REDMAYNE ET AL	RECREATIVE PASTIME BY CARDPLAY	SK-96
LEA, PHILIP (after SAXTON)	22	1689	SAXTON	LEA	LEA	LEA	ALL THE SHIRES OF ENGLAND AND WALES	SK-110
COLLINS, CAPTAIN GREENVILE	23	1689	COLLINS	YEATS	COLLINS	COLLINS	GREAT BRITAIN'S COASTING PILOT.	-
De HOOGHE, Sr. ROMAIN	24	1693	DE HOOGE	DE HOOGE	DE HOOGE	MORTIER	ATLAS MARITIME	-

Antique Maps of Cornwall and the Isles of Scilly

239

INDEX-HEAD	CHAPTER #	1ST DATE	SURVEYOR/DRAWN BY	ENGRAVER	AUTHOR	PUBLISHER	TITLE	SKELTON / HODSON INDEX
GASGOYNE, JOEL	25	1700	GASGOYNE	GASGOYNE	GASGOYNE	DARKER & FARLEY	A MAP OF THE COUNTY OF CORNWALL	-
SELLER, JOHN	26	1694	UNKNOWN	UNKNOWN	SELLER	SELLER	ANGLIA CONTRACTA	SK-115
NICHOLLS, SUTTON	27	1712		NICHOLLS	OVERTON	OVERTON	A NEW MAPP OF THE COUNTY OF CORNWALL	DH-142
SCHENK, PETER & VALK, GERARD	28	1714	JANSSON	SCHENK	MORTIER	MORTIER	ATLAS ANGLOIS	DH-131
LENTHALL, JOHN	29	1717	REDMAYNE	LENTHALL	LENTHALL	LENTHALL	PACK OF PLAYING CARDS	DH-146
BOWEN, EMANUEL	30	1720	BOWEN	BOWEN	BOWEN	BOWLES	BRITANNIA DEPICTA	DH-149
BOWEN, EMANUEL	30	1748	BOWEN	BOWEN	BOWEN	HINTON	THE UNIVERSAL MAGAZINE OF KNOWLEDGE AND PLEASURE	DH-253
BOWEN, EMANUEL	30	1759	BOWEN	BOWEN	BOWEN	MARTIN	THE GENERAL MAGAZINE OF ARTS AND SCIENCES	DH-230
BOWEN, EMANUEL	30	1762	BOWEN	BOWEN	BOWEN	BOWEN & KITCHIN	THE ROYAL ENGLISH ATLAS	DH-233
BOWEN, EMANUEL	30	1767	BOWEN	BOWEN	BOWEN	BOWEN & BOWEN	ATLAS ANGLICANUS	DH-254
MOLL, HERMAN	31	1724	MOLL	MOLL	MOLL	MOLL ET AL	A NEW DESCRIPTION OF ENGLAND AND WALES	DH-173
VAN KEULEN, GERARD	32	1735	VAN KEULEN	VAN KEULEN	VAN KEULEN	VAN KEULEN	NIEUWE AFTEEKENING VAN DE SORLINGES EYLANDEN	-
PINE, JOHN	33	1739		PINE	PINE	PINE	THE TAPESTRY HANGINGS	
BADESLADE, THOMAS & TOMS, WILLIAM	34	1741		TOMS	BADESLADE & TOMS	BADESLADE & TOMS	CHOROGRAPHIA BRITANNIAE	DH-188
DODSLEY ROBERT & COWLEY, JOHN	35	1741		COWLEY	DODSLEY	DODSLEY	THE GEOGRAPHY OF ENGLAND	DH-194
READ, THOMAS & ROCQUE, JOHN	36	1743		ROCQUE	READ	READ	THE ENGLISH TRAVAILLER	DH-197
WALKER, ROBERT & SIMPSON, SAMUEL	37	1744		SIMPSON	WALKER	WALKER	THE AGREEABLE HISTORIAN	DH-204
OSBORNE THOMAS & HUTCHINSON THOMAS	38	1748		HUTCHINSON	OSBORNE	OSBORNE ET AL	GEOGRAPHIA MAGNA BRITANNIAE	DH-205
KITCHIN, THOMAS	39	1749		KITCHIN	KITCHIN	BALDWIN	THE LONDON MAGAZINE	DH-229
KITCHIN, THOMAS	39	1750		KITCHIN	KITCHIN	BOWEN & KITCHIN	THE LARGE ENGLISH ATLAS	DH-221
KITCHIN, THOMAS	39	1764		KITCHIN	KITCHIN	R & J DODSLEY	ENGLAND ILLUSTRATED …	DH-231
KITCHIN, THOMAS	39	1769		KITCHIN	KITCHIN	KITCHIN	KITCHIN'S POCKET ATLAS	DH-258
MARTYN, THOMAS	40	1748	MARTYN	UNKNOWN	MARTYN	SAYER	NEW AND ACCURATE MAP OF THE COUNTY OF CORNWALL	-
MARTYN, THOMAS	40	1749	MARTYN	UNKNOWN	MARTYN	SAYER	NEW AND ACCURATE MAP OF THE COUNTY OF CORNWALL	-
MARTYN, THOMAS	40	1784	MARTYN	UNKNOWN	MARTYN	FADEN	NEW AND ACCURATE MAP OF THE COUNTY OF CORNWALL	-
KITCHIN, THOMAS & JEFFERYS, THOMAS	41	1749		KITCHIN	KITCHIN & JEFFERYS	KITCHIN & JEFFERYS	THE SMALL ENGLISH ATLAS	DH-209
KITCHIN, THOMAS & JEFFERYS, THOMAS	41	1776		KITCHIN	KITCHIN & JEFFERYS	SAYER & BENNETT	AN ENGLISH ATLAS: OR, A CONCISE VIEW	DH-212
BICKHAM, GEORGE (Snr & Jnr)	42	1750	BICKHAM JNR	BICKHAM JNR	BICKHAM SNR	BICKHAM SNR	THE BRITISH MONARCHY	DH-217
BICKHAM, GEORGE (Snr & Jnr)	42	1796	BICKHAM JNR	BICKHAM JNR	BICKHAM SNR	LAURIE & WHITTLE	A CURIOUS ANTIQUE COLLECTION OF BIRD'S EYE VIEWS	DH-218
BORLASE, WILLIAM	43	1754		BORLASE	BORLASE	BORLASE	OBSERVATIONS ON THE ANTIQUITIES OF CORNWALL	-
BORLASE, WILLIAM	43	1758		BORLASE	BORLASE	BORLASE	THE NATURAL HISTORY OF CORNWALL	-
MEIJER, PIETER & SCHENK, LEONARD	44	1757		SCHENK	MEIJER	MEIJER	ALGEMEENE OEFENSCHOOLE	DH-260
GIBSON, JOHN	45	1759	GIBSON?	GIBSON	GIBSON	NEWBERRY	NEW AND ACCURATE MAPS OF THE COUNTIES OF ENGLAND AND	DH-219
GIBSON, JOHN	45	1762		GIBSON	PAYNE	PAYNE	THE UNIVERSAL MUSEUM AND COMPLETE MAGAZINE	-
DURY, ANDREW & ELLIS, JOSEPH	46	1764		ELLIS	DURY	DURY	A COLLECTION OF PLANS OF THE PRINCIPAL CITIES OF GREAT BRITAIN AND IRELAND	-
DE LA ROCHETTE, LOUIS STANISLAS	47	1765	DE LA ROCHETTE	DE LA ROCHETTE	ELLIS	ELLIS	ELLIS'S ENGLISH ATLAS	DH-238
TOVEY (Jnr), ABRAHAM & GINVER, N.	48	1779		TOVEY JNR ?	SAYER & BENNETT	SAYER & BENNETT	COMPLETE CHANNEL PILOT	-
"WALPOOLE, GEORGE" & HATCHETT, THOMAS	49	1784	DE LA ROCHETTE	HATCHETT	"WALPOOLE"	"WALPOOLE"	THE NEW BRITISH TRAVELLER	DH-269
CARY, JOHN	50	1787		CARY	CARY	CARY	CARY'S NEW AND CORRECT ENGLISH ATLAS	DH-285
CARY, JOHN	50	1789	NOBLE	CARY	CAMDEN / GOUGH	CAMDEN/GOUGH	BRITANNIA	HODSON ENDS WITH CARY
CARY, JOHN	50	1790		CARY	CARY	CARY	CARY'S TRAVELLER'S COMPANION	
CARY, JOHN	50	1809		CARY	CARY	CARY	CARY'S NEW ENGLISH ATLAS	
MURRAY, JOHN & LODGE, JOHN	51	1788		LODGE	MURRAY	MURRAY	THE POLITICAL MAGAZINE	
HARRISON, JOHN & SUDLOW, EDWARD	52	1790	HAYWOOD	SUDLOW	HARRISON	HARRISON	MAPS OF THE ENGLISH COUNTIES	
AIKIN, JOHN & JOHNSON, JOSEPH	53	1790			AIKIN	AIKIN	ENGLAND DELINEATED	
BAKER, BENJAMIN	54	1791		BAKER	BENT	BENT	THE UNIVERSAL MAGAZINE OF KNOWLEDGE AND PLEASURE	
TUNNICLIFF, WILLIAM	55	1791	TUNNICLIFF	TUNNICLIFF	TUNNICLIFF	COLLINS ET AL	A TOPOGRAPHICAL SURVEY OF THE COUNTIES	
SPENCE, GRAEME	56	1792			SPENCE	HYDROGRAPHIC OFFICE	A SURVEY OF THE ISLES OF SCILLY	
FAIRBURN, JOHN & ROWE, ROBERT	57	1798		ROWE	FAIRBURN	FAIRBURN	THE GAME OF ENGLISH GEOGRAPHY	

INDEX-HEAD	CHAPTER #	1ST DATE	SURVEYOR/DRAWN BY	ENGRAVER	AUTHOR	PUBLISHER	TITLE	SKELTON / HODSON INDEX
SMITH, CHARLES	58	1801		JONES & SMITH	SMITH	SMITH	SMITH'S NEW ENGLISH ATLAS	NO INDEX OF C19
WILKES, SAMUEL & NEELE, SAMUEL	59	1810		NEELE	WILKES	WILKES	ENCYCLOPAEDIA LONDINENSIS	
DUGDALE, JAMES & NEELE, SAMUEL	60	1814		NEELE	DUGDALE	CUNDEE	THE NEW BRITISH TRAVELLER	
LYSONS BROS & NEELE, SAMUEL	61	1814		NEELE	LYSONS & LYSONS	CADELL & DAVIES	MAGNA BRITANNIA	
PINNOCK, WILLIAM & NEELE, SAMUEL	62	1819		NEELE	PINNOCK	PINNOCK & MAUNDER	PINNOCK'S HISTORY AND TOPOGRAPHY OF CORNWALL	
BUTTERS, ROBERT	63	1803		BUTTERS	BUTTERS	BUTTERS	AN ATLAS OF ENGLAND	
LUFFMAN, JOHN	64	1803		LUFFMAN	LUFFMAN	LUFFMAN ET AL	NEW POCKET ATLAS AND GEOGRAPHY OF ENGLAND AND WALES	
COLE, GEORGE & ROPER, JOHN	65	1805	COLES	ROPER	VERNOR, HOOD & SHARP	VERNOR, HOOD & SHARP	THE BRITISH ATLAS,	
CAPPER, BENJAMIN & COOPER, HENRY	66	1808		COOPER	CAPPER	PHILLIPS	TOPOGRAPHICAL DICTIONARY	
WALLIS, JAMES	67	1812		WALLIS	WALLIS	WALLIS	WALLIS'S NEW POCKET EDITION OF THE ENGLISH COUNTIES	
WALLIS, JAMES	67	1812		WALLIS	WALLIS	ODDY	A NEW AND IMPROVED ENGLISH ATLAS	
WALLIS, JAMES	67	1820		WALLIS	WALLIS	READ	THE PANORAMA: OR TRAVELLER'S INSTRUCTIVE GUIDE	
BAKER, BENJAMIN & ORDNANCE SURVEY	68	1813	UNDER MUDGE	BAKER	ORDNANCE SURVEY	ORDNANCE SURVEY	OS PARTS IID AND III	
ROWE, ROBERT	69	1816		ROWE	ROWE	ROWE	THE ENGLISH ATLAS	
LANGLEY, EDWARD & BELCH, WILLIAM	70	1817		BELCH	LANGLEY & BELCH	LANGLEY & BELCH	LANGLEY'S NEW COUNTY ATLAS OF ENGLAND AND WALES	
CRABB, THOMAS	71	1819		CRABB	CRABB	CRABB	SET OF PLAYING CARDS	
LEIGH, SAMUEL & HALL, SIDNEY	72	1820		HALL	LEIGH	LEIGH	LEIGH'S NEW POCKET ATLAS OF ENGLAND AND WALES	
DIX, THOMAS & DARTON, WILLIAM	73	1821	DIX	DARTON SNR	DARTON JNR	DARTON JNR	A COMPLETE ATLAS OF THE ENGLISH COUNTIES	
SMITH, WILLIAM & GARDNER, WILLIAM ROBERT	74	1822		GARDNER	SMITH	SMITH	SMITH'S NEW ENGLISH ATLAS	
PERROT, ARISTIDE & MIGNARET, ADRIEN	75	1824	THIERRY?	MIGNERET / THIERRY	DEPPING	LE DOUX	L'ANGLETERRE OU DESCRIPTION HISTORIQUE ET TOPOGRAPHIQUE	
GREENWOOD, C & J	76	1834	C&J GREENWOOD	DOWER	C&J GREENWOOD	C&J GREENWOOD	ATLAS OF THE COUNTIES OF ENGLAND,	
TEESDALE, HENRY	77	1830		ROWE / TEESDALE	TEESDALE & CO	TEESDALE & CO	A NEW BRITISH ATLAS	
MURRAY, T. LAURIE & HOARE & REEVES	78	1830		HOARE & REEVES	TL MURRAY	MURRAY	AN ATLAS OF THE ENGLISH COUNTIES	
CREIGHTON, ROBERT & STARLING, THOMAS	79	1831	CREIGHTON	STARLING	LEWIS	LEWIS	A TOPOGRAPHICAL DICTIONARY OF ENGLAND IN FOUR VOLUMES	
COBBETT, WILLIAM	80	1832		UNKNOWN	COBBETT	COBBETT	GEOGRAPHICAL DIRECTORY	
FISHER, HENRY & DAVIES, BENJAMIN REES	81	1832		DAVIES	FISHER, SON & CO	FISHER, SON & CO	DEVON AND CORNWALL ILLUSTRATED	
DUNCAN, JAMES & EBDEN, WILLIAM	82	1833	EBDEN	HOARE & REEVES	EBDEN	DUNCAN	A COMPLETE COUNTY ATLAS OF ENGLAND & WALES	
BELL, JAMES & SCOTT, ROBERT	83	1833		SCOTT	BELL	FULLERTON & CO	A NEW AND COMPREHENSIVE GAZETTEER OF ENGLAND AND WALES	
PIGOT, JAMES & Co.	84	1830		PIGOT & SON	PIGOT & CO	PIGOT & CO	BRITISH ATLAS OF THE COUNTIES OF ENGLAND	
PINNOCK, WILAM & ARCHER, JOSHUA	85	1833	ARCHER	ARCHER	PINNOCK	EDWARDS	THE GUIDE TO KNOWLEDGE	
DUGDALE, JAMES & ARCHER, JOSHUA	86	1846	ARCHER	ARCHER	DUGDALE	DUGDALE	DUGDALE'S ENGLAND AND WALES DELINEATED	
MOULE, THOMAS	87	1836		DOWER	MOULE	MOULE	MOULE'S ENGLISH COUNTIES	

References
By Title

Title	Reference
A Complete Guide to Heraldry.	William Fox-Smith, London, Edinburgh, T.C. & E.C. Jack 1909.
A Map of The County of Devon.	W.L.D. Ravenhill London, 1965.
A Topographical Description of Cornwall.	John Norden. London 1728.
Antique Maps.	P.J. Radford, Portsmouth, 1965.
Britannia...	William Camden, Pub George Bishop & John Norton London 1607.
Britannia: Or, A Geographical Description...	Richard Blome, London 1673.
British Map Engravers.	L. Worms and A. Baynton-Williams. London 2011.
British Maps and Mapmakers.	Edward Lynham, London, 1947.
British Regional Geology, South West England.	Edmonds, McKeown & William HMSO 1975.
Capt. Collins Coasting Pilot. A Carto-bibliographic analysis.	C. Verner, Map Collectors' Series Vol 6, No 58 1-57. 1969.
County Atlases of The British Isles. 1579-1703.	R.A. Skelton. Map Collectors' Circle, London, 1964.
County Atlases of The British Isles. 1704-1789.	Donald Hodson, Terwin Press 1984-1997 Vols 1-3.
Decorative Printed Maps of The Fifteenth to Eighteenth Centuries.	R.A. Skelton, London, 1958.
Historical Account of the Navigable Rivers, Canals & Railways of Great Britain.	Joseph Priestley, Longman, Rees, Orme & Green London. 1831.
Iconic Rhetoric and the Geographical Imagination, Frontispieces as declarations of Ideology.	A. Hernando, Boletín de la Asociación de Geógrafos Españoles, No 51, 2009.
Joel Gasgoyne – 'A Map of The County of Cornwall' 1699.	W.L.D. Ravenhill & O.J. Padel. Devon And Cornwall Record Society, New Series Vol 34. 1991.
Joel Gascoyne, a Pioneer of Large-Scale County Mapping.	W.L.D. Ravenhill, Imago Mundi, vol. 26, 1972.
John Norden's Manuscript Maps of Cornwall And Its Nine Hundreds.	William Ravenhill. Exeter 1972.
Lake's Parochial History of the County of Cornwall.	J. Polsue, Truro 1867-73 Vols 1-4.
Maps and Mapmakers.	R.V. Tooley, London, 1961.
Memoirs of Hydrography including Brief Biographies of the Principal Officers who have served in H. M. Naval Surveying Service.	Dawson, L.S. Keay, Eastbourne 1885.
Norden's Preparative to His Speculum Britanniae.	John Norden, London 1596.
Place Names in Cornwall and Scilly.	Craig Weatherhill, Launceston 2005.
Popular Dictionary of Cornish Place-names.	O.J. Padel, Penzance 1988.
Printed Maps of Devon 1575-1837 2nd Ed.	K. Batten & F. Bennett. 2012.
Re-Engraving – A Beginners Guide.	Ashley Baynton-Williams, The Map Forum, Volume 1, Issue 7.
Richard Carew Of Antony.	F.E. Halliday, London, 1953.
Sea Monsters on Medieval and Renaissance Maps.	Chet Van Duzer, The British Library 2013.
The Isles of Scilly.	Margaret Palmer. Map Collectors' Circle, London, 1963.
The Printed Maps in The Atlases of Great Britain And Ireland: A Bibliography, 1579-1870.	Thomas Chubb, London, 1927.
Zero Degrees: Geographies of the Prime Meridian.	Charles W.J. Withers, Havard University Press 2017.

On Line

There are hundreds of On-line references from Auction Houses to Dealers, Collectors and Academic resources from all over the World. This is a non-exhaustive list:

British Library, The.	*www.bl.uk*
British Printed Images to 1700. Directory of Printmakers, Publishers and Print sellers.	*www.bpi1700.org.uk*
Calculations of Historic Magnetic Declination.	*www.ngdc.noaa.gov*
Camden's Britannia (1722 Ed).	*https://ebooks.adelaide.edu.au/f/facsimile/britannia*
Confederation of Many Academic Institutions.	*www.copac.jisc.ac.uk*
Dictionary of National Biography.	*www.oxforddnb.com*
Family tree records, births, deaths, marriages, public records &c.	*www.ancestry.com*
Harvard University Map Library.	*http://hcl.harvard.edu/libraries/maps*
London Gazette. Records of Legal Proceedings from 1665.	*https://www.thegazette.co.uk*
National Library of Australia.	*www.nla.gov.au*
On-Line Index of Miniature Maps and Playing Cards.	*www.miniaturemaps.net*
The Arundel Family.	*www.landedfamilies.blogspot.co.uk/2015/11/194- arundell-of-trerice-barons-arundell.html*
The Isles of Scilly and the Channel Islands: "bench-mark" hydrographic and geodetic surveys 1689-1980. PhD Thesis, Cyril Everard, 2004.	*https://qmro.qmul.ac.uk/jspui/handle/123456789/1838*
The Burden Private Collection of English County Atlases.	*www.caburden.com*
The Photographer's Ephemeris - historical sun and moon positions	*app.photoephemeris.com*
US Library of Congress.	*www.loc.gov*

Index

Abbey Gardens	158	Bowen, Emanuel	76, 85, 89, 90, 110, 113, 116, 122, 126, 127, 154, 231
Adams, Robert	98, 100		
Agonic meridian	166	Bowen, Thomas	90
Aikin, John	152	Bowes, William	10, 236
Airlie, 1st Earl of	55	Bowles, Carington	89, 90, 91, 113, 117, 123, 130, 131
Airy, George Biddell	166	Bowles, Thomas	85, 87, 92
Amsterdam	7, 10, 11, 33, 41, 46, 49, 72, 96, 126	Bradley, James	166
		Brahe, Tycho	28
Archer, Joshua	216, 220	Bridgerule	230
Arrowsmith, Aaron	40, 128, 138, 192	Brown Willy	119
Arundel, Christopher	60	Brown, Christopher	33, 36, 92
Arundel, Sir John	60	Burghley, 1st Baron of, William Cecil	13
Ashley, Sir Anthony	9	Butters, Robert	168, 176
Azores, The	20, 40, 60, 72, 82, 231	C. Dicey and Co.	5, 6, 33, 36, 68, 236
Badeslade, Thomas	102, 103	Camden Place	19
Baker, Benjamin	154, 168, 185, 238	Camden, Earl of, Charles Pratt	19
Baker, Henry	125	Camden, William	10, 12, 13, 18, 19, 25, 27, 35, 39, 40, 50, 60, 79, 80, 92, 109, 142, 154, 206, 231, 232, 235, 237
Basset, Sir Francis. Lord de Dustanville	60		
Bassett & Chiswell	11, 33, 58, 80		
Bassett, Thomas	36	Camelford	92
Bateman, Christopher	13, 15, 18	Cape Cornwall	28, 29
Bath, Earl of, John Granville	50	Cara Couze in clouze	See St Michael's Mount
Baynton-Williams, Ashley	6, 66	Carew, Richard	12, 17, 60, 80, 224, 235
Belch, William	188	Carew's Salt Pond	12, 60, 80
Bell, James	212	Carnmenellis	227
Bickham, George, Jnr	124, 151	Cary, John	138, 141, 142, 145, 146, 160, 182, 185, 191, 204, 214
Bickham, George, Snr	124		
Bill, John	40, 231, 236	Cheesewring	36, 78, 191, 194, 208
Blaeu, Jan	12, 18, 46, 49, 66, 98, 235, 237	Chislehurst Golf Club	See Camden Place
Blaeu, Willem Janzoon	10, 11, 28, 29, 46, 100, 166, 236	Chiswell, Richard	15, 36
Blome, Richard	28, 50, 51, 52, 53, 54, 98, 156, 235, 242	Claesz, Cornelis	7, 10, 11
		Clark, Rev. Samuel	191
Boconnoc	138	Cobbett, William	208
Bodley, Sir Thomas	40	Coldwind Cross or Blow Ye Cold Wind	58, 60, 87, 127
Bodmin	92, 102, 138, 178, 185, 208, 220, 227		
		Cole, George	178, 227
Bodmin Moor	92	Collins Bros	178
Borlase, William	125	Collins, BC	156
Botallack	110, 191	Collins, Greenvile	69, 72, 78, 96, 132, 158
Bourne, Ebenezer	185	Collins, H.G.	186

244   **Antique Maps of Cornwall and the Isles of Scilly**

Index

Cooper, Henry	104, 181
Cornwall Records Office	71
Cotton, Sir Robert	100
Counties (Detached Parts) Act, 1844	230
Cowley, John	104, 126
Crabb, Thomas	183, 191
Cranbourne, Viscount, William Cecil	15
Creighton, R.	206
Cremyll	87
Crewkerne	56
Crowan Beacon	66, 94
Crutchley, George F.	141, 146
Cundee, James	171
Dartmoor	185, 227
Darton, William Jnr	191
Darton, William Snr	154, 171, 178, 188
Davies, Benjamin Rees	208
de Bry, Theodore	9, 28, 98, 100
de Dunstanville, Reginald. Earl of Cornwall	60
de Hondt, Elizabeth	49
de Hooghe, Romain	72
De la Beche, Sir Henry	146, 185
de la Rochette, Louis Stanislas D'arcy	35, 76, 116, 130, 134, 136, 148
de Mortain, Robert. Earl of Cornwall	35, 68, 228
de Thoryas, Paul Rapin	151
de Valletort, Roger	230
De Wolff	See Wolf Rock
Depping, Georges-Bernard	198
Dexbeer	230
Dix, Thomas	194
Dodman Point	236
Dodsley, Robert	104
Donn, Benjamin	76, 119, 125
Drayton, Michael	39
Dugdale, James	171
Dugdale, Thomas	109, 178, 216
Duncan, James	210
Dunheved	27, 35, 64, 224, 228
Dury, Andrew	128
Earls and Duke of Cornwall	37
Ebden, William	204, 210
Eddystone Lighthouse	92, 199
Edgecumbe, 1st Baron of, Richard Edgecumbe	113
Effingham, 2nd Baron of, Charles Howard	9
Ellis, G.	182
Ellis, Joseph	90, 128
England's End	See Land's End
English Statute Mile	56, 128, 151, 231, 232
Engravers' Act, 1735	100
Ereira, Alan	55
Essex, Earl of, Robert Devereaux	13, 15
Everard, Cyril	71, 243
Exeter	85, 87
Faden, William	119, 130
Fairburn, John	160, 186
Fairthorne, George	55
Fal	58, 76, 119, 235
Falmouth	28, 50, 68, 72, 78, 79, 80, 82, 98, 127, 196, 227
Fisher, Henry & Son	208
Flamsteed, John	166
Fowey	58, 87, 94, 110, 126, 151
Fullerton, Archibald	206, 212
Gardner, Thomas	94
Gardner, William Robert	171
Gasgoyne, Joel	13, 76, 78, 92, 110, 113, 116, 119, 121, 151, 225, 231, 232, 236, 237, 238
Gaveston, Piers. Earl of Cornwall	37, 64, 68
Geological Survey, The	185
Gerbier, Sir Balthasar	25
Gibson, Edmund	18, 19, 60, 237
Gibson, John	127
Ginver, Nicholas	71, 132, 133, 158, 229
Godolphin	227
Grafton, Duke of, Henry Fitzroy	69
Grampound	41, 87, 102

Index

Gravelot, Hubert	98
Great Cross Course	178, 182, 188, 227
Greenwich	20, 60, 122, 154, 164, 166, 167, 171, 182, 196, 200, 208, 220, 231
Greenwood, Christopher & James	13, 214
Guilielmi Camdeni	See Camden, William
Gwennap	119, 220
Hachett, Thomas	148
Haig Fras	227
Hall Drunkard	87, 92, 104, 148, 224
Hall, Sidney	192, 216
Halley, Edmond	166
Hallworthy	87, 92
Hals, William	54
Hansard	208
Harrison, John	151, 229
Harrison, Stephen	25
Hatchett, Thomas	130, 134, 136, 148
Hayle	42
Haywood, James	151, 202
Helston	156, 178, 185, 227
Hinton, John	89
HMS Association	69, 96, 122, 130, 136, 148, 156, 229
Hoare and Reeves	204
Hoare, Henry	94
Hoblyn, Robert	121
Hodson, Donald	109, 116, 122, 134, 138, 141, 239
Hogarth, William	100
Hogg, Alexander	134, 171
Hole, William	13, 18, 39
Holland, Philémon	18, 27
Hondius, Honricus	46
Hondius, Jodocus	9, 10, 18, 19, 20, 33, 35, 36, 37, 46, 49
Hugh Town	69, 96, 122
Humble, George	33, 35, 36
Humble, William	11, 36
Hurlers, The	78
Hydrographic Office	158
International Meridian Conference	166
Isles of Scilly	7, 9, 28, 39, 69, 72, 78, 79, 90, 96, 98, 110, 113, 116, 121, 122, 125, 127, 132, 151, 156, 158, 178, 186, 196, 199, 204, 206, 208
Jamaica Inn	138
Jansson, Jan	46, 49, 72, 80, 82, 231, 235, 237
Jefferys, Thomas	5, 6, 68, 122, 236
Jenner, Thomas	41, 42
Kaerius, Petrus	See Van den Keere, Pieter
Kerrier	66, 71, 121, 181
Kip, William	12, 13, 17, 18, 19, 27, 35, 36, 39, 66, 104, 228, 231, 234, 235, 237
Kitchin, Thomas	60, 76, 89, 90, 92, 113, 116, 117, 121, 122, 128, 130, 154
Land's End	36, 56, 58, 66, 68, 72, 79, 80, 87, 90, 102, 122, 124, 125, 151, 178, 185, 196
Langley, Edward	178, 188, 227, 231
Launceston	27, 35, 36, 59, 64, 76, 78, 79, 84, 85, 87, 89, 102, 104, 124, 128, 130, 136, 177, 178, 185, 214, 228, 235
Launceston - Victoria Railway	210
Laurie, Richard Holmes	154
Laurie, Robert	124, 132, 154
Lea, Philip	5, 6, 18, 56, 60, 64, 66, 68, 78, 92, 236
Leigh, G	125
Leigh, Samuel	192
Lemprière, Clement	98
Lenthall, John	64, 84
Lethowsow	See Lyonesse
Lewis, Samuel	206
Lewis, William	182
Liskeard	42, 87, 102, 125, 178
Lizard	9, 18, 36, 80, 185, 227, 231, 232, 235, 236, 237

246

Antique Maps of Cornwall and the Isles of Scilly

Index

Lodge, John	60, 148, 208, 225
Lombart, Pierre	55
Longitude Act, 1714	229
Longships	71, 80, 98, 154
Looe	5, 17, 27, 58, 60, 68, 78, 84, 87, 89, 94, 122, 130, 185, 186, 196, 204, 208, 214
Looe Is or St George's Is or St Michael's Is	13, 17, 18, 89, 92, 130, 200, 214
Looe Island.	See Looe Is
Lostwithiel	36, 87, 102, 127, 178, 185, 228, 235
Love I	See Looe Is
Luffman, John	177
Lyonesse	226
Lysons, Daniel	119, 171, 173
Madron	76, 141, 156
Marazion	191
Marazion or Market Jew	20, 58, 87, 94, 102, 122, 127, 224, 225
Marsland	230
Martin, Benjamin	89, 126
Martin, P.	182
Martyn, Thomas	60, 78, 119, 121, 125, 156, 225, 231
Matherderna	148, See Madron
Meijer, Pieter	126
Mên Scryfa	121
Mercator, Gerard	17, 18, 20, 49, 166, 231
Mercator, Rumold	20
Mertha-Derua	60
Migneret, Mme	171, 194, 198
Miller, Robert	191
Moll, Herman	92, 94, 102, 106, 109, 151, 231, 232, 238
Morden, Robert	12, 18, 59, 60, 62, 84, 92, 110, 151, 231, 232, 235, 236, 237, 238
Mortier, David	72, 82
Moule, Thomas	17, 219
Mount's Bay	42, 87, 225, 235
Mousehole	7, 9, 41, 80
Mudge, William	185
Murray, J.	148
Murray, T. Laurie	204
Neele, George	192
Neele, Samuel	154, 168, 171, 173, 192
Newlyn	7, 9, 20, 76, 87, 116, 119, 130, 204, 224
Newlyn East	76, 110, 116
Newquay	42
Nicholls, Sutton	18, 49, 80, 82
Norden, John	5, 12, 13, 15, 17, 18, 19, 27, 33, 35, 40, 41, 50, 60, 66, 76, 80, 98, 214, 225, 226, 228, 231, 234, 235, 236, 237, 238
North Petherwin	230
North Tamerton	230
Oddy, S.A.	182
Ogilby, John	55, 56, 58, 59, 60, 68, 85, 87, 89, 92, 94, 100, 102, 109, 225, 226
Okehampton	196
Orange, William of	69
Ordnance Survey	76, 125, 154, 166, 185, 204, 238
Ortelius, Abraham	40
Osborne, Thomas	110
Oundle School	194
Overton, Henry	33, 36, 56, 80
Overton, John	33, 36, 64, 80
Owen, John	85
Oxford, Earl of, Edward Harley	15
Padstow	18, 42, 72, 87, 102, 110, 185, 214
Pendeen	125, 196
Pendennis Castle	20, 28, 72, 82
Penryn	102, 127
Penwith	17, 29, 60, 64, 66, 71, 78, 89, 142, 174, 196, 214, 225, 226, 235
Penzance	7, 9, 20, 58, 87, 94, 102, 122, 125, 127, 141, 178, 185, 196, 199, 224, 225, 226
Perranzabuloe	18
Perrot, Aristide-Michel	198
Philleigh	87

Antique Maps of Cornwall and the Isles of Scilly

Index

Pigot, James	13, 214
Pine, John	12, 15, 98, 100, 228
Pinnock, William	216
Plymouth	9, 56, 58, 66, 68, 78, 87, 94, 142, 185
Polgooth	87
Poly-olbion	39
Porthcurno	29
Porthhellick	69, 96, 122, 132
Proposed Tamar Navigation	141, 142, 171, 214
Ptolomy, Claudius	166
Radnor, 2nd Earl of, Charles Bodville	78, 124
Ramsden Theodolite	185
Rashleigh, Jonathan	121
Ravenhill, William	13, 15, 17, 35
Rea, Roger	11, 33, 36, 80
Redmayne, William	64, 84
Redruth	72, 102, 127, 185, 196, 227
Reform Act, 1832	204
Reuben Ramble	191
Roberts, Hender	52
Rocque, John	106, 110, 119, 128
Rogers, William	33
Roper, John	178, 182, 188, 227
Rough Tor	119
Rowe, Robert	160, 186, 202
Royal Geographic Society	202, 204
Royal Observatory	166
Royal Society of Arts	138
Runnel Stone	29, 80, 154
Ryther, Augustinus	9, 10, 98, 100
Saltash Passage	142, 230
Sancreed	156
Saxton, Christopher	5, 6, 7, 10, 33, 40, 45, 54, 56, 60, 64, 68, 76, 92, 225, 226, 234, 235, 236, 237, 238
Sayer, Robert	119, 121, 122, 124, 128, 129, 130, 132
Schenk, Leonard	126
Schenk, Peter	49, 82, 126, 231
Seale, Richard	89
Seckford, Thomas	5, 64
Seller, John	64, 78, 79
Seller, John Jr	78
Senex, John	94
Sennen	56, 58, 87, 127
Sexegesimal	231
Shepherd, Charles	167
Shovell, Sir Cloudesley	69, 96, 122, 132, 142, 156, 229
Silly	See Isles of Scilly
Silly Islands	See Isles of Scilly
Simmons, Mary	42
Simmons, Matthew	41, 42, 236
Simmons, Samuel	42
Simpson, Samuel	109, 227
Skelton, Raleigh A.	27, 239
Slater, Isaac	214
Smith, Charles	196, 214
Smith, Joseph	82
Smith, William	18, 185
Sorlinges	20, See Scilly Isles
Spanish Armada	66, 98
Speed, John	10, 11, 12, 13, 15, 17, 18, 19, 27, 33, 35, 36, 37, 46, 49, 50, 54, 56, 58, 60, 64, 66, 76, 78, 80, 92, 110, 228, 231, 235, 237
Spence, Graeme	158, 159
St. Agnes	42, 72, 132
St. Austell	58, 185
St. Blazey	87
St. Budeaux	142, 230
St. Buryan	9, 58
St. Clement's Isle	29, 71
St. Columb	102, 185
St. Day	76, 119
St. Ginnys	210
St. Hillary	58
St. Ive	87
St. Ives	42, 185
St. John's & Maker	142, 230
St. Just	9, 29
St. Mawes	20, 28

Index

St. Michael's Isle	See Looe Is	Valk, Gerard	49, 82, 126, 231
St. Michael's Mount	29, 42, 119, 188, 191, 200, 204	Valmue	See Falmouth
St. Paul's Cathedral	36, 60, 68, 154, 191	Van den Keere, Pieter	10, 40, 236
Stanford, Edward	208	Van Deutecom, Baptist & Johannes	7
Stannary Towns	178	Van Keulen, Gerard	96, 132
Starling, Thomas	206	Van Langeren, Jacob	41
Statutes (Definition of Time) Act, 1880	167	Verenigde Oostindische Compagnie	46, 96
Stogursey	186	Virgivian Sea	36
Stratton	89, 185, 196, 199, 208	Virtue, George	219
Sudbury, John	33, 35, 36	Virtue, James	219
Sudlow, Edward	151, 156	Wadebridge	79, 127
Sympson, Samuel	109	Waghenaer, Lucas Janzoon	7, 9, 28, 72, 98, 100
Tamar	36, 46, 58, 76, 87, 102, 119, 124, 214, 230, 235	Wallis, James	178, 182, 188, 227
Tavistock	85, 87, 102	Walpoole, George Augustus	76, 134
Teesdale, Henry	186	Web, William	5, 6, 45, 66, 236
Temple Moors	92, 104	Wheel Dimensurator	56
Terwoort, Lenaert	5, 45, 64	Whittaker, G & WB	188
The Gulfe	See Wolf Rock	Whittle, James	124, 132, 154
The Thames School of Chart-makers	76	Wilkes, John	168
Thierry brothers	198	Willdey, George	5, 6, 68, 236
Tillie, Sir James	50, 54	Withers, Charles W. J.	166
Tindal, Rev. Nicholas	151	Wolf Rock	9, 28, 79, 98
Tintagel Head	235	Woolley Moor	230
Tol Pedn Penwith	29, 71	Worms, Laurence	192
Toms, William Henry	102, 103	Wren, Sir Christopher	166
Tovey, Abraham	69, 132	Zennor	42, 80, 156
Tovey, Abraham Jnr	132		
Treaty of Tordesillas	166		
Tregony	58, 87, 102		
Trematon Castle	230		
Trengwainton	60		
Trevose Head	235		
Trinity College, Cambridge	13, 15		
Trinity House	69, 80		
Truro	56, 68, 72, 79, 85, 87, 94, 102, 178, 185, 196, 214, 232		
Tunnicliff, William	156		
Tywardreath	58, 87, 94		
Vaelmuijen	See Falmouth		